The Practical Guide

to

Pregnancy and Child Care

Karen Sullivan is the Health Editor of Northern Woman Magazine and has written and edited a number of books on all aspects of health care, including *The Complete Encyclopedia of Healing Remedies, Vitamins and Minerals in a Nutshell, First Aid, The Hamlyn Encyclopedia of Complementary Health* and *The Complete Family Guide to Natural Home Remedies.*
She has two children and lives in London.

The Practical Guide

to

Pregnancy and Child Care

Everything you need to know
from conception to 2 years old

Karen Sullivan

Foreword by Professor Lesley Regan, St Mary's Hospital

Photography by Christina Jansen

PARRAGON

To Kathy, Kyla and Tristyn

First published in Great Britain in 1998 by
Parragon
13 Whiteladies Road
Clifton
Bristol BS8 1PB

ISBN 0-75252-577-8

Produced by Grapevine Publishing Services Ltd, London
Editors: Gill Paul, Catherine Blake
Design: Avril Broadley, Joy Fitzsimmon, Yvonne Worth
Illustrations: Joy Fitzsimmon, Sylvie Rabbe
Photography by Christina Jansen
Printed in Italy

NOTE
While every precaution has been taken to check that the information given in this book
is accurate and concurs with up-to-date medical knowledge, each individual's
circumstances can vary greatly so it is not possible to guarantee that all advice will work
for every reader. If you or your baby experience any problems or symptoms that alarm
you, you should consult a qualified professional straight away.

Throughout this book we have alternated the use of 'he' and 'she' when referring to
babies, depending on whether the pictures on each page show a boy or a girl.

Contents

Part Two:

Your new baby

Foreword

by Professor Lesley Regan

Reading this thoughtfully written and well-illustrated guide to pregnancy and childcare has been a thoroughly enjoyable experience. As a mother of young children and a practising obstetrician, I found it a breath of fresh air. Most importantly, the book truly lives up to its titles of 'The Practical Guide' and as such it is a welcome addition to the bookshelf.

In Part One, Karen Sullivan begins by discussing some of the issues that a couple need to consider when planning a pregnancy. Along with practical advice on the best ways to ensure a healthy diet and lifestyle, the biology of how a pregnancy is achieved is explained in a simple and sympathetic manner that is easy to read and understand. The pregnancy experience is then explored and the reader is led step by step through all the stages of pregnancy and childbirth. This part of the book provides a detailed account of the physical changes that a mother can expect to occur during her pregnancy, the emotions she may experience, the medical care that she is likely to receive and the preparations she needs to make for the arrival of her baby. Many first-time mothers will be fascinated and reassured by the week-by-week accounts of what is happening to their body and the stage of development that their unborn child has reached. Potential anxieties and fears are openly addressed and are accompanied by practical tips and sensible advice as to how to deal with them.

This book offers the reader information on both conventional and complementary approaches to pregnancy and childbirth. It encourages the individual to consider all the options available to her and then stands back in order to allow the woman to reach an informed decision. Details of herbal remedies and other alternative therapies are discussed in many of the chapters. I must state here that I have no personal or professional experience of these therapies. However, since this book is not written in a prescriptive manner, the inclusion of these potential treatment options will be a useful addition for some readers.

In my opinion one of the strengths of this book is that Part Two – 'Caring for your Child' – is as detailed and comprehensive as Part One. Many new mothers feel justifiably bewildered by all the new skills that they are expected to learn in the first few months after their baby is born. They often receive conflicting advice from health care professionals, family and friends. Karen Sullivan takes the new mother firmly by the hand and leads her carefully through each task that she needs to become experienced at performing. The text on feeding, changing, bathing and handling the baby is complimented by numerous helpful illustrations and in addition useful sections on a variety of common problems, sleeping patterns and the importance of a daily routine for the baby are included. But the book does not end at the six-week postnatal check. It moves on to discuss the child's physical and emotional development up to the age of two years. This last part of the book highlights the fact that parenting is a unique and very individual task and that there are no hard and fast rules leading to success.

Yes, this is a book that I would have liked to read during my own pregnancy. I feel sure that there are many future mothers who will benefit from the knowledge that it contains and find that it provides them with more confidence in bringing up their young children.

Professor Lesley Regan is head of the Department of Obstetrics and Gynaecology at St Mary's Hospital, London, the only woman in the UK to head an Obstetrics and Gynaecology department. She runs a Recurrent Miscarriage Unit at St Mary's which is the largest in Europe and deals with high-risk referrals from all over the country. She is the author of *Miscarriage: What Every Woman Needs to Know*, published by Bloomsbury. She also has first-hand experience of motherhood with five-year-old twin girls and four stepchildren.

Introduction

Pregnancy is undoubtedly one of the most important and life-changing events we will ever experience. Although most of us have friends, parents or colleagues who have been through it many times over, it is, for each of us, a unique experience, that provokes feelings of doubt and worry, bewilderment and sheer exhilaration.

Our responsibilities to our children begin before conception and continue throughout pregnancy, when it is essential that we maintain our own health in order to give our children the best possible start in life. New-born babies have their own separate needs and patterns of health, which require decisions and choices to be made. And as our children grow up, their needs become more defined, and we are presented with a plethora of conflicting advice about how we should bring them up, and deal with common problems of everyday life.

As a mother of two boys, I found that I was being offered two approaches: go natural, which meant embracing alternatives to the conventional system, or do it the traditional way. Neither seemed exactly right for me. With a healthy respect for the medical profession, and a family history of difficult labours, I found the 'natural' approach to childbirth as daunting as the prospect of full intervention. On the other hand, as an advocate of complementary medicine, which I had practised long before my

children were born, I believed instinctively that I should be encouraging the health of my babies in a more natural way than the conventional system offered. What I needed, therefore, was information that presented both options, from which I could make my own decisions, according to my specific needs, and those of my children. This book sets out to do just that.

Today, we are in the unique position of being able to combine the best of both worlds by using the conventional system when and as it is required, but taking responsibility for our own health and well-being by using natural alternatives that have been tried and tested. This book is a practical guide to the options that are available, and encourages you to make your own decisions about how you want to approach your pregnancy, your labour and, eventually, the upbringing of your children. It is based on the experiences of mothers who have been through it all - from women who have suffered every symptom under the sun during pregnancy to those who have sailed through without a stretchmark in sight; from mothers of babies with colic, spots and unending crying sessions to those whose babies slept through the night from day one, and ate all their vegetables without a murmur. It also takes into account the views of fathers, most of whom have their own secrets of successful parenting.

This is the book that I would have liked to read - a practical, common-sense approach to some of the most fulfilling and worrying years of life, using the best of the 'naturals' alongside conventional wisdom and treatment, in whatever combination suits you best. There are no rules for having babies, or bringing them up, and every parent finds his or her own path. All you need is information, and that is what I have set out to provide, in a comprehensive and easy-to-understand form.

Parenting is a creative art - one in which you amass the skills and tools over years of experience, and with the wisdom and guidance of others. Because it is creative there is no one way to do it - you'll need to draw upon your own beliefs and base decisions on your own instinctive feelings.

There is nothing more exciting than seeing your expanding abdomen become a baby, and then a person. Use the tools that are most appropriate, and the wisdom that seems to work, and you will have the confidence and the peace of mind to give birth to a healthy baby, and watch him or her grow into a happy child.

Karen Sullivan
March 1998

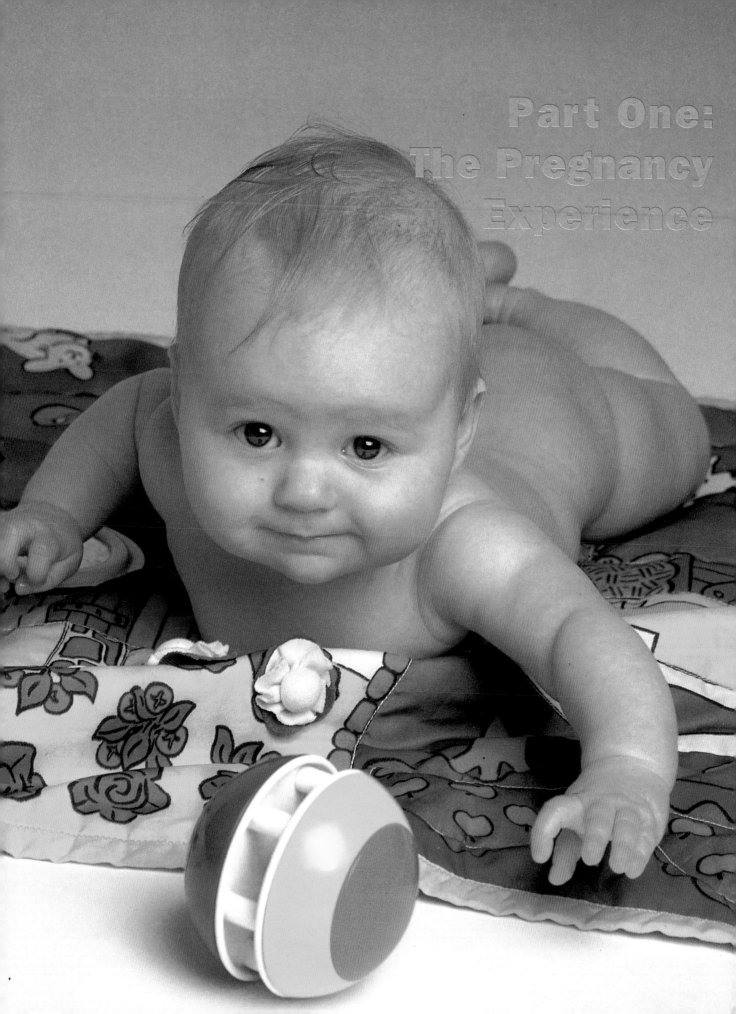

Planning a pregnancy

Getting fit before trying for a baby will help in a number of ways. You may find it easier to conceive if you and your partner are fit and healthy, and your body will be better able to cope with the strain of pregnancy and childbirth as well as the trials of lifting and carrying a new baby.

Many couples do not prepare for pregnancy with the careful planning they devote to other major events, and yet a successful pregnancy and the birth of a healthy baby are among the most important achievements of a lifetime. Starting a family is a huge responsibility for both parents, that will alter your life forever.

Most deeply affected will be those things you have always taken for granted, such as time to yourself, your relationship with your partner and your social life, as well as your financial outlay. A baby does tend to take over your life – in the nicest possible way – so it makes sense to be prepared emotionally, physically and financially for the arrival. Healthy, happy parents are more likely to produce healthy, happy children, so make sure you are fit for parenthood before you decide to start trying for a baby.

It is easy to underestimate the sheer hard work, dedication and patience involved in caring for a baby. Spending time with other parents and their babies when you are planning a family or while you are pregnant will help to give you some idea of what life will be like after the birth. Some of the most important considerations are:

Note: It's normal to have mixed feelings about pregnancy and parenthood. It would be unrealistic to imagine that your life will remain unchanged after the baby comes, and it's better to think ahead.

Money

Studies show that you can expect to spend roughly 20 percent of your family income on your child, no matter how much you earn. This figure covers the cost of food, clothing and equipment, as well as nappies and infant formula if you are bottle-feeding. As your child grows older, you will have to consider the cost of extras, such as holidays, perhaps schooling, presents and parties, and leisure activities such as swimming lessons, gymnastics or a musical instrument.

Relationships

Your relationship with your partner will change with the advent of another family member. Most couples report that their relationship becomes stronger, but you have to be prepared for the tension caused by sleepless nights – particularly in the early days – and the responsibilities of a new, helpless baby. It's not uncommon for new dads to feel left out when their partner is breastfeeding, or absorbed in the care of the new baby, or for new mothers to be overcritical of their partner's attempts to help. On top of all this, any time alone together will likely be compromised. Be aware that both partners will need almost as much reassurance and attention as the new addition.

Time

Many couples are choosing to start their families later in life – in fact, the average age of first-time mothers has increased by over ten years in the past decades. Beginning later means that you probably have the rhythms of work, social activities, recreation and relaxation firmly established. Don't assume that your baby will just fit into your present lifestyle. Babies require a great deal of time, attention and care, and will limit what you would normally expect to achieve. Like anything worthwhile, becoming a parent is a profoundly challenging experience. During the first few years your baby will be totally dependent on you and the way that you respond to her is vital to her happiness and health. You will need to come to terms with the burden of such responsibility, and it is reassuring to know that most of us, given realistic expectations, learn to be good enough parents.

Genes for bodily characteristics like hair and eye colour are carried on chromosomes, which come from the mother and the father. Some genes are dominant, meaning that they will take precedence over a recessive gene. Brown eyes are dominant, for example, so if a baby got a brown-eyes gene from his mother and a blue-eyes one from his father, he would be brown-eyed. But it's not quite so straightforward because people carry and pass on recessive genes as well, so it could be that the brown-eyed mother carried a blue-eyes gene, which mixed with a blue-eyes gene from the father, and the baby would then have blue eyes.

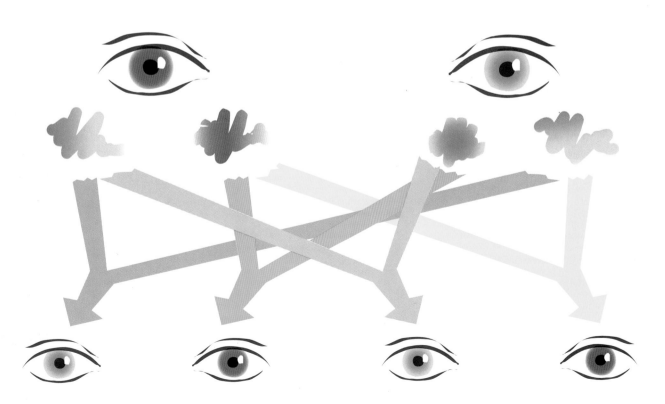

Trying for a baby

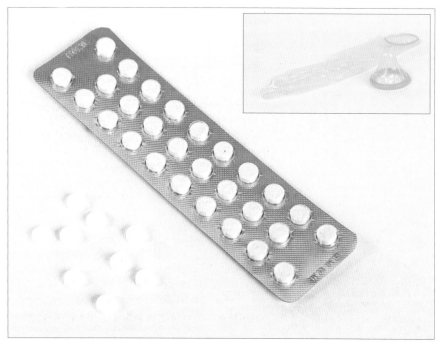

Some women become pregnant immediately after stopping taking the pill, so take other precautions if this would be inconvenient.

Ideally, we would all like to know in advance when we will conceive, in order to make the necessary changes to our lifestyle that will help ensure a healthy baby. In reality, however, planning a pregnancy is not always as easy as we may wish – many women become pregnant accidentally, and in other cases, it can take months, even years, before conception takes place.

It is now recommended that you begin preconceptual care several months before trying to conceive. In practical terms, preconceptual care means taking care of your body, and helping to ensure that everything is working at optimum level by the time you do become pregnant.

Preconceptual care

● See your physician for a thorough physical examination. Although the majority of women are healthy and will conceive naturally, it is always a good idea to pick up any problems which may prevent conception from taking place, or which may need to be monitored during pregnancy.

● Begin keeping track of your monthly cycle. Your chances of conceiving will be

Give up drinking and smoking several months before trying for a baby to give your body time to clean out.

greater if you have intercourse during your most fertile period, and this can vary from woman to woman, depending upon the length of your particular cycle. Ovulation generally occurs in the middle of the cycle (around the fourteenth day of a twenty-eight-day cycle, for example), but some women have irregular cycles, which means that the timing will be less easy to predict. You can purchase a home ovulation kit to help you establish when you do ovulate each month.

● Experts recommend that you update your immunizations – in particular, tetanus, if you haven't had one in the last ten years, and rubella, if you are not already immune. Your physician will be able to do a blood test to check immunity levels. Wait three months after immunization before trying to conceive.

● If you are taking the pill discontinue three months in advance of trying to become pregnant. If you have an IUD fitted, it should be removed.

● Make sure your diet is healthy (see pages 20–23), and cut down on caffeine.

You'll need at least five servings of fresh fruits and vegetables both preconceptually and while pregnant. Wash them carefully to remove any traces of pesticides or other toxins.

● Begin taking a vitamin and mineral supplement specially designed for pregnancy and the preconceptual period. Studies show that even slight deficiencies of some vitamins, minerals and trace elements can lead to problems conceiving. Furthermore, if your nutritional status is good, your baby will have the best chance of being healthy and developing normally. One of the most important vitamins to take during pregnancy is folic acid, which can prevent some birth defects, including spina bifida. The optimum dose is 400mcg daily.

● Avoid pollutants and toxins that may cause damage to the baby by interfering with the healthy multiplication of cells. Studies show that the following things can interfere with the conception and birth of a healthy baby: alcohol, tobacco, lead, overheated cooking oil, charred or barbecued foods, radiation, diazepam tranquillizers, paracetamol

(acetaminophen), drugs, viruses, infections, and the smoke from diesel engines.

● Give up smoking. Smoking can reduce fertility in either partner, and is hazardous to your pregnancy.

● Avoid heavy drinking. A little alcohol every day is likely to do more good than harm while you are trying to conceive, by helping you relax, but drinking in excess reduces fertility and can cause a wide variety of problems in your baby if you are pregnant. Most experts now consider it safe to have the occasional glass of wine during pregnancy.

● Try to relax. One of the most common causes of conceptual problems is stress. Make sure you get some good, regular exercise, and concentrate on getting enough sleep and relaxation.

● If you take prescription drugs, or have a long-standing medical condition, see your physician before attempting to get

pregnant, so that dosages of the medication can be adjusted if necessary.

● If you or your partner have any genetic condition, such as muscular dystrophy or cystic fibrosis, or you have a close relative who does, see your physician for genetic counselling. If you have had more than two miscarriages in the past, genetic counselling may also be advised.

Health considerations

If you suffer from one of the following conditions, you will need to see your physician before trying for a baby:

● Asthma
● Epilepsy
● Kidney disease
● Heart disease
● Diabetes mellitus
● AIDS
● Sexually transmitted diseases

Fertilization

Your baby will be conceived when a sperm from your partner fertilizes an egg (ovum) to form a single cell. A fertilized ovum starts to divide rapidly until a new individual is formed. All the tissues of the body are derived from the single fertilized egg and all the information necessary for planning the body is contained in the genetic code on the set of chromosomes present in each cell. Every time a cell divides and reproduces this set is copied precisely. About two weeks after fertilization, the embryo is implanted in the wall of the uterus. Once fully implanted, the placenta begins to develop.

Ovulation occurs roughly halfway through your menstrual cycle, and fertilization is most likely to take place if you have intercourse between the thirteenth and fifteenth days. Women with irregular cycles may need help in pinpointing ovulation, and there are now home ovulation tests to help you do so. Some women seem to know instantly when conception has been successful; others may not realize they are pregnant until after the first, or even second, missed period.

Every woman is born with a lifetime's supply of eggs in her ovaries, which will be released during her fertile years. The ovaries are located in the pelvis, close to the end of the Fallopian tubes which lead to the uterus. An egg is released roughly every lunar month (about every twenty-eight days). The ovarian cycle is controlled by hormones. The pituitary gland of the brain secretes a follicle-stimulating hormone (FSH) which acts on one of the ovaries to cause an egg-containing collection of cells to develop. This follicle secretes increasing amounts of oestrogen during the first half of the menstrual cycle, causing the lining of the uterus to thicken. In the middle of the cycle the egg is released from the follicle in the ovary, after which the cells of the empty follicle develop into the corpus luteum. This yellow, glandular mass of tissue begins to secrete progesterone, a hormone necessary to maintain the lining of the uterus so that it is suitable to support a pregnancy. If the ovum is not fertilized, the corpus luteum degenerates and progesterone production drops off. This causes the lining of the uterus to be discarded, as menstruation, about fourteen days after the time of ovulation.

A released ovum is swept into the Fallopian tube and carried along towards the womb. While in the tube, it may be met by sperm (spermatozoa). If not, the ovum is simply discarded during the next menstruation. If pregnancy does occur, the placenta begins to secrete a hormone called chorionic gonadotrophin almost as soon as it is established. This is similar to the luteinizing hormone of the pituitary and its function is to keep the corpus luteum going so that the correct hormones are secreted to prevent further ovulation and menstruation during the remainder of the pregnancy.

Sperm is formed in the testes (testicles) of the man. Sperm formation begins at puberty, under the influence of testosterone from the testes, as well as the luteinizing hormone (LH) and follicle stimulating hormone (FSH), which are produced by the pituitary gland, and which act on the testes in the same way that they do on the ovaries. Sperm count can decrease with age, and while production of sperm can speed up at times of sexual activity, numbers may decrease if ejaculation is frequent.

The average ejaculate contains approximately 300 million sperm, of which about 75 percent are motile (which means that they are capable of sustaining movement). Each sperm has a head, which contains its genetic material, and a long, thin tail which allows it to swim up the vagina and into the uterus. Sperm move quite quickly, but they can be slowed down by an acid environment, such as that of the vagina. The uterus is a more 'sperm-friendly' environment, but the sperm must travel a long way to reach the egg, having survived acidic vaginal secretions and cleansing cells in the uterus (which will swallow up stray sperm). Many sperm may enter the wrong Fallopian tube or simply miss the egg.

When a sperm does meet an egg, usually around a third of the way along the Fallopian tube, it fertilizes it. Both egg and sperm carry twenty-three chromosomes, and when they meet, the full complement of forty-six chromosomes is achieved and a new cell is formed.

Boy or girl?

Of the forty-six chromosomes, two determine the sex of the child, and they are known as X and Y. A woman's egg contains a single X chromosome, while the sperm contains either an X or a Y chromosome. If the egg is fertilized by an X chromosome, the baby will be a girl. If the sperm has a Y chromosome, the baby will be a boy.

● Y sperm swim faster, but they are smaller and live for a shorter period of time. If you have intercourse on ovulation day, or just after ovulation, you are more likely to conceive a boy. This explains the fact that a majority of planned pregnancies result in baby boys.

● X sperm are slower, but stronger, and they live longer. Therefore, if you have intercourse two to three days before ovulation, only the female (X) sperm will survive long enough to fertilize the egg, and you will be likely to have a girl.

After ovulation, an egg can only be fertilized for approximately 12 to 24 hours. Sperm can last up to 72 hours, if they survive the hostile vagina, and the long journey to reach the egg in the Fallopian tube.

Twins

When a woman produces more than one egg at a time, non-identical twins may develop from two eggs fertilised by two different sperm. Each will have its own placenta in the uterus. Identical twins come from a single fertilized egg, which divides into two and develops independently. Identical twins share a placenta. Triplets and other multiple births form in much the same way.

Twins and other multiple births are becoming increasingly common – in fact, 2 in every 100 sets of parents can expect to see more than one baby on the ultrasound scan, and those numbers seem to be on the increase. The good news is that with modern technology and enhanced knowledge, women carrying multiple babies are more likely than ever to deliver those babies in good condition.

What to do if you have problems conceiving

For many couples, it may take six months or longer to become pregnant. You will be diagnosed as having fertility problems if you have had unprotected intercourse for one year without conception, and for various reasons fertility problems are on the increase. The most important advice is: don't panic. A huge percentage of fertility problems are caused by tension and related conditions. If you stay calm, and positive, you are much more likely to become pregnant.

Male fertility problems can be linked to underwear that is too tight. Wearing boxer shorts can help by lowering the temperature around the testes, where the sperm are formed.

On average, 25 percent of women will conceive within the first month of having unprotected intercourse; 60 percent will conceive within six months; 75 percent will conceive within nine months; 80 percent within one year; and 90 percent within eighteen months. The remaining 10 percent may need some extra help to achieve a pregnancy.

There are a number of factors which can affect fertility. Apart from women who suffer from anxiety or stress, others who may experience difficulty are older than 35, when fertility begins to decrease dramatically; are underweight; have fibroids, chronic pelvic infections or endometriosis; or have an abnormal womb shape. Female infertility can be caused by a failure to ovulate, blocked

Take a good multi-vitamin supplement, with extra folic acid (for you) and zinc (for your partner) in the pre-conceptual period.

Fallopian tubes, ovulation or hormone problems, smoking, past methods of contraception (in particular the pill) and the production of antibodies to a partner's sperm. Male infertility is more common if you smoke or drink alcohol; wear tight trousers or are obese (both of which increase the temperature around the testes, where the sperm is produced); have had mumps or a previous genito-urinary infection; or again, suffer from stress. Other causes of male infertility include: pollution, which in urban areas has caused the average male's sperm count to halve over the last fifty years; poor sperm quality; sperm stuck together in clumps or sperm which cannot penetrate an egg; an absence of sperm, either because none is produced or because other delicate tubes which carry them are blocked; and hormonal problems.

Practical advice for conception

- The most likely days or nights you will conceive are the thirteenth, fourteenth and fifteenth days before your next menstrual period if you have a twenty-eight-day cycle. Record the dates of your period and time intercourse during the fertile period.

- Abstaining from intercourse for a day or two before these dates ensures a healthy sperm count during the fertile period.

- The best position to conceive is with the man on top. After ejaculation, the woman should remain lying down for about 30 minutes.

- Do not use KY jelly, which may inhibit sperm movement.

- Do not douche after intercourse.

- Stop smoking and drinking caffeine (coffee, tea, chocolate and cola), which can interfere with ovulation and sperm production.

- Try to reach and stay at your normal body weight. Being under or over your usual weight can sometimes interfere with conception.

- As stress can affect the ability to conceive in either partner, take time to relax, and perhaps take up a hobby or sport that you enjoy.

- Don't over-exercise. Intensive training has been seen to reduce sperm count in men and suppress ovulation in women.

- Studies in the US have shown that zinc is essential for sperm formation, and men who have zinc deficiencies may produce zero or reduced sperm counts. Zinc is also linked to the male sex drive, and most men are advised to take supplemental zinc when trying to achieve a pregnancy.

- Eating plenty of wholefoods, rich in vitamins and minerals, will ensure not only that sperm and egg are healthy, but also that the women's body is a welcoming home for the growing embryo. A nutritious diet increases the likelihood of conception and gives the baby every chance of a healthy start.

- Vitamins E and B6 are often linked to a low sperm count. Vitamin E may regulate the production of cervical mucus in women.

- EFAs (essential fatty acids, found in oily fish, fish liver oils, seeds, nuts, pulses, beans, evening primrose oil and unrefined vegetable oils) can stimulate the production of sex hormones.

- Aromatherapists claim that rose oil will increase sperm count and quality, as well as acting as a mild aphrodisiac. Add a few drops to your partner's bath, or perhaps engage in a little gentle massage, with two or three drops of rose essential oil in a mild carrier oil, like sweet almond oil.

- The herb agnus castus is an excellent hormone regulator and will help if you have irregular periods, or are not ovulating for hormonal reasons. It may also be useful you are prone to early miscarriage.

Treatment for fertility problems

The main prescription drugs offered include:

- Clomiphene, which is taken for five days near the beginning of your menstrual cycle to stimulate the ovary to encourage eggs to ripen.

- Tamoxifen or Rehibin has a similar effect.

- HCG (human chorionic gonadotrophin) may be given in addition to the above drugs if the ripened eggs do not seem to be escaping from the ovary.

- Pergonal may be suggested if Clomiphene is unsuccessful. Pergonal is a powerful drug containing a mixture of hormones, which is given in the first half of your menstrual cycle.

When these drugs fail, or the problem is male infertility, or cervical mucus problems that do not respond to treatment, you may want to consider:

- AIP – Artificial Insemination by Partner. This involves collecting your partner's semen on the day that you ovulate. The semen will be washed or prepared in a laboratory and injected into the cervix using a syringe, or passed into the womb using a slim tube. The success rate depends on the fertility of the sperm, but it can take up to twelve attempts before fertilization occurs.

- AID – Artificial Insemination by Donor. This involves using the sperm of an anonymous donor (although you can ask to be matched for race). All samples are carefully screened for Hepatitis B and, if they are frozen, for AIDS. It can take up to eighteen tries to achieve successful fertilization, but the success rate for fertile women trying over a year with frozen sperm is up to 90 percent.

- GIFT – Gamete Intra Fallopian Transfer. This involves collecting the eggs by a laparoscopy under general anaesthetic, usually after the woman has been given an ovulation-stimulating drug to produce several eggs rather than the usual one. They are mixed with a fresh sample of semen in a test tube, and then about four are replaced straight back into the Fallopian tubes with the sperm. GIFT uses either your partner's sperm or donor sperm. Some couples try up to six times before conceiving, while for others it doesn't work at all. The success rate is about 15 percent.

- IVF – In Vitro Fertilization is much the same as GIFT, except that once the eggs have been collected they are placed one at a time with a washed sample of sperm in a series of glass test tubes or dishes. The lab technicians check each one 48 hours later to see if it has fertilized and an embryo begun. Any embryos will be placed directly into the woman's womb, using a syringe and plastic tubing inserted through the cervix. IVF may require up to eight or even nine attempts, after which there is a 20 to 35 percent chance of achieving pregnancy.

- Adoption is an option for couples who either cannot get pregnant, cannot afford fertility treatment, or who find the treatments too stressful. Waiting lists can be long, so if you are considering adoption it is a good idea to get your name registered with a local adoption agency as soon as possible. There are at present at least twenty couples waiting to adopt for every baby available.

- Surrogate mothers are women who bear your child for you, having been fertilized by your partner (either by sexual intercourse or by AID), on the understanding that the child will be yours when it is born. Your physician will be able to advise you about this option.

You are pregnant

Probably the earliest sign that conception has been successful will be an instinctive knowledge that you really are pregnant. Some woman feel energized by early pregnancy, but most notice a very profound tiredness – usually unlike anything they have experienced before. Many women report dropping off to sleep in the middle of the day, or being unable to stay awake in the evening – probably as a result of the increased progesterone in the blood in early pregnancy.

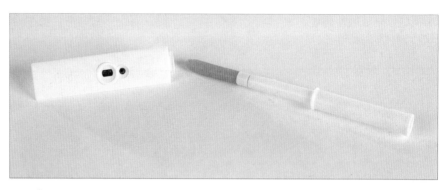

Modern home pregnancy tests are now accurate enough to record a positive reading just days after your first missed period. Try to test your urine first thing in the morning, when it is more concentrated, and hormone levels are more likely to register.

Other classic signs include: missing a period when you were previously having regular periods; having a short, scanty period and tender, swollen breasts with darkened nipples; feeling nauseous; needing to urinate more frequently; having an increased vaginal discharge; or suddenly losing your taste for some foods.

Diagnosis of pregnancy

If you miss two menstrual periods and you are usually regular, then may well be pregnant and should see your physician to confirm it. At this stage, your physician can usually diagnose pregnancy by a pelvic examination.

If you want to confirm your suspicions before this, you can try a do-it-yourself pregnancy test at home, or arrange a test through your physician, a family planning clinic, or a reputable pregnancy-testing service (many chemists now offer this).

Pregnancy tests

A blood test can be performed by your physician, and it can accurately detect the hormone HCG (human chorionic gonadotrophin) which is present in the

To estimate your delivery date, find the first day of your last period on the chart, and check the number directly below it. This is the date around which you can expect to give birth. Don't rely on this, however, as babies often have their own plans!

Week 1		Week 2	Week 3	Week 4	
28	1 2 3 4 5 6 7	8 9 10 11 12 13 14	15 16 17 18 19 20 21	22 23 24 25 26 27 28	1

First day of your last monthly period — Ovulation, conception — 4 weeks pregnant

January	1 2 3 4 5 6 7 8 9 10 11 12 13 14 15 6 17 18 19 20 21 22 23 24 25 26 27 28 29 30 31	January
October	8 9 10 11 12 13 14 15 16 17 18 19 20 21 22 23 24 25 26 27 28 29 30 31 1 2 3 4 5 6 7	November
February	1 2 3 4 5 6 7 8 9 10 11 121 13 14 15 16 17 18 19 20 21 22 23 24 25 26 27 28	February
November	8 9 10 11 12 13 14 15 16 17 18 19 20 21 22 23 24 25 26 27 28 29 30 1 2 3 4 5	December
March	1 2 3 4 5 6 7 8 9 10 11 121 13 14 15 16 17 18 19 20 21 22 23 24 25 26 27 28 29 30 31	March
December	6 7 8 9 10 11 12 13 14 15 16 7 18 19 20 21 22 23 24 25 26 27 28 29 30 31 1 2 3 4 5	January
April	1 2 3 4 5 6 7 8 9 10 11 121 13 14 15 16 17 18 19 20 21 22 23 24 25 26 27 28 29 30	April
January	6 7 8 9 10 11 12 13 14 15 16 7 18 19 20 21 22 23 24 25 26 27 28 29 30 31 1 2 3 4	February
May	1 2 3 4 5 6 7 8 9 10 11 12 13 14 15 16 17 18 19 20 21 22 23 24 25 26 27 28 29 30 31	May
February	5 6 7 8 9 10 11 12 13 14 15 6 17 18 19 20 21 22 23 24 25 26 27 28 1 2 3 4 5 6 7	March
June	1 2 3 4 5 6 7 8 9 10 11 121 13 14 15 16 17 18 19 20 21 22 23 24 25 26 27 28 29 30	June
March	8 9 10 11 12 13 14 15 16 17 18 9 20 21 22 23 24 25 26 27 28 29 30 31 1 2 3 4 5 6	April
July	1 2 3 4 5 6 7 8 9 10 11 121 13 14 15 16 17 18 19 20 21 22 23 24 25 26 27 28 29 30 31	July
April	7 8 9 10 11 12 13 14 15 16 17 8 19 20 21 22 23 24 25 26 27 28 29 30 1 2 3 4 5 6 7	May
August	1 2 3 4 5 6 7 8 9 10 11 12 13 14 15 16 17 18 19 20 21 22 23 24 25 26 27 28 29 30 31	August
May	8 9 10 11 12 13 14 15 16 17 18 19 20 21 22 23 24 25 26 27 28 29 30 31 1 2 3 4 5 6 7	June
September	1 2 3 4 5 6 7 8 9 10 11 12 13 14 15 16 17 18 19 20 21 22 23 24 25 26 27 28 29 30	September
June	8 9 10 11 12 13 14 15 16 17 18 19 20 21 22 23 24 25 26 27 28 29 30 1 2 3 4 5 6 7	July
October	1 2 3 4 5 6 7 8 9 10 11 12 13 14 15 16 17 18 19 20 21 22 23 24 25 26 27 28 29 30 31	October
July	8 9 10 11 12 13 14 15 16 17 18 19 20 21 22 23 24 25 26 27 28 29 30 31 1 2 3 4 5 6 7	August
November	1 2 3 4 5 6 7 8 9 10 11 12 13 14 15 16 17 18 19 20 21 22 23 24 25 26 27 28 29 30	November
August	8 9 10 11 12 13 14 15 16 17 18 19 20 21 22 23 24 25 26 27 28 29 30 31 1 2 3 4 5 6	September
December	1 2 3 4 5 6 7 8 9 10 11 12 13 14 15 16 17 18 19 20 21 22 23 24 25 26 27 28 29 30 31	December
September	7 8 9 10 11 12 13 14 15 16 17 18 19 20 211 22 23 24 25 26 27 28 29 30 1 2 3 4 5 6 7	October

18

Try to get into a regular exercise routine designed to keep you fit and supple throughout your pregnancy.

Early concerns

It is not unusual to experience mixed reactions to the news that you are about to have a baby. You may be worried about a drinking binge you had when you didn't realize you were pregnant, or perhaps you are an older mother and are concerned about the effect that will have on your pregnancy and your baby. No matter how much you wanted to become pregnant, feelings of elation may nose-dive when you realize that the next eight months will change your life forever.

Whatever your concerns, there are tests that can be done early in your pregnancy to reassure you that your baby is growing normally (see page 29). Pregnancy is a time of great physical change, and it can also be an exciting period of emotional growth and personal discovery. In these months, you have the potential to improve your health and vitality, and to influence your baby's development in the most positive way possible. The majority of us become more health-conscious when we are pregnant, and perhaps the most important way to begin is by embracing the essentials of a healthy diet, which will help you give your baby the best start in life. Eating well and keeping fit are crucial for a healthy pregnancy.

urine of a pregnant woman about two weeks after the first missed period. A blood test is almost 100 percent accurate, and can actually date a pregnancy by measuring the exact amount of HCG in the blood, since HCG values alter as the pregnancy proceeds.

Kits for do-it-yourself pregnancy testing are widely available, and they also work by detecting the hormone HCG. A negative result (that you are not pregnant) is less reliable than the positive result (that you are pregnant), especially if you are taking antidepressant drugs, nearing menopause, or having irregular or infrequent periods. To get the most accurate results, it is best to test your urine first thing in the morning, before you drink anything. Most tests will work about a fortnight after conception, but you may get a more reliable result if you wait three to four weeks.

Pelvic examination

From about four weeks after conception, your physician will be able to undertake an internal examination, which will show the distinct signs of pregnancy, including a slightly enlarged uterus, and a purplish cervix and vagina.

Your baby's arrival

When your pregnancy has been confirmed, you will be able to estimate when your baby is due. Only 4 percent of women give birth on their due date, because most full-term pregnancies can last anywhere from thirty-eight to forty-two weeks. The chart opposite gives you an estimated date for delivery (EDD). Find the first day of your last period, then look at the figure below it. That's your baby's EDD.

Try not to be tempted to drink coffee in the early months of pregnancy. While the odd cup will not do you any harm, caffeine is a toxin and will be passed to your baby.

A healthy diet

From the moment that you conceive until you give birth, and during breastfeeding, your body will provide all the essential nutrients required to nourish your growing baby. Food molecules pass from your blood into your baby's bloodstream through the placenta (see page 28). While your own circulation and that of your baby remain quite separate, you will breathe, eat and excrete for your baby throughout the pregnancy and labour.

A nourishing and balanced diet is extremely important during pregnancy, both for your own health and that of your baby. Eating fresh, wholesome and nutritious foods will not only help to give your baby a good start, but also act to suppress some of the more unpleasant symptoms of pregnancy. Although you will probably be hungrier during pregnancy, it is unnecessary to eat 'for two'. Concentrate on eating as many fresh, unrefined foods as possible, with plenty of variety and a good balance of proteins, fats, carbohydrates, vitamins and minerals. If you combine a healthy diet with regular exercise, you will have plenty of energy and strength to see you through the pregnancy, and help you recover from the birth.

Calcium is essential for the healthy development of bones and teeth, and is a natural tranquillizer, ensuring the normal function of nerves and muscles. Good sources include salmon, broccoli, sesame seeds, soya beans, dairy produce, and sprouted seeds.

Protein is made up of amino acids, which are called the 'building blocks' of our cells. These are particularly important in building the cells of your unborn baby, and an inadequate intake can mean a lower birthweight baby. Try to get at least 60 to 75 grams of protein every day from good sources, such as cheese, lean meats, fish, nuts and seeds, wholegrains, eggs, vegetable proteins and milk.

Supplements for preconception and pregnancy

It is important not to take too many supplements when you are pregnant (this can have a detrimental effect on your unborn baby), but to use them prudently, in combination with nutritious food. It is an indisputable fact that the chances of conceiving and giving birth to a healthy baby are increased by a good diet – in both parents. Studies show that poor diet and environmental factors may be responsible for a much larger proportion of birth defects, still births and miscarriages than previous believed.

● Take a good multi-vitamin and mineral tablet with high levels of antioxidants and zinc. Antioxidant vitamins and minerals help to prevent cell damage caused by oxidation, which can be crucial as your baby is developing.

● Avoid taking more than 10,000 iu of Vitamin A, which can cause birth defects in your unborn baby. Take Vitamin A as beta carotene, which is safer.

● Take a zinc supplement at 10mg per day.

● Take at least 400mcg of folic acid, which will help to prevent birth defects such as spina bifida.

● Partners should take 1000mg (1g) of Vitamin C daily in the preconceptual period, and 200 iu of Vitamin E, as well as extra zinc (up to 25mg daily).

Tips for healthy eating

In pregnancy, your diet should contain approximately 40 percent cereal foods, 25 percent vegetables, 30 percent proteins and 5 percent fresh and dried fruit.

● Select a diet that is rich in wholefoods and antioxidants (Vitamins A, C and E, and the mineral selenium), as well as

Vitamin C will help your body to absorb iron, boost your immune system, and establish a good immune system in your baby, which will kick into action when she is born. Vitamin C is also a natural antibiotic, and helps your body to fight infection and illness. Good sources include leafy green vegetables, citrus fruits, strawberries, blackcurrants, raspberries, watermelon, potatoes and cabbage.

Fibre is found in most 'raw' or unrefined foods, and is essential for keeping bowel movements regular, helping to prevent gestational diabetes, and preventing nausea. Most fibre-rich foods are both filling and low in fat –an ideal combination if you want to avoid putting on too much weight in pregnancy. Foods that are rich in fibre also tend to supply necessary trace minerals and vitamins, which are essential for the health of your baby, and you.

foods that are known to reduce damage caused by 'toxic substances', such as cigarette smoke, pollution and food additives. Foods or nutrients which neutralize mutagens (substances capable of causing the mutation of cells, which can occur as a result of toxins in the body) include burdock, mint, broccoli, green pepper, apples, shallots, pineapples, ginger, cabbage, aubergine, parsley and grapes. The beneficial effects of these seem to be lost when the plants are boiled. Unrefined olive oil and linoleic acid from nuts and seeds may also work against a large number of mutagens.

● Eat five or six portions of fresh fruits and vegetables each day – organic if you can get them, because organic produce can have up to 100 percent more nutritional value than commercially grown varieties. Try to choose seasonal varieties, and vary them throughout the week. Make sure you remove the skin or carefully scrub the surface area of all fruits and vegetables.

● Eat wholemeal breads and cereals, and brown, unpolished rice. You should aim for a minimum of five portions of wholegrain cereals or rice each day, six if you are vegetarian. Try whenever possible to eat whole rather than refined foods. Parts of the food are removed during the refining process and vital nutrients and fibre are lost.

● Pregnant women will need about three daily servings of dairy foods, or alternatives, made from protein or calcium-rich plants.

● Choose two or three portions of foods that are rich in protein, such as fish, lean meats, peas, beans, lentils, nuts, seeds and eggs.

● Always drink according to your thirst in pregnancy (you may find that you are very thirsty), and you may prefer bottled mineral or spring water to tap water. Avoid fizzy drinks, and instead of tea

Folic acid, which is a member of the B-complex family of vitamins, is required in twice the normal quantity during pregnancy, to help build red blood cells, and to develop your baby's nervous system. Good sources include leafy green vegetables, root vegetables, oysters, mushrooms, almonds, orange juice and dates.

Iron is an essential ingredient of haemoglobin, which carries oxygen in your blood, and as much as a third of your iron intake is used by your baby to make blood and build up stores for after the birth. Iron-rich foods include: dried fruit, eggs, beef, sardines, brewer's yeast, cocoa, wholegrain bread, beets, broccoli and leafy green vegetables.

and coffee drink mild herbal teas and grain coffees. Fresh fruit and vegetable juices are highly nutritious, and are best drunk immediately after preparing.

● If you find that you need to snack regularly to keep your blood sugar levels stable, eat small, nutritious meals four or five times a day, rather than three main meals. In between meals, nuts and raisins make a good, nourishing snack.

● Lightly steam, stir-fry or bake fish and vegetables to retain maximum nutritional value. Buy fresh local produce that has not been stored for long periods of time. You are better off eating frozen vegetables if you tend to let them linger in the refrigerator.

Important vitamins and minerals during pregnancy

Iron

Iron is essential for the developing blood supply of your baby, and for your own increasing blood supply. Try to get as much iron as possible from your diet (see opposite) and take a good multi-vitamin and mineral supplement with at least 30mg of ferrous iron. Iron is best absorbed when taken in combination with vitamin C, so drink a glass of orange juice with your raisins midmorning, or use a lemon dressing on your spinach salad.

Folic acid

Studies now confirm that folic acid is essential for the healthy development of your baby - in particular, the nervous system. Make sure that you include plenty of wholegrains and leafy green vegetables in your diet, to ensure that your baby is getting all he needs, and consider taking a supplement of at least 400mcg per day.

Zinc

The mineral zinc helps to encourage growth and healing, and there is some evidence that it may help to prevent nausea. Good sources include beef, seafood, nuts, carrots, sweetcorn, bananas and wholegrains.

Calcium

Your baby needs calcium in order to develop normally, and if there is a shortfall in your diet, your body will draw upon calcium stores in your own body (in your bones) which can cause serious problems in later life. Calcium is found in dairy produce, and in many leafy green vegetables, including broccoli.

B-complex vitamins

The B-complex vitamins are crucial for the normal function of the nervous system, and they have a range of other important functions in the body. Good sources include yeast, eggs, organ meats, soya beans, fish, wheatgerm, avocados and nuts.

Beta-carotene

Beta-carotene is essential during pregnancy both for its antioxidant activity (see above) and to ensure that your baby develops normally. Good sources include brightly coloured fruits and vegetables, in particular carrots.

Vitamin C

Vitamin C is necessary for both you and your baby - to repair and form tissues, heal wounds, ensure healthy growth and for the development of strong bones and teeth. Your baby cannot store vitamin C, so it is essential that you eat vitamin C-rich foods several times a day. There are dozens of sources of vitamin C (see page 21), and the fresher the source, the higher the levels of vitamin C.

QUICK GUIDE TO VITAMINS

VITAMIN	SOURCES
A	Dark green and yellow fruits and vegetables
B1 Thiamine	Wholegrain foods, brown rice, seafood and beans
B2 Riboflavin	Milk, cheese, yoghurt, leafy green vegetables, fruits, bread, cereals, meat
B3 Niacin	Meat, fish and poultry
B5 Pantothenic acid	Liver and kidney, fish, eggs, wholegrain creals
B6	Meat, wholegrains and yeast
B12	Fish, dairy produce, liver and kidneys, eggs
Folic acid	Fresh leafy green vegetables, yeast and liver
C Ascorbic acid	Fresh fruit and vegetables, potatoes, leafy herbs and berries
D	Dairy produce, eggs, fatty fish, fish oil. Synthesized in the skin from sunlight.
E	Nuts, seeds, eggs, milk, wholegrains, unrefined oils, leafy vegetables, avocados and soya
K	Green vegetables, dairy produce, molasses, cod liver oil, apricots, wholegrains. Synthesized in the intestines

Studies show that the healthiest babies are those born to mothers who took steps to eat well throughout their pregnancies. Consider everything you eat while pregnant, bearing in mind that good eating habits can affect the course of your pregnancy, and help to prevent complications.

What to avoid and why

● Refined and processed foods are best avoided, since they tend to have a high sugar and/or salt content, and a number of additives that may harm your unborn baby.

● Try to avoid spicy or fatty foods, which can cause indigestion, and which are, largely, unhealthy. Fatty foods, apart from having little nutritional value, will be laid down as maternal fat almost immediately, and it can be difficult to shift after the birth. Poor diets are related to a higher incidence of miscarriage, neonatal death and low birthweight babies.

● Avoid food additives, such as sodium nitrate, and flavour enhancers, such as monosodium glutamate. Nitrates can react with the haemoglobin in your blood, which will reduce its oxygen-carrying power. MSG can cause dehydration and headaches. Food

additives will be preceded by an 'E' number on the packaging, and for safety purposes, it is suggested that you avoid as many as possible.

● Caffeine (in tea, coffee and chocolate) is a stimulant and should be avoided in pregnancy. Tannin in tea will also interfere with iron absorption.

● There is no safe established level for alcohol-drinking in pregnancy, although most physicians generally agree that the odd glass of wine or beer will not damage your baby. However, to be safe, it is best to avoid drinking during the first three months. Fetal alcohol syndrome refers to birth defects caused by consumption of alcohol during pregnancy. The condition occurs most often in the children of women who are binge drinkers or consistent drinkers, but it is possible that even small amounts of alcohol may produce a lower-than-average birthweight and less

obvious adverse effects, as well as increase the risk of birth defects and miscarriage.

● Excessive intake of red meat is associated with high blood pressure, and should be avoided. Try to stick to fish and lean white meats.

● Avoid eating liver, which can have excessive quantities of Vitamin A (now linked with birth defects).

● Avoid raw eggs, and chicken meat that has not been thoroughly cooked. Always cook eggs and chicken well to prevent the risk of salmonella. Symptoms include headache, nausea, abdominal pain, diarrhoea, shivering and fever. See your physician if you experience any of these symptoms.

● Toxoplasmosis is caused by a parasite that can seriously harm your baby, causing brain damage, blindness and sometimes fatalities. The greatest danger is during the third trimester. Don't eat raw or undercooked meat, particularly steak and pork. Don't garden in soil used by cats and wear gloves when gardening. Try to avoid

Sex in pregnancy

Unless there is a threat of miscarriage, or your doctor has suggested otherwise, it is perfectly safe to continue making love throughout pregnancy, and indeed many women find that they are more in touch with their bodies during this time – particularly in the second trimester.

As your baby grows larger, you may wish to experiment with different positions, such as on your side, with your partner behind you.

Many couples prefer to engage in foreplay rather than penetration during late pregnancy, because they feel uncomfortable or afraid that it may damage the baby in some way.

Unless your pregnancy is high risk, there is no need to worry. The uterus does contract more strongly during orgasm in pregnancy, but it will not bring on labour unless the cervix is 'ripe'.

Foods to avoid in pregnancy are those that contain large numbers of listeria bacteria –such as soft cheeses, unpasteurized milk or honey, ready-prepared coleslaw, chilled convenience foods, pâtés and, in some cases, shellfish. Some of the suspect products can be eaten if they are heated to piping hot, which will kill any bacteria present.

cleaning your cat's litter box. If you cannot avoid it, wear rubber gloves and carefully wash your hands afterwards with an antiseptic soap. Cook meat to an internal temperature of at least 54 degrees C/140 degrees F, the temperature at which bacteria is killed. Wash your hands after gardening or petting animals.

● Foods that contain large numbers of listeria bacteria include soft cheese, unpasteurized milk, ready-prepared

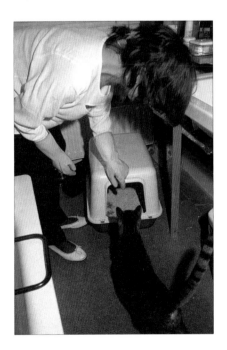

If you have a cat, make sure you wear gloves when cleaning the litter tray and wash thoroughly afterwards to avoid contamination with the toxoplasmosis parasite, which could seriously harm your baby.

coleslaw, cooked chilled foods, pâtés, and improperly cooked meat. Pasteurization normally destroys the bacteria, as does heat, so take care to cook foods until they are piping hot, and avoid reheating in the microwave. Reheat food thoroughly only once and then throw it away. Avoid dented and rusty tins, and don't risk any food that looks or smells as if it might be off. Thoroughly defrost all food, particularly poultry, and ensure it is cooked through.

● Avoid hot baths and saunas, which have been implicated in fetal abnormalities, particularly of the nervous system.

● Avoid using aerosol sprays, which are a source of potentially harmful chemicals, as are fumes from petrol, paint, glue and other such substances.

● In the first twelve weeks of pregnancy, try to avoid contact with anyone who has

a high fever, particularly children. Rubella is particularly dangerous (see page 12), and mumps increase risk of miscarriage. Chickenpox, although rare in adults, can cause fetal malformations. Some very virulent flu viruses can cause miscarriage, so play it safe.

● Avoid X-rays and any other forms of radiation, unless absolutely necessary. The likelihood of damage to the foetus from X-ray exposure is slight, but there are hazards.

Caution: Avoid taking drugs, unless prescribed by your physician. Specific drugs that may cause damage to your baby include:

● amphetamines
● anabolic steroids
● tetracycline
● streptomycin
● antihistamines
● anti-nausea drugs
● aspirin
● diuretics
● narcotics
● paracetamol
● cannabis
● sulphonamides

The pregnancy experience

The first few months of pregnancy represent a period of enormous change and adjustment, both emotionally and physically, and you and your partner may shift between feeling pleased or elated to being anxious or fearful. It is normal to experience these mixed feelings, and with high levels of hormones raging around your body, you may feel you have lost all control of your emotions.

Be prepared in advance and plan for the future; talk to health professionals, learn about the stages of pregnancy and what to expect at each stage, and organize your time carefully. It will make you feel a lot more in control.

Many partnerships start to fail after the birth of a child. As a couple, you and your partner should discuss how you think your lifestyles will be affected by the pregnancy and parenthood, perhaps with the help of friends or family who have recently been through the experience. Your relationships and personal freedom will change, and your financial situation, housing arrangements and mode of employment will all have to be reassessed. Talk about which parts of your present lifestyle are most important to you, and what you would most hate to give up; try to foresee possible difficulties and tensions

It's important to discuss your views on childrearing and issues like discipline before the baby arrives.

between you and think of ways to minimize them. Forethought, love and understanding will help you to get through this period of your life. Keep talking to each other and try to remain close.

Lovemaking is safe and often heightened during pregnancy, and unless your physician has suggested otherwise, it is perfectly all right to carry on normally. Be aware of any changes in your own and your partner's desires, and be open with each other when discussing your needs. You may want to concentrate on loving rather than intercourse, depending upon how you both feel, and this time together can be a source of joy and comfort for both of you. Try to involve your partner in the pregnancy process; explain what and how you are feeling, and reassure him of his importance. As your baby develops, he will want to experience those first flutters and kicks, so make sure you have time to be alone together as a couple.

Your first antenatal appointment is an intensive information-gathering session (see page 29) and many women like to have their partners along for that initial discussion about what to expect from the healthcare system over the next eight months. Try not to compare yourself with other pregnant women. Some women sail through pregnancy, get their figures back immediately and seem to be able to take part in their old social life a few short weeks after the baby is born. These women are lucky, not the norm, so you shouldn't feel discouraged if you are one of the many who suffer from the more unpleasant side-effects, put on a little too much weight, or find the whole experience

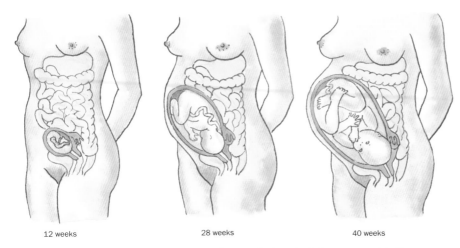

12 weeks   28 weeks   40 weeks

Your skin, muscles and ligaments are going to be stretched gradually to accommodate the expansion of the womb over the following months.

Kegel exercises

Kegel exercises, or exercises for the pelvic floor, are crucial throughout pregnancy, and should be done at least three times daily. The benefit of these exercises is that they can be done anywhere, at any time. Pelvic floor muscles are comprised of a sling of muscles that lie in two main groups, forming a figure eight around the urethra, vagina and anus. The layers of muscle are at their thickest at the perineum. You can exercise the pelvic floor by tightening and pulling in the muscles around your vagina and anus, as if you were stopping the flow of urine. Think of your pelvic floor as an elevator, and move it up the floors, holding for about 10 seconds at each 'floor', and then slowly bringing it back down again. These exercises will help during labour, and they strengthen the muscles of the vaginal and perineal area, preventing things like a prolapsed vagina or uterus, and stress incontinence. If you find that you leak a little when laughing or coughing, your pelvic floor muscles probably need some attention. During pregnancy, an increase in progesterone causes the muscles to soften and relax, but these exercises will help you to counteract this.

emotionally draining. No two pregnancies are alike, just as no two women are. Pregnancy offers you a wonderful opportunity to learn about your body, to get in touch with it, and to understand the miracle that is occurring within you. Gather information from others, but process it and adapt it to your own needs. Only you will know what is right for you.

It will take time to adjust to your changing body shape, and you may feel strange, even unrelated to the body you now find yourself in. Many pregnant women have simply forgotten their size and found themselves stuck in a narrow doorway, or knocked over a whole display in a shop. Changes occur fast and furiously. You may feel overweight and unattractive, particularly during the first months when there is no obvious 'bump' to indicate that you are pregnant. Try to learn to feel proud of your new feminine shape, and your

increasing curves. Many women feel extremely feminine during this time, and you may have an increased awareness of your own sexuality and fertility (although, don't worry if you don't, that is equally normal!). Remember that the hormones that are causing the mood swings are the same ones that will eventually give you shining hair, supple, glowing skin, and an aura of tranquillity and contentment – the bloom of expectant motherhood.

Kegel or 'pelvic floor' exercises should be practised several times each day throughout your pregnancy, and after. These simple exercises tone the muscles of the vagina, anus and perineal area, strengthening them in preparation for delivery, and helping to ensure a speedy recovery after the birth.

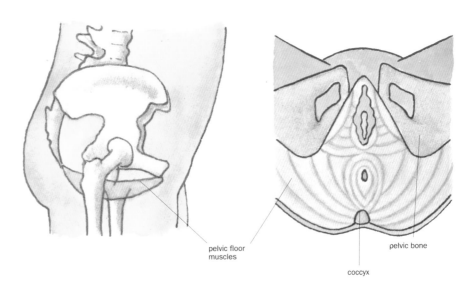

pelvic floor muscles

pelvic bone

coccyx

First four weeks

Pregnancy is measured in weeks, rather than calendar months; in fact 'nine months' is a rather misleading calculation since you may actually be pregnant for closer to ten. The weeks of actual pregnancy begin from the date of your presumed conception. Physicians refer to your weeks of pregnancy from the date of your last menstrual period, so although you may effectively be four weeks pregnant from the date of conception, you are officially six weeks pregnant.

In this book, the trimesters are described from the date of conception.

Trimesters are not of equal length and are defined by the baby's growth rather than calendar months. The first trimester represents the first twelve weeks of your baby's life, from two weeks after your last period; the second trimester ends at twenty-eight weeks, and the third trimester covers the remainder of your pregnancy.

Your baby's growth

During the first four weeks, the fertilized egg is implanted in the lining of the uterus, and the outer layers begin to form the placenta, which starts to develop a blood supply from your blood vessels. The inner cells are beginning to group into three layers, which will grow into three different parts of your baby's body, making him a complete and unique individual. Before you may even know you are pregnant, your baby will have reached a critical stage of development. By the second week, a rudimentary spinal cord will have appeared on the back of the embryo,

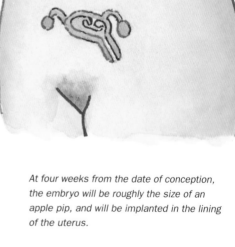

At four weeks from the date of conception, the embryo will be roughly the size of an apple pip, and will be implanted in the lining of the uterus.

A light, green salad to accompany a meal is a good way of getting one of the five daily servings of fresh fruit and vegetables you need.

and by the end of the third week your baby will have a heart that has begun to beat. The third week is the most important of your baby's development, when all the major organs are forming. By the end of the first four weeks, your baby will be approximately 4mm long, and will weigh less than a gram.

Changes to your body

Once the embryo has been implanted in the lining of the womb, you will not ovulate again until after your pregnancy, and you should not get any further periods, although some women do experience spotting or a light blood flow at the time of their regular period each month. The cervical mucus thickens to form a plug in the neck of the cervix, which will remain in place until you go into labour. Your uterus will begin to enlarge almost immediately.

You may experience

- some fatigue
- frequent urination
- nausea
- indigestion or heartburn
- breast changes, including tingling, fullness, tenderness, heaviness and darkening of the areole
- aversions to foods and drinks
- a heightened sense of smell
- mood swings, tearfulness alternating with elation

Antenatal visits

Your first visit to your physician will confirm your pregnancy, and you may make an appointment with the antenatal clinic as soon as you have a positive result. At the first visit you will be asked about your health, personal medical history, allergies, medication, previous illnesses, your family's medical history, your age, occupation and lifestyle, including whether or not your smoke, drink alcohol, exercise regularly and what you eat. You will also be asked about your gynaecological history, including other pregnancies and miscarriages, the regularity of your periods, and the date of your first menstrual period. Your physician or midwife will take your blood pressure, and probably weigh you, although

many hospitals are now avoiding regular weigh-ins (see page 50).

Routine tests

There are a number of routine tests that are undertaken at your first antenatal visit, and the most common of these are:

- a blood test, to determine your type of blood and to check for anaemia
- a urine analysis (make sure you drink plenty of fluids before your appointment), to check for sugar, protein, white blood cells and bacteria
- blood screens to determine whether or not you are immune to diseases like rubella

Other tests, which will be performed if required, include:
- tests to disclose the presence of infections such as sexually transmitted diseases, hepatitis and AIDS.
- tests for sickle-cell anaemia or Tay-Sachs disease
- a cervical smear
- tests for gestational diabetes

You will also be given details of maternity benefits, and notified of your rights in pregnancy.

Try to carry on with your normal exercise routine in early pregnancy, cutting back when you feel tired or uncomfortable. Keeping fit can help to ensure the health of your baby, and make your labour easier.

Five to eight weeks

The second four weeks often herald the beginning of the side-effects of pregnancy, which some women greet with relief, since it confirms that they are truly pregnant. Your baby will be growing rapidly and this is a crucial stage of development. The placenta will be also be developing during this period.

Your baby's growth

Your baby will, by the end of the sixth week, be recognizably human and the size of a small plum. He floats inside the amniotic fluid which is contained within a double layer of membranes called the amniotic sac. The tiny heart will be pumping blood around the embryo and out along the umbilical cord to the placenta. The head is almost half the size of the embryo, the side of the ears is evident and the eyes will have some colour. There is a perceptible face, and a mouth with a tongue. In the seventh week, the soft cartilage of the skeleton has started to change to bone, and the first movements can be detected by ultrasound. Your baby's limbs will have changed from being flipper-like appendages to limbs with joints, hands and feet with fingers and toes. All of the internal organs will be present and most major structures will have been formed.

Changes to your body?

Your metabolism will increase, which means that you will probably be hungrier, and will require more calories than usual. Your breasts will normally start to swell, and to become larger, and you will feel more tired than usual, and may even feel faint. The huge rise in the amount of oestrogen and progesterone in your body may cause, among other things, water retention, morning sickness,

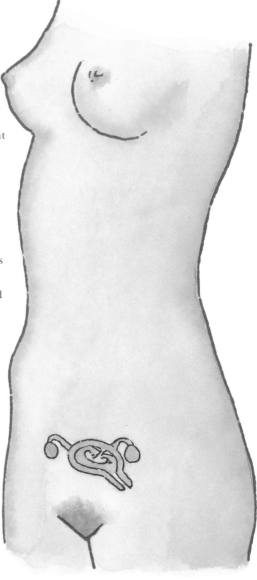

At around eight weeks from conception, the foetus will be the size of a strawberry.

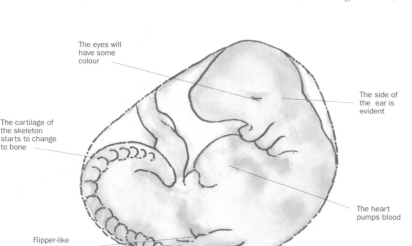

The eyes will have some colour

The side of the ear is evident

The cartilage of the skeleton starts to change to bone

The heart pumps blood

Flipper-like appendages become limbs with joints

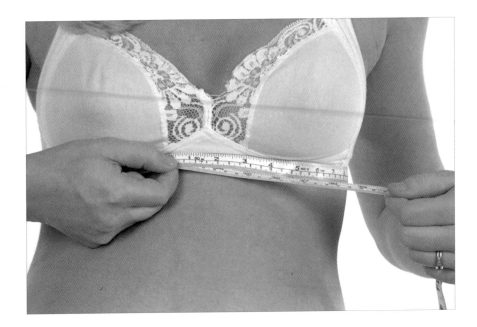

If your breasts become uncomfortable in the early stages of pregnancy, or you notice that they have grown, or appear swollen, take the time to be measured for a good support bra, which will help to ease discomfort and prevent stretchmarks and sagging later on.

and the relaxation of muscle tissues and ligaments, and you may experience some of the symptoms of PMS. The amount of blood and fluid in your body will be increasing, and you may need to urinate more frequently. Some women begin to feel pregnant for the first time during this period, and you may notice a slight swelling of your abdomen.

You may experience

- fatigue
- frequent urination
- nausea
- excessive salivation
- constipation
- occasional faintness or dizziness
- breast changes
- food aversions and cravings
- indigestion or heartburn

Antenatal visits

Your second appointment will take place during this period, and if you have not already had them, you will have the battery of tests necessary to provide basic information for your physician or midwife (see page 34).

At the second appointment, you can expect to be weighed, and have your blood pressure taken. Your urine will be tested for sugar and protein, and you may be asked to bring along a urine specimen in a sterile jar. You will be checked over for any swelling, and asked about any worries. Never be embarrassed about concerns that you may think are trivial. Health professionals are there to put your mind at ease, and to follow up anything that might be unusual.

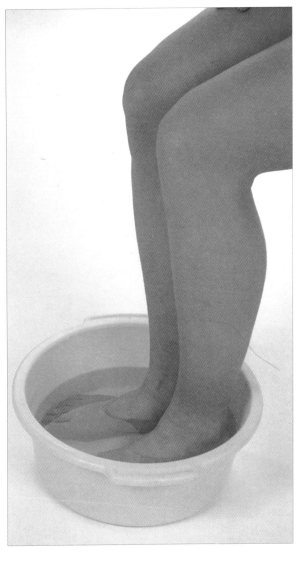

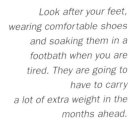

Look after your feet, wearing comfortable shoes and soaking them in a footbath when you are tired. They are going to have to carry a lot of extra weight in the months ahead.

Nine to twelve weeks

The third month of your first trimester will probably mark the end of nausea and some of the fatigue associated with the first few months of pregnancy. Your body will begin changing rapidly – it may seem as if it grows larger overnight – and the hormones that have been wreaking havoc with your system will begin to settle down. All in all, you will begin to feel more like yourself, and able to enjoy your pregnancy.

Your baby's growth

By the end of the first trimester, your baby's organs will have formed and begun working, and his intestines will be sealed in the abdominal cavity. There will be ears, a nose and recognizably male or female genitalia. Eyelids will have formed and closed over the eyes, which are continuing development, and nails will grow on fingers and toes. Your baby will be moving now, and you may feel some fluttering – some women describe it as the flopping of a goldfish out of water. His toes can curl and he can frown and open his mouth. Most of the time he is in the fetal position (with his chin down and his knees curled up). Fine hair covers the whole of the body.

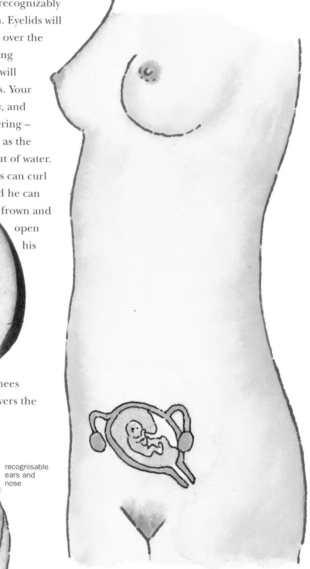

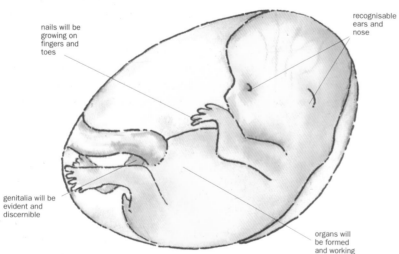

nails will be growing on fingers and toes

recognisable ears and nose

genitalia will be evident and discernible

organs will be formed and working

Your baby is now the size of a slice of apple, about 2 inches (5cm) long and weighing a little under 2 ounces (28gm).

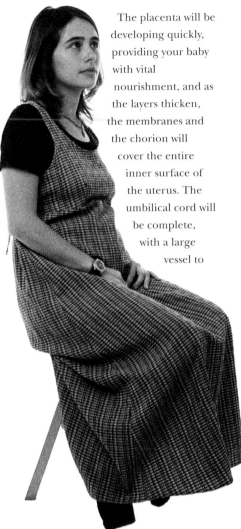

The placenta will be developing quickly, providing your baby with vital nourishment, and as the layers thicken, the membranes and the chorion will cover the entire inner surface of the uterus. The umbilical cord will be complete, with a large vessel to carry nutrients and blood to the foetus, and two smaller veins to remove waste products and blood that the baby has depleted of oxygen.

Changes to your body

You will begin to put on more weight during this period, as your baby begins to grow more quickly, and your physician will be able to feel the baby by gently palpating your abdomen. As your hormones settle down, you will feel more at ease with your body. Arteries and veins in your hands and feet will relax, as your cardiac output increases, and you may begin to feel warmer. You may notice increased skin pigmentation on various parts of your body, including a brown line (the linea nigra) which may appear up the centre of your abdomen. There will be a more definite rounding of your belly, and you may have occasional backache and sometimes sharp twinges or pain, or aches lower down the sides of your abdomen.

You may experience

- a slight lessening of fatigue as the weeks pass
- frequent urination
- occasional headaches
- venous changes; vessels may become visible through the skin
- breast changes
- constipation
- indigestion or heartburn
- nausea, although it should begin to wane toward the end of the trimester
- mood swings and other PMS-like symptoms, but a new feeling of tranquillity

Antenatal visits

Your third appointment will be much the same as your second, and your physician will establish the size of the uterus by feeling outside the body, to check the accuracy of your EDD, and the height of the fundus (the top of the uterus). You will have your urine tested for sugar and protein, and your blood pressure taken. You may also be weighed, and your hands and feet checked for any unusual swelling. The fetal heartbeat can be heard quite clearly now, and you may be offered the opportunity to hear it yourself using your

Chorionic villus sampling

CVS is a procedure that enables the accurate diagnosis of certain genetic disorders, and is usually undertaken between the tenth and twelfth weeks of pregnancy, and in the US, between the sixth and tenth weeks. Because CVS is carried out so early in pregnancy, parents have the option of deciding whether or not to terminate the pregnancy if the developing embryo is found to have a genetic disorder. In CVS, a small piece of the placenta (the chorionic villi: fingerlike outgrowths on the edge of the chorion, which contains the same genes as the embryo) is removed under ultrasound control, either through the cervix by means of a minor suction procedure or through the abdomen, and examined for disorders. CVS carries a small risk of inducing a miscarriage (about 2 percent). For this reason, the test is performed only when there is a clear risk of serious genetic disorder (see page 13). CVS cannot detect all inherited disorders, and, in certain cases, must be postponed until between the sixteenth and eighteenth weeks of pregnancy, when amniocentesis (see page 64) and fetoscopy (see page 65) can be performed. You will usually receive the results of your CVS test within about 24 to 48 hours.

physician's or midwife's stethoscope. This is an opportunity to discuss any concerns that have arisen, and to point out unusual symptoms. If you are at risk of having a Down's Syndrome baby, or if there are reasons to suspect that there may be a genetic problem, you may wish, or be advised to have, chorionic villus sampling.

Start your day with a good fibre-rich cereal, like muesli with a combination of fresh and dried fruits. Rich in complex carbohydrates, cereal is both filling and nutritious, and will help to keep your blood sugar stable throughout the morning.

Routine tests in the first three months

Blood tests

Your first blood tests will establish a number of criteria that will enable your physician to treat you accordingly. It is important to establish your blood group, particularly if you are among the 15 percent of women who are rhesus negative (Rh negative). Problems only arise when a rhesus negative mother has already given birth to a rhesus positive baby. In the next pregnancy there is a risk that the mother's body may consider the rhesus factor in her baby's blood to be foreign, and manufacture antibodies against it, which could destroy her baby's blood cells and cause serious anaemia. Occasionally, the unborn baby will be given a transfusion in the uterus. Almost all Rh negative mothers are given an injection which contains a rhesus antibody within 48 hours of delivery, miscarriage, or the termination of a first pregnancy, which prevents rhesus factor problems in subsequent pregnancies.

Many rhesus negative women are offered two anti-D injections during a first pregnancy, as well as one afterwards, for extra safety. If you are Rh negative in your second, or later, pregnancy, the level of antibodies in your blood will be checked. It is unlikely that the level will be high enough to put the baby at risk, but if it is, you will be given special care and may be referred to a specialist centre.

Haemoglobin level

Your haemoglobin level – the oxygen-carrying power of your red blood cells – will be measured. A normal level is between 12 and 14 grams; if it falls below 10 grams, you will be treated for anaemia (see page 66). Anaemia can make your system less able to cope with haemorrhage, which can occur suddenly in late pregnancy or at delivery, as well as making you extremely tired.

Rubella antibodies

Your test will show whether or not you are immune to rubella (German measles; see page 12).

AFP (alpha-fetoprotein)

AFP is a protein that is first produced by the yolk sac of the embryo, and later by the liver of your baby. The AFP varies

Your doctor will advise on the tests you need.

throughout your pregnancy. If the levels are unusually high in mid-pregnancy, there may be neurological problems, such as hydrocephalus, which is an excessive amount of cerebrospinal fluid within the brain. High levels may also be caused by a multiple pregnancy, inaccurate dating of the pregnancy, and a number of other factors, which your physician will discuss with you. An abnormally low level of AFP may mean that your baby has Down's Syndrome. If there are concerns about your AFP, you will be offered amniocentesis (see page 64).

Blood pressure

Your blood pressure will be checked at each appointment. Blood pressure is the

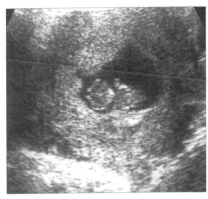
It's not usual to have a scan in the first trimester but if you do, you will see a distinct head and body and possibly the baby's limbs.

pressure at which your heart pumps blood through the veins in your body. The reading will be comprised of two numbers. The upper number, or systolic pressure, is measured when the armband is tight. This is the rate at which your heart pushes out blood, or beats. The lower number, or diastolic pressure, is taken as the armband deflates, and it measures the resting pressure between beats. An average reading is 120 over 70, but it will differ from woman to woman.

High blood pressure may have been present for some time before pregnancy, or it may be related to the pregnancy. Anxiety alone can raise blood pressure for short periods of time. If anxiety is the cause, the blood pressure will return to normal. It is common for blood pressure to fall slightly during the middle weeks of pregnancy and to rise slightly at the end. There are generally no symptoms, but extremely high blood pressure is associated with pregnancy complications and can harm the foetus. High blood pressure in the last three months of pregnancy can be a symptom of pre-eclampsia (see page 84). If you have high blood pressure, you should have frequent examinations. Not only will your blood pressure be monitored, but blood and urine tests will also be done to check on the function of your kidneys and the condition of the foetus. Ultrasound scanning is used to see if the foetus is developing at the usual rate. Your physician may advise you to rest, and if your blood pressure is above a certain level, one or more drugs may be prescribed to lower it. Most women with the condition have a normal delivery.

Weight

Many physicians and midwives choose not to weigh you regularly, because women can become overconcerned about normal weight gain and may be tempted to diet. The reason for weighing you is to ensure that you have not suddenly put on a great deal of weight, which can give an early indication of problems such as pre-eclampsia (see page 84), or to detect very slow weight gain, which may indicate slow fetal growth. If you are not weighed regularly during your antenatal visits, you will be asked to weigh yourself at home. Tell your doctor if at any time your rings become tight on your fingers or your ankles swollen as this could be a sign of toxaemia.

External examinations

Your abdomen will be gently palpated to determine the size of your baby. At about ten to twelve weeks, it will be possible to feel the top (fundus) of your uterus, which will be just above the pubic bone at this point. A measurement of the distance between your pubic bone and the fundus will be taken at each visit, and your physician or midwife will also be able to assess the quantity of amniotic fluid.

Internal examinations

You may not require an internal examination until later in your pregnancy. The purpose of this is to check the cervix, your pelvic size (to ensure that it is big enough for a vaginal delivery), and any pelvic disproportion, which will make a vaginal delivery difficult.

Urine tests

You will be required to provide a urine sample at each antenatal visit, which will be tested for a variety of things:

Sugar in the urine

If you have high levels of sugar in your urine, you may be at risk of developing gestational diabetes, a type of diabetes that usually only remains for the course of the pregnancy. The urine sample will also be tested for ketones, a high level of which indicates that diabetes is already established. Diabetes can lead to a number of problems in pregnancy and must be carefully controlled throughout. If you do have gestational diabetes, you will be given a diet to follow, which is normally successful in managing the condition. Some women may need insulin if dietary changes are not successful, and many suffering from diabetes mellitus or gestational diabetes will have their babies induced a little early, or have a Caesarean section, to avoid any potential problems.

Protein in the urine

Your midwife or doctor will test for protein in the urine, to see if your kidneys are coping well with pregnancy. Everyone has some protein in their urine, and pregnant women normally have a little more than usual, so tests often pick up traces. But in late pregnancy, protein in the urine can be an sign of pre-eclampsia (see page 84).

Fetal heartbeat

Your physician or midwife will monitor your baby's heartbeat early in the pregnancy. Your baby's heart beats approximately twice as often as your own, so don't be alarmed if it doesn't sound the same. It can be very reassuring to hear the heartbeat, particularly if you have been concerned about the health of your baby.

What happens in miscarriage

Miscarriage (known medically as a spontaneous abortion) occurs when a pregnancy ends naturally before the beginning of the twentieth week counted from the first day of the last period. After that time, the natural end of a pregnancy is called stillbirth if the child is born dead and a premature delivery if the child is born alive.

Miscarriage is very common, occurring in 20 percent of women who know they are pregnant, and many pass unnoticed as a particularly late and heavy period. Miscarriage results when the developing foetus and the placenta separates from the inner wall of the uterus. This may occur because of a developmental defect in the foetus or because the placenta is not attached properly. At least 50 percent of miscarriages result from a chromosomal abnormality in the foetus, but often the cause of miscarriage is not known. Miscarriages from falls or other injuries are uncommon, because the foetus is well protected inside the uterus.

Some women have what is called a 'threatened' miscarriage in early pregnancy, when there is usually spotting from the vagina. However, there is sometimes slight bleeding when

the fertilized egg implants in the uterus, and this may be misinterpreted as a threatened miscarriage. About one in five women has some bleeding during the first three months, but if care is taken, the pregnancy usually proceeds normally.

An 'inevitable' miscarriage occurs when the foetus has died, so nothing can be done to prevent miscarriage. In an 'incomplete' miscarriage, parts of the foetus and placenta remain in the uterus. A 'missed' miscarriage means that the foetus has died in the uterus, but there are no symptoms. Any type of miscarriage can be very emotionally distressing.

What are the symptoms?

The first symptom you are likely to notice when a miscarriage begins is bleeding from your vagina. This can range from a few drops of blood to a heavy flow. The bleeding may start with no warning or may be preceded by a brownish discharge.

A threatened miscarriage is often painless, but an inevitable miscarriage is usually accompanied by cramping pain in the lower abdomen or back. The pain may be either dull and constant or sharp and intermittent. At some stage during an inevitable miscarriage, you may pass some solid tissue through your vagina. As gruesome as it may seem at the time,

Caution: If you are pregnant and have bleeding from the vagina, with or without pain, contact your physician. If the bleeding stops or is not very heavy, your physician may recommend that you rest at home. However, if bleeding is heavy or pain is severe, you should see your physician immediately.

it is important to collect this tissue and take it to your physician for analysis, where it can be tested for chromosomal abnormalities.

In an incomplete miscarriage, you may have either constant or intermittent bleeding and pain for several days. With a missed miscarriage, you may have no bleeding or pain, but the symptoms of early pregnancy will disappear. Often the only symptom is that your uterus has not increased in size.

If the pregnancy seems to be continuing, even though you have had some bleeding, your physician may arrange for you to have another pregnancy test, and perhaps an ultrasound scan, to confirm that the developing embryo is still alive. It is best not to have sexual intercourse for a few weeks after bleeding, to give the pregnancy a chance to become more stable. Talk to your physician about other precautions.

In the case of a threatened miscarriage, there is no medical treatment, and you may simply be told to rest in bed as much as possible.

If your miscarriage is inevitable, missed, or incomplete, you may have the remains of the foetus and placenta removed from your uterus by your physician, usually in hospital but sometimes in your physician's office or in a clinic. Often the uterus can be emptied by a simple suction procedure but sometimes a D & C is necessary.

Recent studies show that women who have had one miscarriage are more likely to miscarry again, and the risk seems to increase if conception occurs too soon after the miscarriage. Experts recommend that you wait at least three months before trying to become pregnant again. There is a simple test, carried out before pregnancy, which can help to identify women who are likely to miscarry again. During the menstrual cycle, too high a level of LH (luteinizing hormone) before ovulation increases the risk of miscarriage. Some women do miscarry repeatedly, but your physician will undertake tests to ascertain the reason why, and take steps to rectify any problems.

Coping with miscarriage

There is a large number of support groups that can offer help and comfort after a miscarriage, and your physician can normally arrange some counselling. It is normal to feel guilt and despair, and you may find that friends and family find it difficult to discuss your loss, just when you need the most support. It is natural, and indeed, healthy, to mourn the loss of a baby, and it will take time to adjust both emotionally and physically. Your partner will also be distressed, and may be reluctant to share his feelings. Talk it through, and don't be afraid to express your grief together. Some couples find it helpful to name their baby, or to do something in his or her memory.

Keeping fit

It is perfectly safe to continue your usual physical activity while you are pregnant, unless you have had a history of miscarriage or your physician recommends some changes. Exercising regularly may help you feel well and keep you in good physical condition, which make your pregnancy and birth easier. Walking and swimming are the easiest and most gentle form of exercise recommended. Try to avoid strenuous sports and sports that carry a risk of injury. But as a general rule, after discussion with your physician, you can continue the forms of exercise you enjoy as long as you do not overtire or overstrain yourself.

Swimming is good for aerobic fitness and you will also find it one of the most comfortable forms of exercise, particularly in late pregnancy, as the water supports your weight.

The benefits of exercise

Exercising during pregnancy is good for you and your baby, and joining an antenatal exercise class can also provide an opportunity to meet other expectant mothers. The benefits are numerous – here are some of the most rewarding:

● The release of the hormone adrenaline triggered by exercise can lift your spirits and improve your sense of well-being. Your baby will also experience an emotional lift.

● Your body also releases hormones which act to soothe and tranquillize, and you will feel calmer and happier. Your baby will also feel happy and content as a result of the hormones released.

● Your circulation will improve, which means that you are likely to suffer fewer pregnancy-related ailments, and your baby will get the optimum level of oxygen in her blood as you exercise. This is important for her development – particularly that of her brain.

● You will regain your shape more quickly after pregnancy if you are fit. Labour will be easier and you will have more energy to cope.

● Exercising regularly helps to prevent stress, release tension and protect your spine, so that your body can accommodate the changes of pregnancy more easily.

● You will become more in tune with your body, and it will be easier to understand what is happening as your body changes and your baby grows within you.

What kind of exercise?

The best forms of exercise for pregnancy are those that do not place undue strain on your body, or raise your heart rate beyond 140 beats per minute (your exercise instructor will show you how to measure this by taking your pulse).

When lifting anything – from children to groceries – bend your knees until you are stable, keeping your feet well apart.

Use the muscles of your thighs and arms to take the weight rather than knees and elbows, to avoid straining joints that may be looser than usual.

Keep your back in a straight line from the back of the head down to the bottom and don't bend at the waist.

Aerobics

Aerobics that are specially designed for pregnancy can be an excellent way of getting fit and improving your cardio-vascular health. As long as you do undertake anything too strenuous, you'll see benefits within a few weeks. Always stop when you feel tired, dizzy, or are short of breath.

This is the wrong way to lift heavy loads. Bending at the waist can cause you to become unbalanced, and puts unnecessary pressure on your back.

Walking

Walking is an often underrated form of exercise which greatly enhances the health and fitness of even the most out-of-condition mother-to-be. If walking is your primary form of exercise, try to walk about a mile each day, in a pair of good, flat shoes. Take care to keep your shoulders back and tuck your bottom under your spine, so that you aren't putting too much strain on your musculo-skeletal system. Take a bottle of water or juice along with you, and sip regularly. Always stop if you become short of breath, or get a stitch.

Swimming

Swimming is an excellent form of exercise for pregnancy. It works to tone a large number of muscles in the body, as well as improving stamina, and because the water carries most of the weight of your body, you are unlikely to hurt yourself, or to strain muscles or joints in the process. Antenatal aqua aerobics classes are very popular, allowing you to get a good workout without straining yourself. It's particularly useful for women with knee or other joint problems, and for expectant women who are overweight.

Yoga

The extra progesterone in the body also relaxes ligaments that hold the joints together, so that your skeleton becomes more flexible and will expand more easily during the birth. Yoga is the ideal exercise, as it incorporates relaxation therapy to take advantage of this improved flexibility, and you will respond to the exercises more readily

Crouch on all fours on the floor, with your hands resting flat underneath your shoulders, knees slightly apart.

than if you were not pregnant. Yoga will improve all your vital bodily functions, including circulation, elimination and respiration, and will raise your level of stamina, energy and health in general.

You may wish to join a yoga class, and there are some designed for expectant mothers that focus on relaxation and breathing, as well as whole-body fitness and well-being. The following exercise comprises a lovely series of movements that loosen and energize the entire body.

Salute to the Sun

1 Stand tall, feet together, palms touching in front of the chest as if you are praying.

2 Inhale and stretch arms up and backwards. Tighten buttocks.

3 Exhale, bend forward and place hands on or near to the floor. Take head towards the knees. Legs are kept straight.

4 Inhale and extend right foot as far back as possible, toes touching the floor.

5 Exhale and draw left foot back to meet right. Head, back and legs form a straight line. Hold breath.

6 Turn the hands in slightly, bend the arms and knees so that the toes, knees, chest, hands and forehead are touching the floor.

Stretch your back upwards, feeling the muscles loosen, and then sink back to the starting position again.

7 Inhale, straighten the arm, as you bend backwards, the lower body resting on the floor.*

8 Exhale and raise the hips into the air, hands and feet stay on the floor.

9 Inhale. Bring the right foot forward, knee to chest, and raise the face to look up.

10 Exhale. Draw left foot to join right. Draw head to chest. Keep legs straight.

11 Inhale. Raise the arms above the head and bend backwards.*

12 Exhale and draw the arms together in front of the chest.

Perform the whole sequence twice and relax on completion for a few minutes. You may develop the number of rounds with practice.

When sitting back on your heels, ensure that your knees are pointing in the same direction as your feet.

* Omit backbend if you suffer from chronic back pain. Do not hold your breath if you have high blood pressure or epilepsy.

Posture

During pregnancy, the weight of your baby and uterus changes the posture of your body, so that the natural curves of the spine are accentuated. It is important to take good care of your posture during this time, which will help to prevent conditions like backache, sciatica, and even things like headaches and poor digestion, which can be exacerbated by poor posture.

Try to prevent any stresses to the body by wearing flat shoes and walking with your head up, rather than hung down. Tuck your pelvis under your belly and bring your body into alignment so that your abdomen is well supported. You can do this by loosening your knees. Try not to hollow or arch your lower back, which will throw the weight of your belly forward, placing strain on the abdominal muscles and the lower part of the spine.

Avoid crossing your legs when sitting, and straighten your spine by lengthening your lower back.

Stretch each leg in turn behind you, pulling the back straight.

When you are lifting a child or an object, bend down in a squatting position, rather than leaning forward from full height. Use your feet and leg muscles to propel you upwards, to avoid straining the lower back.

Yoga is a particularly good exercise throughout pregnancy – helping you to relax, keep supple and improving your circulation. It will also give you a chance to focus on your baby, which can be difficult for people with busy lifestyles.

Tips for exercising

● If you are not accustomed to exercise, begin slowly and don't exhaust yourself. Try to join a class where the exercises are specially designed for pregnant women, and do apply too much strain to the muscles and ligaments, which become softer during pregnancy.

● Always start with 10 minutes of warm-up exercises, which will stretch your body and prevent sore muscles. End with 5 to 10 minutes of cooling down. Stopping abruptly traps blood in the muscles, reducing the blood supply to other parts of the body. You may feel dizzy, faint or nauseous as a result.

● Make sure you are eating enough to compensate for the calories you will be burning off. Pregnancy is not a time for weight loss, and although you may become fitter and stronger and, as a result, lose some excess fat, you will need to eat plenty of good, nutritious foods to feed your body and your baby. Similarly, drink plenty of fluids throughout exercising.

● Wear loose, comfortable clothing that allows freedom of movement, and invest in a good pair of training shoes.

● Keep exercise to a maximum of one hour a day, even if you feel that you can do more. For most women, 20 to 30 minutes daily is quite adequate.

● Three or four times a week is usually enough to keep you fit, but try to keep your exercise routines regular. Exercising once one week and four times the next is counterproductive, and you won't develop the stamina and fitness you want.

Caution: If you have had repeated miscarriages during the early weeks of past pregnancies, or if you have recently had spotting, talk to your physician about whether you should exercise during pregnancy.

Common ailments

The first three months of pregnancy can be host to many unpleasant symptoms and ailments, which vary in severity from woman to woman. Although some women seem to sail through pregnancy with hardly a twinge or a moment of ill-health, others feel that their bodies have been invaded by aliens (or one big one) for most of the gestational period – with many disagreeable side-effects. The good news is that there are a wide variety of simple, practical treatments which can ease the discomfort of the first three months, and help you to prepare for the rest of your pregnancy and childbirth.

The first trimester is often the period in which many women suffer most, partly because your body is adjusting to the huge physical and emotional demands of pregnancy, and partly because you may feel slightly nervous or unsure about what to expect, particularly if this is your first pregnancy. Below you'll find explanations of why the most common symptoms occur, and what you can do to make life easier.

Morning sickness

The first and foremost complaint of many newly pregnant women is morning sickness – the ultimate misnomer, since the nausea and vomiting can occur at any time of day, and sometimes all day long. Morning sickness affects about half of all expectant women, and although there are many theories about its causes, no one knows for sure why some women get it while others do not. The most likely reason is a higher level of the pregnancy hormone HCG in the blood. Other causes or exacerbating factors include the rapid stretching of the muscles of the uterus, an enhanced sense of smell, less efficient digestion and, of course, stress, which can be the root of both fatigue and nausea. Whatever the cause, it can be either mildly irritating or completely debilitating. The good news is that symptoms usually last no longer than the first three months, although women carrying twins or other multiple pregnancies may suffer more severe or long-term symptoms. Only rarely does the condition interfere with nutrition enough to harm your baby, but if you are concerned, see your physician.

Note: Very rarely (about seven in two thousand pregnancies) vomiting is severe enough to cause dehydration and loss of body salts and minerals. This condition is known as hyperemesis, and requires hospitalization, where you will be given anti-emetic drugs to control the vomiting, and a drip to replace lost fluids.

What you can do

● Blood sugar levels can drop suddenly in pregnancy, and one of the symptoms can be nausea. It is a good idea to eat little and often throughout the day, avoiding fatty, spicy, sweet or refined foods in favour of small nutritious meals and snacks that will help to keep blood sugar levels even. A handful of nuts, an apple, cheese and biscuits, or a box of raisins are ideal snack foods. Eat foods that are high in protein and complex carbohydrates, and drink plenty of fresh, bottled water, particularly if you are vomiting frequently.

● Try to get lots of rest. Fatigue can enhance symptoms, and similarly, debilitating morning sickness can increase fatigue.

● Some women find that eating a high-protein snack before bed, such as a sandwich, or few nuts, and then a couple of crackers in bed upon waking, will help to prevent nausea in the mornings.

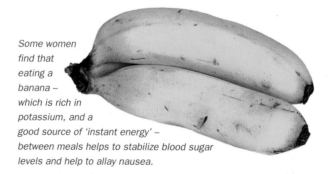
Some women find that eating a banana – which is rich in potassium, and a good source of 'instant energy' – between meals helps to stabilize blood sugar levels and help to allay nausea.

● Carbonated mineral water often settles the stomach, and adding a little fresh lemon juice will help to gently cleanse your body.

● Tobacco smoke and strong smells can exacerbate the problem, so avoid them if you can.

● For severe nausea, there is a homeopathic remedy called Ipecacuana, which can be taken three times a day for five days (stopping earlier if the symptoms cease). Get the 6x potency, and take care not to eat or drink for 30 minutes on either side of taking the remedy. Homeopathic remedies are completely safe in pregnancy.

● There are a number of gentle herbal remedies, and one of the most popular is ginger. Try chewing a raw ginger root, or if you find it difficult to keep anything down, infuse a lemon and ginger teabag, adding a little extra honey (pasteurized) and powdered ginger, and then freeze as ice cubes or lollies to suck when needed.

● Peppermint tea, sipped with a little cleansing lemon and honey, will also help to ease nausea.

● Dr Bach's flower essences are enormously useful. Try a few drops of Rescue Remedy (rub them on your pulse points if you can't keep anything down) to relieve the distress of vomiting. Crab apple may help any mental aspects of feeling nauseous.

● Nutritionists find that improving your diet and supplementing it with Vitamins B12, B6, folic acid and zinc help to improve fatigue and morning sickness. Talk to your physician about Vitamin B6 and safe levels in general (see page 21).

● An acupressure wrist band may be effective. These are marketed in the UK as 'sea bands', and are designed to prevent nausea – such as travel sickness or morning sickness – by pressing on specific acupressure points on the wrists.

Fatigue

Fatigue is an overwhelming feature of early (and often late) pregnancy for many women, as your body adjusts to demands placed upon it by a growing baby, and the high levels of hormones. When the placenta is complete (at about the fourth month), you should feel less tired; indeed, many women feel full of vitality at this time.

What you can do

● Feeling weary and extremely tired is absolutely normal, and is usually a message from your body indicating that

you need to rest more. In some cases, however, your diet may not be sufficiently nutritious (particularly if you suffer from vomiting or nausea). Suggestions for healthy eating are given on pages 20–23; make sure particularly that you get plenty of iron and protein. Drinks containing caffeine may provide short-term relief, but don't be tempted to try them , because you will feel much worse when the effect wears off. Your physician will test your blood to ensure that you are not anaemic (usually a deficiency of iron), and if you need more iron, you may be offered supplements. Do make sure you eat regularly, to keep energy levels constant.

● Try to get some more sleep. For working women it is often difficult to find a few moments to rest and relax, but be kind to yourself. Put your feet up during your lunch break, and try to take a short nap when you return

home from work. If you are at home during the day, a mid-afternoon nap of only 25 minutes can make all the difference. Many women need an extra 2 or 3 hours of sleep each day, so don't hesitate to turn in early, or turn off the alarm clock at the weekends to catch up on sleep then.

● Try to get a little exercise (see page 38). If you are fit, you will have more energy and stamina. Under exercising can actually cause fatigue, so try to take a short walk each day, or enjoy a relaxing form of exercise like yoga, or gentle swimming.

● Don't hesitate to pass on some of the household chores to your partner, or to friends or family. The first trimester will quickly pass, and it will help if some of the burden of day-to-day life is lifted from your shoulders.

Frequent urination

This occurs, particularly during the first and last trimesters of pregnancy, primarily because of the increased volume of body fluids, and the improved action of the kidneys, which help to rid the body of waste products more quickly. Your uterus is also growing, making less room for your bladder, which may not be able to expand to its normal size. When the uterus rises into the abdominal cavity in about the fourth month, you should feel some relief from these symptoms.

What you can do

● Try to empty your bladder each time you urinate – you can do this by leaning forward. Don't be tempted to reduce your fluid intake – you will find that you need a great deal more to drink during pregnancy, and it is necessary for both your own health and the health of your baby.

● Try massaging a little lavender oil, diluted in a carrier oil like grapeseed or apricot kernel, into your abdomen. This will help to reduce stress on the bladder, and will discourage any inflammation.

Moodiness or tearfulness

The high levels of hormones in the body can cause symptoms that are similar to PMS, including mood swings, irritability, tearfulness, irrational behaviour and even mild depression. While it is distressing to feel little control over your emotions, these symptoms will soon pass. Ambivalence about your pregnancy, particularly if it was unexpected, and overwhelming fatigue or morning sickness can all contribute, and it's more important than ever to take time for yourself, to talk to friends and your partner. It is also normal to feel anxiety and fear, particularly before you have had your first ultrasound scan. Don't hesitate to see your physician about any concerns you may have. There are wide boundaries for what is normal in pregnancy, and the chances are that the symptoms you are experiencing are well within them.

Many women choose to use natural remedies while they are pregnant, as they become more in tune with their bodies. Aromatherapy oils and herbal treatments can help you feel your best and can also deal with many of the niggling symptoms you might experience.

What you can do

● Drops in blood sugar can exacerbate symptoms, so make sure you eat small meals regularly, with plenty of nutritious snacks. Sweet, refined foods, alcohol and caffeine can make the symptoms much worse, so avoid them at all cost.

● Get lots of sleep, and naps when you can manage them. It's not always easy, particularly if you have older children, but try

As ligaments soften and your abdomen becomes larger, it can be difficult to find a comfortable position. Sleeping on your side, with a pillow under your abdomen, can help to ease the discomfort and ensure a good night's sleep.

to conspire with them to let you sit down and put your feet up, or take a nap when they do. If you find you are being irrational or overly irritable with older children, or your partner, gently explain that you are feeling low because of your pregnancy. It's amazingly reassuring for children to know there is a cause, and your partner will be more likely to be supportive if he feels involved.

● Take a relaxing aromatherapy bath every day. There are a number of oils that are safe in pregnancy that will help to calm you. Try a few drops of lavender or chamomile oils in the bath, or put a few drops on the lightbulb to soothe you. Your partner may also be able to give you a massage with a few drops of each of these oils in a carrier oil like sweet almond or grapeseed.

● Dr Bach's Rescue Remedy or Jan de Vries' Emergency Essence are both ideal standbys in pregnancy. Take a few drops on your tongue if you are feeling angry, frustrated, or emotional. Mimulus is great for fear of unknown things, such as the impending birth, or concerns about the health of your baby. Olive will help with overwhelming fatigue.

● Sip a cup of chamomile tea to ease symptoms – it's particularly nice with a little pasteurized honey and a squirt of lemon juice.

● Most important of all, don't feel guilty about your feelings or emotions, even if you find yourself losing control more often than you would like. Try to make your life as stress-free as possible; there is no doubt that stress exacerbates symptoms, and makes you feel less in control.

Food cravings

Some women experience food cravings from the very earliest days of pregnancy, others only later, and still others not at all. Don't be concerned if you don't crave the obligatory pickles and ice cream, but by the same token, it is normal to crave some foods and feel enormous distaste for others. Many women 'go off' coffee and alcohol, a result of your body's natural defensive mechanism. Cravings are often messages from your body that you are lacking certain nutritional elements, whether they are specific vitamins and minerals, or even proteins and fats. If you suddenly crave nursery foods like sausages and jam puddings, you may not be getting enough calories – specifically fat calories – in your diet. If you crave chocolate or sweet things, you may need more energy foods, while the craving for savoury foods like pickles and crisps is often related to a need for a little more salt.

What you can do

● If you have cravings, give in to them within reason. Try to find healthy substitutes for sweets or refined foods – nuts and raisins may not be as immediately satisfying, but they will provide good long-term energy. It doesn't matter if you succumb to the occasional piece of cake, or the odd bar of chocolate. Most foods in moderation will not harm you, if you take care to eat a balanced diet. If you find you are hungry all the time, eat lots of fresh fruits and vegetables, or low-fat organic yoghurts, which will fill you up without adding lots of calories that may be laid down as fat that is difficult to shift after the pregnancy.

● There is a possibility that you may have a mild chromium deficiency. Chromium is a mineral which helps to balance blood sugar levels in the body. If you are taking a good multi-vitamin or mineral tablet, you will be getting 'insurance' level quantities. Foods that are rich in chromium include: wholegrain cereals, meat and cheese, brewer's yeast, molasses, mushrooms and egg yolk.

Studies show that prudent use of supplements during pregnancy can help to ensure the health of your baby. A good multi-vitamin tablet, with at least 400mcg of folic acid, is now recommended for pregnant women of every age.

Cramps, twinges and unexpected aches and pains

Your body will be adjusting a great deal over the first trimester, and it is normal to feel the occasional sharp pain or twinge in your abdomen, as pressure is put on the ligaments that support the uterus. Cramps in the legs are common – usually later in pregnancy – and they are often caused by changes in circulation, possibly a deficiency of calcium and magnesium, and also the extra weight you are carrying.

What you can do

● If you are feeling achy or uncomfortable, try a relaxing massage or bath with a few drops of chamomile or lavender aromatherapy oils. This will help to reduce some of the symptoms. For cramps, blend a few drops of chamomile oil in a little grapeseed or apricot kernel oil, and massage into the affected area.

When to see your physician

You are the best judge of your own body, and if you feel that things are not right, don't hesitate to see your physician about your concerns. While the occasional grumbling pains or twinges are normal, do see your physician if you experience:

● bleeding of any description

● fluid leaking from the vagina

● severe pain in the abdomen

● cramping in the abdomen that doesn't subside within a few hours

● debilitating exhaustion that doesn't improve after a few good nights' sleep

● severe headaches

● severe nausea and vomiting (more than three times each day)

● fainting or dizziness

● visual disturbances

● unusual swellings or puffiness of the hands, face or eyes

● sudden need for increased fluid intake without the same degree of urination

Some women claim that a slice of fresh pineapple after every meal prevents heartburn.

● The tissue salt Mag phos (at 6x dilution) can be diluted in a little warm water, and sipped slowly in an attack of cramp.

● Calf cramps can be eased by leaning forward against a wall, and pulling out the muscles of the affected leg by placing the foot flat against the floor.

Indigestion and heartburn

As your uterus grows larger, it may push up into the abdominal cavity and reduce the amount of space available for the digestive organs. The high levels of progesterone also cause the muscle between your oesophagus and your stomach to relax, slowing the passage of food from stomach to gut. Some women find that digestion is much slower and less efficient. Heartburn itself is a burning sensation in your upper chest, felt when the acid from the stomach rises up. Heartburn is, surprisingly, extremely debilitating, and some women can suffer from this condition for the whole of their pregnancy.

What you can do

● Eat little and often, so that you stomach does not become too full.

● Avoid drinking anything with meals, as this dilutes the digestive juices and makes them less efficient.

● Avoid very fatty or spicy foods that may exacerbate the problem.

● One trick, which is infallible, is to eat a slice of fresh pineapple after every meal (tinned will not do). This seems to neutralize the stomach acid and prevent heartburn altogether.

● Sip a little peppermint or chamomile tea after a meal, to soothe the digestive tract.

● Some women claim that having a half glass of milk

Homeopathy is safe and effective throughout pregnancy.

before meals helps to ease symptoms.

● Raise your head and shoulders when lying in bed, and try not to lie down after a meal for at least a couple of hours.

● The homeopathic remedy Calc carb will help if your heartburn is caused by over-acidity, and heartburn without obvious acidity will respond to Pulsatilla. Homeopathic remedies are safe during pregnancy, and can be taken as required, for up to five doses, 30 minutes either side of food or drink.

Sore or aching breasts

Your breasts do become larger and fuller during pregnancy, in preparation for breastfeeding, and many women experience discomfort ranging from tingling to aching. Your breasts may also become the site of a network of visible blue veins, which will eventually form the system through which nutrients and fluids will be delivered to your new baby.

What you can do

● Make sure you have a good support bra that is professionally fitted. This will help to prevent the breasts sagging, and ease some of the discomfort. If you have full breasts normally, you may even need to wear a good bra at night-time.

● Gentle massaging of the nipples with a soothing cream, with a chamomile or calendula base, will help to ease soreness and prepare the nipples for breastfeeding.

Constipation

As the progesterone levels in the body rise, the muscles in the intestines relax, so that excretion is less efficient. More water is absorbed from the faecal matter during its longer journey, and as a result, it can become hard and dry, and less easy to pass.

What you can do

● Make sure you drink plenty of fresh bottled water and fruit juices (freshly squeezed are best), and eat plenty of fibre-rich foods, such as fruits, vegetables and wholegrains.

● Try to get some exercise each day, as it helps to improve the function of all the systems in the body, and will keep the digestive system working efficiently.

● Liquorice is an excellent natural laxative. You can purchase liquorice capsules in the chemist or healthfood shop (read the label carefully before taking) or buy fresh liquorice and add it to foods for flavouring. Figs, prunes and freshly squeezed fruit and vegetable juices will also work as a gentle laxative.

● Geranium and ylang ylang essential oils can be added to the bath to prevent constipation. A few drops of one or a blend will be sufficient. You can also add a few drops to a light carrier oil, such as sweet almond, and massage it into your abdominal area.

Moderate physical activity is now considered to be safe for pregnant women, and beneficial for both mother and baby. A good exercise programme –one which fits your daily lifestyle – will keep you fit and encourage a good blood supply to your baby.

Thirteen to sixteen weeks

The second trimester, or the middle months of pregnancy, can be characterized by a wonderful sense of well-being, as your pregnancy is well-established and many of the complaints of early pregnancy have passed. Your renewed vitality can make you feel able to achieve much more in a day without tiring.

Your appearance will also improve – most women have a clear complexion and a healthy 'glow', along with thick, shining hair. You will look pregnant over these months, as your body grows with your baby, and you will begin to feel your baby's movements, which can be an enormously rewarding and comforting sensation. You may need to invest in some maternity clothes to accommodate your growing waistline, although don't be alarmed if you seem to be either smaller or bigger than other pregnant women. Every woman grows at different stages, and muscles stretch at a different rate. Your physician or midwife will let you know if there are any problems with your baby's growth, and if they are satisfied, you have no need to worry. You can expect

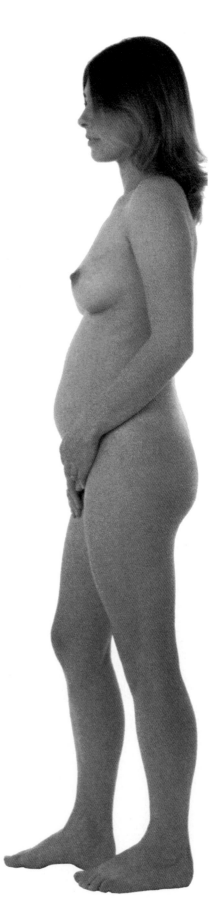

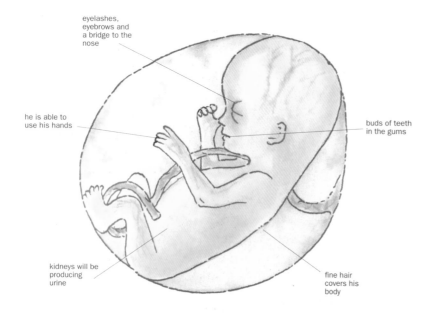

eyelashes, eyebrows and a bridge to the nose

he is able to use his hands

buds of teeth in the gums

kidneys will be producing urine

fine hair covers his body

to put on around 12 pounds (6 kilograms) during this period, although many women put on less, and many others much more than this.

Thirteen to sixteen weeks

The second trimester is usually the point at which you will have any extra tests to ensure that all is well with your baby. If you are over thrity-five, you will be offered amniocentesis (see page 64) and other tests. All women will have an ultrasound scan (see page 65) and you may want your partner to come along for this particular antenatal visit.

The thirteenth week marks the beginning of the second trimester of pregnancy, and you will probably begin to look pregnant for the first time, as your uterus rises above your pubic bone and begins to expand into the abdominal cavity.

Your baby's growth

Your baby will be steadily growing and by the end of the sixteenth week he will weigh about 6 ounces (180 grams), and grow to about 6 inches (13 centimetres) in length. Your baby is fully formed, and from now until the end of the pregnancy, the organs will continue to grow and improve their functioning. He is now completely nourished by the placenta. The kidneys will be producing urine, which will be discharged into the amniotic fluid. He will be beginning to breathe, swallowing the amniotic fluid, which is continually increased by your body. He now has a covering of fine,

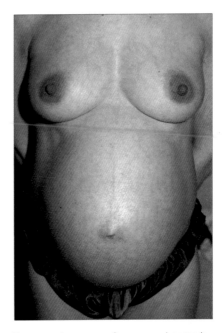

Pregnancy hormones often cause changes in skin pigmentation, and are responsible for the darkening of the linea alba – the white line which runs down the centre of your abdomen to the top of the pubic bone. During pregnancy, it is renamed the linea nigra, or 'black line'. Fair-skinned women may not see any changes in skin pigmentation.

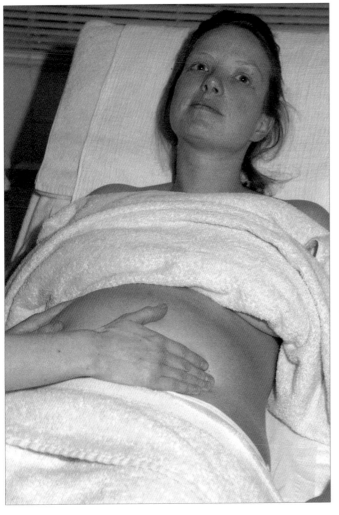

When your doctor or midwife palpates your abdomen, they are checking the size of the uterus to see how it correlates to the estimated date of delivery (EDD), or due date. They will also measure the height of the fundus (the top of the uterus) when it expands above the pubic bone.

downy hair, and will develop eyelashes and eyebrows, and a bridge to his nose. The eyelids are fused shut, and will not open until the sixth month of pregnancy. Your baby will begin to make facial expressions, frowning, pursing his lips, grimacing and appearing to squint. He will be able to use his hands, and grasp his other limbs. Some babies already find their thumbs and begin rudimentary sucking. Other reflexes, such as swallowing, will be developing.

The buds of his teeth will already be in his gums, and his fingernails and toenails will be more definite. The bones inside the ear will begin to harden, and your baby will be able to hear you, your heartbeat and other sounds of your body, which will comfort him.

Your baby will be active by this point, as connections are made between nerves and muscles, and he looks much more human, although the head is still large in proportion to the body. The external genitalia are being formed, and are becoming more obvious. The vaginal plate of a female baby is developing, and the testes of a male baby will begin to descend into the scrotum. It may be possible to see your baby's sex on the ultrasound scan, although many technicians will not disclose it unless you specifically ask.

Changes to your body

Your abdomen will become definitely rounder, and you may experience some backache because of the increased blood supply to the area, and the softening of the ligaments caused by the extra hormones in the body. If you continue to feel unwell, and your expectations of renewed well-being and vitality remain unmet, do not be alarmed, as this is not a sign that there is anything wrong. If you haven't already experienced a fluttering sensation, you will normally feel something around the fourteenth or fifteenth week. Women who have had previous pregnancies tend to be aware of fetal movement before women who are pregnant for the first time.

Your breasts may also begin to secrete a little colostrum, which is the early milk on which your baby will begin feeding when he is born. Your nipples may become darker, and your skin more deeply pigmented. Some women continue to suffer from sore, tingling breasts as they become heavier, but many merely experience an increased sensitivity, which can be pleasant.

Your heart will be working harder to push around the extra blood in your body, and all of your other organs will be under increased pressure as your baby grows larger.

Some women complain of being distracted and forgetting things they would normally remember. You may also have trouble concentrating, and experience some nasal congestion that also makes you feel as if your ears are slightly blocked.

You may experience

- some fatigue, but usually a general increase in energy
- relief from nausea (not always)
- constipation
- indigestion, heartburn and some flatulence
- increased vaginal discharge
- an increased appetite
- occasional headaches, faintness or dizziness

Weight gain in pregnancy

As your pregnancy progresses you may be feeling very heavy and bloated, and find it hard to believe you will ever regain your pre-pregnancy size. Weight gain in pregnancy varies from woman to woman, but if you have exercised regularly, and taken care to eat a healthy, balanced diet, chances are that you will lose any weight you have gained within the first couple of months after the birth.

In the past, doctors tried to limit pregnancy weight gain to 15 pounds (a little over 6 kilograms), but it is now recognized that this gain was insufficient, and babies were more likely to be born premature and underweight and to suffer growth problems in the uterus. Conversely, it is equally dangerous to put on too much weight in pregnancy, partly because of the strain it places on your body, causing symptoms such as severe back pain, leg pain, fatigue and varicose veins. Overeating during pregnancy can also make your baby too large for a normal vaginal delivery, and you may have to have a Caesarean section (see page 112).

The average woman can expect to put on about 3-4 pounds in the first trimester, about a pound a week during the second trimester, and a pound a week until about the eighth month, when weight gain drops off and you may even lose a pound or two. The total average weight gain is between 25 and 35 pounds, depending on your build, but if you have been eating a good, healthy diet of regular meals, you shouldn't be concerned if you have put on more. Some women have gained up to 60 pounds, and lost it almost immediately. Don't fight your body. If you are hungry, eat – just take care to eat nutritious meals and avoid high-calorie foods with little nutritional value.

If you find that you have put on too much weight, don't be tempted to diet. Losing weight in pregnancy can release toxins stored in the body fat into the bloodstream, which will reach your baby and may cause damage. Furthermore, your baby will have increasing nutritional requirements that must be met by your food intake, so cutting down on food will affect your baby much more than it will you, and leave you feeling tired and unwell. Change your eating habits to include fresh fruits and vegetables and plenty of wholegrains and low-fat proteins, and your weight gain will even out. It is useful to know that of about 30 pounds (12–13 kilograms) gained, only 7 pounds (3.25 kilograms) will actually be maternal fat – and that fat will be quickly used up if you plan to breastfeed your baby.

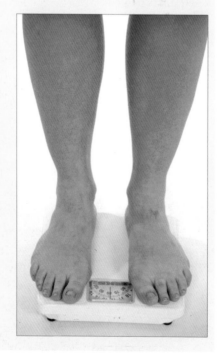

- sore, occasionally bleeding gums
- varicose veins
- haemorrhoids (piles)
- enlarged breasts, sometimes with tenderness
- mild swelling of the hands, feet, face and ankles (anything more than mild should be reported to your physician)
- trouble concentrating
- emotional highs and lows

Antenatal visits

The routine tests will be made, and the AFP (alpha-fetoprotein) test may be undertaken towards the end of this month (see page 34). You may also be asked if you have experienced any fetal movements, and the date at which these occurred will be recorded. If you have noticed any unusual symptoms, including swelling, headaches or sudden weight gain, let your physician or

midwife know, and they can run any necessary checks. Most physicians will also arrange a blood test around this point to check your haemoglobin levels.

If you are over thirty-five, or if your AFP test comes back with a low reading, you may wish to have amniocentesis. This involves drawing amniotic fluid from the amniotic sac, which is then analysed (see page 64). Some women may also choose to have the Bart's test (see page 34), which will help to predict the chance of your baby suffering from Down's Syndrome.

The incidence of Down's Syndrome is around 1 in every 700 births but it varies markedly depending on the age of the mother. For young girls, there is a 1 in 2,000 chance but for women in their forties, the chances are 1 in 40. The test will generally be offered to all mothers over the age of 35.

Choose clothes that are comfortable and not constrictive; even women who don't 'show' until later in pregnancy are likely to find their pre-pregnancy clothes tight around the waist and abdomen.

For many women, any nausea experienced in the first trimester of pregnancy will have passed, and you will feel more interested in food and in your diet. You may also find that you are hungry frequently throughout the day. Try to avoid filling up on unhealthy snacks, choosing a variety fresh fruits and vegetables – organic if you can get them – which will provide both you and your growing baby with the vitamins, minerals and other trace elements that you both need.

Seventeen to twenty weeks

The middle weeks of the second trimester are often the best of the entire pregnancy, and you will probably feel more like yourself than you have at any time. Because your pregnancy is now more established, you are likely to feel less fearful about your baby's safety. For many parents, this period offers them the first opportunity to see their baby 'on screen', in the ultrasound scan.

Your baby's growth

Your baby's development will have started to slow down now, although the weight gain will continue apace. A sheath will begin to form around the nerves in the spinal cord, to protect them from damage, and parts of his body will be covered in a substance known as 'brown fat', which started to form earlier in the second trimester, and which will continue to grow and cover the body in order to produce body heat and maintain his internal temperature. He will have a rudimentary immune system, which means that he is able, to a slight extent, to fight off some invading organisms. The skin will be red and wrinkled, and covered with the fine hair called lanugo. The body is also covered

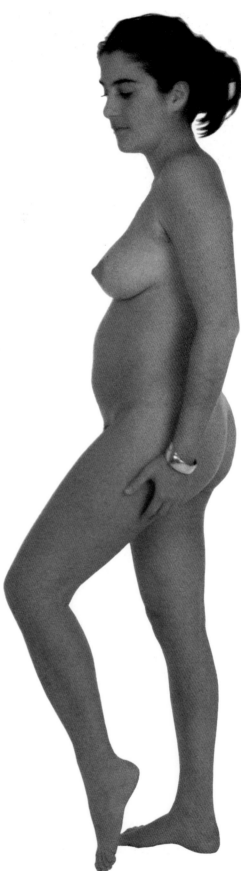

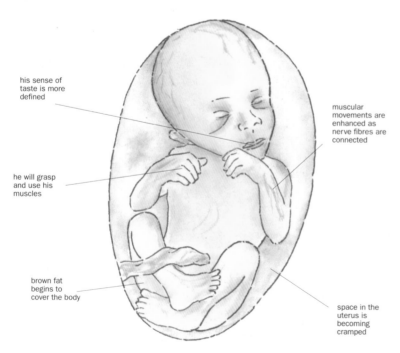

his sense of taste is more defined

he will grasp and use his muscles

brown fat begins to cover the body

muscular movements are enhanced as nerve fibres are connected

space in the uterus is becoming cramped

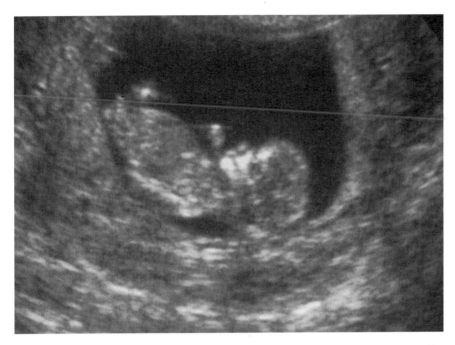

In this scan, taken at 20 weeks, the baby's head, body and limbs can be clearly made out, and its facial features are also visible.

hear you, and he will respond to music and rhythm. He will find your voice soothing, and you may find that he will respond when you speak or sing to him during a quiet moment. The noise level inside the uterus is high, with your gurgling digestive system, and the loud beating of your heart, but he can distinguish between external and internal sounds, and may even try to reach out towards the sounds. His sense of touch is more defined by this month, and he will be able to distinguish between sweet and salty tastes.

By the end of this month, your baby will be about 7 inches (18.5 centimetres) in length, and weigh about a pound (0.5 kilograms). If your baby is female, she will have ovaries and a hollow vagina in place, as well as nipples. If you baby is male, his scrotum will be solid, and he will also have developed nipples.

Changes to your body

As your waistline grows, you may find stretchmarks appearing on the skin of your abdomen, your lower back and upper legs. Your skin may also show tiny red marks called spider naevi, which are in fact dilated blood vessels caused by your high oestrogen levels. These may appear across your face, shoulders and

with a waxy substance known as vernix caseosa, which coats the skin and protects it from 'waterlogging' by the amniotic fluid. Premature babies will have distinctly less brown fat than full-term babies, and may have a heavier coating of vernix caseosa. Your baby will begin to put on weight, and his shape will become increasingly 'babylike', with a more rounded abdomen, and more fat on the chest, neck and limbs.

Muscular movements are enhanced, as your baby's nerve fibres become connected, and he will be much more active, turning, grasping and using his muscles on a regular basis both to improve motor skills and to strengthen the bones. He will become stronger, and you will feel his acrobatics as he practises his new skills. Your baby will

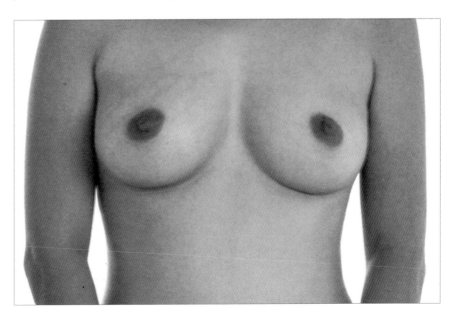

Your breasts will be heavier and may be feeling sensitive. Your nipples might darken and you may need to wear a bra in bed for extra support.

arms, and in most cases they disappear shortly after the birth. Blood vessels in your breasts will be more prominent, appearing as bluish lines leading down to your areole. Your breasts will be heavier, and remember you can wear a bra at night if you are concerned about sagging. The ligaments supporting your uterus may stretch and you may feel the odd twinge of pain or aching at the bottom of your belly. Your linea nigra (see page 49) may be more prominent (some fair-skinned women do not get one), and there may be skin pigmentation changes on your abdomen or your face, caused by the hormonal changes of pregnancy. Darkening of the skin will fade after pregnancy, but if you feel self-conscious, you can usually mask the changes with a good foundation. You can expect to feel hungrier, as your baby grows and requires more nutrients, and the demands on your body increase.

Most women feel comfortable with their pregnancy by now, and as mood swings settle, they are more able to enjoy it. Your baby's movements will be very definite, and you may feel anything from fluttering or a bubbling sensation to full-blown kicks. As your baby's hearing has developed, you will feel him respond to your voice, and to music. Some babies have been known to kick in rhythm!

Your baby's heartbeat will be strong enough to hear with an ordinary stethoscope, which can be exciting, and with an ear pressed to your belly, your partner may also be able to hear it, and to feel some movement. Make the most of this special bond between you, particularly when you are feeling fit and well, for it will help you to weather any tensions to come. As the reality of parenthood approaches, discuss the way you'd like to have your baby, and raise him. It is common to start evaluating each other in light of your new roles, and it may be difficult to cast your partner in the role of father, particularly if you have always had set ideas about how children should be brought up. Try to be patient and honest with each other, and accept early on that neither of you is likely to be the perfect parent, no matter how much you want to be.

Anxieties have a habit of manifesting themselves as dreams, and many women report having vivid, sometimes disturbing dreams while pregnant – often beginning around the second trimester. Remember to talk your fears over with your partner, doctor, friends or family, as this really does help to quell anxiety.

You may experience

- lower pain in the abdomen
- backache
- constipation
- haemorrhoids (piles)
- an increased sensuality
- cramping in your legs
- enhanced sense of smell
- larger appetite
- bleeding gums
- changes to you skin pigmentation
- heartburn, indigestion, flatulence
- occasional headaches, dizziness or faintness
- some swelling of the extremities, and your face
- varicose veins
- increased vaginal discharge
- some congestion of the nasal passages, and ears
- absentmindedness
- irritability
- a sense of calm and increased vitality

Antenatal visits

As well as the normal checks on blood pressure, swelling, weight and urine, and your baby's heartbeat, you may have your first ultrasound scan around this time (see page 65), which can be both alarming and exciting. Your baby's heartbeat will be checked, and you will be asked to report on any sensations or movements you have noticed. Your uterus will be palpated, and the height of the fundus measured. Take along a list of any questions you may have about symptoms, or a lack of them. You may also need to discuss your maternity rights with your physician or midwife, and you will receive official confirmation of your pregnancy, which may be required for any benefits to which you are entitled, as well as for your place of employment if you are working.

Many women will experience back pain and other muscular aches during this period, and it is a good idea to invest in a pair of sensible, flat shoes, with good arches to provide support. High heels are not recommended in pregnancy, and some doctors advise that you opt for wide heels to help keep the body properly aligned.

Twenty-one to twenty-four weeks

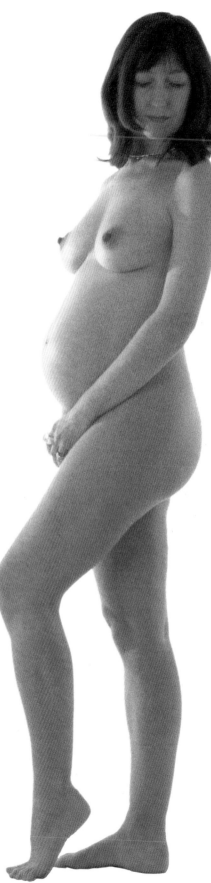

By the end of the sixth month, you will probably be very noticeably pregnant, and may even be growing tired of the focus of attention on your baby and your body. With the ultrasound under your belt, you may feel confident enough to think about decorating a room for your baby, or purchasing some basic articles of clothing or equipment. You may also want to consider signing up for a childbirth class, which you can attend on your own or with your partner to learn some of the techniques which will be helpful in labour.

Your baby's growth

As you near the end of the second trimester, your baby will be about 13 inches (33 centimetres) long, and will weight about 1¾ pounds (about 675 grams). Your baby will have thin, shiny skin with little underlying fat, but he will be sufficiently developed to stand a chance of survival in an intensive care unit, if he were born now. Although the lungs are still immature, they are developing quickly, and he will begin to practise breathing. He may even cough or hiccup – felt as a tiny rhythmic beat from the lower abdomen, which may last up to 30 minutes.

There will be more defined periods of wakefulness and sleepiness, and an early routine may appear obvious to some

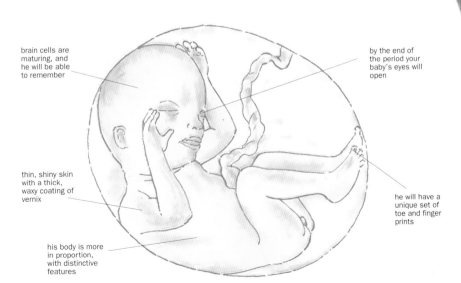

brain cells are maturing, and he will be able to remember

thin, shiny skin with a thick, waxy coating of vernix

his body is more in proportion, with distinctive features

by the end of the period your baby's eyes will open

he will have a unique set of toe and finger prints

mothers. The vernix on the body will be thick, and very waxy, and will appear white. By the end of this period, your baby's eyes will open. Most babies' eyes are blue at this stage, and will not change to their final colour until some weeks after they are born. A few babies, are, however, born with brown eyes. Your baby now has his own unique set of finger and toe prints, and a grip strong enough to support his own weight. His body will appear to be more in proportion, with distinctive features. Legs and arms will have the normal amount of muscle, and the centres of the bones will be hardening. Brain cells are now maturing, and your baby will be able to remember things, and to learn. He can also hear sound frequencies that we do not hear, and may move in response to them. From this month, he will be able to remember music, sounds and voices, and will respond accordingly. Songs that are played to your baby while he is in the womb are likely to soothe him when he is born, because of their familiarity. Your baby can also distinguish between father and mother, and will recognize your voice as soon as he is born.

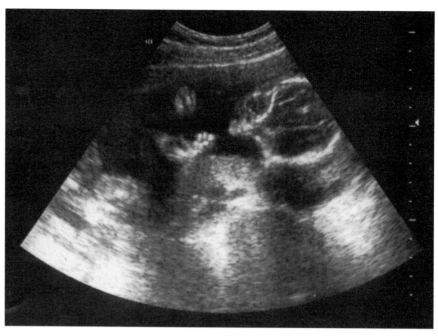

Not long after 20 weeks, your baby will be too large for the whole of it to appear in one picture and you will only see individual parts if you have a late scan, depending on the position the baby is lying in.

Changes to your body

You can expect to put on about 1lb (4g) a week from this point, although many women put on more. Your baby is growing quickly now, and your uterus will be pushing upwards against your ribcage, decreasing the space available for your stomach and other internal organs, and causing your lower ribs to spread outwards. You may experience some rib pain as a result, and suffer from some indigestion or heartburn. As the muscles of your uterus stretch, and the ligaments supporting it are strained, you may feel sharp pains or stitches, or a dull ache in your lower abdomen. Some women experience strain of the ligament holding together the pubic bone – the pubic symphisis – which can make sitting or standing for long periods quite painful. You will feel your baby on a regular basis, and will soon learn when to expect activity – often when you take a moment to put your feet up at the end of the day. Rest is also likely to be disrupted by leg cramps, particularly at night, and for the first time you may find it difficult to sleep comfortably.

Some women suffer from haemorrhoids, which can be itchy and painful, accompanied by some constipation as the digestive system becomes less effective. Remember to eat smaller meals, as your stomach is unable to expand to its normal size. The skin on your belly may also become itchy as it is

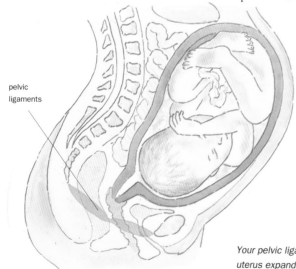

pelvic
ligaments

Your pelvic ligaments will be stretching as your uterus expands. You may feel sharp pains as they are strained.

stretched and pulled taut across your abdomen, and stretchmarks may become more prominent.

Mothers-to-be complain of being mentally fuzzy and absentminded. It is a natural side-effect of pregnancy to become more forgetful, a consequence of the hormonal changes in your body, but with rest and nutritious food you should feel a little sharper. Many women experience dental problems as their gums become swollen and inflamed, with a tendency to bleed more easily because of the same hormones.

With the date of the birth drawing nearer, you may be concerned about the labour, and the pain. Joining a childbirth class will help to alleviate some of your worries by sharing them with the other women, and by doing something positive, such as learning methods of pain control.

You may experience

● occasional headaches, faintness or dizziness
● pain in your back and abdomen
● tightening of the lower abdomen (early, mild contractions as your uterus shapes up for the labour)
● vaginal discharge
● constipation and haemorrhoids
● congestion of the nasal passages and ears
● leg cramps
● bleeding, sore gums
● enlarged breasts, and a larger, browner areole
● itchy skin across your abdomen
● stretchmarks
● changes to the pigmentation of the skin, including facial skin
● mild swelling of the face and extremities
● varicose veins
● increased appetite
● definite activity of your baby
● some anxiety about the birth and becoming a mother

● more energy and an enhanced sense of well-being

Antenatal visits

Apart from the regular checks on your blood pressure, urine and weight, you may have a further blood test this month to check haemoglobin levels, particularly if you are feeling more tired than usual. Your physician or midwife will listen to your baby's heartbeat, and you will usually be offered the opportunity to hear it yourself. The height of the fundus will be measured, and your abdomen will be palpated to check the size of the uterus and the position of the foetus. You will be asked about any unusual symptoms or concerns, and it is a good idea to go armed with a list of questions. Your midwife or physician will be able to offer practical advice about the common ailments of pregnancy, and may even be able to advise you of a good childbirth class in your area.

Learning to have a baby

Although women have been having babies for countless thousands of years, modern women do not have the support structure of an extended family, or indeed, experience of large families or labours where female family members are called upon to lend a hand. Many women become pregnant without ever having held a baby or with no knowledge of the nature of childbirth in any form. Furthermore, because more and more women work, there are fewer opportunities for pregnant women to come into contact with new mothers, or women who are also expecting. Our mothers are likely to have given birth with anaesthetic, with little prior preparation or understanding of what was to follow, so we are unlikely to have discovered the secrets of a successful, controlled labour from them. Today, with anaesthetics reserved for emergencies, and pain controlled rather than eliminated, it is important to be prepared for what is to follow, and your childbirth will be easier, less frightening, and more satisfying as a result.

A childbirth class offers you the opportunity to meet other pregnant women, and to learn some of the techniques that will help you to get through the labour. The benefits are numerous, and include:

● a chance to learn the most up-to-date information on issues surrounding childbirth and early childcare

● talking with other women and an expert instructor, who can help to eliminate your fears and concerns by giving you practical advice to help you through every eventuality

● the opportunity for your partner to become involved in the process, from which he may, until now, have felt rather excluded. Men often wish to take part in an active labour, and to be present in the delivery room; they will feel more confident and at ease with the situation if they know what to expect, and what practical steps can be taken to help you to cope. Many classes are for women only, however, with a special session for men.

● the chance to ask questions that you may find difficult to ask your physician, including symptoms that crop up on a weekly basis that are not worrying enough to warrant contacting your physician between visits, but which may prove irksome or irritating

● the opportunity to share advice and practical strategies for coping with pregnancy

● confidence in yourself to cope with the labour, and to deal with the technology available

● the opportunity to learn breathing and relaxation techniques and pain-control methods

● setting up a network of other parents-to-be which will help you to get through the early days of motherhood. Many women become firm friends with other parents in childbirth classes, and there are often reunions after the birth to encourage friendships and a good support system.

Relaxation techniques

Studies show that you may feel pain more acutely if you are frightened or tense. By learning how to relax and to breathe properly, you will feel calmer and will be able to cope better with your labour. Many childbirth classes focus on exercises for breathing and relaxation, which you will be able to put to use in the labour room, and in the later stages of pregnancy, when you may be feeling tense or uncomfortable.

Breathing is particularly useful for labour, and it isn't necessary to learn a whole series of complicated manoeuvres to benefit. Breathing is essential to life,

and is, traditionally, the key to health and peace of mind. Next time you are feeling anxious or upset about something, focus on your breathing and concentrate on taking slow, measured, deep breaths. Your body will respond immediately by relaxing, and you will feel a significant change in your emotional outlook as well.

While you are pregnant and during labour, you are breathing for yourself and for your baby, so it is important to ensure that you are breathing well. Spend a little time each day deep-breathing and concentrating on your breath, to help you use your resources to cope with any difficulties that may arise. Breathing deeply helps to make you feel grounded and enables you to release tension.

Deep-breathing exercise

Close your eyes and concentrate on each breath, and the feelings it inspires in your body. Focus on drawing the air deep into your lungs, and as you exhale,

relax your whole body. Find a comfortable position – the yoga position is ideal – and let your pelvis settle on the ground by releasing and lengthening your lower back. Stretch out your neck by letting your chin drop towards your chest and let your shoulders fall downwards. Your abdomen and your pelvic floor should also be relaxed. Put your hands on the lower part of your abdomen, and try to feel the rhythm of your breathing. Breathe out through your mouth and in through your nose.

Inhale slowly and lightly – try not to overbreathe. Feel the air come into your body and imagine it filling every space. Concentrate on relaxing all of your muscles as you do so. As you breathe out, imagine the air drawing out pain and tension, up through your lungs and out through your mouth. You should be able to feel the movement of the breath in your abdomen with your hands, while your chest remains calm and still.

When you breathe deeply, your baby's movements usually increase, centring your awareness on her. It is an enormously rewarding feeling to concentrate exclusively on your baby and her movements in your body.

During labour it is helpful to take shallow breaths in groups of three, when contractions are very strong, and you are finding it difficult to keep up ordinary, slow breathing. Try to breathe as you feel the need – not too fast and not too deeply, concentrating more on the breath out.

A basic relaxation exercise

Take a deep breath and sigh as you exhale. Let your body relax and the muscles go loose all over. Relax one arm and then another, and then your legs, one by one. Feel the tension ebb away from your shoulders and your neck, and imagine being able to pull pain away from your abdomen by relaxing and contracting with the contractions themselves. You may find it useful to practise this exercise with pillows.

Some women find it helpful to keep their eyes open and focus on one particular spot in the room – this will help during labour by preventing you from retreating too much into your own world, where you concentrate only on the pain.

Other forms of relaxation

● Many women find massage enormously relaxing, and the physical and emotional comfort of touch is important, particularly if you are feeling very isolated, alone or afraid. Your partner can massage you whether you are lying down, standing or squatting, and it is especially useful for backache. If your partner is massaging your back, ask him to concentrate on deep, downwards movements, as if he is helping to push out the baby with his hands. Massage in a circle around the centre of the lower back, just above the cleft of your buttocks.

● Water can also be therapeutic, and it will help to take pressure off aching muscles. It is usually possible to take a bath during labour, but make sure your bathwater is not too hot, which can constrict blood vessels and make the pain much worse.

● Visualization is a way of creating images in your mind. Before the birth, practise 'visiting' a place that you find calming or soothing – maybe a warm sunny beach, or a cool, moonlit lake. Explore this place in your mind so that you are familiar with it, so that when you are in labour, it will be easier to 'visit' it. It also helps to imagine your body doing its work. As a contraction comes, try to think of it as a productive and powerful wave that is washing your baby out of your body. Giving pain another 'visual' meaning will help you to control it.

● Many women find it helpful to shout and to sing in labour, which will release tension that may be exacerbating the pain of contractions. Don't be embarrassed about being noisy. A study done in the 1980s showed that Italian women, who are much more vocal in labour, suffer far less than their more reserved European contemporaries and tend to have shorter, less painful labours.

● If you have been attending yoga classes, you'll be taught special exercises for relaxation, which you can use for breathing through contractions.

Massage will help to relieve some of the aches and pains associated with later pregnancy, and can help to keep you calm if you are feeling anxious about the birth and your baby's health as the delivery draws near.

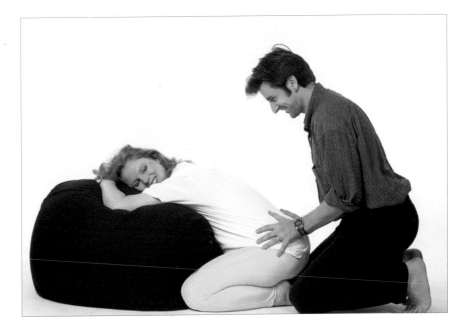

Twenty-five to twenty-eight weeks

The final month of the second trimester takes you to the end of the twenty-eighth week from the time of conception (thirty weeks since your last period), and you may start to become tired again, as your baby grows larger and places additional demands on your body. Many women find this a good time to think about their birthplan (see page 78).

Your baby's growth

By the twenty-eighth week, your baby will weigh about 3 pounds (1.5 kilograms) and will measure approximately 11 inches (28 centimetres) in length. These measurements will be confirmed by your ultrasound scan (see page 65). He will now have a mature respiratory system, and his lungs will begin preparing for the first breaths he will take when he is born. His growth over this period is increasing, and it is the last month in which he will be able to turn completely in the womb. His muscles are developing, through constant use, and while he will remain head up for most of this period, towards the end of the second trimester he will probably settle

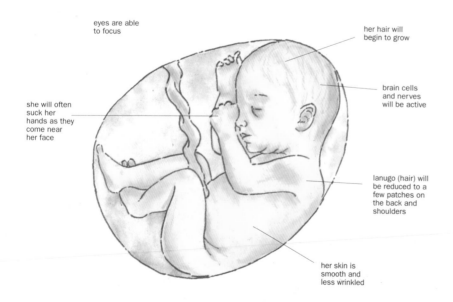

eyes are able to focus

her hair will begin to grow

brain cells and nerves will be active

she will often suck her hands as they come near her face

lanugo (hair) will be reduced to a few patches on the back and shoulders

her skin is smooth and less wrinkled

Stretching regularly will help to alleviate problems such as sciatica, and keep you supple as your body changes and has to cope with the extra weight on softening ligaments.

about a pound (half a kilogram) in weight each week. This weight is largely made up of the mechanisms of pregnancy, such as the placenta, the extra blood and other fluids, and the baby itself, so don't be alarmed if you seem to be getting heavier overnight. Your baby will be much larger now, and pressing against your bladder, so you will find that you need to urinate more frequently. Try to empty your bladder fully to help prevent a urinary tract infection, which is common during later pregnancy. You may also experience pain in your lower back, once again caused by the hormones softening your pelvic ligaments, and the size of your baby throwing off your centre of gravity. And you may suffer from sciatica, which is characterized by pain down the lower back, buttock and leg, and is often caused by the pressure of the enlarging uterus on the sciatic nerve in the spine.

From this point, your sleep may be broken by trips to the lavatory, and difficulty in finding a comfortable position. Many babies are more alert in the late evenings, which can also disrupt

into place for the delivery ('engage'). The bone marrow will produce all the necessary red blood cells, and he will begin to urinate regularly into the amniotic fluid.

If your baby were to be born now, his chances of survival would be good. Your baby is beginning to develop a layer of white fat under the skin, which will help him to control his own body temperature, and as a result the skin appears smoother and less wrinkled. As the fat is laid down, the lanugo (hair) will be reduced to a few patches on the back and shoulders. His sucking reflex is also near to being fully developed, and he will often suck his hands or his fingers as they come near to his face.

There are a huge number of developments in your baby's nervous system this month, and his brain will grow and fold over to fit inside the skull.

The brain cells and nerve connections will be active, and a sheath begins to cover the nerves to allow impulses to travel more quickly and more effectively. His eyes are able to focus, and the eyebrows and eyelashes are fully developed. Finger and toe nails are also in place, and growing all the time. The hair on the head will begin to grow, and he is beginning to look much like he will when he emerges in a few short months.

Changes to your body

You will be much bigger by this point, and can expect to carry on gaining

Until your baby turns into the head-down position, and settles lower into the pelvic cavity (towards the end of the second trimester), you may experience some breathlessness as the growing uterus expands up into the upper abdomen.

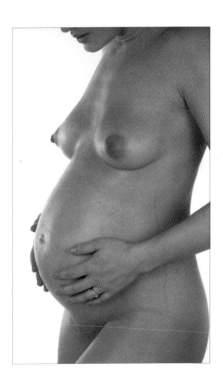

your sleep, as can vivid dreams, which may be disconcerting. If you experience swelling of your face, hands, ankles and feet, always tell your doctor. It may help to keep feet raised for an hour or so each day, to help redress the balance of fluids in the body, and take some of the load off your heart. You will be shorter of breath, as the uterus pushes up into the abdominal cavity, and may not be able to exercise as often or as long as you used to.

Your breasts will be full, and by now many women experience a slight secretion of the colostrum. Your vaginal discharge will become heavier, but it should be odourless and not irritating. Many women have their first contractions, called Braxton-Hicks contractions, which are usually fairly painless, but which indicate that your uterus is preparing for the labour to come. Your thyroid gland is more active, and your basal metabolic rate (the rate at which your body expends energy at rest) increases during pregnancy, so you will feel warmer – sometimes very flushed and overheated – and you will

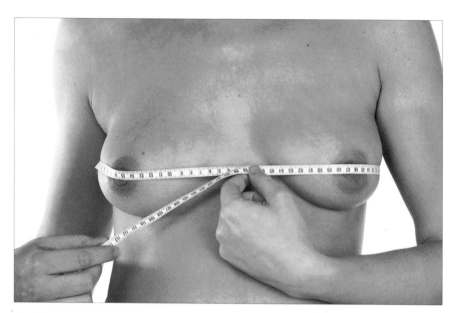

Your breasts will be full, in preparation for breastfeeding, and if you have not already done so, now is the time to be measured for a well-fitting bra. Women with heavy breasts may also need to wear a comfortable bra to bed.

perspire more freely, which helps to rid your body of waste products and cool you. You skin may be itchier, and most women suffer from stretchmarks as the abdomen expands to accommodate the growing baby.

Your baby will be very active, and you will feel kicks, somersaults, hiccups and all kinds of movement at different times of the day. With a hand on your belly, it is often possible to feel your baby's heartbeat.

Emotionally, you may find that you are increasingly nervous about the birth, and about your baby's health, as the delivery date draws closer. You may also find that you daydream more, and have decreasing powers of concentration. You may become anxious about how you will ever be a mother when you have no short-term memory to speak of, and you seem to knock over everything in your path, but be reassured that all this will pass as soon as your baby is born. Try to share your concerns with your partner,

Many women find relief from the common problems associated with pregnancy through yoga or meditation. Pregnancy can be a time of high anxiety, which can both cause and exacerbate symptoms such as fatigue, headaches, mood swings and aches and pains.

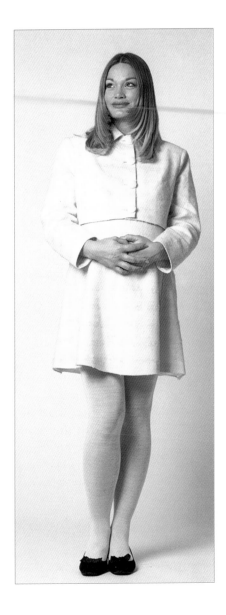

who will probably also be feeling anxious about the impending birth, and if you haven't already done so, try to find a childbirth class so that you will feel more confident about what is to come.

You may experience:
- sciatica and/or lower back and abdominal pain
- strong activity by your baby
- vivid dreams, daydreams and fantasies
- increasing fatigue
- increasing vaginal discharge
- constipation and haemorrhoids

If you are still working or have to attend smart functions, opt for co-ordinates without a waistband that allow you to move freely.

- some headaches, faintness and dizziness
- leg cramps
- disrupted sleep
- frequent urination
- Braxton-Hicks contractions
- varicose veins
- clumsiness, absentmindedness, anxiety about the impending birth
- sore or bleeding gums
- some swelling of your face, hands, feet and ankles
- itchy skin and/or stretchmarks
- shortness of breath
- weariness, feeling as though you have been pregnant forever

Antenatal visits

From this month, you may be asked to visit your antenatal clinic or physician more frequently, so that you and the baby can be monitored carefully in the weeks leading up to the birth. Your blood pressure will be taken, and you may be weighed. Your urine will be checked for protein and sugar, and your physician or midwife will listen to your baby's heartbeat and usually let you listen too. Some physicians ask you to record your baby's movements, and being forced to concentrate on these sensations can be reassuring. Many women are concerned that they do not feel enough

Many women choose to make a feature of their 'bump' rather than try to disguise it wearing smocks. If you've got it, why not flaunt it?

movement, but it becomes obvious, when you begin recording details, that this is usually far from the case. If you do not think your baby is active enough, or if he is inactive for long periods of time, talk to your physician or midwife, who will be able to reassure you.

The size and position of the foetus will be ascertained by palpation, and the height of the fundus will be measured. Some women may need a further blood test at this point, particularly if they have developed some anaemia (which is not uncommon in later pregnancy). Any oedema (swelling) you may have will be carefully checked (see page 68), and you will be asked if there are any unusual symptoms to report. You may wish to ask for advice on preparing your birthplan, which should be done some time over the coming weeks.

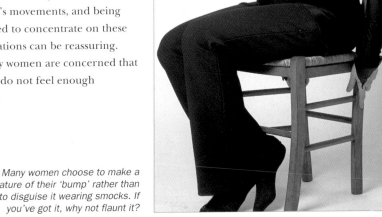

Tests in the middle months and what they mean

There are a number of common and less common tests which may be undertaken in the second trimester, according to your age, your health, and your specific needs.

Amniocentesis

Amniocentesis is usually undertaken in the early months of the second trimester, and it is an optional test for women who have a higher than average risk of carrying a baby with genetic problems, such as Down's Syndrome. If you have already had a child with a severe birth defect, if there is a family history of some abnormality, or if you will be thirty-five or older when the baby is due, amniocentesis may be performed between the fourteenth and eighteenth weeks of pregnancy, although it can be done a little earlier if necessary.

Amniocentesis is also used to determine the level of maturity of the developing foetus's lungs if premature labour is expected, or if the baby is to be delivered by Caesarean section. Your physician will insert a hollow needle through the abdomen and the uterine wall into the amniotic sac to withdraw a sample of amniotic fluid, which surrounds the foetus. An ultrasound scan is performed before amniocentesis to determine the exact position of the foetus and placenta, and your abdomen is numbed with a local anaesthetic before the needle is inserted. The fluid is withdrawn and spun in a centrifuge to separate the cells shed from the baby from the rest of the liquid. The cells are cultured for about two to five weeks, and therefore you cannot expect results until after that period.

These tests can identify many genetic abnormalities, and can also determine, amongst other things, the amount of oxygen your baby is getting, or whether a rhesus positive baby will require an intrauterine transfusion. By testing the acidity of the fluid, your physician can also detect fetal distress, and run a chromosome count to check for deviations. The procedure involves a slight risk of terminating the pregnancy (about 0.5 percent). Amniocentesis can also reveal the sex of your baby.

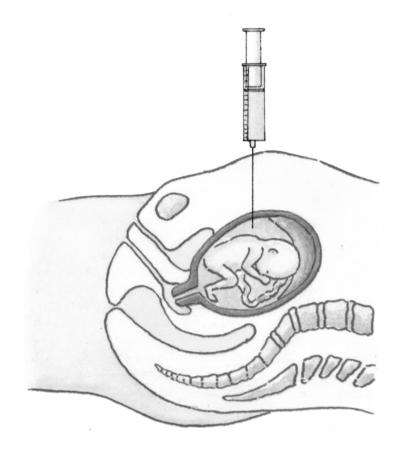

Amniocentesis involves drawing a small amount of amniotic fluid from the uterus for examination. The foetal cells, chemicals and micro-organisms in the amniotic fluid provide a wide range of information about your baby, including her genetic make-up, present condition, and her level of maturity.

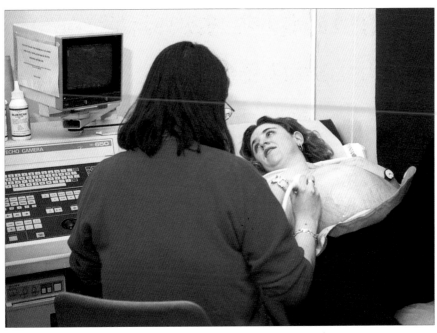

You will be able to see your baby moving on the screen during ultrasound.

Umbilical vein sampling

This procedure is used to examine the blood of your baby, and for an intrauterine blood transfusion if he has fetal anaemia, or if there is rhesus incompatibility. Under ultrasound control, a hollow needle is passed through the abdomen and uterus, to a blood vessel in the umbilical cord, where it removes a small quantity of blood for testing. There is a risk to the foetus of about 1 to 2 percent.

Ultrasound

Ultrasound is a device that transmits sound waves through body tissues, records the echoes as the sounds bounce off tissues inside the body, and transforms the recordings into a photographic image. When used on a pregnant woman, the surface of the abdomen is first covered with a film of oil, and the transmitter is then moved slowly over the surface of her abdomen. Ultrasound is performed as a matter of course in almost all pregnancies, and usually takes place between the twelfth

and twentieth weeks, depending on the policy of your physician or clinic. You may have further 'scans' at various stages, if they are required.

Ultrasound can be used to measure the size and shape of the foetus to help establish the stage of a pregnancy, to detect twins, to show the rate of development if growth problems are suspected, to determine the position of the baby during late pregnancy, to locate the position of the placenta if placenta praevia (see page 85) is suspected, and to detect any problems with your baby.

Ultrasound is an entirely painless procedure with no apparent side-effects for either you or your baby, and you will be able to see your baby moving, and hear the heartbeat. Some clinics will

give you a print of the image. You will need to drink plenty of water before the procedure, as a full bladder is required for a clear picture.

Fetoscopy

Ultrasound techniques allow your physician to obtain very clear images of the baby at all stages of pregnancy. In some cases, however, the physician may require a closer examination of the foetus, which can be undertaken after the twenty-second week.

With a fetoscopy, a laparoscope is passed into the uterus through a tiny incision above the pubic bone, in a technique similar to amniocentesis. Occasionally the laparoscope may be passed through the vagina. Once the laparoscope is inside, the physician can examine the foetus. He or she may also remove a blood sample by using a special attachment on the laparoscope. The physician may even perform an operation during this procedure. The entire procedure is monitored by ultrasound (see above). Fetoscopy is used only rarely, when there is reason to be concerned about the health of the baby.

Bart's Triple Test

A relatively new test, developed by St Bartholomew's Hospital in London, takes a sample of your blood at around sixteen weeks to measure the levels of oestriol, human chorionic gonadotrophin and alpha-fetoprotein. The results will be used to assess the chances of your baby suffering from Down's Syndrome. If the chances appear to be higher than the average of 1 in 700, you will be offered amniocentesis. If they are low, you may decide that amniocentesis is unnecessary in your case and that you would rather avoid the discomfort and the slight risk to the baby involved.

Common ailments

The second trimester is host to a variety of pregnancy-related symptoms which range from being merely irritating, to downright debilitating. The common problems discussed in the first trimester may continue into the second and third, and there are other symptoms which may crop up as well. You may suffer from any combination of ailments, or, if you are lucky, none at all. A troublesome pregnancy does not in any way mean that there will be problems with either the birth or your baby. If you are concerned about any health problems, see your physician.

Anaemia

One of the most important components of blood is haemoglobin, a protein that carries oxygen to the body's tissues. If the haemoglobin in your body falls below an adequate level, you are considered to be anaemic. The most common cause of this problem is a deficiency of iron in the body. Another possible cause of anaemia is an inadequate amount of folic acid. You may not notice mild anaemia, but if the condition is more pronounced, you might have any of the following symptoms: paleness, weakness, tiredness, breathlessness, fainting, palpitations, or an abnormal awareness of your heartbeat. Even if you have an adequate amount of iron and folic acid in your diet, you may become anaemic when you are pregnant. In addition, in about the fifth month of your pregnancy, the developing foetus will use more iron and folic acid.

What you can do

● You can help prevent anaemia during your pregnancy by eating foods that are rich in iron, such as beef, wholegrain bread, eggs, and dried fruits. Try to eat plenty of citrus fruits and fresh vegetables, because the Vitamin C in them helps your body absorb iron more efficiently. Make sure you eat plenty of green vegetables, since these are one of the best sources of folic acid.

● Constipation can be a problem if you are taking iron supplements prescribed by your physician, but can be avoided if you opt for a good iron-rich tonic, made from food and herbal sources rich in iron such as dandelion leaves, nettles, chives, sorrel and coriander leaves.

● The homeopathic remedy Kali carb is useful for anaemia, when your back feels weak and tired and there are dragging pains.

● Olive flower essence will ease symptoms of fatigue.

Varicose veins

Many women suffer from varicose veins during pregnancy, and the problem is especially common in the last three months. When you are pregnant, your blood vessels are forced to accommodate an increased volume of blood in order to supply the needs of your developing baby. As the uterus enlarges and presses on some of the major veins, the flow of blood from the leg veins up to the pelvis slows down. This combination of factors sometimes produces pressure that causes the veins in the calves and thighs to become swollen and painful. The veins around the entrance to the vagina and rectum may also be affected as a result of the same kinds of pressure.

What you can do

● Wear loose clothing, particularly around your legs and waist, and avoid standing for long periods of time. Rest with your feet up as often as possible. If you are working and you spend a lot of time on your feet, sit down and rest as much as possible. Excessive weight gain during pregnancy can also put additional strain on the system.

● Elastic stockings relieve the discomfort of varicose veins significantly. You can ask your physician to prescribe specially fitted stockings or buy them over the counter. Put them on first thing in the morning, before you get out of bed.

● Calendula, marjoram and comfrey are astringent herbs and they can be soaked in warm water applied to the legs or vulva as required to ease the symptoms of varicose veins.

● An infusion of peppermint tea will help to improve circulation and treat varicose veins. Drink as required.

● Some women report that an application of neat lemon juice, which is an astringent, to the varicose veins in your legs relieves the irritation, and helps to reduce swelling. Witch hazel has the same effect. Never rub a varicose vein, always dab carefully around the site.

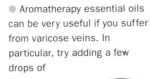

● Aromatherapy essential oils can be very useful if you suffer from varicose veins. In particular, try adding a few drops of thyme, 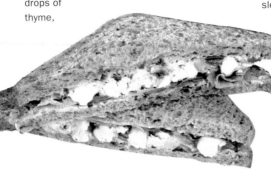 lavender and lemon oils to the bathwater to strengthen the veins and increase circulation.

● Vitamins C and E and bioflavonoids, zinc and brewer's yeast will help to heal damaged blood vessels causing varicose veins. If you are taking a good multi-vitamin and mineral supplement, you should be getting an insurance level dose of each; however, it is wise to increase your intake of foods containing these nutrients.

Headaches

Occasional headaches are common in pregnancy, due to the hormonal changes and the extra stress on your body. Your posture will change, putting pressure on the muscles of your back and neck, which may also cause you to feel achy. Fatigue, low blood sugar, hunger or stress and anxiety can also exacerbate the problem.

What you can do

● Try to find ways to relax, whether you enjoy a long, leisurely walk or a swim, or curling up with a good book and a cup of chamomile tea. Many women find that yoga is an excellent form of exercise and relaxation, and that it reduces some of the problems associated with pregnancy.

● Make sure you get enough sleep. If you are having trouble sleeping, see page 86 for tips on getting to sleep and staying asleep.

● Eat regularly – eating small meals will often help to keep your blood pressure even. Carry nutritious snacks in your handbag, to get you through the periods between meals.

● Try to stand properly (see page 40); slouching can cause headaches. A good technique is to place a couple of books on the floor, lie on your back and place your head on them, so that the back of your neck, just where it reaches your skull, is resting on the edge of the top of the pile. Let your shoulders sink towards the floor. Pull your chin towards your chest, and then raise it up again. Rest on the books for about 10 minutes, and headaches caused by muscular or structural problems will be eased significantly.

● Many women find that a drop of lavender essential oil, applied neat to the nostrils, or added to the bath (use two or three drops) will help to ease the pain of headaches and help you to relax and sleep well.

● Rescue Remedy or Emergency Essence can be rubbed into the temples during a headache to relax you, and reduce pain.

Caution: If you have a headache that lasts for more than a few hours, or that is recurrent or accompanied by fever, call your physician immediately.

Faintness and dizziness

Dizziness is common in pregnancy, particularly in the early stages of pregnancy when the blood supply is inadequate for the increasing circulatory needs. In the second trimester, it may be caused by the pressure of the uterus on the blood vessels. You may feel dizzy or faint when you suddenly rise from sitting or lying down, or in a crowded, overheated room. You may also experience a drop in blood sugar levels that makes you feel faint. Fainting is quite rare (although you may feel very faint), and should be reported to your physician.

What you can do

● Always stand up slowly after sitting or lying down for extended periods of time.

● Eat little and often, to ensure that your blood sugar levels remain stable.

● Try to avoid hot, crowded rooms, but if this is impossible, wear loose, cool clothing, and try to position yourself next to a source of fresh air.

● If you do feel as though you are going to faint, sit down, and elevate your feet or, alternatively, put your head between your knees (if you can!) until the symptoms pass.

● Rescue Remedy or Emergency Essence contain a blend of flower essences which can help you to cope with feelings of faintness and dizziness. If you

feel dizzy, or faint, take a few drops under your tongue. Many pregnant women carry a bottle with them in case it is needed.

Mild oedema

Swelling of the hands and feet and, later, the face and ankles, is a natural part of pregnancy and the result of extra fluid in the body. Most oedema is not a cause for concern, but you should always inform your doctor in case it is a sign of toxaemia.

What you can do

● Try to lie down for an hour or so each day with your legs raised, or at least sit down with your feet up as often as you can. Avoid standing for long periods if possible.

● Drink plenty of fresh bottled water to help flush your system. Water is the best natural diuretic, and you will notice an improvement within a few hours.

If you suffer from varicose veins, gently massage the area around the varicosities, always working in an upward motion (towards the heart).

● Support tights can help if the swelling is uncomfortable.

● Dandelion root coffee is a mild diuretic, which will help with swelling. It is a terrific alternative to coffee or tea, and also works as a tonic to the liver, which, like all organs in the body, will be under increased pressure during pregnancy.

● Nettle tea is a good source of iron, and it also acts as a mild diuretic. It's delicious with a little honey and lemon, and will help control swelling.

Haemorrhoids

Haemorrhoids, or piles, are swollen veins of the rectum, and almost 50 percent of all women suffer from them at some point in their pregnancy, when the veins of the rectum are more susceptible to varicosities (as the pressure of the growing baby bears down, the veins bulge and can collapse, causing bleeding and itching). Constipation can exacerbate the problem, so take steps to rectify that (see page 47), and try not to bear down too hard when passing stools.

What you can do

● Sleep on your side, to avoid

putting pressure on the rectal veins. Similarly, sitting or standing for long periods can exacerbate the problem.

● Pelvic floor exercises (Kegel exercises, see page 27) will help to improve the problem if they are done regularly.

● Keep the area scrupulously clean to avoid infection.

● Chamomile is a gentle laxative, and safe in pregnancy. It will also help to soothe and heal haemorrhoids. Try to drink several cups of camomile tea a day with a little organic, pasteurized honey stirred into it. Nettle will also help with haemorrhoids, and you can drink nettle and chamomile tea together with a little fresh apple juice.

● A witch hazel compress (a wad of cotton wool soaked with witch hazel) can be applied to the affected area to soothe and encourage healing.

● Eating fresh garlic encourages the health of the circulatory system, and can help to heal haemorrhoids. Take it in capsule form to avoid bad breath.

● You may wish to sit on a rubber swimming ring, if symptoms become too unbearable. This helps to take the pressure off the rectal veins, and makes it more comfortable to sit down. A rubber ring may also come in handy later on, if you have stitches following the birth.

Caution: Report any rectal bleeding to your physician immediately.

Sore gums

During pregnancy, your gums will become swollen and

inflamed, and may bleed during brushing, because of the extra hormones in your body.

What you can do

● Brush carefully with a soft toothbrush, and rinse your mouth with a little salt water to encourage healing. You will also need to floss regularly, to prevent gum disease and tooth decay, which seem to be more common in pregnancy. Soak your floss first in a little antibacterial mouthwash, or a drop of clove oil diluted in water, to prevent infection.

● Eat plenty of fresh fruits and vegetables that are rich in Vitamin C, to encourage the health of your gums.

● Gargle with a tablespoon of cider vinegar in warm water to help prevent infection and to soothe sore gums.

Stretchmarks

The ultimate, lasting legacy of pregnancy. Some women, particularly those with fair skin and hair, have an increased tendency to stretchmarks, which will first appear as red welts on the abdomen, buttocks, hips, upper thighs and even arms and breasts. In time, these marks will fade to a silvery white, and will be less noticeable; when they first appear, they can be quite vivid, and alarming. Stretchmarks occur when your skin stretches beyond its normal elasticity, and tears occur just under the top layer of your skin.

What you can do

● Try to keep your skin supple by using plenty of rich moisturizers, such as coconut oil, which can be applied liberally before a bath and allowed to soak into the skin while you are bathing.

● Rub Vitamin E oil into the skin, which helps to encourage the elasticity and health of the skin. Also, make sure that you get plenty of Vitamin E in your diet – a good source is avocados. Some women swear by rubbing the rind of the avocado (pulp side down) on the skin where it is likely to stretch most.

● Calendula flowers can be infused and added to coconut oil and rubbed into the skin to prevent stretchmarks.

● A light massage of lavender and neroli essential oils, in a rich carrier oil like avocado or apricot kernel, can help to prevent stretchmarks.

Breathlessness

Many women experience breathlessness beginning in the second trimester, which increases as the pregnancy progresses. Hormones cause the capillaries of the respiratory tract to swell, and they relax the muscles of the lungs and bronchial tubes. As your baby gets larger, the uterus pushes up against the diaphragm, which leaves less room for the lungs to expand.

What you can do

● At a childbirth or yoga class, you can learn techniques to

make breathing more efficient and effective, emptying the lungs each time you exhale, and ensuring that your body gets plenty of oxygen-rich air.

● Don't push yourself. You will tire more easily if you are unable to breathe effectively, and you may find that you feel dizzy or faint after overexertion.

Backache

During pregnancy, the joints of the pelvis loosen to allow your baby to be born, and other ligaments are also softened by the pregnancy hormones so that your entire skeletal structure may feel slightly off-kilter. Your growing baby will also put enormous strain on the muscles and ligaments in and around the abdomen, which can be painful.

What you can do

● Beware of excessive weight gain, which can increase the strain on your muscles and joints.

● Avoid wearing high heels, and invest in a good pair of shoes with a solid arch and a sole that is designed for back health.

● Try to avoid lifting or carrying heavy things if you can help it, and if you must lift, for instance a child, take

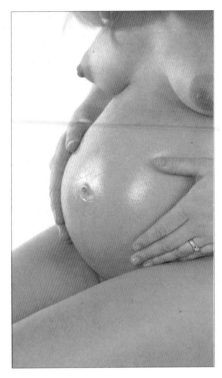

Use an oily moisturizer on your abdomen from the early days of pregnancy to try and prevent stretch marks.

care to squat down and carry the weight on your legs rather than your back.

● Try to avoid standing for long periods of time, and raise your feet if you need to sit at a desk for hours on end.

● Invest in a good mattress, or put a board between the box springs or frame of your bed and the mattress, to provide firm support. Try to sleep on your side, which prevents strain on the spine.

● Add a few drops of lavender oil to your bath, or add to a carrier oil and ask your partner to massage the affected area. The lavender will relax your muscles and encourage the relief of any stress exacerbating the condition.

● Roman chamomile and marjoram are excellent in a full-body Massage to ease the muscular pains of pregnancy.

● Use a hot compress on the affected area to loosen the muscles, or make a warming rub by blending a teaspoon of cayenne pepper in about a quarter of a cup of warm olive oil. Rub into the lower back.

● Try the exercise to reduce headaches (see page 67), where you lie on your back with your head supported by a coule of books. It has the effect of lengthening the spine, which can reduce muscular tension.

Getting ready for your baby

Preparing for the birth of your baby can be great fun, and encourages positive anticipation and excitement. Being prepared for the arrival of your baby not only helps you to relax, but also makes the prospect of having a baby more believable. It's hard to imagine what it will be like to have a baby when you are pregnant, and purchasing those first clothes and baby equipment can help you to focus on what your baby's needs are likely to be.

Your baby's room

If you have a room available for your baby, you may wish to decorate it in cheerful colours that will still be suitable as your child grows older. Babies will respond to bright colours, but remember they can also be invigorating, and may make it more difficult to settle your baby down to sleep.

You'll need

● A chair, for night feeds. Something low and comfortable, with arms, is best. Rocking chairs can be useful for soothing a baby, but they may be more difficult to feed in.

● A chest of drawers for your baby's clothes. You may wish to buy one that is the right height to use as a change table as well.

● Well-lined curtains to keep out the daylight when your baby needs to sleep, and the draughts, if it is windy or cold.

● Soft lighting. You may wish to invest in a dimmer switch, so that you can adjust the level of light in the room to suit your baby's needs. Otherwise, a table lamp, with a low-voltage bulb will be useful. Don't place it near to your baby's bed, where she can reach it.

● Shelves on which to keep your baby's necessities, such as cream for her bottom, baby wipes and powders.

● You may wish to invest in a basket to keep nappies (cloth or disposable) close to hand.

● A mobile will both stimulate your baby, and help to lull her to sleep, depending on her mood, and it might be useful to purchase one that can be removed, or moved to the other end of the cot, if your baby is overly excited by it.

● Your baby's first bed may be a Moses basket, which will keep him snug, or perhaps a bassinet or a rocking cradle. Many women like to choose a first bed that can be moved from room to room while your baby is sleeping. A carry cot that fits on to your baby's pram frame is a particularly good idea. As your baby gets bigger, you will need to move her to a cot. Ensure that you choose one that is strong and safe, and if you have borrowed one, or bought it second-hand, it is wise to invest in a new mattress.

Baby equipment

● From the first trip home from the hospital, your baby will require a car seat. Choose a brand that is safe and which can be tipped back when your baby is sleeping. Many women prefer portable seats that can be moved from the car into the house, so that a sleeping infant will not have to be disturbed. These act as a baby rocking chair as well.

● Prams or pushchairs. Many pushchairs now come with detachable fittings, which means that you can clip on a carry cot to make a pram when your baby is very young, and change it over to a reclining seat as your baby gets older. Make sure you choose a model with a good sturdy frame and handles at a comfortable height, that is light and easily collapsible. If you choose a pushchair instead of a pram, which can be cumbersome, particularly

if you have little storage space and lots of steps to negotiate, make sure you choose one that will recline flat. You will need some sort of protection for your baby's head, so ensure that your pram has a bonnet or a clip-on protective covering.

● A bouncing, portable chair is useful to keep your baby occupied, and to help you to rock her to sleep when your hands are required elsewhere.

● You may wish to buy a baby bath, as it can be difficult to manage a baby in a normal-

sized bath (although the sink is fine). Choose a light but sturdy bath that can either fit inside your own bathtub, or sit on a stable stand.

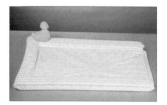

● Unless you have purchased a specially made change table, you will need a change mat for your baby. Choose one that is plastic-covered for easy cleaning, and padded to ensure that your baby is comfortable.

● A baby sling is extremely useful in the early days, as your baby will love being close to your body, where she will be able to hear your heartbeat and feel your warmth. It is also a practical

way of transporting your baby, and holding her close to you while you go about household tasks.

● A washable bag, with a portable changing mat, is indispensable for trips and visits.

Essential clothes and accessories

Buying baby clothes can be very enjoyable, so try not to leave it to the last minute, when you may find shopping difficult or uncomfortable. There is a great tendency to buy far too much for your baby (particularly first babies) and it is useful to remember that you are likely to be given clothing as gifts in the early

days. You will also have no idea how quickly your baby will grow, and you may find that you are left with dozens of little garments that will never be worn. Concentrate on the basic necessities, if you can restrain yourself, and wait to see what your baby needs as she grows.

What to look for

● It is pointless buying expensive clothing that may only be worn a handful of times. You are much better off buying mid-price clothes that are durable and of good quality (particularly if you

plan to have more children). Choose cotton and other natural fibres, which will be easier on your baby's skin, and will stop her getting too hot.

● Try to find clothes that are easy to put on. Look for large necks, easy-to-use fastenings at the legs, and a minimum of fussy ribbons and ties, which can be time-consuming and may catch your baby's fingers.

● Choose clothes that are generously cut – your baby will need plenty of room to move around, and she may be frustrated by tight or constraining garments.

● Choose machine-washable clothes. Babies can be very messy in the early days, and handwashing and dry-cleaning are luxuries you probably won't be able to afford.

You'll need

● A baby hat – either a warm bonnet or a sunhat, depending on the season.

● Seven cotton vests with a wide neck. Whole body vests are useful and won't ride up.

● Seven stretchy sleepers in a good-quality cotton. Make sure the fastenings are easy to manage, for nappy changing.

Disposable or cloth nappies?

Cloth nappies are more environmentally friendly, but it can be time-consuming to wash and dry them. There are now nappy services available that will deliver freshly laundered cloth nappies to your door, and take care of cleaning them, and if you can afford it, this might be a good option.

If you choose cloth nappies, you may wish to invest in fitted nappies, which are fastened with Velcro. These are much the same shape as the disposable variety and are much easier to put on and take off.

Cloth nappies will work out to be cheaper in the long run, especially if you have more than one child, and there is no problem with their disposal. Worn with waterproof pants, they are now pretty much leakproof. Cloth nappies do, however, require soaking, rinsing, and possibly washing and drying, and if your drying facilities are at a minimum, you may want to think carefully about the prospect of having drying nappies hung around the house.

Disposable nappies work out to be quite expensive, and create a great deal of rubbish. However, they are quick and easy to put on and take off, and you won't be saddled with constant washing and drying.

Some women choose cloth nappies for the home, and the disposable kind for outings or holidays, where it is not practical to carry large quantities of soiled or wet nappies or where washing facilities are unavailable.

● Two nighties. In the early days, nighties are practical and facilitate quick night-time changes. Choose ones that are long enough to keep your baby warm, and easy to put on.

● Two warm sweaters. Again, cotton may be best, for ease of care and kindness to your baby's skin.

● One all-in-one outdoor suit, depending on the season. Choose one that protects your baby's hands and feet, and which has a hood, and a long zipper to allow you to dress and undress her quickly and easily.

● Four pairs of cotton socks. Beware – baby socks have a habit of disappearing both from the wash and your baby's feet. This is one article of clothing that you may have to replace on a constant basis.

● Between two and four cotton blankets. Choose two 'sheet'-style blankets, in which you can swaddle your baby (don't be surprised if she becomes attached to it very early on; it might be helpful to have two the same, which can be interchanged), and two thermal blankets, perhaps cotton cellular blankets, which are easy to clean and allow the skin to breathe.

● A box of nappies in the smallest size, if you are using disposable, or at least twenty-four cloth nappies.

● blunt-edged scissors, for cutting your baby's nails

● bottom cream, to protect against nappy rash

● muslin or cotton squares, to protect your clothing against regurgitated milk and other baby 'leaks'

● a mild baby bath, ideally one that can be used as a shampoo

● between two and four soft baby

washcloths, both for the bath, and for 'topping and tailing'.

● two soft new towels

● cotton wool

● disposable baby wipes

● non-biological laundry detergent.

Feeding your baby

You will need to decide how you want to feed your baby, and stock up on all the necessities (see the pros and cons of breastfeeding and bottle-feeding on page 00). You may wish to combine breastfeeding with bottle-feeding, to fit in with your lifestyle. Here's what you'll need for both.

Breastfeeding
You'll need:
● breastpads

● two good, well-supported nursing bras that allow easy access to your breasts
● you may wish to purchase a breastpump, in order to express milk

● bottles (see below) if you plan to use expressed milk for some of the feeds – a nice idea if your partner or

another child wants to be involved

● a soothing nipple cream, which may be necessary if you suffer from sore or cracked nipples in the early days. Try to choose one that doesn't need to be washed off before the next feed.

Bottle feeding
You'll need
● teats

● caps

● bottles (at least six)

● bottle brush

● sterilizing tablets and a sterilizing tank, or a steam sterilizer

● measuring jug

● infant formula (your doctor or midwife will advise you on the most appropriate brand to buy)

Twenty-nine to thirty-two weeks

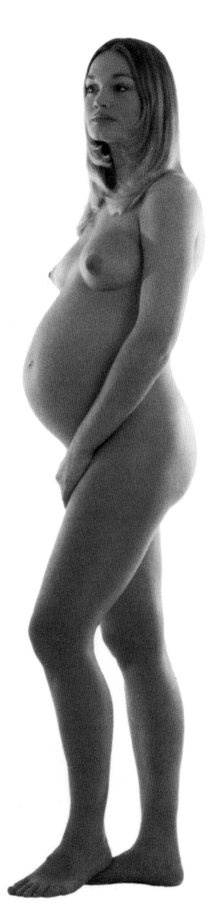

The final trimester of pregnancy runs from the twenty-ninth week to the thirty-eighth week after conception. It is the shortest trimester, but it may appear to pass slowly, particularly if you are feeling tired or somewhat preoccupied. Your size will be increasing rapidly (you can expect to gain about 10 pounds, or 4 kilograms), and you may find that you become very tired and uncomfortable.

However, the last trimester can also be a time of useful activity, as you attend childbirth classes, prepare your baby's clothes and equipment, and come to terms with the imminent birth. Braxton-Hicks contractions may become more frequent, and may even begin to be painful, and you will see your doctor or midwife more often.

Your baby will be perfectly formed by now, and many women are comforted by the knowledge that he would survive if born prematurely. If you experienced a burst of energy in your second trimester, you may now find that the fatigue that characterized the early months is back. Your baby will be very active in the womb, and you can expect to feel strong, regular kicking and see the occasional elbow or knee pressing your

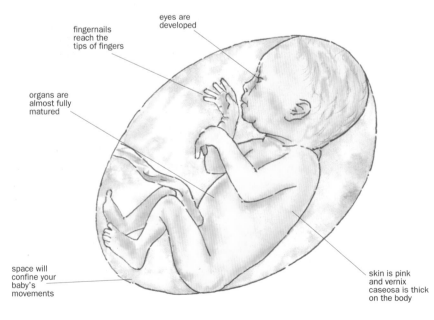

eyes are developed

fingernails reach the tips of fingers

organs are almost fully matured

space will confine your baby's movements

skin is pink and vernix caseosa is thick on the body

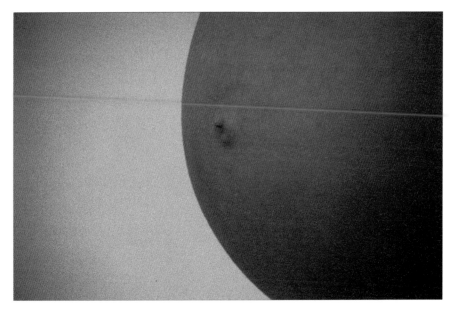

As the skin stretches across your abdomen, some women may find that their navel starts to protrude. This is nothing to worry about and it will return to normal after the birth. Continue to massage oil into your abdomen to help prevent stretchmarks, and try not to put on weight too rapidly. If you are one of the unlucky ones who gets stretchmarks despite the precautions – and some skin types are more prone than others – be assured that they will fade from red to silver in a short time.

developed, and she will open and close her eyelids, blink, and be able to focus. The fingernails are long enough to reach the tips of the fingers, and the toenails are still growing. She may have a full head of hair by now, and she will look very much like the newborn baby you will soon see yourself. Movement will be strong, but slower, as the lack of space begins to confine activity.

Changes to your body

Your weight gain will continue apace as your baby grows (see page 50), but unless it increases drastically, or you suffer from sudden swelling or water

uterus outwards. As your EDD looms nearer, you may start to worry about the pain of the birth, and the responsibility of caring for a newborn. Now is the time to educate yourself on the stages of labour, and the early days of being a parent, so that you will feel more confident when the day arrives.

Your baby's growth

Many babies (particularly first babies) will turn in the womb to position themselves face down some time between the first month of the last trimester and the thirty-sixth week. Don't worry if your baby doesn't engage until the very end of pregnancy – this too is normal. Your baby's organs will now be almost fully matured, although her lungs are not completely developed. The layers of fat laid down on the body are increasing, and the skin is now pink, rather than red and wrinkled. The vernix caseosa is now thick on her body, which will protect her from being

immersed in amniotic fluid for so long. Over this period, your baby will continue to put on about a pound a week (comprised of muscle and fat), and by the end of the month she will weigh about 5 pounds (2.5 kilograms) and measure about 12 inches (32 centimetres). The eyes are now

As you become larger, and your baby places increasing demands on your body, it's important to stop and rest. Being physically and mentally prepared for the birth will help you to cope.

retention, there is no need to be concerned. Your pelvis will have expanded quite dramatically, in preparation for the birth, and you may experience discomfort and pain, particularly in your back, or where the pubic bone is jointed together. As your baby increases in size, the uterus will push up against the lower ribs, which expand, and may become quite painful. Breathlessness increases during this month, but it should settle down when your baby engages, dropping lower into the pelvis. Many women suffer from the symptoms of anaemia for the first time this month – a low haemoglobin level is common, and you will be advised to rest more, and to eat plenty of iron-rich foods (see page 22). Your linea nigra will become more prominent, as may any stretchmarks, and your navel will invert, as the skin stretches over your abdomen. The stretching of the skin may cause rashes and some itching, which is natural. Contact your doctor if itching becomes severe, and you appear slightly jaundiced because these symptoms could indicate a condition known as choleostasis where your liver is not functioning properly.

Many women find that their hands, feet, ankles and face swell up during the last trimester, but this is no cause for alarm unless the swelling is sudden or extensive, and doesn't disperse after rest. The pressure on your bladder increases, and you may be slightly incontinent, particularly if you laugh or cough. Leaking urine is nothing to be worried about, but it is a sign that you should be doing your pelvic floor more often (see Kegel exercises, page 27).

Sleeping difficulties become more pronounced this month, and you may need to adopt a different position, and reduce your fluid intake just before bed, in order to get a sound night's rest (see page 86).

By this time, many women are tired of being pregnant – and tired of feeling tired! Others are sad in the knowledge that their pregnancy is nearly over and they will soon be alone in their body again. To counter this feeling, there is the excitement at the prospect of the new baby and the preparations to be made – you may wish to begin discussing names. It's normal to feel preoccupied about the labour and the delivery, to spend long periods daydreaming or worrying, to find that your attention span is shorter, and that it's difficult to concentrate or remember things, even in the short term. Try to think of practical things you can do to prepare for the birth, so that you don't become overanxious. These last months of pregnancy also present a good opportunity to spend time alone with your partner, and to talk through the way you envisage the weeks to come.

You may experience

- sciatica and/or lower back and abdominal pain
- strong activity by your baby
- vivid dreams, daydreams and fantasies
- increasing fatigue
- increasing vaginal discharge
- increased constipation and haemorrhoids
- some headaches, faintness and dizziness
- leg cramps
- disrupted sleep
- frequent urination
- stronger Braxton-Hicks contractions
- varicose veins
- anxiety about the impending birth
- sore or bleeding gums
- some swelling of your face, hands, feet and ankles
- itchy skin and/or stretchmarks
- shortness of breath
- clumsiness, absentmindedness

Take frequent rests with your feet up to help prevent swelling of the feet and ankles.

- weariness, feeling as though you have been pregnant forever

- difficulty sleeping

- anxiety about the birth and caring for a newborn

- nasal stuffiness and occasional nosebleeds

- colostrum leaking from your breast

- excitement and anticipation

Antenatal visits

You will probably be asked to attend your clinic once a fortnight instead of every month, if you don't already, and you will be carefully monitored to ensure that all goes well in the final trimester. Your weight and blood pressure will be checked, and your urine will be tested for protein and sugar. The height of the fundus will be measured, and for the first time your midwife or doctor will be able to provide you with an idea of your baby's weight and position, which they can ascertain by palpating your abdomen. Any swelling you may have will be checked, and as usual, you will have the opportunity to discuss any unusual symptoms or concerns.

This month you will also be offered the opportunity to visit the hospital where you plan to have your baby, and you will be given a list of things you will require. It is a good time to think carefully about your birthplan, because you may wish to arrange for special equipment, such as a birthing pool, or perhaps a TENS machine, which may need to be ordered (see page 96). You may also want to discuss the possibility of having your baby at home (see page 99). Don't hesitate to ask any questions you may have about the labour itself, or the preparation for it. You'll need time to plan and get to grips with it all, and the midwife and doctor are there to help you do so.

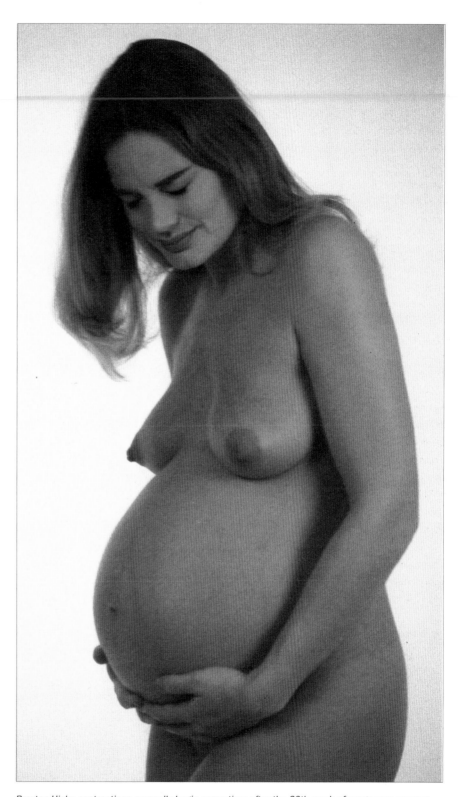

Braxton-Hicks contractions normally begin some time after the 20th week of pregnancy, as your uterus begins to prepare or 'practise' for the contractions of labour. The contractions are often painless (you'll feel a tightening of the uterus, which gradually spreads from the top to the bottom) and they usually last around 30 seconds. As pregnancy draws to a close, the contractions may become more frequent and intense, and even quite painful – use your breathing exercises to get you through them.

Your birthplan

In the UK, women have been encouraged to prepare birthplans in advance of the labour for many years, and now this practice is becoming more common in the US and Canada. Women increasingly want to be involved in making as many of the decisions about their childbirth as possible, and if you have prepared a birthplan, your wishes are down in writing for anyone attending the birth to consider.

The birthplan should always be discussed with your doctor or midwife, as it will be necessary for you to fall in with hospital policy to a certain extent, and it may need to be modified according to your individual pregnancy and needs. There is no point, for instance, in insisting on an anaesthetic-free labour, if chances are that your labour may be long and protracted. Discussing your birthplan will help you to keep an open mind, and set parameters that are acceptable both to you and whoever will be attending your birth.

Your birthplan will deal with a huge variety of subjects, and you should familiarize yourself with the options available (see page 94) before beginning. It is also crucial that you understand the stages of labour, and know what to expect at each, before you decide on how you want to handle them. You may want to consider:

● Who you would like to be present during the delivery. Some women specifically request that student midwives or doctors do not attend, or if they do, that they are not involved in the administration of pain relief or stitching. You may find that you don't mind extra people around, many of whom may have good ideas to help you cope. You may want your partner to be present for the entire labour and delivery, or you may wish him to leave for some procedures. Alternatively, you may wish to have a friend or family member with you instead.

● How long you would like to remain at home before going to hospital (if you plan to have your baby there). Many women want to remain at home for as long as possible, but it is useful to be aware of the signs of an

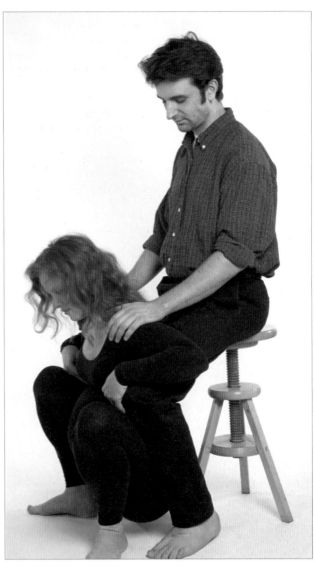

Discuss with your partner the ways in which he can help you during labour and the positions that might be most useful.

imminent delivery so that you don't end up having your baby in your bathtub or in the back of a taxi. Many midwives recommend that you make your journey to hospital when you are no longer confident about coping with the pain, and certainly when contractions are no less than 5 minutes apart. Remember that second labours are often much faster than first.

● How active you want to be in labour. Many women find that it helps to move around during labour, and do not wish to be constrained by fetal monitors unless absolutely necessary.

You may want to go for walks, if labour is prolonged, and you should check what the procedure is for leaving the labour room.

● Whether you would like to have a bath or a shower during labour, or spend some or all of the labour in a birthing pool. Some hospitals have these facilities available but, if not, you may be permitted to make arrangements to have a pool delivered to the hospital.

● What extras you want to bring with you. Many hospitals will allow you to bring in a cassette player or radio, and your personal pillows or beanbag chairs; other hospitals supply their own. Decide on what you would like to have to help you get through, and make a note of it on your birthplan.

● How you feel about medical induction and the techniques used (including having your waters broken). These are all matters that should be considered with your hospital team or midwife.

● When you would like to be allowed to eat and drink, and

whether this would be appropriate.

● What pain relief, and when to have it. Many women wish to have a natural delivery, and avoid pain relief in any form (see page 94). Others are happy to have a shot of pethidine or use the gas and air that will be available. You may wish to have an epidural, to make the labour as painless as possible. The best advice is to keep an open mind. Certainly express your wishes in your birthplan, but set up a contingency plan. For example, note that you would like a natural labour, but that you will consider gas and air if you are finding things more difficult than anticipated. Never rule out any type of pain relief, unless you are adamant that you want to cope on your own.

● Whether you want to use natural remedies. Many women choose to use aromatherapy oils, or homeopathic remedies during labour. Others bring along a hypnotherapist, an acupuncturist or even a reflexologist, to help to ensure a good labour. Once again, discuss your plans with your doctor. In theory, your midwife will not be

able to administer herbs or homeopathic remedies in the hospital, but they may sanction their use if they know in advance what you are taking and why.

● Hospital policy on things like catheterization,

intravenous fluid administration, fetal monitoring and episiotomy (see page 110), and make decisions that will be acceptable both to you and to the hospital. If you feel very strongly that you do not want something to happen, then say so.

● Whether or not you want oxytocin used to induce the birth, or to increase contractions.

● Emergency situations, and the possibility of Caesarean section.

● What positions you want to use for delivery. If you are being monitored, or are on a drip, you may need to be confined to the bed, but there are positions that can be adopted to facilitate an easier delivery, even if you do have to stay still (see pages 98–105). Talk to your partner about positions that would be most useful for you, and request help with them on your birthplan.

● The use of syntometrine in the final stage to speed up the delivery and expulsion of the

placenta, to prevent it from being retained. You may wish to discuss this with your physician.

● Whether you would like your baby placed on your breast before the cord is cut. Would you like her to be washed before she is presented to you? Would you like to hold her before the first tests are undertaken, or are you happy to wait until the all-clear is given?

● The role of your partner. He may wish to be involved in the delivery, and even cut the cord himself. Some hospitals will allow this, but you will have to check first.

● Some procedures involving your newly born baby, such as the administration of Vitamin K (see page 109), the type of feeding you would like to use (bottle or breast, see pages 132–9), having other children present in the delivery room, perhaps allowing them to hold your baby first, and circumcision (see page 116).

● How long you would like to stay in hospital, and if you would like to have your baby with you in your room or cubicle, or whether you would like the night staff to take her so that you can get some sleep.

● Postpartum medication or treatment for you and your baby.

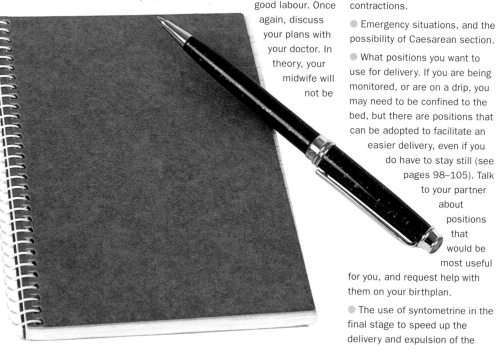

Thirty-three to forty weeks

Your delivery date will be approximately thirty-eight weeks from the date of conception, and forty weeks from your last menstrual period. In the six weeks leading up to this date, your baby and your body will prepare for the birth, and you will also be adapting your home to accommodate the new arrival.

Most women feel excited and nervous about the birth and about having a baby, and you may experience pains that feel like the real thing several times before the actual labour and birth.

Your baby's development

Your baby will be snug inside the uterus, which, by the end of the pregnancy, can only just contain him. He will be curled up tightly, usually head down (about 96 percent of all babies present head first – the vertex position) while the remainder are in one or another breech position (buttocks first) by the thirty-sixth week.

Your baby will lose most of the lanugo that is covering his body, and his skin will be soft and smooth, although there may still be vernix caseosa in parts which will make it easier for his body to pass down the birth canal. Most babies' eyes are blue at this stage (although a few babies are born with brown); if they are going to change colour, they will do so in the first weeks after the birth. His adrenal glands are producing large quantities of cortisone, which helps to mature the lungs and

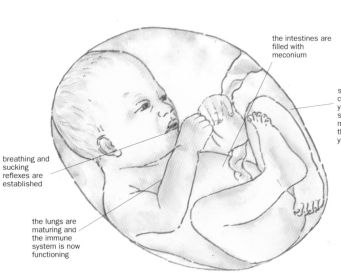

the intestines are filled with meconium

space is cramped and you will often see limbs moving across the surface of your abdomen

breathing and sucking reflexes are established

the lungs are maturing and the immune system is now functioning

make it easier for him to breathe on his own when he is born. Growth will begin to slow down as the placenta's reserves start to diminish, and most babies do not grow much more if pregnancy continues past the expected delivery date. Breathing and sucking reflexes are now well established, and he will be able to feed if he is born at this stage.

The immune system will be functional, and he will have a defence against a wide range of infections through the transfer of antibodies from your blood. When he is born, he will get further antibodies from your breast milk. The intestines are filled with a substance called meconium, which is a dark, sticky green secretion that will be passed as his first bowel movements when he is born. Some babies pass meconium during the birth.

Preparing for labour

In the weeks approaching labour, you will need to get plenty of sleep, and eat small, nutritious meals to keep your energy levels high. Don't wear yourself out cleaning and organizing your house. If you are feeling nervous or panicky about the impending birth, practise your breathing exercises, and take time to relax, perhaps in a warm bath with a few drops of chamomile oil. Take lots of breaks with your feet up, and sip chamomile tea and read something distracting. If you are truly frightened about what is to come, talk through your worries with your partner, or your doctor or midwife, who may be able to reassure you. There are a couple of very useful natural remedies that help with fear and apprehension, including the homeopathic remedy Arg nit, which can be taken in 6x dilution, three times daily, in the weeks leading up to the birth. This will help to keep you calm, and settle your nerves. The flower essence Mimulus is also terrific for fear of unknown things, and you can put a few drops in a glass of water and sip as required, to help put things into perspective and dispel your fears.

Most babies reach between 6 and 8 pounds (3 to 4 kilograms) by the end of the thirty-eighth week, and will measure between 14 and 15 inches (35 to 37 centimetres) in length. The body will be plump and rounded now, and his movements will be slower, although you should still feel them. You will likely see protruding limbs pressing against the uterus as he moves to make himself comfortable, and because there is less amniotic fluid in the amniotic sac, you will be able to feel parts of his body quite clearly.

Changes to your body

The hormones produced by the placenta will cause your breasts to swell and fill up with milk, some of which can leak or even squirt from them unexpectedly. Not all women experience this symptom, and it is also normal for the milk not to appear until after your baby is born. Throughout your pregnancy, your tissues have softened and become more elastic, so that the vaginal opening can gradually stretch to let your baby out. The ligaments which bind the bones of your pelvis have often softened to allow expansion of your birth canal, so there will be extra room for your baby to pass. This may cause pain throughout the lower abdominal area, particularly as

your baby prepares for the birth. Sleeping may be increasingly difficult, so it is important that you rest as much as possible during the day. If you are suffering from swelling, which becomes more prominent as the pregnancy progresses, take time to sit down with your feet up, and rest flat on your back when you get the opportunity.

Most women experience practice contractions (Braxton-Hicks) as they near the end of the pregnancy, and they may last longer. As your baby drops into your pelvis in preparation for the birth, you will feel less breathless and may even experience a sudden burst of energy. Many women report a 'nesting instinct', in which they feel a sudden desire to clean and prepare for the birth. Experts recommend that you fight the urge to do too much late in the

If you suffer from leg cramps, try placing your feet in a footbath with a few drops of lavender or peppermint oils, or massage a blend of lavender and chamomile oils into the calves. Most importantly, take time to relax and rest – to prepare for the impending birth.

pregnancy, but practically, it can be difficult to resist and you may find that you can only relax when you know that the baby's things are clean and ready, and that your home is immaculate in anticipation of the new arrival. Don't be surprised if you suddenly decide to paint the sitting room, or steam-clean the carpets. Many women find that as soon as they feel their home is ready they go into labour, and it can be a tremendous emotional or mental release to know that things are well prepared. The same sense of reassurance can be derived from packing early for the hospital – your doctor or midwife may recommend that you have your suitcase ready by about the thirty-fourth week.

Your weight gain will slow down, or even stop, and your posture will probably change quite dramatically as your centre of gravity shifts again with the weight of your baby. You may also find that your vaginal discharge increases; it may contain more mucus, possibly brownish in colour, or even streaked with blood. If you are concerned about any bleeding, see your doctor, but don't be concerned if your baby seems to be less active – he will have very little room in which to manoeuvre, and movements will be slower and more defined.

You may feel great relief that you are almost there, or you may be terrified by the prospect of the birth. Many women feel quite nervous about the impending birth, and the sudden realization that they are about to have a baby. Being pregnant can seem very dissociated from the reality of a new baby, and as you recognize signs that you are nearing labour, you may feel a sense of panic that you will be unable to cope. Rest assured that most women feel very sensitive just prior to the birth, and you may swing from excitement to despair in a few short minutes. You may also feel impatient and restless, and unable to concentrate on anything for very long. Try to spend time

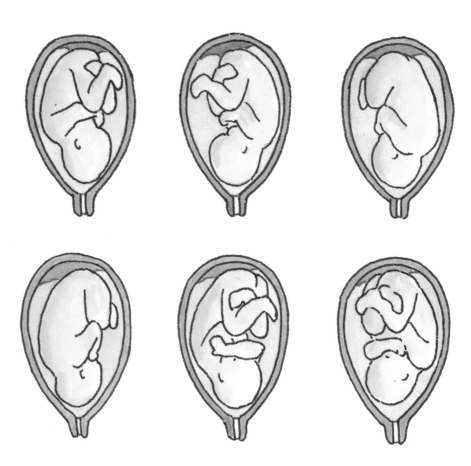

Your baby may be lying in any of the above positions. The technical names for them are, clockwise from top left: Right Occiput Transverse; Left Occiput Transverse; Left Occiput Anterior; Left Occiput Posterior; Right Occiput Posterior; and Right Occiput Anterior. Occiput means the crown of the baby's head.

with your partner, and practise your breathing and relaxation routines. They will help to keep you calm in the weeks leading up to the birth.

You may experience

- sciatica and/or lower back and abdominal pain
- slower activity of your baby, as he adapts to the confines of the uterus
- vivid dreams, daydreams and fantasies
- increasing fatigue alternating with periods of enormous extra energy
- a hearty appetite, or a complete loss of appetite
- increasing vaginal discharge, sometimes accompanied by streaks of blood
- heartburn and indigestion, which can become increasingly debilitating
- increased constipation and haemorrhoids
- some headaches, faintness and dizziness
- leg cramps
- disrupted sleep
- frequent urination, which becomes worse when your baby drops
- stronger Braxton-Hicks contractions, which may now be painful
- varicose veins
- clumsiness, absentmindedness, anxiety about the impending birth
- sore or bleeding gums

● backache and pain in the pelvis and buttocks

● increased swelling of your face, hands, feet and ankles

● itchy skin and/or stretchmarks, and a protruding navel

● shortness of breath, which improves when your baby engages

● weariness, feeling as though you have been pregnant forever

● nasal stuffiness and occasional nosebleeds

● colostrum leaking from your breasts

● excitement and anticipation, alternating with fear and trepidation

● over-sensitivity and perhaps tearfulness

Antenatal visits

Your doctor or midwife will want to see you weekly from about the thirty-fourth week, to ensure that everything is going well. Your blood pressure will be taken, and it may be a little higher than normal, although slight increases are nothing to worry about. Your urine will be tested for sugar and protein, and you may have another blood test for haemoglobin levels, especially if you are feeling very tired and run down. The height of the fundus will be measured, and your doctor or midwife will listen to your baby's heartbeat, which is now strong and regular.

Your abdomen will be palpated to ascertain the position of the baby, and to see if he is engaged, and to what degree. You will be given a good idea of the size of your baby by this point, and you'll know quite soon whether a normal vaginal delivery is on the cards. If your baby is in a breech position, your doctor may request another ultrasound scan to see if it will be possible for you to deliver your baby naturally. Your cervix may also be examined (internally) to check

Keep the skin on your abdomen moisturized to ease the itchiness that is common during the last month or so of pregnancy. Many women enjoy a gentle abdominal massage, and you may be able to distinguish the different limbs, and feel your baby respond to your touch.

effacement (when the cervix thins in preparation for delivery) and dilatation, which may begin some time before you actually go into labour.

Your doctor or midwife will also discuss any unusual symptoms with you, and provide advice for the labour, particularly if it seems imminent.

They will be more concerned than usual about any sudden weight gain or swelling, because of the risk of pre-eclampsia (see page 84). Always make sure that you advise your doctor of any changes in symptoms, or of anything that worries you, or seems slightly out of the ordinary.

Complications in pregnancy

In a small minority of cases, there are problems or complications which occur during the pregnancy which may threaten the health of the mother or the baby.

Ectopic pregnancy

In ectopic pregnancy, the fertilized egg develops outside the uterus, usually in one of the Fallopian tubes. The egg burrows into the surrounding tissue, which usually tears and causes internal bleeding. The tissue cannot sustain a foetus, and the pregnancy cannot continue. In this condition, you may have cramping abdominal pain, often with vaginal bleeding. About one percent of all pregnancies is ectopic, and most of them are discovered in the first month or two.

You may not suspect you are pregnant. If you experience abdominal pain that lasts for more than a few hours, see your physician as soon as possible. There is a risk of severe internal bleeding that can lead to shock and even death. An ultrasound scan may allow an accurate diagnosis, but in some cases a laparoscopy (an examination of the inside of the abdomen with a specialized tool) may be required.

Once an ectopic pregnancy is confirmed, surgery is performed immediately. The developing foetus and surrounding tissue are removed and the damaged blood vessels are repaired. Occasionally an ectopic pregnancy can affect fertility, and they may recur, so if you become pregnant again, you should see your doctor immediately.

Incompetent cervix

In this condition, the cervix opens up during pregnancy, usually after the fourteenth week. The foetus and placenta escape from the uterus, which causes a miscarriage. Weakness of the cervix may trigger this, but usually the cause is not known. If your physician suspects that you may have an incompetent cervix, a miscarriage can be prevented by surgery during early pregnancy. Under general anaesthetic, your cervix will be literally sewn shut. The thread is cut when labour starts or at about the thirty-eighth week of pregnancy if labour has not yet started.

Hydramnios

Hydramnios is normally a harmless condition that may occur in the middle or late stages of pregnancy, when an excessive amount of amniotic fluid is produced around the foetus. In most cases, the swelling of the uterus is only slightly greater than normal, and the condition produces either no symptoms or a gradual onset of symptoms such as breathlessness, indigestion and tension in the muscles of the abdomen. In some cases, swelling may be pronounced, symptoms may begin suddenly and may be accompanied by nausea, and there is risk of premature labour.

Hydramnios is more common in women with diabetes, in cases when a foetus has a malformed gastrointestinal system or spine or brain malformations, or with twins or other multiple pregnancies. In minor cases, a physician may obtain a detailed ultrasound scan to rule out fetal malformations. If hydramnios comes on suddenly, your physician may advise you to rest completely and may prescribe drugs to relax your uterus and reduce the risk of premature labour. Rarely, amniocentesis is performed to reduce pain.

Pre-eclampsia and eclampsia

Pre-eclampsia is a disorder that occurs during late pregnancy, in which your blood pressure rises and there is excess fluid in your body. A common signal that there is pre-eclampsia is protein in the urine, which is one of the reasons why your urine is tested so regularly in antenatal visits. Salt and water retention causing swelling of ankles and fingers can also be a symptom. Pre-eclampsia may lead to eclampsia (seizures), which are hazardous to both you and your baby.

Mild pre-eclampsia has few symptoms, so it is important that you visit your antenatal

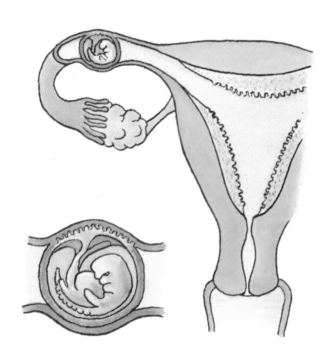

clinic regularly, where they should be detected. The symptoms of more severe pre-eclampsia, which can develop during the last three months of pregnancy, are headaches, blurred vision, intolerance of bright light, upper abdominal pain, nausea and vomiting, and salt and water retention.

Pre-eclampsia seems to occur particularly in the first pregnancies of women between ages eighteen and thirty, and in women who have diabetes, high blood pressure, or a family history of high blood pressure. Your physician may prescribe a drug to control your blood pressure, and you will be advised to get plenty of rest.

If you develop symptoms of severe pre-eclampsia or eclampsia, contact your physician immediately. You may be admitted to a hospital, where you can be given drugs to lower your blood pressure, remove excess fluid from your body, and prevent other complications. Your baby may have to be delivered early, either by inducing the labour (which could be problematic if it is impossible to control your blood pressure), or by Caesarean section.

Antepartum haemorrhaging

Antepartum haemorrhage is any bleeding from the vagina after the end of the twentieth week of pregnancy. Earlier bleeding is known as a threatened miscarriage (see page 36). The condition may be the result of placenta praevia (see below), a burst varicose vein in the vagina, damage to the cervix, or partial or complete separation of the placenta from the wall of the uterus. In most cases, antepartum bleeding is mild and harmless. An antepartum haemorrhage caused by placental separation can cause problems with your baby's growth, however, and if there is

heavy bleeding, both you and your baby will be in danger.

If you have bleeding during pregnancy, call your physician as soon as possible. He or she may arrange for blood tests and an ultrasound scan. If bleeding is severe, you will be hospitalized, and you may receive transfusions. The baby may be delivered as soon as possible, either by inducing labour or Caesarean.

Placenta praevia

Placenta praevia occurs in about one in two hundred pregnancies, after the twenty-eighth week. In this condition, the placenta develops low in the uterus, either partially or completely over the cervix. Any part of the placenta that is near the cervix will be poorly supported and prone to damage. The cause is unknown, but it occurs more frequently in women who have already given birth to several children or who are pregnant with twins. Some women have a low-lying placenta early in pregnancy, but it normally shifts position as the pregnancy progresses and is therefore not threatening.

There are often no symptoms of this condition, but if the placenta becomes partly detached from the uterus, you will have sporadic, painless bleeding from the vagina, usually late in the pregnancy. If you have bleeding from the vagina during pregnancy, call your physician immediately and lie flat on your back until you are advised to do otherwise.

If your cervix is only partially covered by the placenta, your physician may recommend an ultrasound scan to determine whether or not it is safe to have a normal vaginal delivery. If the condition is more serious, with profuse bleeding, you may require a blood transfusion, and your baby will be delivered by Caesarean.

Premature rupturing of the membranes

When labour starts, the membranes surrounding your baby may rupture, releasing amniotic fluid. In this situation, it is said that your 'waters have broken', and it may be the first indication that labour has begun. Occasionally, the membranes may rupture before labour has begun, and there are risks associated with this condition, including premature labour or an infection of the uterus.

If your membranes have ruptured prematurely, contact your physician, who will examine you and may admit you to hospital. Fluid from your vagina may be collected, or an amniocentesis may be performed to ascertain whether or not your baby's lungs have developed enough for him to survive. If your expected delivery date is imminent, and tests confirm that your baby is mature enough to live, labour may be induced. However, if it is still quite early in the pregnancy, you may require hospitalization or complete bed rest until labour. If your pregnancy is further ahead, you may be hospitalized for bed rest until labour begins or evidence of infection makes delivery necessary. Sometimes a small tear in the membranes surrounding the foetus heals naturally and allows the pregnancy to continue to a full-term delivery, but the risk of infection of the uterus remains, so your pregnancy will be carefully monitored.

Intrauterine death

Very rarely, a baby will die in the uterus after the twentieth week of pregnancy, usually as a result of severe pre-eclampsia or eclampsia, a haemorrhage, postmaturity (see below), or a severe abnormality. In some cases, the cause is not known.

Usually, the only sign is that you no longer feel any movement or activity. If your physician is unable to find a heartbeat, a fetal electrocardiogram (ECG) and ultrasound scan are carried out.

If the baby has died in the womb, you may go into labour naturally, or labour will be induced. Throughout your antenatal care programme, your doctor and midwife will do their best to ensure that any dangers to your baby are picked up before anything serious occurs, and stillbirth, or death in the womb, occurs in less than one percent of all pregnancies. If you do not feel your baby move for 6 to 8 hours, call your doctor immediately. In nearly all cases, it will be a false alarm. If a baby has died, a woman will know about it before the labour, and her doctor or midwife will explain all they can about what may have gone wrong. There are also many support groups to help parents cope with the tragedy of stillbirth and neonatal death. Having a stillborn baby does not indicate a recurrent problem.

Postmaturity

In the vast majority of cases, labour begins when your baby is fully mature and able to survive. When you do not go into labour until long after this stage, your baby may be in some danger. This condition is known as postmaturity. An ageing placenta can fail to provide a large baby with enough oxygenated blood, and this can result in brain damage or even death. Postmaturity may be more likely to occur if you have a family history of diabetes, and becomes more common if you have been carrying your baby for more than forty weeks. If postmaturity is suspected, your physician will probably induce labour, monitoring both the labour and the delivery carefully.

Common ailments

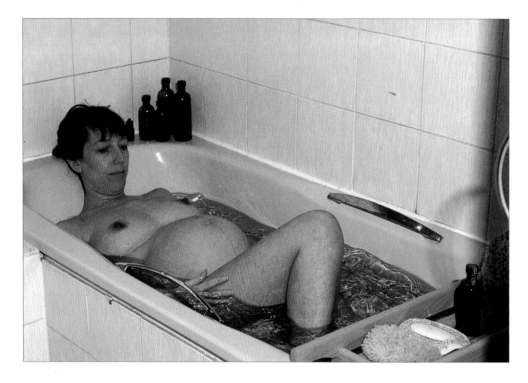

Sleeping problems

Difficulties in sleeping are common in the later months of pregnancy when it may be hard to find a comfortable position, and your baby's movements or a full bladder may wake you. If you have trouble getting to sleep or tend to wake in the middle of the night, try not to worry, as this can make the situation worse. Many women also suffer from vivid nightmares and dreams, so their sleep is less restful.

What you can do

● Take a warm (not hot) bath before bedtime, with a few drops of lavender or roman chamomile essential oils, which can help you to relax.

● Try to get some exercise, even if you are feeling fatigued, because it can actually work to improve sleep and provide you with more natural energy.

● If heartburn is causing you to lose sleep, try eating a slice of fresh pineapple after your last meal, and avoid eating for at least 2 hours before bedtime. A glass of milk at bedtime may help both to encourage sleep and to ease the heartburn.

● Try to avoid sleeping on your back, which rests the entire weight of your uterus on the back, intestines and the veins responsible for returning the blood from the lower body to the heart. This can exacerbate backache and haemorrhoids, among other things, and interfere with digestion, breathing and circulation, which can lead to sleeping problems.

● If you are exhausted by lack of sleep in the later months of pregnancy, your doctor may prescribe a sleeping tablet, but it is advised that you try more natural methods, since these drugs can cross the placenta and affect the baby.

● Find a means of controlling pain, and learn some relaxation techniques to help you get through the tense hours of early waking.

● Stop working or doing anything strenuous (mentally or physically) at least an hour before bedtime, and try reading something light or watching television until you feel sleepy.

● If you cannot get to sleep, switch on the light and read, or do something different, and then try to go back to sleep later.

● Many women suffer from night sweats (see below). Keeping cool can help you to sleep better.

● If you are overtired when you go to bed, try taking a short afternoon nap, to break the cycle.

● Find the right bed: a good mattress is essential for good quality sleep. As a general rule, the more expensive, the better the quality, but decide which gives most comfort and support. It is not true that firm mattresses are better.

Increased vaginal discharge

It is normal to have a thin, odourless or mild-smelling vaginal discharge in pregnancy (called leukorrhoea), much like the discharge that many women get just prior to their periods. Although it may be uncomfortable, there is nothing to worry about unless it becomes thicker, yellow, green or smelly, or is accompanied by redness, itching or pain, which can indicate an infection. Infections such as vaginitis rarely pose a risk to the baby, but you should report it to your doctor, who will prescribe a safe treatment.

Thrush is also easily treated by your doctor (and see below). If you are diagnosed as having a sexually transmitted disease, you will be advised to avoid intercourse until you are free of the infection, and you will be prescribed appropriate treatment to ensure that you do not pass on the condition to your baby at birth. Never douche when you are pregnant, unless it is recommended by your doctor.

What you can do

● Wear loose-fitting clothes and cotton underpants, and avoid tights and anything nylon.

● Keep your vaginal area scrupulously clean, and pat dry with a clean towel. Try not to use soaps and bubble baths, which may cause irritation.

● You may wish to wear a sanitary pad as the discharge increases, but do not use a tampon under any circumstances.

● If you suffer from thrush, eat plenty of fresh, live yoghurt, which helps to balance the body's healthy bacteria (flora) and fight off fungal organisms.

● You can also apply live yoghurt to the entrance of your vagina, to ease the itching.

● Add a few tablespoons of apple cider vinegar to some warm water and gently bathe the affected area. You can also add about 6 ounces (180 ml) of vinegar to your bath water, which will have the same effect.

● If you have thrush, cut down on foods containing sugar and yeast, as both of these can exacerbate the problem.

Itchy skin and rashes

As your skin stretches, it can become itchy and more easily irritated. You may also find that you get rashes in the folds of your skin, partly because of the increased perspiration, and partly because some areas of your body may chafe against others as you grow larger.

What you can do

● Avoid using any perfumed soaps or bath products, which can irritate your skin, and use a non-biological laundry detergent.

● Wear cotton clothing that allows your skin to 'breathe', and use talcum powder in areas that are prone to sweating.

● Add a few drops of roman chamomile and lavender essential oils to a light carrier oil, such as grapeseed, and rub it into the affected area to soothe and encourage healing.

● Soothing herbs such as chamomile can be added to the bath (a handful will do as you are running the bath water).

● A cream or ointment containing calendula can be rubbed into the affected area to ease the discomfort, and to encourage the skin to heal.

● Consult your doctor if itchiness persists as it could indicate a rare liver condition known as choleostasis.

Nose problems

Nasal congestion, often with nosebleeds and a feeling of stuffiness in your ears, is commonly associated with pregnancy and results from the high levels of hormones circulating in your body, which cause the mucous membranes to soften and swell. The congestion may be worse in the winter months, when you are spending more time inside, perhaps in a centrally heated house.

What you can do

● Place pans of water on the radiators, or get a vaporizer, which will ensure that the air is less dry and therefore less irritating. A few drops of tea tree oil in the vaporizer or water will help you to breathe more easily.

● Take some extra Vitamin C each day, which can encourage the health of your capillaries, and reduce the chances of bleeding. 250mg per day is adequate.

● If your nose does begin to bleed, pinch it between fingers and thumb for about thirty seconds. This should stop the bleeding but you could also try soaking a piece of cotton wool in a little fresh lemon juice and

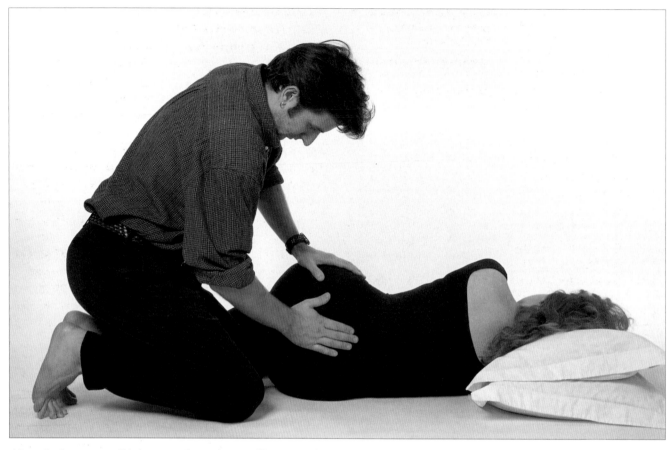

A lower back massage will help to ease the strain caused by your growing baby, and will help you to relax. Ask your birthing partner to practise massage that you may wish to use in labour in the weeks leading up to the birth – it can be particularly useful to relieve any pain associated with Braxton-Hicks, or 'practise' contractions.

inserting in the offending nostril to staunch blood flow.

● Drink a little elderflower tea, which can reduce mucus secretion and catarrh, and relieve the pressure on your nasal passages to prevent nosebleeds.

Night sweats

In pregnancy, the increased blood supply causes your blood vessels to dilate and radiate warmth that can, at times, be excessive. It is also believed that pregnancy hormones cause extra sweating and flushing, which may be uncomfortable, and make it difficult for you to sleep.

What you can do

● Make sure that your night garments are made of cotton, so that you will remain cooler.

● Try not to be too active before bedtime.

● Take a lukewarm bath before bed to cool you down, and leave a window open so that you don't become too hot.

● Add a few drops of essential oils of chamomile or lavender to your bathwater, which will help to cool and relax you.

● Make sure that you eat plenty of oats, which can help to restore balance to the nervous system – the idea being that the nerve fibres supplying the blood vessels would become less irritable and therefore less likely to swing between dilation and constriction, causing sweats.

Rib pain

As your uterus increases in size, it pushes up into the abdomen, compressing the ribs. Your growing baby can also bruise your ribs by punching or kicking, which can be enormously painful. You may find that the pain is worse when you are sitting down, and there is extreme tenderness and soreness just below the breasts. You should experience some relief when the baby drops down into the pelvis (engages).

What you can do

● Wear loose clothing that won't apply pressure to your ribs, and try to improve your posture, which will help to open up the rib cage.

● Place a cushion behind your head and back when lying down.

● Try massaging a few drops of melissa or lavender oil in a light carrier oil into the affected area to ease pain and reduce any inflammation.

● An osteopath will be able to work on the ribs to relieve pain and prevent problems recurring. He will also be able to relieve stress in the rib area, to restore joint mobility. Many osteopaths specialize in treating pregnant women, so look around for one who does.

Sciatica

Sciatica is the name given to the aching or pain along the route of the sciatic nerve. This is the largest nerve in the body, running from the spinal cord, through the buttock and the back of the leg. Sciatica is usually caused by pressure on the roots of the sciatic nerve, and is common as your baby becomes larger. It is also exacerbated by the loosening of the ligaments caused by the pregnancy hormones. The type of pain varies from mild to more severe and 'shooting', and you may experience some numbness, pins and needles, pain in the legs and buttocks, and a burning sensation.

What you can do

● Try to improve your posture (see page 40), which will help to relieve some of the pressure on the sciatic nerve.

● There are a number of homeopathic remedies which can help, including: Colocynth for shooting pains down the right leg to the foot, causing numbness; Rhus tox, for tearing pain, which improves with heat and movement; Lycopodium, for pain in the right leg, which is worse between 4 and 8pm; Carbon sulph, for pain in the left leg, which is worse with heat and cold; and Gelsemium, for burning pains that are worse at night. Take homeopathic remedies in the 6x dilution, every 3 hours as required, and stop when the symptoms disappear. Homeopathic remedies are safe to take in pregnancy.

● Lavender oil is antispasmodic and anti-inflammatory. Try adding a few drops to your bath, or to a light carrier oil, such as grapeseed, and massage into the affected area.

● Rub fresh lemon over the affected area – it's a traditional remedy that really works.

● Sciatica and other forms of back pain may be eased by lying on the floor for 15 minutes. Prop your head up on a small pile of paperback books and keep your knees bent. Repeat daily.

● Yoga and stretching exercises will help to relieve the discomfort of sciatica by relieving the pressure on the sciatic nerve. See page 39 for some suggestions or consult your exercise teacher.

Problems associated with multiple pregnancies

Multiple pregnancies are normally discovered early on, usually as a result of the first blood test, and certainly by the first ultrasound scan (although one twin has been known to hide behind the other). In any case, many women guess fairly soon that they are carrying more than one baby – perhaps because they are more likely to be larger earlier, or because they may feel much more tired or sick. If you are carrying twins, your pregnancy will be monitored closely, and in particular your midwife or doctor will keep a close eye on your blood pressure, and watch for oedema, anaemia and pre-eclampsia (see page 84). You will therefore be required to have more antenatal visits.

Because you will be feeling much more tired, and the strain on your body will be virtually double that of a single baby pregnancy, you will probably be urged to avoid strenuous exercise or work, either in the home or in the office, and many women are advised to have complete rest from the fifth month onwards. Multiple pregnancies are much more likely to end in premature labour, so ensuring that you take time to rest often is much more important than it would be normally. Twins are normally born at thirty-seven weeks rather than forty weeks of pregnancy (from your last menstrual period), largely because of the restricted space in the womb. As a consequence, they are smaller and weigh less than single babies.

As there are risks to twins in labour, delivery always takes place in hospital, under the guidance of a senior member of staff. There are potential problems for the second-born child, who will have to suffer the contractions of the uterus twice, and who may become deprived of oxygen when the uterus starts to contract after the first twin has been born. Many twins are delivered by Caesarean section for this reason. If you are carrying more than two babies, you will undoubtedly have a Caesarean, as doctors will not chance a vaginal delivery in these circumstances.

Preparing for the birth

As the days draw closer, you'll need to prime yourself emotionally and physically for the birth, and make sure that you have everything ready at home. By now, you will have prepared a birthplan (see page 78) and investigated the facilities at your hospital.

If you have decided upon a home birth, your midwife or doctor will help you to get ready for delivery in your own environment, and most health practitioners will provide you with a 'delivery kit'.

There are a few practical considerations that must be undertaken before your baby is born:

● Think about how you will get to the hospital at different times of day. If parking is difficult, you may wish to consider a taxi, or make a list of friends who are prepared to give you a lift. Plot out how long it will take you to get to the hospital in rush-hour traffic.

● Think about childcare if you have other children. Write out a list of their favourite activities if your child is unaccustomed to being with another carer, and leave contact phone numbers in the event of an emergency.

● Prepare a list of people you would like to advise of the birth, with their numbers. Your partner may wish to ring friends and relations from the hospital, and it is helpful to have this list ready before you go into labour.

● Pack your hospital suitcase (see below).

● Prepare any items you may wish to have along with you at the birth, including things like a cassette player, aromatherapy oils, homeopathic remedies, snacks and drinks, and perhaps a deck of cards or a game, if things become protracted (see below).

● Be relaxed in the knowledge that you have everything ready for your baby.

Choose a lightweight holdall for your hospital bag. Pack a couple of weeks before your due date and leave the bag in a convenient place.

Your hospital suitcase

If you plan to stay longer than a few hours after the labour, you will have to pack a few things for yourself and your baby, including:

For you

- a night garment that will allow you to feed easily
- at least a dozen maternity pads
- a box of breastpads
- nipple cream, if you plan to breastfeed
- at least six changes of underpants (disposable pants might be useful, since you can expect to go through about three or four pairs of underpants in the first day)
- two or three nursing bras, if you plan to breastfeed, or firm-support bras if you do not
- a book or a couple of magazines
- money for the telephone and other sundries
- a toothbrush and toothpaste
- slippers or warm socks
- a dressing gown
- a towel and wash cloth
- soap and deodorant
- any oils or remedies you plan to take after the birth to encourage healing (see pages 126–7)
- tissues
- shampoo and a hair brush
- bottled water or boxed drinks
- a notebook or some paper and a pen (there is nothing like a new baby to bring on the urge to make lists!)
- perhaps your birth announcement cards, to get an early start

- a camera and a roll of film for early shots of your baby
- a change of clothes for going home – remember that you won't be at your pre-pregnancy size for some time, and loose, comfortable clothing is best.

For your baby

- two or three sleep suits
- two or three vests
- disposable nappies and baby wipes

- cotton wool
- baby bath and bottom cream
- a soft cotton blanket
- a warm sweater or jacket for the trip home
- a pair of socks
- a first toy, that you can place at the side of her cot to attract her attention

In addition to provisions for your hospital stay, think about what you would like to have with you during the labour, and have it ready from about the thirty-sixth week after conception (thirty-eighth week of pregnancy). You may want to consider:

- a pair of warm socks, for the later stages of labour
- a change of loose, comfortable clothing
- a small towel for your face
- a natural sponge, from which you can suck small amounts of cool water if you become hot, or use it to gently sponge your body if things become difficult to cope with
- lip salve

- massage oils
- a beanbag chair
- a hot water bottle
- food and drink (for you and your partner; choose small, easily digested snacks for you, such as raisins or fruit, and perhaps some sandwiches and a bar of chocolate for your partner)
- magazines and board games
- natural remedies to help you get through the labour and delivery (see page 103)
- a glucose drink or tablets, such as Lucozade or Gatorade
- a flask containing frozen cubes of fruit juice, to suck
- a cassette player and some soothing tapes
- your camera
- a copy of your birthplan

Are you overdue?

The estimated date for your baby's delivery is determined by doctors, not babies, and only about 5 percent of babies arrive when they are expected. The large majority are born more than a week after the expected date, so don't panic if your delivery date comes and goes without any sign of labour beginning.

Many women have irregular cycles, which makes the date of conception difficult to pinpoint, and unless you are absolutely sure of your dates, the estimated delivery date will be fuzzy at best. Your ultrasound scan will give you some idea of the age of your baby, and if you are unsure, a later scan can be arranged to determine the correct dates. Women of different races seem to have different gestational periods, and it is useful to talk to your mother or sisters, if you have any, to find out when their babies were born. If you have a family history of late babies, your doctor or midwife will probably allow you to go a little later before making the decision to induce.

It is, however, not safe to go far beyond your estimated date, primarily because the placenta may be unable to sustain the baby over an extended period (see Postmaturity, page 85), and also because a large baby may be more difficult to deliver. There may be causes for failure to go into labour, including pelvic disproportion, which means that your baby's head is too big to pass through your pelvis, and he may not engage. Some women simply do not begin labour naturally, making an induction necessary.

If your baby is late, your doctor or midwife will keep a close eye on you to ensure that all is well, and may use several means of monitoring the baby,

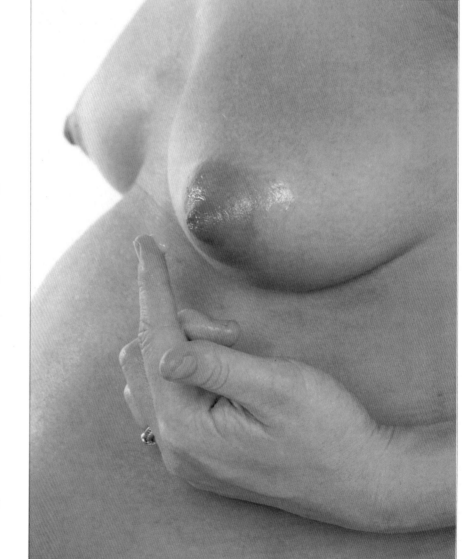

Gentle stimulation of the nipples can encourage uterine contractions and may bring on labour if you are overdue. Many women regularly massage their nipples with a gentle oil like calendula, to help prepare them for breastfeeding.

including:

● Electronic monitoring of the baby. Your baby's heartbeat may be monitored electronically, usually by a belt that is strapped around your abdomen. If all is well, it is likely that you will be left to go into labour naturally. If there seems to be some distress, labour may be induced.

● Recording fetal movements. You can do this yourself, by making a simple chart and recording when your baby moves throughout the day, across several days. If movement is regular, there should not be a problem. If you do find that your baby ceases to be active, or is much less active than in previous days, you should contact your doctor immediately.

● In some hospitals, the doctor may test the amount of oestriol in your urine. Production of oestriol usually drops off before labour. If your levels are lower than they should be for several days without result, it could mean that your placenta is not functioning properly.

● Some doctors inject a small quantity of oxytocin, which causes the uterus to contract. Your baby will be monitored during the contractions and if there is any foetal distress, induction is usually recommended.

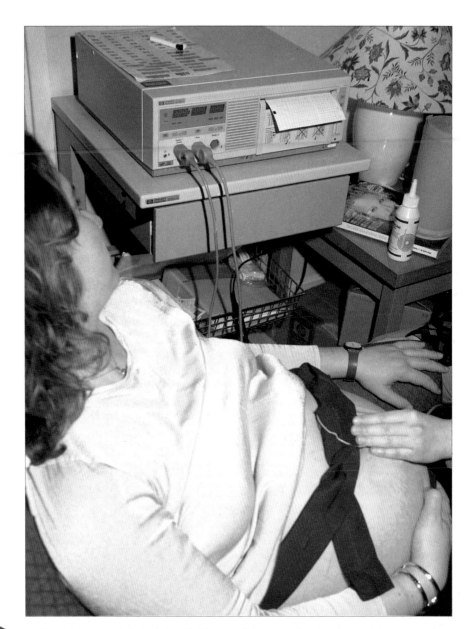

If your labour needs to be induced at the hospital, you may be placed on an intravenous drip, which provides oxytocin to stimulate uterine contractions. During an induction, your baby's heartbeat may also be monitored electronically.

Some women claim that spicy foods like curry or pepperoni can start labour. Others say that gentle exercise helped to make their contractions start and some women find that sex can bring it on.

Note: If your doctor or midwife decides that labour should be induced, you may wish to try some natural means before they intervene (see left). However, in an emergency situation, it is best to allow them to use whatever methods are necessary to ensure the health of you and your baby.

Pain relief

The intensity of pain in labour varies significantly from woman to woman, and is partly influenced by your expectations. You may not need pain relief during labour, but if you do, there are several options available. Try to keep an open mind about pain relief when you are preparing your birthplan. Even if you don't end up using anything, it is comforting to know that it is available.

If the first stage of labour is very painful, you may be given medication to help reduce tension and pain. This is done only if your physician is fairly sure that delivery is not imminent, because the drug can affect your baby's breathing if given late in labour.

Pudendal block

Vaginal pain can be relieved by an anaesthetic injected into the tissues of the vagina, known as pudendal block. It is often used just before a forceps delivery or before an episiotomy, in which an incision is made in the vagina to aid delivery. Caudal anaesthesia is administered by an injection into your spinal area and may be used for short-term relief if the birth involves forceps or ventouse extraction (see page 111).

Paracervical block

A paracervical block is a local anaesthetic injected on either side of the cervix, usually towards the end of the first stage of labour, when the dilation of the cervix may be most uncomfortable. It works by numbing the nerves as they leave the uterus and travel with the uterine arteries, towards the side wall of the pelvis. It is sometimes used for forceps delivery, and only takes a few minutes to work.

Epidural anaesthesia

A painkilling method called epidural anaesthesia involves injecting an anaesthetic into the base of your spine to temporarily deaden the nerves running to the lower half of your body. A catheter is then usually placed in the lower part of your back and small doses of anaesthetic are given if needed as labour progresses, or during delivery. Epidurals may be recommended if you are having a long and difficult

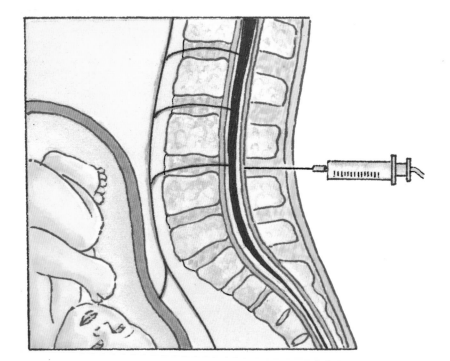

The epidural block (also called lumbar epidural) is becoming popular for both vaginal and Caesarean births, and provides almost complete relief from the pain of labour. A needle is inserted into the back (after a local anaesthetic numbs the area) and the drug (usually bupivacaine, lidocaine or choloroprocaine) is administered as required throughout the labour, into the space between the spinal cord and the outer membrane. The drugs can be stopped at any time throughout the labour, and then restarted if required.

The pain of labour

It's difficult to understand why a natural process should be so painful, but there are many reasons it is so.

● Your pelvic ligaments, and the soft tissues and joints, are stretched, which stimulates the nerves that run through them.

● When your muscles contract, the metabolic rate in the tissues of the surrounding area is increased. This can speed up the onset of pain.

● Tension builds up in muscles during labour, which makes them sore. Try not to stiffen when you have a contraction. When muscles become stiff and tired, they are more susceptible to injury.

● The reduced blood supply to the muscles causes pain and cramping. When oxygen is unable to reach the muscles, and waste products are unable to be released, the muscles become ischaemic, or starved of oxygen, and go into spasm. The build-up of waste products can also cause enormous pain.

● The pain begins in the muscles of the uterus when you have a contraction, and they become worst at the height of the contraction, when nerve fibres are stimulated.

● Pain results from the stretching and dilating of the cervix as it effaces.

● In the second stage of labour, pain is caused by the stretching of the vagina, vulva, perineum and pelvic joints, as the baby works her way down the birth canal.

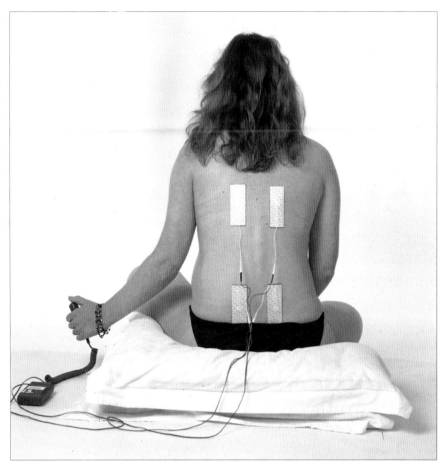

A TENS (transcutaneous electrical nerve stimulation) machine uses electrodes to stimulate nerve pathways to the uterus and the cervix. It is believed that this stimulation prevents other sensory travel along these pathways, including pain. The intensity of stimulation will be controlled by you, in the form of a hand-held mechanism. TENS machines also work to raise the level of endorphins, the body's natural painkillers, thus easing the discomfort of labour pains.

labour, and finding it difficult to cope and to summon energy to continue. Most Caesareans are now done under epidural instead of a general anaesthetic, so that you can stay awake during the birth. You'll need to let your midwife know in advance if you want an epidural. The hospital anaesthetist will need to be summoned, and it usually takes about 20 minutes to prepare. You will need to have an intravenous drip if you are using an epidural, and some forms of epidural will make it necessary for you to remain in one position. Try to make sure you are propped up rather than lying flat on your back or on your side, to make the labour and delivery easier.

Gas and air

Gas and air, or Entonox, can be controlled by you, as you require it, and it works by numbing the pain centre of the brain. Using a mask, you will inhale deeply as a contraction starts, and carry on until the contraction peaks. Breathe normally without the mask.

Narcotics

The most commonly used narcotic is pethidine, which is injected into your thigh or buttock during the first stage of labour to dull the pain. Try a small injection first, to see how it affects you; it will probably be administered with an anti-emetic, as pethidine can cause nausea. Some women don't like the feeling of drowsiness that it can encourage. Narcotics take longer to work than an epidural, and you can expect to wait about 20 minutes for relief.

Natural pain relief

Apart from the relaxation and breathing methods discussed on page 58, there are a number of other natural methods of pain relief which will help you to get through labour without the use of drugs, if that is what you wish. Your body has its own natural painkillers called endorphins, which build up as contractions get worse. The more natural your labour, the more quickly the endorphins are produced and put into action.

TENS

TENS stands for Transcutaneous Electrical Nerve Stimulation, and it involves using an electric current to stimulate the production of endorphins and block the pain impulses conducted by your nerves. You will be given a battery-powered stimulator, which is connected by wires to electrodes that are placed on either side of your spine. A hand-held set allows you to control the amount of stimulation required, increasing or decreasing through contractions.

It is worth knowing that endorphins build up over time and require constant stimulation. If you have a TENS machine, you will need to use it consistently through the labour for best effect. You won't, for instance, be able to

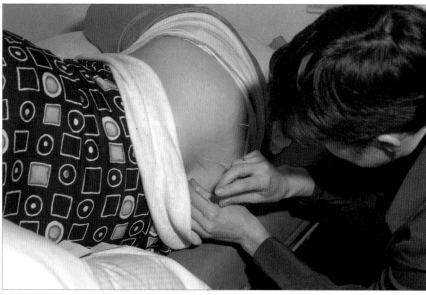

Acupuncture points across the body can be stimulated throughout labour to ease pain, and to encourage a more efficient delivery. A qualified and experienced acupuncturist may even be able to turn a breech baby prior to labour, and to start contractions if you are overdue.

have a bath while wearing it, and if you take it off for a bath, the effect will be reduced.

Acupuncture

Many women use acupuncture for pain relief, both before and during the labour, and several documented studies show that it is an extremely successful means of pain control and relief; indeed, in China, it is often used as total anaesthesia for Caesareans instead of epidurals. Some women also report that it eases other symptoms of labour, such as nausea. Acupuncture involves stimulating the flow of energy in your body with very thin needles, and there are several documented studies which show that it does have enormous success in relieving pain.

Aromatherapy oils can be used to improve mood and emotional outlook in labour, and many oils have specific properties to ease pain, reduce tension, alleviate cramping, and stimulate the release of endorphins, your body's natural painkillers. Oils can be used in massage, or in the bath, while in labour, or in a vaporiser, which will fill the room with your chosen scent.

Aromatherapy

Aromatherapy oils can be used in a variety of ways for a range of purposes, including pain relief and relaxation. It is believed that the essential oils trigger the central nervous system to provide pain relief by stimulating the release of chemicals including endorphins. Aromatherapy has been successfully used as a method of pain relief in several maternity units in the UK, and they also help to relieve nausea, increase the rate or strength of contractions, ease emotional symptoms, and soothe the pain of labour. Because they work with your body, there are no side effects. Some of the best oils to use in labour are those listed on page 103.

Other natural treatments

● Homeopathic remedies and flower essences encourage a positive response to pain, and can be used in a variety of situations. It is a good idea to contact a therapist to get the right dosage and remedy. There are, for example, over two thousand homeopathic remedies available, and you may need assistance choosing the one that is best for you.

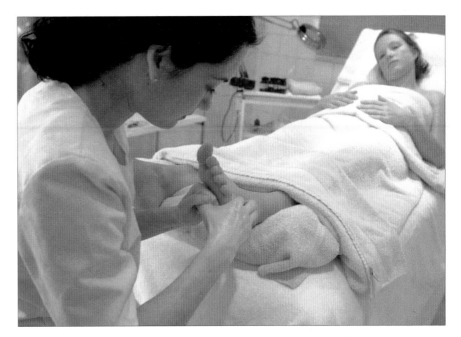

A reflexologist will massage points on your hands and/or feet in order to relieve pain, and encourage the action of the uterus and other organs of the body. Studies show that women who have reflexology treatments prior to labour have a shorter and less painful delivery, and a reflexologist can also provide supportive treatment during the labour itself.

The tried and tested remedies for labour are listed on page 103.

● Herbs have a wide range of therapeutic and pharmacological properties, and can be as powerful as any drugs, if used correctly. They have no side-effects, however, and they work with your body rather than merely sedating it.

There are a wide variety of homeopathic remedies that are appropriate for childbirth, to encourage the action of your body, and to help you to cope with pain and discomfort. Following the birth, remedies can be prescribed to ensure a speedy recovery, to minimize bruising, to ease pain, and help deal with any infection or trauma.

Herbs should be prescribed by a therapist, but it is safe to use tisanes in labour, and useful herbs include those listed on page 103.

● Hypnotherapy will have to be taught to you in advance of the labour, but it can be useful at any stage, as well as afterwards, for post-delivery problems. Studies show that it can reduce the duration of labour and the pain of contractions, as well as improving your emotional state.

● Reflexology involves gently massaging or pressing certain areas of feet (and sometimes hands) which relate to different body parts, to relieve pain, encourage the action of the uterus and other organs in the body, and even help to dilate the cervix and speed up the labour. If you have treatment throughout pregnancy, you may suffer from fewer side-effects. Your therapist will be able to teach you or your partner where and how to manipulate the points on your feet during labour.

The first stage of birth

Every woman's labour is different, and it is impossible to predict how long or how demanding yours will be. Studies show that women who approach labour with a positive attitude, and a belief that they will cope, do on average have shorter and less painful labours. A woman spends over nine months being pregnant, and only a tiny proportion of that time actually delivering the end result, but those hours of labour and birth preoccupy women throughout their pregnancy, and, indeed, afterwards, when you will probably feel an irresistible urge to discuss it in great detail.

Think of your labour as a marathon for which you are training. By going into it thinking positively, with a strong, well-rested and well-fed body, you are more likely to fly through. If there are problems, or your labour is more protracted than you had hoped, it helps to know that labour and delivery have never been safer than they are today. Your hospital team will be prepared to handle any eventuality, and you can rest assured that they will do everything in their power to make you as comfortable as they can, and to bring your baby into the world in the easiest possible way.

The stages of birth

As labour starts, many women have a 'show', which means that they lose the mucus plug that has formed a barrier between the uterus and vagina during pregnancy. You may discover that you have a mucousy, blood-streaked discharge before you have any other symptoms, and many women find this alarming, as it does usually indicate the onset of labour, and also because it may be the first blood you have discharged for nine long months.

Another sign of labour is the bursting of the membranes that surround the amniotic fluid in which the foetus floats. When this occurs, you may have a slow trickle from your vagina or you may have a sudden gush. If your waters break, but there is no sign of regular contractions, inform the hospital as soon as possible (see page 85).

Notify your hospital team when you have any of these signs of labour, and they will advise you when to come in. If you have planned a home birth, your physician or midwife should be called.

Are you in labour?

There are several signs that indicate you are in labour. The first is contractions of the muscles of the uterus. Initially, these contractions may feel like cramping, painful gas in the intestines, or a regular, lower back pain. If the contractions begin coming at regular intervals, and occur increasingly closer together, you are likely to be in labour, although many women experience 'false labour', which can be characterized by contractions which come and go, but which do not increase in frequency or strength.

The first stage

This can last anywhere from 2 to 24 hours, and it begins with the first contractions, which help open the cervix, through which your baby will leave the uterus. The average duration of the first stage is about 10 to 12 hours, which decreases to between 4 and 7 for subsequent babies. If you have had several children, you may have a first stage that lasts only a few minutes.

With each contraction, the cervix is gradually pulled open and up (dilated). Effacement is the thinning and shortening of the cervix, when it merges with the walls of the uterus. Full dilation is reached when the opening of the cervix with the baby's head protruding is about 4 inches (10 centimetres) in diameter.

Coping with the first stage of labour

Most labours begin gradually, and build up to stronger and more painful contractions. You may wish to move around, particularly at the beginning, which helps you to cope with the pain and keeps the contractions coming. You might find that contractions slow down when you rest, but that may prolong the labour, and if you can continue to be active, the duration should decrease. Many women like to take a long walk, which will keep up the contractions, and also help to distract them from the pain.

If you need to have your baby monitored, ask if you can do so in a way that allows you to remain active for as long as possible.

As the labour progresses, you may find that the pain roots you to the spot. It may be more comfortable lying down, or

A home birth

Many women are put off by the thought of having their baby in hospital, and feel more comfortable with the idea of giving birth in their own environment. Home births have many benefits, and some women do find they have an easier labour when they do it on their own terms. A baby who is born at home, into the environment that he will

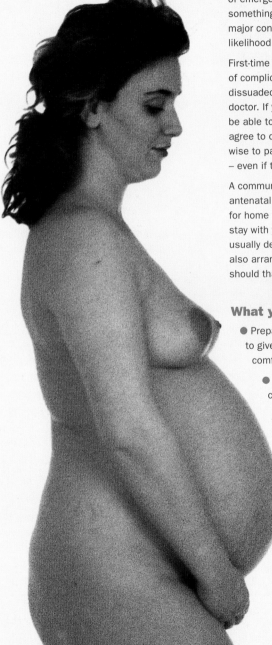

become a part of, will not be disrupted by the transition from hospital to home, and he will be welcomed by family and friends into a loving atmosphere.

If you are considering a home birth, it is a good idea to discuss it at length with your doctor and midwife, to ensure that it is a safe option for you. It is important to remember that you won't have the benefit of emergency facilities readily available if something were to go wrong, and that is a major consideration if there is any likelihood that you may need them.

First-time mothers, or women with a history of complications in childbirth, will be dissuaded from a home birth by their doctor. If you are very determined, you may be able to find another doctor who will agree to care for you at home, but it is wise to pay attention to your doctor's views – even if they seem to be overcautious.

A community midwife will oversee your antenatal care and advise you on preparing for home labour and delivery. She or he will stay with you during your labour, and usually deliver your baby herself. She will also arrange for emergency back-up, should that be necessary.

What you need to do:

● Prepare the room in which you intend to give birth, and make sure you will be comfortable but have some privacy.

● You will need to have several clean sheets (which can be discarded afterwards) available, as well as towels and plastic sheeting. Your midwife may be able to provide you with a ready-prepared pack containing everything you need.

● Talk to your doctor about the safety of a home birth, and ensure that you have regular antenatal care up to the birth so that any changes in your condition are noted, and the situation reassessed.

● You will need to have facilities available for washing

● Prepare clothing for yourself and the baby (see page 91), just as you would for a hospital birth.

● Ring the hospital when your contractions are 15 minutes apart, and your midwife will come, according to arrangements you will have made with her.

● Your midwife will bring along several things, including a stethoscope or sonic aid, for listening to your baby's heart, gas and air (Entonox), sticks to test your urine, a local anaesthetic, materials for suturing tears or an episiotomy, intravenous equipment, Syntometrine and resuscitation equipment.

With the help of an experienced midwife, you should be able to have a safe and natural labour at home, without complications. However, you must be prepared for the possibility that an emergency situation may arise (see page 110), and you may need to be transported quickly to hospital. If all does not go according to plan, you will likely feel disappointed, so it is best to be prepared for the eventuality beforehand.

When a home birth is not safe

There are a variety of conditions that will preclude a home birth, and for the safety of you and your baby, you should not consider one if you have any of the following:

● previous complications in childbirth or pregnancy
● breech baby
● premature baby
● multiple pregnancy
● high blood pressure
● anaemia
● diabetes
● placenta praevia
● pre-eclampsia
● abruptio placentae
● excess amniotic fluid
● a baby that is too large to pass through your pelvis

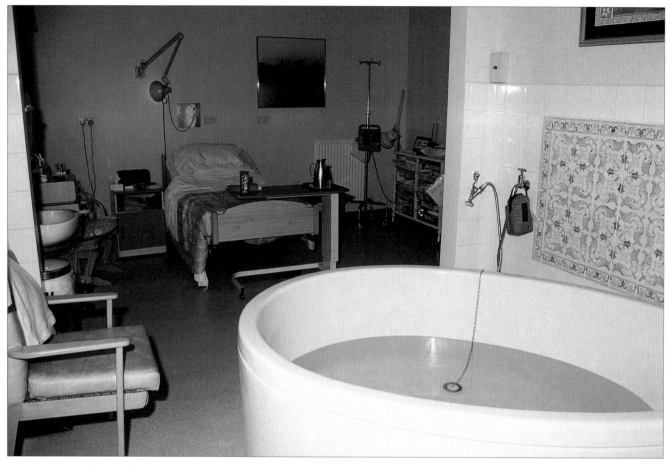

Water births are becoming more common and you may wish to find out if your hospital offers this facility. Even if you don't give birth in a birthing pool, you will find that a warm bath during early and even advanced labour can soothe the pain of contractions.

finding a position on your hands and knees that makes the contractions less painful. Lying flat on your back will not help the progress of your labour. Change positions as often as possible, and try to put into practice the breathing lessons you have learned.

You may find the pain unbearable, and require some anaesthetic (see page 94). There are, however, a number of steps you can take to make the labour easier, and make it possible for you to cope. Your perception of the pain may be enhanced if you feel alone, so make sure you involve your partner or midwife in the process. If you are tired or hungry, you are likely to feel worse, so it is a good idea to eat something light and easily digested in the early stages, and

take regular drinks of water or diluted fruit juice. If you find that you can't stomach food, suck a cube of frozen fruit juice, or try a glucose tablet or drink, which will provide you with energy. Try to rest between contractions, and practise your breathing. If your partner or a midwife is able to give you a massage, you may feel less alone and more able to relax.

It is quite natural to feel as if you have lost control, and given the choice, you would probably decide at that point that you would rather not have a baby than proceed. Focus on the reward at the end of it all, and try to keep yourself in a positive frame of mind. Remember that the pain is normal, that it will soon be over, and that you are experiencing

nothing worse than what countless millions of women have experienced since the human race began. Your partner can also help by encouraging you and endeavouring to distract you.

You may be feeling:

● discomfort with the contractions, including backache, leg pain

● growing fatigue and a fear that you aren't able to cope

● restless and loss of confidence

What you can do

● Before you go to the hospital, try to keep active, or if your labour comes on in the middle of the night, try to get a good night's sleep. Chances are, the contractions won't be strong enough to

Admission to hospital

If this is your first baby, you will know you are in labour when you have contractions every 10 minutes, or more frequently, for at least 2 to 3 hours. You may wish to stay at home for as long as possible, but it is recommended that you ring the hospital and prepare them for your arrival when contractions are about 10 minutes apart. It is now recommended that you make your way to hospital when contractions are not less than 5 minutes apart, or sooner if you have a long journey ahead of you. If you are having a second baby, contractions may be quite mild and infrequent until your labour is quite advanced, so you may need to get to the hospital earlier – even if contractions seem to be quite weak.

You will also need to go into hospital if there is any bleeding (not to be confused with the 'show', see above). Bleeding in early labour, or at any stage of your pregnancy, must be checked out by your doctor immediately.

When you arrive at the hospital, you will need to be admitted, so it is best to allow some time for this procedure.

● You will need to give your personal details, and you may need to provide your antenatal records if they are not already at the hospital.

● You will have to provide details of when the contractions started, how far apart they are, whether or not your membranes have ruptured, and some details about the type of pain.

● You will need to sign routine consent forms.

● You will be taken to an examination room, or perhaps the labour room itself, where you will be examined by a midwife.

● Your blood pressure will be taken, and your midwife will check your pulse,

respiration and temperature. She will also request a urine sample, and listen to your baby's heartbeat with a stethoscope, or hook you up to a fetal monitor.

● You'll have an internal examination, in which your midwife will check for any blood or liquid in the vagina, and she will place two fingers in the vagina to see how far you are dilated, which will give you a good idea of how far the labour has progressed. If it is possible, she will feel for the intact bag of waters, and check for cord pulsation through it. If the membranes have already broken, she will check to see if the umbilical cord can be felt, and if you are sufficiently dilated, she will be able to tell what position the baby is in (see page 82). Try to relax when she is examining you, and make sure you tell your midwife when a contraction is coming, so that she is not examining you at that time. It may help to bear down slightly as she inserts her fingers, and then practise your breathing exercises.

● If you have opted for epidural anaesthesia (see page 94), an IV may be started.

● Your partner or whoever you have chosen to be with you throughout the labour may be asked to leave you alone for the duration of the examination, but if you feel more comfortable having them present, say so.

● If labour is progressing, you can make yourself at home in the labour room, and change into the clothes in which you want to give birth. Some hospitals may ask you to wear a hospital gown; others are happy to allow you to wear whatever feels most comfortable, or to take everything off. An over-sized T-shirt may be the best option, because you'll have room to move around, and your midwife will be able to check the status of your labour more easily.

your breath.

● Try to move around and change positions as often as possible.

● Keep your energy up by eating small, frequent snacks, if your hospital will allow it.

● Try to remember to urinate as often as possible; you may not notice a full bladder with the distraction of the contractions.

● Think about pain relief, and don't be too hard on yourself if you decide that you will need some assistance after all. Discuss how you are feeling with your midwife or doctor. You may be past the point where it will be necessary. Many women often give in to pain relief for the first time just before transition (see page 104), when delivery is imminent.

● Try some natural remedies (see page 103).

● Take a bath. The warm water will help to ease the symptoms, and may calm you. It's a good idea to add a handful of chamomile flowers, or a little lavender essential oil to enhance the effect.

What your partner can do

● Try to create a calm atmosphere by playing a little soft music, perhaps dimming the lights, and shutting the door to the labour room.

● Use aromatherapy oils, or perhaps a little baby oil, to massage your partner wherever it most helps. Some women appreciate having their lower back massaged; others can't bear to be touched, and may respond better to a hand or foot massage, or simply having their temples rubbed.

keep you awake, and you'll be better off if you start with a solid rest under your belt.

● Eat while the contractions are not too strong; your digestion slows down as labour proceeds.

● Practise your breathing exercises. If you haven't learned any, your midwife

will be able to give you some practical suggestions. Some women find that breathing doesn't help in the way they had hoped, or that under stress they forget all they had learnt; but don't worry about that. It's perfectly possible to have a baby without using them. Just remember to breathe out, and not hold

● Keep calm, no matter how frightened or frightening your partner is, and don't be offended if she becomes abusive.

● Help her to breathe through contractions, and encourage her as they become more painful. Remind her that she is almost there, and that it will all be over soon.

● Regularly offer sips of juice or water, or small bites of food, if she is hungry.

● Remind her to urinate frequently.

● Try to think of diversions – read to her from a favourite book or magazine, or set up a board game or a deck of cards. Tell her a funny story, the latest gossip, or whatever else will get her attention for a few moments.

● Sponge her face if she is hot, or put a pair of socks on her if she is cold. Try to keep tabs on what she is feeling; she may not be responsive to your questions, but if you know her well, you may have an instinctive understanding.

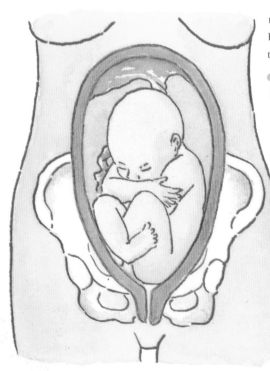

In many cases of breech presentation, your labour will be allowed to proceed as normal but delivery will be slow and controlled by the medical team.

Special types of labour

Most labours are straightforward, but there are cases where it may become slightly more complicated, and you may need extra help.

A posterior baby

The majority of babies are not only engaged head first, but presented with their spine facing outwards. If your baby's head is facing outwards, he is in what is called a 'posterior' position, which means that instead of the crown of his head pushing open the cervix, the front of the head emerges first. In this position, your baby's neck may not be properly flexed, and a larger proportion of the head than normal is presented, which may prolong the labour and cause considerable pain in your back as his head presses up against your spine. In many labours, your baby will eventually rotate into the anterior position, but if he fails so to do, your doctor may need to deliver him using forceps. Posterior labours tend to begin slowly, and take longer than their anterior equivalents, but there are a few things that may help:

● Local massage of your lower back with a few drops of lavender oil in a light carrier oil will help to ease the discomfort, and encourage relaxation of the muscles.

● Try to spend as much time as possible on your hands and knees, which takes the pressure off your back. Rocking back

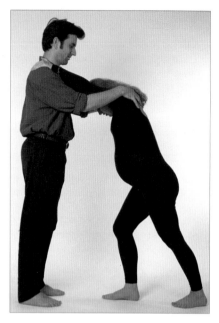

Many women find that adopting an upright position will help to encourage the contractions and speed up the labour. Lean on your birth partner for support, and adopt a stance that allows you to maintain your balance and breathe through the contractions.

and forth on hands and knees is usually helpful.

● Go for a walk to speed up the labour, and try to avoid lying on your back, which will prolong it even further.

● If you need to lie down, do so on the side that your baby is turning towards (your midwife will advise about this).

A breech birth

In a breech presentation, your baby will be positioned with its buttocks down, and one or both feet may emerge first. Breech presentation is common in premature labour (see opposite) because babies often do not assume a normal position for delivery until late in pregnancy. In some cases of breech presentation, a physician will be able to manipulate your baby into the normal presentation position during the last few weeks of pregnancy. If breech presentation persists, but there are no other problems, your physician may suggest that you allow labour to start naturally, while being prepared for a Caesarean section if labour is difficult. When your baby's bottom is delivered first, the head is more vulnerable to pressure as it passes along the birth canal, because the passage has not been sufficiently enlarged by the buttocks.

Extended labour

Your labour may be extended or prolonged when normal contractions do not bring about a delivery. In some cases this is caused by the inability of the cervix to dilate, or the failure of the baby to descend into the birth canal. There is also the risk of an obstruction,

Some women find that squatting is the most natural position to adopt during labour, but make sure you have some support as your leg muscles may tire easily.

which may be caused by a large or breech baby, or one that is lying in a transverse or oblique position (across the uterus rather than facing up or down).

If your labour is taking much longer than expected, you will be closely monitored. If your contractions are weak and infrequent, and your cervix seems to be dilating slowly, your uterus may not be working efficiently. In many cases, labour will speed up of its own accord, as your uterus begins to co-ordinate the muscular activity. In other cases, your doctor may need to rupture the membranes, or administer syntocinon, to encourage contractions. If activity does not increase at this stage,

Natural remedies for childbirth

HOMEOPATHIC REMEDIES

Homeopathic remedies are safe to take both in pregnancy and during the labour itself. You should try to avoid taking them at least 30 minutes on either side of eating or drinking. Homeopathic remedies are widely available in a number of strengths. For labour pains, you will probably want to get 6x strength. Take them as required.

● Coffea is for violent, unbearable pain that causes you to cry out. You will feel nervous between contractions.

● Belladonna is for when contractions, are violent, and you have staring eyes.

● Nux vomica will help when the pains are accompanied by irritability and a need to pass water or faeces.

● Secale can speed a slow labour, when the uterus seems unable to contract any longer.

● Carbo veg is useful when you feel exhausted during the labour.

● Caulophyllum is for contractions that are weak and irregular.

● Gelsemium will help if you become anxious and tremble, and your contractions are not productive.

HERBS

You can bring along some herbal teabags, or a flask of pre-prepared infusions. The best herb to try is chamomile, which will calm you and help to ease the pain. If you find it difficult to sip tea, you might want to make an iced tea in advance, with some cooled chamomile tea, a little lemon juice, and some fresh honey. Sip as required, or freeze into ice-cubes and suck throughout the labour. You can also add a raspberry leaf teabag to the blend before it cools; raspberry leaf helps to tone the uterus.

FLOWER ESSENCES

Flower essences are used to improve your mental state, which can have an enormous effect on your physical well-being. You normally purchase them in small bottles, adding a few drops to a glass of water and sipping. The following are particularly useful in labour.
● Rescue Remedy can be used to ease anxiety and tension, and to help you if you are feeling shocked or traumatized.

● Olive is useful for overwhelming fatigue.

● Take vervain when you have been struggling and straining with little results.

● Sweet chestnut is good for utter despair, when you are about to give up, and think that the baby will never be born.

AROMATHERAPY

You can bring small bottles of essential oils into the labour room, or blend them in advance for your partner to massage into your back as required.

● Clary sage, jasmine and rose can be massaged into the lower back to relax you between contractions.

● Melissa oil has been traditionally used to help with the pain of labour. Use throughout either in a massage, or put a few drops in a bath.

● Rub lavender oil into your lower back or add to the water of a birthing pool, to ease pain. A few drops on the lightbulb in the labour room will help you to relax.

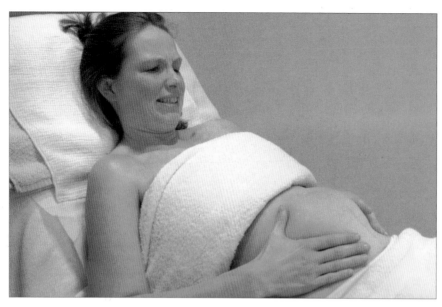

If you need to lie down during labour, you need not be on your back. Lying on your side can be more comfortable and encourages the uterus to contract efficiently.

and there is reason to believe that continuing with the labour will cause harm to either you or your baby, you will probably be advised to have a Caesarean or a forceps delivery.

Premature labour

Premature or early labour occurs some time before the thirty-seventh week of pregnancy, and it has to be said that the cause of most cases of prematurity are unknown. In some instances, however, it may occur as a result of the premature rupturing of the membranes, multiple pregnancy, pre-eclampsia, cervical incompetence and abnormalities of the uterus. You are likely to be in labour if your contractions occur every 5 to 10 minutes on a regular basis, and if an examination by your physician indicates that your cervix is more than an inch dilated. Occasionally, premature labour turns out to be false, the symptoms will subside and your pregnancy will proceed normally. However, if it is discovered that you are in premature labour, your physician will likely hospitalize you and try to delay or suppress the labour. If it

appears that your baby is in some distress, or if you have high blood pressure, diabetes, an infection or fever, or an abnormally placed placenta, you will probably be advised to have a Caesarean, before labour proceeds any further.

Premature labour does tend to be shorter and easier than full-term, but there is an increased risk to the baby, partly because he may not be ready to breathe on his own, and partly because

he may not be physically ready to cope with the trauma of the birth. If you do go into labour prematurely, you will be given Vitamin K at 6-hourly intervals, as a premature baby does not yet have a mature blood-clotting mechanism.

Transition

When the cervix is fully dilated, there is a transition period between the first and second stages of labour. Transition is usually the shortest and most intense phase of labour, lasting for no more than an hour (although it may feel like a lot longer). Your contractions will last between 60 and 90 seconds, with only short intervals between them. You may find it difficult to relax during transition, and you may also feel a very strong urge to push, although you will be discouraged from doing so until the midwife judges that you are ready. Many women find transition the most emotionally upsetting stage of pregnancy, and feel as though they cannot carry on. In general terms, when you are at the end of your tether both physically and emotionally, you are probably in transition and delivery is only a few short minutes away.

In transition, you may feel nauseous and chilly, and you may find that you are falling asleep for seconds between

Find the position that is most comfortable for you, and relax while you focus on your breathing. If your labour runs across a night, try to sleep a little between contractions.

An upright position can accelerate labour, and if you prop some pillows behind you, you can relax back between contractions. Lean forward as you breathe, and meditate, if it helps you to focus.

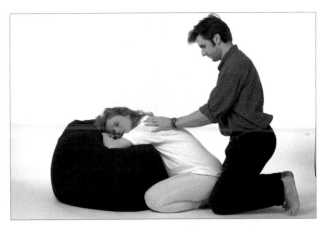

Leaning forward onto a comfortable chair or beanbag is an ideal position for the early stages of labour. Encourage your partner to massage your back wherever it is most painful, and to help ease the tension in your neck and shoulders.

contractions as oxygen is diverted from your brain to the lower part of your body. Don't be surprised if you are abusive to your partner and the hospital team; it's common to feel intense irritability, anxiety, fury and disorientation.

Coping with transition

● Try to remember that when labour is at its worst, it is usually very nearly over. If you can make it to the end of this stage, your cervix will be fully dilated and you will begin to push your baby out into the world.

● If you find the urge to push is overwhelming, pant or blow out instead.

● Try to relax for the short time during contractions, and give in if you find your are nodding off (or passing out!) between them.

● Don't be afraid to shout or cry. The natural release of emotion will ease the pain. Studies show that anxiety is linked

directly to the severity of pain, by causing the muscles to tense and reducing the quantity of natural opiates (pain killers) released by the body.

What your partner can do

● Encourage and praise your partner, and focus on how far she has come, and how well she has done, rather than the pain at present.

● Encourage her to show her emotions, and to cry out with pain or frustration. There is evidence that women who are more verbal and emotional in their response to labour suffer less pain and are less traumatized.

● Keep her warm if she is shivering, and make sure she sucks cubes of frozen fruit juice, or has sips of water or glucose drinks.

● Help her to breathe through contractions, if she wants to, and massage her back if it will help.

● Listen to her requests and don't be offended if she doesn't want you to touch her, or be involved in the process. Some women focus so exclusively on the birth process, that they seem to be in a world of their own, and do not want any interruptions from either hospital staff or their partner.

In the early stages of labour, your cervix will dilate as the contractions of the uterus push your baby out and into the birth canal. By the end of the first stage, you will have dilated to a full 10cm, at which time the cervix is thin enough to stretch over your baby's head (effacement).

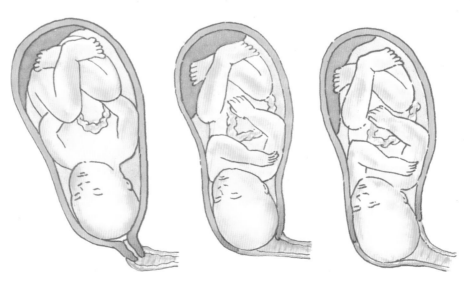

The second stage of birth

As the second stage begins, contractions may be accompanied by an urge to push the baby out and down the birth canal. As the baby moves through the birth canal, it presses on the rectum and may make you feel that you are about to have a bowel movement. You will be advised to push only when you are having a contraction.

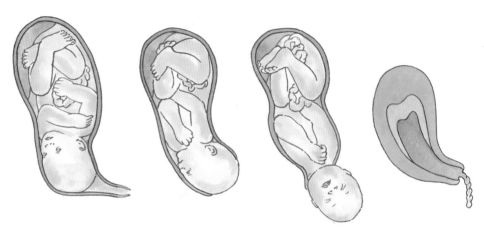

In the first stage of labour, your cervix dilates as the uterus contracts, pushing the baby into the neck of the cervix. The first and second stages are linked by 'transition', a short and intense period of labour when the cervix is fully dilated. In the second stage (third from left), you will push your baby down and out of the birth canal in a series of concerted efforts. This is the first point at which you can actually do something productive to deliver your baby. The final, third stage (shown on the right) is the delivery of the placenta, which is expelled as the uterus continues to contract.

Preventing tearing

● In the weeks leading up to the birth, it will help to keep your perineum soft and supple by rubbing a little olive oil into the area daily.

● Keep your pelvic floor strong by doing your Kegel exercises regularly.

● Some birthing positions may help to avoid episiotomy and tearing, including variations of the squatting position, which seem to be the most natural ways to give birth.

● Some women find that giving birth in warm water helps, and many experts confirm that it results in fewer tears and helps to reduce the need for an episiotomy.

● Hold hot compresses against the perineum during the second stage of labour, to help the tissues relax and stretch more.

This is so that the two physical forces (your pushing and the contractions) combine to expel the baby and you can conserve energy by resting as much as possible between contractions. Episiotomy (see page 110) may be performed toward the end of the second stage of labour, before the baby emerges, to avoid irregular tearing of the vagina, which may be difficult to repair.

The second stage of labour ends when the baby emerges completely from the birth canal. The second stage can last up to 2 or 3 hours for a first baby (or longer!), and up to 1 or 2 hours for a subsequent baby.

Many women find the second stage the most rewarding since you will be actively involved in the birth process for the first time. Contractions will continue as they did in the transition stage, but they may be further apart, giving you the opportunity both to rest and to collect yourself in between. They may also be less painful, perhaps because you are working with them rather than trying to control them.

Coping with the second stage

● Many women find it easier to deliver their babies in a squatting position. You may wish to be supported by your partner and a midwife, or prop yourself up on cushions so that the pull of gravity is used to best effect.

● Rest between contractions, and mentally prepare yourself for the next push. When you feel a contraction, bear down and make sure you breathe as you push. Many women unconsciously hold their breath, which will both exhaust you and make the push less efficient. It's better to give three or four good pushes in a contraction than trying to push for the length of it.

● Pant or blow when you are advised to stop pushing by your doctor.

● Try not to worry about your bowels emptying, or the embarrassment of grunting and groaning. Almost everyone pushes out the contents of their bowels, and some urine, in the second stage of labour, and it will be cleaned up immediately.

● Concentrate on the pushes, and count towards them. Every efficient push brings your baby nearer to being delivered, while inefficient, confused pushing will only waste time.

You may be feeling:

● a burst of energy

● a strong, often irresistible urge to bear down

Once the baby has been delivered, the cord is cut. Your partner can do this if he wants.

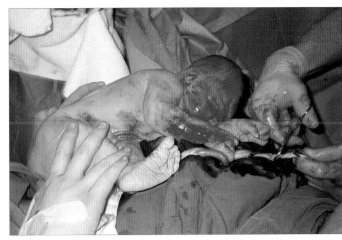

● as if you want to open your bowels, because of the pressure of your baby's head on your rectum

● irritable or frustrated – particularly as your baby's head slides back. When you are pushing out your baby, her body will press out, and then slide back in again, so it may feel as if you are making little progress. It helps to know that you are getting somewhere – for every push, she will slide back about half the distance you have achieved, so it is a slow operation, but progress nonetheless.

● pain and stretching in the perineum

● cold and shivery

What your partner can do

● Help your partner to relax between each contraction, and make sure she has plenty of sips of water, or place slivers of ice between her lips.

● Hold her back or legs in whatever position is most comfortable for her, and provide constant gentle encouragement.

● Encourage the midwife or doctor to keep you abreast of developments. It is helpful to know, for example, when the baby's head has crowned, or when the head is being delivered (see page 108).

Your baby is born

As your baby's head descends, it may feel like a large lump, and you may experience an intense stretching feeling which is released as your baby slips back a little after each push. When the maximum diameter of the baby's head has been delivered, it is said that he has 'crowned'. If you put your hand down, you will be able to feel your baby's head. This can provide enormous motivation to carry on.

When your baby is just about to emerge, you will be asked to pant, which stops you pushing so that the baby can be delivered more slowly and gently. You may feel a stinging sensation as your baby's head stretches the entrance to your vagina. When you experience this,

Your baby will be swaddled in a towel. Let the medical staff know if you want to hold her before she is cleaned up.

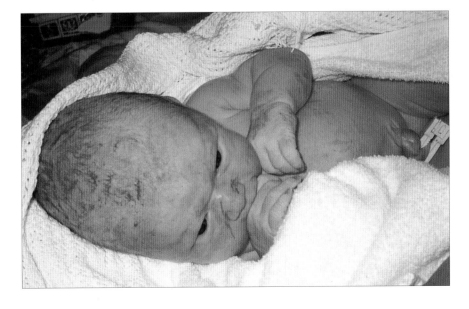

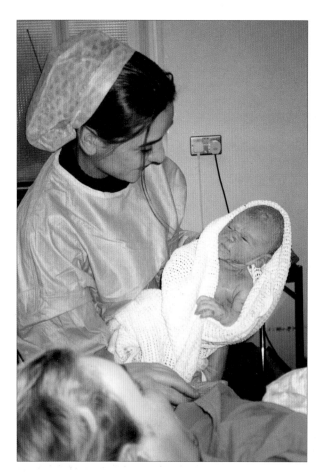

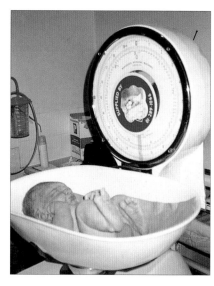

New babies will be sensitive to bright light.

Your baby will be weighed and the Apgar score determined (see page 115).

try to stop pushing and relax the muscles of the perineal floor. Allow the contractions of your uterus to finish off the job.

When the head has been delivered, your baby will be face down. Her head will quickly twist up so that she is facing your thigh, and the midwife or physician will wipe her eyes, nose and mouth, and clear fluid from her nose and air passages. The delivery of the head is a huge relief, and there will be a slight pause before the shoulders

and then the remainder of the body is delivered in a rush of blood and amniotic fluid.

Your baby may be handed to you before the cord is cut, and your partner may wish to cut the cord himself, which is easier than it sounds. If she is slow to breathe, she may need some oxygen from a mask, and occasionally a tube is placed into her windpipe to help get her started. You may want to have your baby cleaned and wrapped up before being given to

you to hold. Because babies are born wet, they have to be quickly wiped and wrapped up before being given to you to hold for any length of time. If you are going to breastfeed, you may want to put the baby on to your breast immediately. Some babies suckle naturally, and others may take a couple of days to become accustomed to the idea.

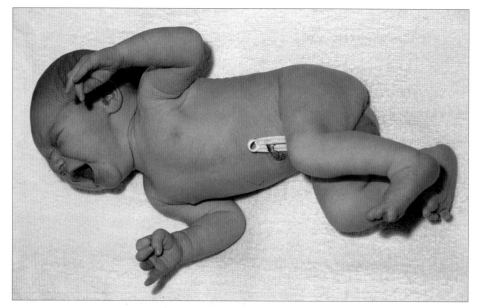

The cord is clamped within minutes of the birth. This is left in place for around 48 hours and the cord stump then shrivels and drops off 3 to 7 days after birth..

The third stage of birth

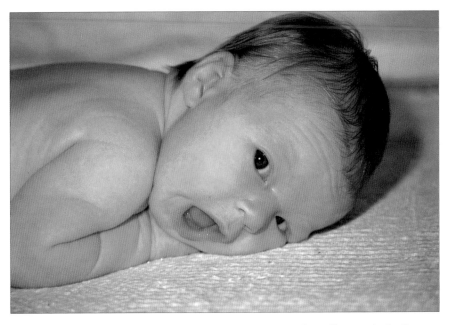

Almost all newborn babies have blue eyes. Their permanent eye colour will appear by the time they are three months old. A few dark-skinned babies have slightly brown eyes from the start.

The third stage is the delivery of the placenta (afterbirth). After your baby is born, your uterus contracts to expel the placenta. There is some bleeding, and the umbilical cord moves a little farther out of the vagina. The third stage of labour lasts about 15 minutes. Usually no attempt is made to deliver the placenta until there are signs that it is separating from the uterine wall, and moving downwards into the vagina.

The delivery may be encouraged by gently pulling the cord, and pressing above the rim of the pelvis to control the expulsion. When the placenta has been delivered, your hospital team will examine it to make sure that none of it has been left behind. If any of the placenta remains in the uterus, there can be haemorrhaging, so it should be removed as soon as possible.

There are two types of drugs which may be used in the third stage:
● ergometrine prevents excessive bleeding, by causing the uterus to contract without relaxing. The placenta will very quickly separate from the uterine wall.

● syntometrine is a combination of syntocin, which stimulates uterine contractions, and ergometrine, which can, on its own, cause some nausea. You will be given a shot of syntometrine in a muscle, usually in the upper leg, when your baby's head crowns, and it is often used to prevent postpartum haemorrhage.

After the placenta is delivered, you may shiver and your teeth may chatter, but you will probably feel an overwhelming sense of exhilaration and relief. Many women are elated by the delivery, and cannot wait to hold their babies. Others feel exhausted, and do not feel an immediate attachment to the little body that has caused so much trauma. Both reactions are natural, and you must try not to feel guilty if you don't feel overwhelming love from the word go.

After the placenta has been delivered, any tears or incisions in the vagina are cleaned and stitched. You will be given a local anaesthetic before stitching, so you are unlikely to feel any pain.

Vitamin K

Vitamin K is often given routinely to newborn, especially premature, babies to prevent haemorrhagic disease. Newborn infants have a low Vitamin K level due to the lack of gut bacteria in the first few days of life. There is considerable debate about whether it is necessary to give your baby Vitamin K, which will be administered by injection directly after the birth, or by oral drops which will be required in two doses. Unless your birth was traumatic, or your baby is premature, it may not be necessary, but it is wise to ask the advice of your doctor or midwife before making a decision against having it. A study which linked Vitamin K with childhood leukaemia has now been discounted, and there is nothing to suggest that it will cause any damage to your baby. However, it is worth talking to your physician if you are concerned.

Special deliveries

Induction of labour

Inducing labour may be necessary for a variety of reasons (see page 92), particularly when the risks of allowing the pregnancy to continue appear to outweigh the risks of induction. You may be induced by having your waters broken, which entails making a small, painless incision in the membranes to drain the fluid.

Sometimes this is enough to start labour. If not, you may receive an intravenous injection of the synthetic hormone oxytocin, which encourages the uterus to contract as it would in natural labour. However, in about one in fifty inductions, the uterus fails to respond to the hormone. In such cases, the baby may be delivered by Caesarean section (see page 112).

When labour is induced, the condition of the foetus is checked throughout delivery by fetal monitoring and by frequent physical examinations. Usually, labour proceeds safely to a normal delivery, but there are some slight risks involved any time that labour is induced. There is also a chance that you will have a premature baby with the associated risks, because it is sometimes difficult to identify the exact stage that a pregnancy is in before inducing labour.

If your doctor has discussed induction with you, and has, perhaps, set a date on which the induction will take place, you may wish to encourage labour yourself. The following tips may help:

● Some women find that stimulating their nipples encourages uterine contractions and may bring on the labour.

● Sexual intercourse can encourage labour naturally, as the prostaglandins in

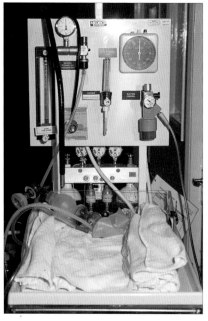

All the delivery rooms in hospitals have special equipment to deal with emergencies.

your partner's semen can soften the cervix and help your womb to contract.

● A spicy meal seems to bring on labour in a large number of cases – try a pepperoni pizza or an Indian curry.

● Drink a glass of orange juice with a few tablespoonsful of castor oil, which can help to evacuate the bowels, and lead to the onset of labour.

● A long walk or an energetic swim can help to trigger labour.

Episiotomy

An episiotomy is an incision sometimes made during labour to widen the opening of the vagina. It is often performed when labour is premature, especially when a forceps delivery is necessary, because your baby's head is vulnerable to pressure in the birth canal.

Episiotomy may also be performed to avoid tearing the vagina as the baby's head emerges from the birth canal. The incision is usually made after injecting a local anaesthetic. After delivery, the cut is sewn up, generally with stitches that gradually dissolve. The incision heals rapidly, although the scar may cause discomfort for up to three months.

To relieve any discomfort in the area around the incision, use an ice pack, sit in a shallow tub of warm water, or on an inflatable pillow. To help prevent infection, rinse the area with warm water and pat dry every time you go to the lavatory.

Forceps

Obstetrical forceps consist of two wide, curved blades designed to fit around a baby's head. There are several different types of forceps, and they are used to assist delivery when, for example, your uterus is not contracting efficiently, or when a baby appears to be suffocating and needs oxygen as soon as possible. Forceps may also be used to protect the baby's head in a breech presentation. When you have had an epidural, forceps are often needed to bring the baby out (an episiotomy is usually needed

The forceps are slipped in to the vagina on either side of the baby's head, to guide it out of the birth channel.

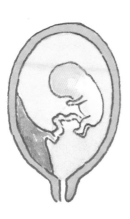
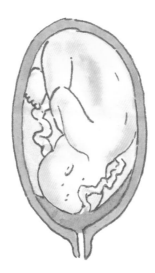

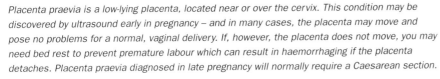

Placenta praevia is a low-lying placenta, located near or over the cervix. This condition may be discovered by ultrasound early in pregnancy – and in many cases, the placenta may move and pose no problems for a normal, vaginal delivery. If, however, the placenta does not move, you may need bed rest to prevent premature labour which can result in haemorrhaging if the placenta detaches. Placenta praevia diagnosed in late pregnancy will normally require a Caesarean section.

If the umbilical cord is found wrapped around the baby's neck, the midwife or doctor will move quickly to free it.

beforehand). The forceps are then inserted into the birth canal, and the baby is gently lifted out. The risks of using forceps range from temporary marks on the baby's cheeks or ears, to damage to the baby's nerves, or to your vagina. However, a forceps delivery is usually less risky than a Caesarean section.

Vacuum extraction

The vacuum extractor, which is also called a ventouse, is often used as an alternative to forceps. It consists of a metal plate or cone-shaped cup, which is placed over the baby's scalp. A pump creates a vacuum that causes the cup or plate to stick to the baby's head, so that it can be drawn out or rotated. Although a ventouse tends to leave a bruise on your baby's head, it is usually less painful than a forceps delivery, and does not necessarily require an episiotomy.

Electronic fetal monitoring

Electronic fetal monitoring (EFM) is used routinely in many hospitals,

particularly if there is any risk to your baby, and its primary purpose is to detect fetal distress. You will have to have EFM if you are being induced, or if your labour is being accelerated. You will also need to have your baby monitored if you have an epidural.

There are two kinds of electronic monitors – external and internal. Early in labour, an external monitor is commonly used, and it can be put on and taken off as required. Wide straps are placed around your stomach. The upper strap records the contractions of your uterus, and the lower strap records your baby's heartbeat. Internal monitors involve having belts strapped round your body, and a tiny electrode being clipped on to your baby's head. Your contractions and the baby's heartbeat are recorded on a paper printout, and there is a video screen which records the contractions and heartbeats. A new type of EFM, known as telemetry, uses radio waves and allows you to walk around as the baby's monitor is attached to a transistor strapped to your thigh. Internal monitors do require your waters to be broken.

If a baby dies

In a very, very small number of cases, a baby dies before, during or very soon after birth, and there can be a variety of reasons, including problems with the placenta, injury to the baby during labour, breathing difficulties, and, in some cases, unknown causes.

Ask someone to take a picture of your baby, and hold him for as long as you need to. It might also help to name your baby, and to bury him in a formal ceremony, which acknowledges the fact that he existed and helps provide a focus for your grieving process. It is important that you grieve for your baby, which will help you to come to terms with his death. It is common and indeed natural to feel angry and isolated, and to blame hospital staff or even each other for the death of a long-awaited baby. It is, however, counterproductive to foster negative feelings. Try to accept that everyone did their very best – including you and your partner – and focus on healing and getting well again. Try to get some support from a group of parents who have been through a similar trauma, and don't be embarrassed about talking to friends and family, or even a counsellor, and sharing your feelings and your grief.

Caesarean section

Caesarean section is a surgical procedure that enables the safe, quick delivery of a baby. Many Caesarean sections are performed under a general anaesthetic – particularly in an emergency – but spinal, or epidural anaesthetics are increasingly being used, so that you can stay awake during the birth, and will suffer fewer side-effects.

In Caesarean section, an incision is made in your lower abdomen, just above the pubic hair, and into the uterus, through which the baby is removed. Within a few minutes, your baby will be delivered, and the umbilical cord clamped and cut. While the placenta is being delivered and the incisions being stitched, you will be able to hold your baby. The stitches in your uterus will be made with an absorbable fabric, which will dissolve naturally. Your external stitches will be removed about a week after the operation. Recovery from the surgery takes longer than it would from a vaginal birth, and the procedure has the risks of a major operation. You are usually able to go home in three or four days.

The number of babies born by Caesarean section has been increasing in recent years and in some parts of the country accounts for as many as a quarter of all deliveries. The reasons for this trend include an increase in the number of women having their first child late in life, when the risks of

pregnancy and birth are greater to both woman and foetus.

Babies who are born by Caesarean will not have the same 'squashed' features as a baby born naturally, and they may appear to be calmer and less traumatized. They will, however, need more time to adjust to the outside world because of their sudden entry into it. Vaginal delivery also helps to clear amniotic fluid from your baby's lungs, and stimulate circulation, so a Caesarean baby may need more attention when she is born and perhaps some assistance to breathe.

You may feel disappointed if you have an unplanned Caesarean, and it is natural to feel this way. It will help to

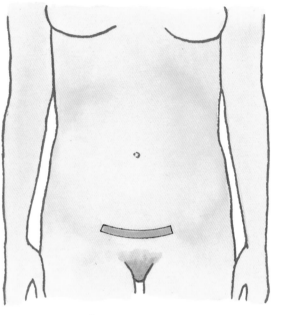

talk your feelings through with your partner and your hospital team, who will be able to explain why it was necessary and the steps leading up to it. Try not to feel as though you have failed. The whole point of pregnancy and birth is to

Emergency Caesarean

A Caesarean may be scheduled before labour for some of the following reasons:

● Maternal diabetes, when pre-term delivery is considered necessary and your cervix is not 'ripe' enough to induce labour.

● Herpes or other STDs, which can be passed to your baby in the birth canal.

● Placenta praevia (see page 111), when labour may cause the placenta to detach prematurely.

● Abruptio placenta, when there is an excessive separation of the placenta from the uterine wall and your baby may be in danger.

● Pre-eclampsia, which doesn't respond to treatment.

● Fetal or maternal distress, which makes labour more dangerous.

● Failure of labour to progress.

● An unusual presentation – perhaps breech or transverse (see page 102), which would make vaginal delivery difficult.

● Pelvic disproportion, when the baby's head is too large to pass through your pelvis.

● Suspected or diagnosed fetal illness.

● High blood pressure in the mother (hypertension) or kidney disease, which may mean that labour will be too dangerous or traumatic.

● Twins that have become locked together so that neither can be delivered.

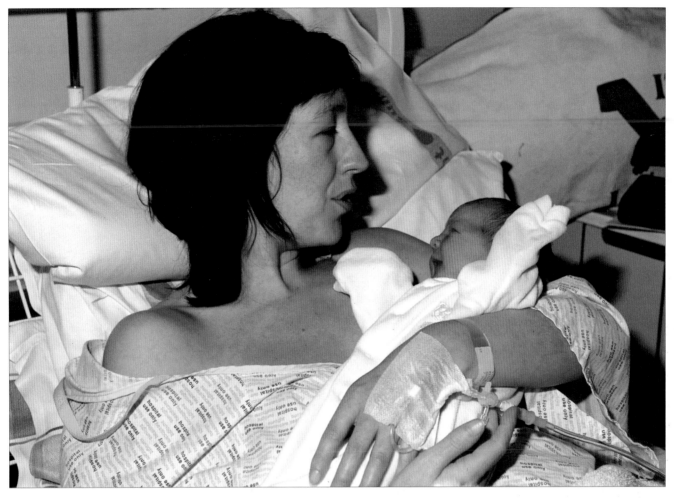

You will be able to hold your new baby as soon as she is born, if you have had your operation under epidural anaesthesia. If you have had emergency surgery, under general anaesthetic, you will be able to hold her as soon as you are feeling well enough to do so. Ask for her cot to be placed by your bed, so that you can touch her as you lie back.

have a healthy baby at the end of it all, and if you have achieved that, by whatever means necessary, you have been successful.

It is useful to know that most women who have delivered a baby by Caesarean section can have a successful vaginal delivery at the end of a subsequent pregnancy. The incision is so low that womb muscles generally don't weaken significantly, so it will not cause any problems with subsequent pregnancies. If you have previously delivered a baby by Caesarean section and are considering having a vaginal delivery in this pregnancy, talk to your physician.

Recovering from a Caesarean

Apart from vaginal problems, you can expect to experience all of the same post-natal discomforts, including after pains, fatigue and hormonal changes; you will also, however, have an incision to consider, and you may suffer from some side- or after-effects of the anaesthesia.

Although Caesareans are performed routinely, and are safer now than ever before, it is important to remember that you have undergone major surgery, and your body will have been traumatized and need time to recover.

Pain around the incision is common, and you will probably be given pain relief as required, which may also help you to get some sleep. Try to get up between 8 and 24 hours after the operation, and

stand for a few moments. It is important to take a few steps, and to sit upright as early as possible, to improve the healing process and help you to stay mobile. It is natural to feel dizzy and sick, and you should sit down as soon as you experience any of these symptoms.

It is also normal to feel frightened of moving, and to hunch your shoulders when sitting and walking. Use your breathing exercises to help with the discomfort and any fears, and try to relax and enjoy the support of the nursing staff.

You won't be able to lift your baby for a few days, but you will still be able to hug and feed him, placing him on a pillow over the incision.

Your new baby: what to expect

The first moments after the birth may be among the most rewarding of your life, and you have every right to feel proud of your achievement. You may experience a combination of exhilaration and exhaustion, and you may also feel emotionally drained by it all. Not all first-time parents feel a rush of love for their new baby – emotional bonds may take some time to develop, and that is entirely natural. You might find that you are disconcerted by your baby's appearance (see below), or disappointed if you longed for a baby of the opposite sex.

Babies are usually covered by vernix, which can make them look greasy and waxy. The vernix may also be streaked with blood, which can be quite alarming if you aren't expecting it. Your baby may begin crying immediately after the birth and unless there are problems with her breathing, there is no reason why she can't be handed to you immediately. She will be calmed by your voice, and by the comfort of your arms, and if you plan to

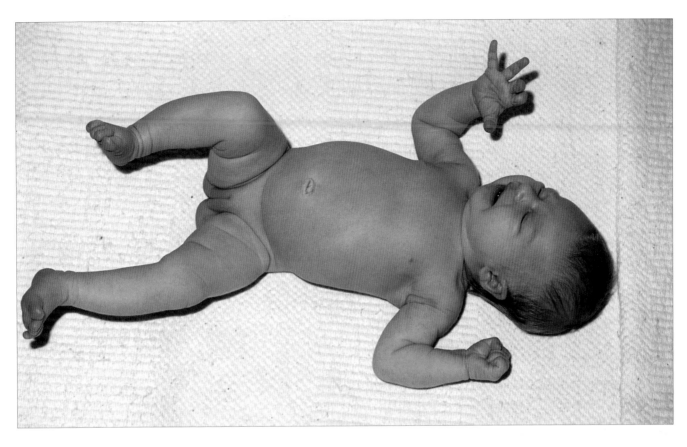

breastfeed, it is a good idea to put her to your breast, which stimulates uterine contractions that can help with the delivery of the placenta. The cord will have been clamped and cut as soon as it stops pulsating (unless it was cut earlier in the labour – if it was wrapped around your baby's neck, for example). One minute after the delivery, and again, 5 minutes later, the midwife will do a simple check of your baby's condition, which is recorded as an Apgar score, with points given out of 10. Zero, 1 or 2 points are given for each of the following signs:

Heart rate

If this is over 100, 2 points are given. Under 100 is considered to be slow, and only 1 point is given.

Respiration. A baby who makes a lot of noise would show mature lungs, and would get a score of 2. Irregular breathing gets 1 point.

Muscle tone

The baby's movements are watched, and if she is active, she'll score 2. Some movement scores 1, and limpness scores 0.

Reflex irritability

Crying and grimacing can indicate that your baby is responding to stimuli. Crying is a good response, and scores 2, whimpering scores 1, and silence 0.

Colour

Babies are normally blue or purplish at birth, but their colour changes rapidly as they begin to breathe for themselves. Caucasian babies should turn a pinkish colour, and black babies can look quite pale.

If the lungs are working well to oxygenate the blood, the skin will turn the correct colour and your baby will score 2. If there are bluish extremities, she will score 1. Blue skin scores 0.

Most babies score between 7 and 10, and a second test will be done about 5 minutes later. A very low score (0 to 4) may mean that emergency care is needed.

When you have had a chance to wash and put on clean clothes, you will be given some time alone with your baby. Ask for it if you don't get it.

Hold your baby next to your heart, which will comfort her, and spend some time getting to know her. If you hold her about 8 inches (20 centimetres) from your face, she will be able to see you clearly, and will soon begin to recognize you, and your voice. Babies will respond best to high vocal pitches, so try to talk to her in a lively voice. Make sure your

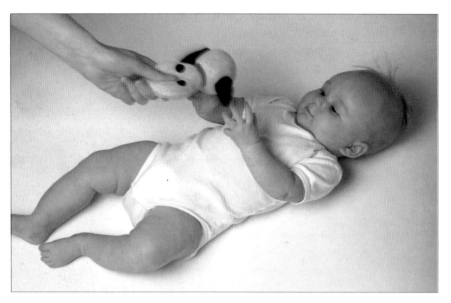

Your new baby will have a 'grasping' reflex, which means that she will automatically grab hold of a finger put into her hand, and can grasp it strongly. Her feet will also curl in a kind of grip.

partner has an opportunity to hold your baby as soon as possible, because it is important that he bonds with her from the earliest moments.

Shortly after the birth, your baby will be examined by a doctor or a midwife for specific things:

● The anus is checked to make sure the opening is clear, and the genitals are checked to verify the sex of the baby.

● The feet are examined for club foot; the hips are examined for congenital (present from birth) dislocation of the hip.

● The mouth is examined for cleft lip and cleft palate, and the face is examined for features that suggest Down's Syndrome.

● The spine is examined for any swelling or ulcer that may indicate spina bifida, and the navel is examined for any swelling resulting from umbilical hernia.

If there are problems, your doctor will advise you on the best and quickest course of treatment. Don't worry if your baby has to be taken away to the special care baby unit – this is a standard procedure in many hospitals, and doesn't necessarily indicate a problem with your baby's condition. You will have a chance to bond with your baby soon after.

The sucking reflex is incredibly strong in a new baby, and they are born knowing how to suck and how to 'root' for the nipple. When they feel skin (or anything else!) against their cheek, they will turn towards the touch with an open mouth.

Your baby will be weighed, her body length with be measured, as will the circumference of her head. Your baby will then be given a plastic identification bracelet, which must remain on her wrist or ankle (or both) for the remainder of the time that she is in the hospital. In some hospitals, your baby's footprint will be taken, and her cot may be marked with her name and an identification number.

The grasp reflex

Your baby will grasp anything placed in her palm, and is able to hold on so tightly that her body can be supported if she grabs your fingers with both hands. The soles of her feet will also curl over if you touch them.

Moro reflex

If she is startled, your baby will extend her arms and legs as if she is reaching out to catch hold of something.

Your baby's appearance

After the birth, it is not unusual for your baby to look quite blue, until her own circulation is able to move oxygenated blood around the body. The head may also look elongated, due to the moulding process as it passes through the birth canal. Her face may also look a

Circumcision

Most doctors in the UK advise against circumcision, as it is an unnecessary surgical procedure. If you feel strongly that you want it performed for religious or other reasons, you will probably have to pay for the operation, which is done in just a few minutes, or you may be able to arrange for a rabbi to undertake the circumcision. One advantage of circumcision is that it seems to discourage urinary tract infections. Although complications are rare, only healthy infants should be circumcised shortly after birth, to avoid possible problems with blood clotting

Why your baby cries

Crying is the way your baby signals to you that she needs something, and you will soon be able to distinguish between the different cries and respond to them. Her first cries may be anything from lusty and agitated to a soft whimpering or even spluttering. Her features will probably tighten up when she cries, and her body will tense. She may even change colour to an alarming dark red, but this is normal. Your baby will cry:

● When she is hungry. She will not stop until she has been fed, either by breastfeeding or bottle-feeding.

● When she is lonely. Your baby has been accustomed to the comfort of the womb, where she has been tightly contained (held) for the last months. In the womb she has been used to the sounds of your digestion and heartbeat (loud to her), and it can be frightening for her to find herself alone and unheld, in a quiet environment. She will love to be held, and will thrive on physical contact.

● When she is tired. She will need some help settling down to sleep. When you were pregnant, she was rocked constantly as you walked or went about your daily jobs. She will be accustomed to being rocked or lulled off to sleep by movement, and in the beginning she may find it difficult to fall asleep without some comfort.

● When she is uncomfortable. Many babies will cry when they have wet nappies or tight clothing – anything that makes them feel not quite right. It may take some time for you to remember to check her nappy regularly, and to discover what type of clothing makes her the most comfortable.

bit swollen, or seem bruised, which is quite normal. You will probably be unaware of your baby's rather messy appearance in the excitement of seeing her for the first time. Over the following days, any bruising will disappear.

Babies vary considerably in size and appearance, all of which fall within the boundaries of what is considered to be normal. Babies' heads are larger in

proportion to their bodies than are older children's and adults', and although her brain is well developed, it will grow until it reaches adult proportions at around the end of her second year.

● In newborn babies, the bones of the skull are not completely fused, so that it can be compressed to adapt to the shape of the birth canal when she is born. This also allows the skull to expand as the brain continues to grow over the next few years. The bones at the top of the skull are attached by a piece of tough membrane, and this area is called the fontanelle. You may notice it pulsating, and be alarmed by the fragility of the head, but it is tough enough to protect your baby, and it can be touched and handled normally.

● Your baby's skin may be blotchy and wrinkled, and there may be a few spots or a rash, which normally disappears within a few days. Some babies have pink areas on their foreheads, eyelids or around the back of their neck. These marks are called stork bites, and they fade over the months to follow. Your baby may also have a red 'strawberry' birthmark, which also fades with time. Port wine stains are darker, and may be slightly raised, and they normally require some treatment. Darker-skinned

babies may have Mongolian patches, which are patches of pigmentation which look blueish in colour.

● The breast and the genitals may look large and even swollen because of the increased hormones they have been in contact with during the pregnancy. Soon after the birth, they will take on their normal shape and size.

● The umbilical cord has been cut, but a small stump will remain clamped with a plastic clip. The clip will be removed after a few days, and you will be shown

Babies' knees bend outwards like frogs'. Your doctor may test for congenital dislocation of the hip, which is more common in girls and babies born by breech presentation.

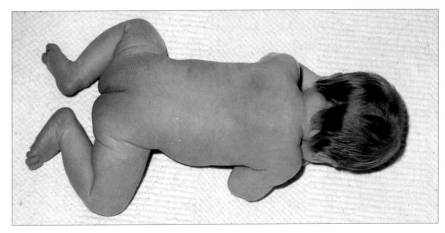

Many babies enjoy the security of being 'swaddled', or wrapped tightly in a soft blanket or towel. Place the blanket flat on a bed or table, with a corner above your baby's head.

Draw the bottom corner up over your baby's legs and abdomen, so that his legs are extended but comfortably wrapped.

Pull the left corner of the blanket up and over your baby's body, and tuck it snugly under his other side, rolling him over slightly to do so.

Draw the final portion of blanket up and over the cocoon you have created, and tuck the top edge into the front of the blanket, just below his chin. He will be snug within the blanket, without it being too restrictive. You can bring down the top corner of the blanket over his head, to keep him warm and free from draughts.

how to clean around the cord until it dries and falls off, at about a week.

Senses

Your baby can see, hear, smell and taste, and she will respond best to touch. She will like to be cuddled, held and rocked, and these are important means by which you can comfort her, and communicate with her. Be gentle and loving, and she will feel relaxed and secure in your arms. She will need to be kept warm from the first moments after birth, so try to find some soft, comfortable clothing. She will feel more secure if you hold her as often as you can, near to your breast. She may cry, or become frustrated if she can't feed immediately. She may also be

hungry, and will express any needs by crying.

● Her sense of smell and taste are well developed, and she will recognize your smell and that of your partner soon after the delivery.

● She will be aware of your voice, and will remember it from the time she was in the womb. She will like soothing, sing-song talking, and songs and rhymes. She will also respond to songs or rhythms that she heard while you were pregnant.

● She can see you, if you hold her about 8 inches (20 centimetres) away, and she will soon be able to focus on things at this range. She may appear to have a squint, but this normally settles down by about three months.

Reflexes

Your baby will likely spend most of the first few days sleeping, or just looking around and feeding.

She may breathe irregularly, and may have bouts of hiccups or shivering, all of which is normal. You may recognize an established pattern of sleeping of waking, which is often the same as it was when you were pregnant. Babies have a number of inborn or instinctive responses to stimuli, some of which will remain while others are lost.

Walking reflex

If you hold your baby upright, she will move her feet and legs as if she were walking. This reflex disappears after a few days.

Sucking reflex

After she is born, your baby will suck

Your hospital stay

If you stay in the hospital for the first day or so, you will receive some expert advice about all your baby's requirements, and it can be reassuring to have some help in those early days. If you have had your baby at home, you may want to arrange for a family member or friend to come round and give you a hand. Someone who has had a baby – maybe your mother, or your partner's mother – may be useful, because they will know what to expect.

After the birth, your temperature will be taken, and your pulse rate and blood pressure recorded. They will be checked every 4 hours while you are in hospital, and during the post-natal care offered to you either at home or in the hospital. You may be given ice packs or prescribed painkillers for any pain, and stitches or tears will be checked regularly to ensure that they are healing properly.

If you have had a Caesarean under general anaesthetic, you will probably feel a bit nauseous and dizzy. The incision of any Caesarean will be painful, and you will probably stay on an intravenous drip for some time. It is normal to stay in hospital for about a week to ten days after a Caesarean, so your condition can be monitored by hospital staff.

If your baby is healthy, you can normally have her with you all the time – whether you have had a Caesarean or not – which gives you the opportunity to get to know her and her needs. Many hospitals will take your baby away for

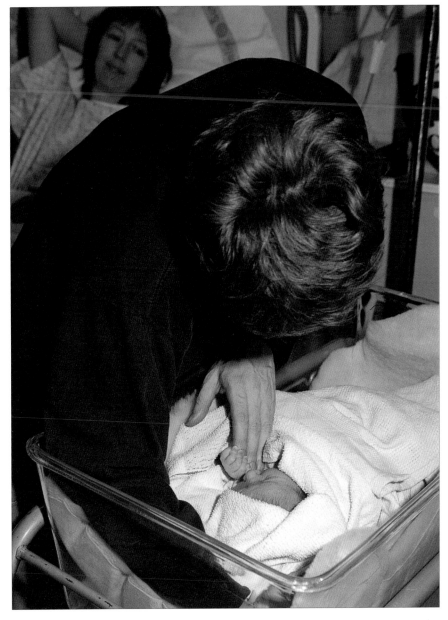

Your baby will be given a cot for the duration of your stay in hospital, and most are set on wheels, so that your baby can be easily transported without you having to lift her. Most hospitals will allow you to keep your baby with you at night, but are happy to take a turn watching her, and ensuring she is content, if you would like a break to catch up on sleep, or recover from the trauma of the birth.

in response to pressure on the palate, just beyond the upper gums.

Rooting reflex

If you stroke your baby's cheek, she will turn her face in that direction and be ready to suck. Even in the womb your baby will have responded to pressure around her face or mouth by sucking –

indeed, many babies suck their hands, fingers or thumbs in the womb and this can sometimes be seen in their scans.

Swallowing

Your baby has practised swallowing in the womb, and she will be able to swallow with ease.

periods, if you wish, so that you can rest or get some sleep. You will be offered advice on feeding, which can be helpful, particularly if this is your first baby.

Some women find the routine of the hospital too stifling – and it can be noisy, particularly if you are on a ward with other mothers and babies. If you find it difficult to sleep, try to take cat naps during the day when your baby is sleeping, and ask the nurses on the ward not to wake you unless it is absolutely necessary. In many hospitals, you will be woken for meals, but it is usually possible for you to keep a supply of non-perishable food yourself, or to have your partner bring you some light meals, so that you can eat when you feel hungry.

If you find it depressing to be in the hospital, ask if you can leave a little sooner than you had planned. You may feel more comfortable to be in your own environment, and if you have set up a support network of family and friends to help you out, the early days of motherhood can be more relaxed and rewarding in your own home.

Leaving the hospital

Before you leave the hospital, a doctor will examine you, by checking to see that your uterus is returning to its normal size, and that your stitches (if you have any) are healing.

Your breasts will be checked, and discharge and bleeding will be examined to ensure that there aren't any clots or persistent bleeding that

could indicate that some of the placenta has been retained.

You will be asked about contraception (which is likely to be the furthest thing from your mind at the moment), and given advice about what birth control methods may be most suitable for you. You may feel sore or uncomfortable after the labour, and find the prospect of intercourse unfathomable, but it is worth remembering that a significant proportion of new mothers are actually pregnant again by ten weeks, having wrongly assumed that they are protected by breastfeeding or because they haven't yet had a period.

If you have had a Caesarean, your incision will be checked and your stitches will be removed before you leave the hospital.

If your blood tests show that you did not have an immunity to rubella during your pregnancy, you will now be immunized against the condition.

You will be shown how to clean your baby's umbilical stump, and you may be given some spirit to do so. Your midwife or doctor will explain the importance of keeping it clean, and will tell you what to do if it appears to become infected.

You will be given a date for your first main post-natal check up, which usually takes place about six weeks after the birth, when you and your baby will both be examined.

It is perfectly natural to feel uncomfortable after the birth, and there are a variety of post-natal ailments which

Raspberry leaf tea can be helpful to tone the muscles of the womb after childbirth.

plague even the healthiest women. These are discussed on pages 126–7.

Looking after yourself

You will need plenty of fresh, nutritious food, and lots to drink (particularly if you are breastfeeding) in the weeks after the birth, so it is a good idea to stock up the refrigerator before your baby is born, and have someone available to purchase necessities as they are required. Eat when you are hungry, and if you concentrate on healthy foods, such as wholemeal sandwiches with plenty of fresh vegetables and perhaps some protein – maybe cheese or meat – a big dish of pasta, some nutritious, warming soup, or some chicken with vegetables, you will find it easier to cope with the strains of new motherhood. The stress of it all can be very draining, and you will find you reach the end of your tether sooner if you haven't eaten properly. Eat plenty of small snacks between meals if you are hungry, and

Your diet in the early days after the birth, and throughout breastfeeding, is as important as it was during pregnancy. Ensure that you eat three, well-balanced meals each day, and choose healthy snacks if you are hungry between meals.

Registration of the birth

You will need to register the birth within six weeks of the birthdate, except in Scotland where the birth must be registered within three weeks. This is done at your local registry office, details of which are available at the hospital or from your midwife. The registrar will give you a birth certificate and a form with your baby's National Health Service number on it. You'll need this form to register your baby with your family doctor.

don't worry about losing weight. That will come eventually.

Try to set up a routine for yourself around your baby's needs, sleeping when he sleeps, and eating when he is happy looking around for a few moments. New motherhood seems sometimes to be an endless series of unfinished meals, cold cups of tea, and half-finished household tasks. Always keep in mind how important it is to take care of yourself, so that you can cope with the demands on your body and your time.

Keeping active

Unless you have had a Caesarean, or a very difficult birth, you can begin to move around by about 6 hours after the birth. You may feel very weak and shaky, and it may be painful to sit, or to walk normally, but try to walk a little, even if it is just to take a shower, or make yourself a cup of tea. By moving around you will regain your strength more quickly, and it will help your bowels and bladder recover. The increased circulation caused by movement will also help you to feel more alert.

Try not to worry about exercising or getting your figure back in the early days of motherhood (many women are surprised by the fact that their shape is quite different from pre-pregnancy days, and how no longer having a baby inside

Talk to your baby, and make eye contact, from the very first days. She will be fascinated by your face, and your voice – which she will recognize – and will be comforted by being in your arms.

them seems to have made little difference to their bellies). Movement is good in moderation, but if you feel unwell, faint, or too tired, or if you bleed profusely after movement, you

may have overdone it. It is best to lose the extra weight gradually over the next weeks and months and this may well happen naturally without dieting, especially if you are breastfeeding.

Parentcare: how to cope during the first few days

The joy of having a new baby, and the exhilaration of having made it through the labour, may be quickly tempered by profound exhaustion. There is nothing to match the exhaustion of new motherhood, as you will soon discover, but it does help if you can establish a routine and be prepared for caring for your baby in those early days.

Your partner will likely be anxious to be involved, and although you may feel as though you don't want your baby to leave your side, it is important to ensure that he feels included and loved. Try not to focus all your attention on your baby (which may be difficult) and try to find ways for your partner to share the care. If you have older children, they too will need to be included, and given lots of extra love and attention.

Share the work of looking after your baby, if you can, particularly in the first weeks, when you will be feeling tired and perhaps a little let down. Don't worry about housework – things will all get done in due course, and forget about trying to maintain your pre-baby standards in the early days. You may be inundated with visitors, who are keen to see the new arrival, and while it may be a

pleasure to show off your baby, you may be feeling too tired to deal with a constant stream of well-wishers. Make sure you take some time for yourself, and rest, relax and sleep whenever you can. Of course you will need to consider your baby's needs first and foremost – just make sure your own needs aren't last.

You may feel terrific after the birth, and experience a state of bliss that seems like it will go on forever, or you may find yourself growing low and over-emotional. This is not unusual. You will probably discover that looking after a baby is harder than you ever imagined, especially if she baby doesn't feed well, cries a lot, or sleeps little. Extreme tiredness, combined with stress, can play havoc when you have just been through the trauma of birth and your hormones have not yet settled down. If you feel low, find someone to talk to, and, if necessary, a shoulder to cry on. Having a new baby can be very isolating,

The walking reflex disappears a few days after birth.

particularly if your partner has gone back to work, the day passes and you feel as if you have achieved nothing, so it is a good idea to have some company round, or perhaps visit the baby clinic in your area, where you will meet other mothers and get a chance to pick up some good practical advice.

The new father

You partner will have his own worries, quite apart from the shared responsibility of a new baby, and it is important to acknowledge them, and keep the channels of communication open during the first weeks after the birth. With the amount of attention focused on you, your achievement, and the new baby, he may feel left out, especially if you are breastfeeding. It helps if he has been involved in your pregnancy from the beginning, attended some of the antenatal appointments and been your close confidante throughout. If he has now been through the birth with you, you can discuss it together. It is common to feel moody and distant with your partner at this time, when your baby takes up your time and energy, and even fulfils much of your need for warmth and affection. If he understands how you are feeling, he will be better able to cope.

He may also be wondering about when you can have sex

again – which may be the last thing you could countenance at this point. Explain to him how you feel (if you are in pain, too tired or whatever else might be killing the urge) but try at least to set aside some time for yourselves alone, perhaps when the baby is sleeping, to hold one another and perhaps just cuddle. Sex will come in good time, when you feel physically and emotionally ready.

It is not unusual for men to be traumatized by the birth as well, and to feel concerned about your health and that of your baby. Let him help with the baby, and give him an opportunity to bond, which will ease his worry as he gets to know the new arrival and becomes accustomed to her routines and needs. His growing competence will enable you to feel more confident in letting him look after her for a while, and give you a break. Let him help you around the house, take some of the pressure off you, and perhaps prepare some meals. Allow him to feel that he can do something positive on the road to your recovery.

It is also normal for both of you to feel anxious about the way your life has changed, so set aside time to talk through the problems that are worrying you, and discuss everything from the division of childcare, the financial implications of a new baby, and the changes that you can now see it will make to your lifestyle and your relationship. If you both know what to expect, and find a happy medium, life together will be much easier.

Caring for your baby

The first week after your birth will be challenging in many ways, particularly if you are a first-time mother. Many women seem to know what to do instinctively, but even the most natural of mothers may find the sheer dependence of a new baby daunting. Even if you don't have any particular worries you will probably feel under pressure to begin with.

Very few babies are predictable in their feeding and sleeping habits, and they are often unsettled for the first few days and nights. Such behaviour is normal, and your baby might seem to be unhappy for no obvious reason. Unless you believe your baby is ill, try not to worry. Spend the first week or so getting to know her – don't fret about what is going on around you, for you need this time to bond and to establish a relationship, even if it does seem to get off to a rocky start.

Friends, family and health practitioners will all have differing (and usually contradictory) views on how you should cope. The best course of action is probably a combination of everyone's tips and guidance – sift through the ideas and practices that sound dated, but always do what seems right for you. You will know your body and your baby best, and you must decide how you want to cope with things on your own terms. Use your common sense and your

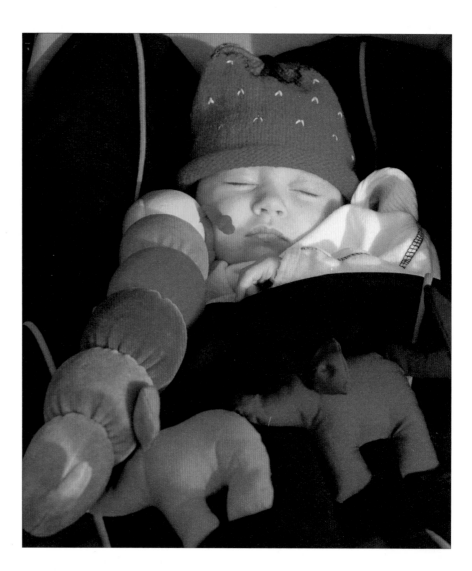

instinct, and you will soon find that you are able to cope.

How to hold your baby

Hold your baby in any way that feels comfortable to you, remembering to support his head over which he will have little control for the first month or so. Many babies respond to being swaddled (wrapped snugly in a blanket, which makes them feel secure), and this also makes them easier to hold. Babies have

an instinctive fear of being dropped, and they are only relaxed and happy when their bodies are supported. Try to keep a firm but gentle grip on him, and don't lift him until he feels comfortable in your hands. It may take some time before you can pick up your baby easily, and hold him without any concern. Think of him as a rag doll, and remember that they need support at both ends, and shouldn't be picked up in the middle or they will flop!

When you pick your baby up

1 Slide one hand underneath your baby's neck and head, and support his back and bottom with your other arm.

2 Continuing to support his head and back, lift the baby very carefully and gently.

Always hold your baby close to your body, as it will help him to feel secure. If you hold him upright, it is easier for him to expel any air. Many women like to place a muslin square or a blanket over their shoulders, to catch the inevitable drips and sick.

Keeping your baby clean

Although you will probably be taught how to bath your baby at the hospital, he is unlikely to need a full bath until he is several weeks old. He will need to be kept clean, certainly, but the best way to deal with that in the early days is to top and tail him – that is, wash the bottom end and the top end, and any of the bits in between that you think might need attention.

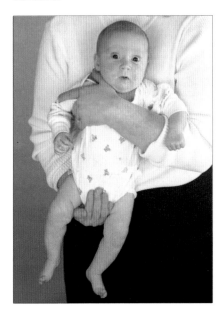

Prepare the things you'll need in advance, which will include a nappy, some cotton balls, a basin of warm,

Place your baby on a towel on the bed or on a changing mat. Wipe each eye with a separate damp cotton ball, moving from the inner corner to the outer corner. Use another cotton ball to wipe around his ears and neck. Use a further cotton ball to clean around his mouth and nose.

Using a clean wet washcloth, wash his hands . . .

. . . and feet, checking for any sharp fingernails which may need to be trimmed. If you do find that your baby's nails are long, and need cutting, use a small pair of specially designed nailclippers or blunt scissors to cut them. Some mothers find it easier to gently bite them off themselves.

Remove his nappy, and wash him with a damp washcloth. If he has soiled his nappy, you may wish to use a nappy wipe first, to remove the faeces.

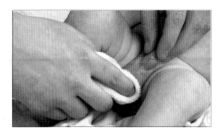

Dry him carefully, and apply any creams you may wish to use.

previously boiled water, perhaps a washcloth and a soft towel, and any creams or powders you wish to use.

Aftercare

You can expect to be visited by a midwife every day for the first week or so after your baby is born, which gives you a good opportunity to ask for practical advice on everything from common worries to feeding difficulties. Don't hesitate to ask her about any unusual symptoms you may be experiencing. If you had a home birth, or left the hospital early, your doctor may visit you at your home to check you and the baby. Some time after the birth, often in your own home, on about the sixth day after the birth, your baby will need to give a small sample of blood, usually taken by pricking the heel. This is tested for a condition called phenylketonuria, and a number of other rare disorders. It will also establish your baby's blood type, which is useful to know.

Your baby's bowel movements

In the first few days, your baby will excrete meconium, which is a blackish-green substance comprised of waste that has collected in the bowels during the time in the womb. After this meconium (which can be very difficult to clean away) has cleared, the stools change. A breastfed baby will have runny, yellow or orange coloured stools. Those of a bottle-fed baby will be darker and more solid, and may have a distinct odour.

Common problems

Almost all women suffer from problems of some kind following the trauma of childbirth, whether physical or emotional, and the first weeks can be difficult to cope with if you are feeling under the weather.

Pain in the perineal area

Even if you were lucky enough to escape an episiotomy or tearing, your perineum is bound to be sore and bruised after having a baby squeezed through it.

What you can do
● Change your sanitary pad often, to ensure that the area stays dry.

● Infuse some calendula (marigold) flowers in some boiling water, cool and strain, and apply to the area to encourage healing and help ease the pain.

● Dilute a drop or two of lavender essential oil in a little apricot kernel oil and rub gently into the affected area to relieve pain. Rubbing olive oil into the area will also soothe and help to heal.

● A cold compress with a little witch hazel will help to reduce swelling and disperse any bruising.

● Take the homeopathic remedy Arnica after childbirth, whatever your symptoms. It is a great natural healer, and helps to prevent and treat bruising. You can take it three or four times daily, at 6x dilution for as long as required.

Painful stitches

If you have had an episiotomy or torn badly enough to require stitches, you may experience pain and discomfort, particularly as the stitches dry and tighten. You may also find the area itchy, or worry about it becoming infected.

What you can do
● Use a bidet or sit in a sitz bath. Add a drop of lavender oil to the water to encourage healing and reduce the pain. Lavender acts as a natural local analgesic, and it also works to prevent infection.

● Pour warm water over the affected area after urinating or defecating, and pat it dry with gauze pads.

● Soak a piece of cotton or a clean cloth in witch hazel and apply to the affected area to encourage healing and reduce the symptoms.

● Lie on your side, and avoid long periods of standing or sitting, which can strain the area. Sit on a pillow or a rubber ring to take the pressure off the area.

● Try to continue doing your Kegel exercises (see page 27) as often as possible after the delivery to stimulate circulation to the area, which will promote healing and improve muscle tone.

Painful bowel movements

The entire lower part of your body may be painful, and you may be afraid to have a bowel movement for the first time after the birth. Try to get over the psychological hurdle of having the first movement – the longer you wait, the more likely it is to cause you discomfort and the harder it will be to bring yourself to do it. You may not need to have a bowel movement straightaway, if the contents of your bowels were evacuated during labour, and the birth may well have caused some bruising or trauma to the bowel, which will slow down digestion.

What you can do
● Try not to worry about it, and brave yourself to make a private visit to the lavatory when you feel the urge.

● Try to be as active as possible, within safe guidelines – this will stimulate activity in the bowels

● Eat plenty of fibre-rich foods, such as fruit, wholegrains, vegetables and, if you find you are constipated, some bran cereal or a handful of prunes to get things going.

● Drink lots of water or juice, to help soften the stool – you will need plenty of extra fluid if you are breastfeeding.

● Try not to strain, which can be painful, and lead to haemorrhoids.

Exhaustion

You are likely to feel very tired after the birth, and this will be compounded if your baby sleeps irregularly or is difficult to settle. You may have lost a night's sleep while in labour and the loss of blood during and after the birth can also make you tired. Breastfeeding has the same result, as your body expends more calories.

Make sure there is plenty of fibre in your diet to avoid constipation and keep bowel movements soft.

What you can do

● Try to sleep or rest as often as possible, and don't feel guilty if you need to take naps during the day. Sleep whenever you can, and certainly when you feel tired.

● Make sure you are eating well – exhaustion is exacerbated by a poor or inadequate diet, and your energy reserves will flag if you are not taking in enough calories. Take a good multi-vitamin and mineral tablet if you don't think you are getting enough of the correct nutrients in your diet: the B-vitamins, chromium and iron are essential following labour.

● Try to get some help with the housework and even some of the baby care to give you a little time to yourself.

● There are three main homeopathic remedies which may be useful: China for exhaustion following loss of blood; Carbo veg for exhaustion with sweating; and Sepia for exhaustion with bearing-down pains.

● Drink a cup of nettle tea – an excellent tonic for exhaustion, and rich in iron (which you may require after the birth).

Pain after a Caesarean

A Caesarean section can be enormously painful, and it is important not to underestimate the effect it may have on your body – it is, after all, a major operation. There are many natural treatments available to help with the discomfort.

What you can do

● Apply compresses to the wound to promote healing, soothe inflammation and prevent an infection from developing (although it is a good idea to wait until the stitches have settled a bit before beginning). You can apply an infusion of comfrey or St John's wort, using clean lint when the infusion has cooled to blood temperature. Alternatively a compress can be made using a few drops of essential oils of lavender, tea tree and myrrh added to warm water. Once the wound has closed over, then comfrey ointment can be massaged in daily to reduce scarring.

● You can drink raspberry leaf tea, to promote healing and to help tone your uterus.

● The homeopathic remedy Arnica will help to prevent infection and promote healing, and it should be taken at 30C dilution for about five days. The remedy Bellis Perennis is also useful after a Caesarean to relieve discomfort and promote tissue healing. Try taking 30C each day for five days following the Arnica.

● If you are feeling nauseous, try drinking a little ginger ale or ginger beer, which will help to settle your stomach. Eat small meals, and avoid anything that is greasy or too spicy.

Afterpains

Following the labour, your uterus will begin to shrink back to its original size, through a series of contractions. You may experience mild cramping, or, particularly if it is a second or later child, extreme pain, especially when breastfeeding, which stimulates the action of the uterus. Afterpains normally subside between four and seven days after the birth.

What you can do

● Use your breathing exercises when you experience pain, especially while breastfeeding.

● There are three main homeopathic remedies suggested for afterpains, including Coffea, when you have sharp pains and feel exhausted; Nux, when your afterpains are associated with a need to pass water; and Pulsatilla, if there is reason to suspect that part of the placenta has been retained.

● The herb cramp bark is used therapeutically for uterine infections, pain and cramping. Drink an infusion twice daily, prepared according to the manufacturer's instructions.

● Chamomile essential oil can be massaged into the abdomen to relieve cramping. Use a few drops in a carrier oil like grapeseed or apricot kernel. You can also add chamomile oil to baths.

Part Two:
Your new baby

The newborn baby

The first weeks of life with a new baby can be both taxing and rewarding, and you will probably swing between feelings of utter bliss and fulfilment, and sheer exhaustion, even panic. Babies are demanding, so do not expect too much of yourself. If you manage to have a bath, put together a basic meal or two, and keep your baby fed and happy, you have achieved a great deal in the early days.

Over the coming weeks, life will begin to take on a pattern, and you will find yourself capable of more and more as the days pass. You will soon be able to establish a basic routine for your baby, which will help her to feel secure and make your life easier to plan. As the months pass, your tiny dependent baby will change rapidly as she grows stronger and more aware, and the excitement and exhausting chaos of the early weeks settle down.

Confidence will soon come, and you will not have to think carefully every time you change a nappy or prepare to take her out; caring for your baby becomes easier and your pleasure will increase. When your baby first smiles, at around four to six weeks, all will be forgiven, and the overwhelming affection she gives you, and the pleasure she gets from your company, are incredibly rewarding.

However, in the beginning, your sheer exhaustion can seem insurmountable, and if you ever have the feeling that the problems of new parenthood are outweighing the joys, never keep them to yourself or try to struggle on. Share your feelings with your health visitor, partner, your parents, a sympathetic friend, or your doctor if you feel you need to, and take care to look out for the signs of depression, which can be a part of post-natal illness (see pages 148-9).

Your baby will be born with her own character traits, likes and dislikes, and if your personalities are well suited and you find that handling her comes naturally, the early days will be easier. Don't be surprised, however, to find that you and your baby have to make adjustments to each other – you may have yearned to cuddle your baby and find that she simply doesn't like physical constriction; or you may be a happy-go-lucky person with a positive outlook and find that you have a baby who is miserable for no obvious reason. Eventually your baby's behaviour will affect your handling, and you may be able to encourage her to respond to things in the same way that you do. You must also be open to the idea that your baby may change, and that a jumpy newborn isn't necessarily a highly strung child, or that a wakeful baby will never settle down to a routine. Try to spend time getting to know her personal needs, and as you grow closer and develop an understanding of each other, and the way you react to one another, you will both be happier and be able to establish a mutual and loving relationship that grows and changes as she does.

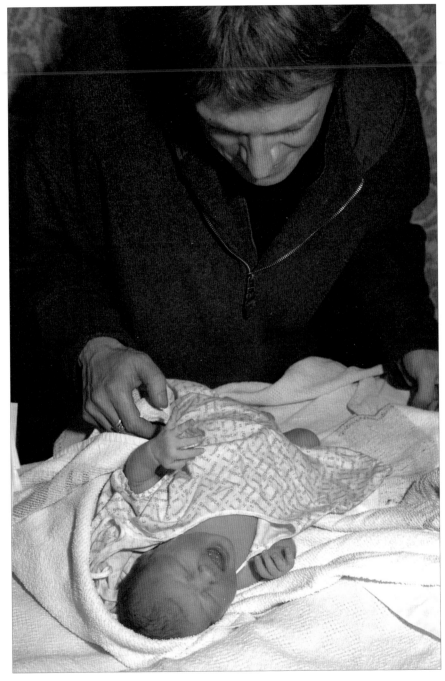

The sheer helplessness of a new baby can be a daunting prospect – particularly for first-time parents. Rest assured that you will soon slip into some kind of routine, and life will begin to settle down.

What you can expect in the first weeks

You may be feeling the trauma of the birth, and still be in some pain or discomfort. You may also experience:

● continued discharge from the vagina, which will eventually turn brown and then yellow before it ceases

● often overwhelming fatigue

● hair loss, as the hormones that kept your hair shiny and healthy drop off

● gradual loss of weight

● reduced pain

● constipation and perhaps haemorrhoids as a legacy of pregnancy and childbirth

● aching arms and backache from feeding and carrying your baby

● a gradually flattening abdomen, as your uterus begins to shrink back to its normal size

● excitement alternating with bouts of depression

Your baby

Your new baby will be making himself at home in your household, and even if you are feeling low or exhausted, you will not be able to resist feeling some pleasure at the enormous change and growth that occurs during the first six weeks:

● Your baby may seem to cry more often as he gets older, as he learns to exercise his lungs and express his needs

● Feeding may settle down into a type of routine – you may find that he wakes at much the same time every evening, or during the night, and sleeps for longer periods at certain times of the day. You will also find that he will learn to feed more efficiently, and any pain you have been suffering as a result of breastfeeding should settle down.

● Be alert to sounds, at around one month.

● Smile, at around four to six weeks – some babies smile earlier, but experts claim that it is wind, rather than emotion, that provokes that first happy look

● Look at faces at about one month, and recognize you.

● Follow an object with his eyes, at around two months.

● His neck will become stronger, and he will not seem to be so floppy.

Feeding your baby

Only you should decide how to feed your baby, based on your own needs and the needs of your newborn. While there are definite advantages to breastfeeding, there is no doubt that bottle-fed babies thrive equally well in most aspects of physical and emotional health. Don't be forced into doing something that does not feel right for you; reluctant breastfeeding can be difficult and frustrating, and will do no one any good; mothers who are persuaded to bottle-feed will also be unhappy in the long run.

If you are uncertain, try breastfeeding first, because you can always stop and change to the bottle, but it is unusual to be able to do it the other way round. You may wish to combine both methods to suit your lifestyle, or to involve your partner or other children in the care of your new baby. The best way to feed your baby is the way that is right for you.

Breastfeeding

Many women find breastfeeding a rewarding and nurturing experience, which establishes a physical bond between you and your baby, and helps to strengthen an emotional one. There are many advantages to breastfeeding, the first and foremost being nutritional.

Breastfeeding has psychological benefits for you and your baby because it helps promote a warm, close relationship between mother and child. Also, breast milk provides the ideal balance of nutrients for your baby, and can help protect him from infections to

Your breasts

The breast is a glandular organ which secretes milk from the end of pregnancy until the stimulation to breastfeed stops. The breast is a modified sweat gland, medically described as the 'mammary gland'.

The breast consists of a round mass of glandular tissue divided into fifteen to twenty lobes, each with a milk duct leading to an opening on the nipple. The size of the breast is determined more by the amount of fat than by the amount of glandular tissue. Connective tissue strands form a kind of skeleton of the breast and these are connected to supporting strands from the underlying tissue (fascia) and the flat pectoral muscles under the breast.

What happens when you breastfeed?

During pregnancy, the placenta and the ovaries secrete high levels of the hormones oestrogen and progesterone, which stimulate the glands to produce colostrum. Colostrum provides your baby with water, protein, sugar, vitamins, minerals and antibodies, to protect him against infection. The production of colostrum eases off around three days after the labour, and then the milk 'comes' in. When your baby sucks, nerve endings are stimulated in the areolae, and the signals from these nerves are received in

which you are already immune. The composition of breast milk also seems to vary with your baby's needs, whereas the composition of formula stays constant. You can put your baby to your breast as often as he seems to want it, and he will not gain weight too quickly, but a baby may become overweight with too much bottle-feeding.

In most women, breast milk is always available and requires no preparation. You will have the advantage of being able to feed your baby virtually anywhere – which can be useful in an emergency, such as being stuck in a traffic jam, or when a holiday runs over time. You can

the hypothalamus in the brain, which in turn sends out signals to the pituitary gland. The pituitary gland then releases a hormone called prolactin, which stimulates the production of milk. It also releases oxytocin, a hormone that causes the muscles around the milk glands to contract, squeezing the milk from the glands into the milk ducts – a process known as the 'let-down' reflex. When your breasts are full, it can be triggered by the sound of your baby's crying (in some cases the crying of other babies!), by his sucking, and often merely by his presence.

Note: If you have any problems in the first few days of breastfeeding, do not be discouraged. Talk to your physician for support and advice, or ask your physician's office for information from or a local telephone number for La Leche League International, a group that offers practical advice and moral support for women who are breastfeeding.

also feed your baby while you are lying down in bed, and many women can successfully sleep while they feed. There may be times when you need to be elsewhere at feeding time, or you may be tired or ill. You can arrange for someone else to feed your baby either by expressing milk manually or with a breast pump into a sterile bottle or by substituting a bottle of formula.

Your milk supply

Your milk supply is stimulated by constant feeding, and your body is in most cases able to produce enough milk for your baby, to meet his growing demands. If your breasts become engorged (swollen with milk), they are unable to produce milk efficiently, and you may also find it uncomfortable to feed your baby, which compounds the problem. Engorgement is easily dealt with (see page 135), and it helps to express a little milk before each feed if your baby is unable to latch onto the breast. Some experts suggest that you empty one breast completely before switching to the other, but if your baby doesn't completely empty your breast during a feed, don't worry – your body will adjust to your baby's changing needs.

While you are breastfeeding, it is essential that you continue the good eating habits of pregnancy, and don't be surprised if you feel very hungry for a good proportion of the time. Try to eat three good meals, as well as snacks in between to maintain your blood sugar levels. If you feel that your eating habits are preventing you from losing your pregnancy weight, don't worry. The milk, 'equipment' and maternal fat stores laid down for breastfeeding may remain quite constant while you are feeding, and it is not unusual to suddenly lose about 5 to 8 pounds when you stop.

Exhaustion can play havoc with your breastfeeding routines, and some women find that they simply don't produce enough milk at stressful times of the day – perhaps at mealtimes, if you have a larger family. Continue trying to breastfeed through these periods, and your body will soon rise to the challenge. If you are very worried, you

Why breastmilk?

Breastmilk is designed to provide complete nourishment for a baby for several months after its birth. Before milk is produced the mother's breast produces colostrum, a deep-yellow liquid containing high levels of protein and antibodies. A newborn baby who feeds on colostrum in the first few days of life is better able to resist the bacteria and viruses that cause illness. The mother's milk, which begins to flow a few days after childbirth when her hormones change, is a blue-white colour with a very thin consistency. If the mother eats healthily, the milk provides the baby with the proper nutritional balance. The fat contained in human milk, compared with cow's milk, is more digestible for babies and allows for greater absorption of fat-soluble vitamins into the bloodstream from the baby's intestine. Calcium and other important nutrients in human milk are also better utilized by babies. Antigens in cow's milk can cause allergic reactions in a newborn baby, whereas such reactions to human milk are rare. Human milk also promotes growth, largely due to the presence of certain hormones and growth factors. Breastfed babies have a very low risk of developing meningitis or severe blood infections, and have a 500 to 600 percent lower risk of getting childhood lymphoma. Breastfed babies also suffer 50 percent fewer middle ear infections.

Many breastfeeding mothers find that there are particular foods that may cause wind, or tummy upset in their babies. As a rule of thumb, it's best to avoid wine, garlic, onions and spicy foods if your baby seems to react badly. Babies with colic may react to wheat and dairy produce in your diet, so you could try cutting down or eliminating these foods to see if they are having any effect.

could try a bottle a day in these period – either formula, or expressed milk; your milk supply may be more plentiful when you are well rested, and many women choose this time to express.

Breastfeeding tips

1 Cradle your baby's head in the crook of your arm so that her well-supported head is above the level of her stomach. If you hold her flat, she may get bubbles of air that are difficult to discharge when burping her. Try to sit up straight, so that you don't get backache.

2 Leave her outside hand free so that she can stroke you or your breasts.

3 When she is feeding correctly, her mouth will be wide open and her tongue and jaw muscles will work to suck milk from your breast. Your nipple should be completely inside her mouth, her lips sealed round the areola. This is important because feeding from the nipple only may cause it to become sore and cracked, and your baby will not be able to stimulate a good flow of milk.

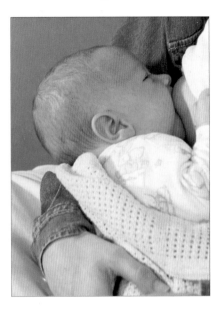

4 Advice differs on whether you should empty one breast completely, or let your baby drink from both breasts. When breastfeeding is established, it is important that your baby gets both the thirst-quenching foremilk, and the nutrient-rich hindmilk, so you will need to ensure that she has had a good drink from one breast – empty it if you can – before you start on the other. You can tell hindmilk from foremilk by the colour – hindmilk is thicker, and perhaps slightly yellow in appearance, while foremilk looks bluer and quite thin. If you are using both breasts, begin with the breast that is heavier and let your baby suck for as long as she likes. If she seems to empty one breast, by all means

move on to the other and allow her to have as much as she wants.

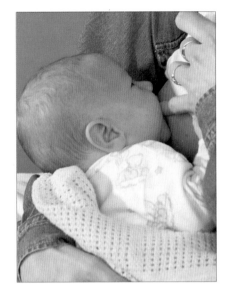

5 To remove your baby from the breast, insert a clean little finger into the corner of her mouth and gently release the seal.

6 You may wish to wear breastpads, which will help to absorb any leaks, and it is essential that you get a good nursing bra, which both supports your breasts and allows you to access them easily.

Breastfeeding problems

Refusing to feed

Your baby may occasionally refuse to feed – some babies are sensitive to your monthly cycle, and seem to be put off about the time of menstruation; other babies are not affected. Your baby may simply be sleeping more and seem to require less, or there may be problems latching on – which can sometimes be improved by changing your position, or ensuring that he has the whole nipple and part of the areola in his mouth. If you are too engorged for your baby to get a successful grip, you can try expressing a little milk before the feed.

To keep your supply active, it is a good idea to express milk in periods when your baby seems to require less (see right).

Breast engorgement

Breast engorgement is common in the early days, as your body adjusts to your baby's demands, and it is important to control it – partly because it is enormously painful if it is left unchecked, and partly because your milk supply will be affected if you do not reduce the swelling of the milk-producing glands (see page 136).

Express a little milk before the feed, and apply cool compresses between feeds to slow down the build-up of milk in the breasts and a warm cloth just before feeding to help the milk flow. The essential oil of peppermint can be added (a drop or two) to the cold compresses applied between feeds to reduce engorgement, but take care to wash your breast carefully before the

next feed. Talk to your midwife or breastfeeding counsellor about how often you are feeding, and when, to see if a change in your routine will help. Normally, feeding on demand will eventually ensure that you have a regular milk supply.

Blocked ducts

A blocked duct appears on the breasts as a small red lump on the breast, or a white spot on the nipple. This is usually caused by not letting your baby determine when the feed ends, or by missed or hurried feeds, which may cause part of the breast not to be emptied completely. It helps to feed from the affected breast first, and to gently massage the milk down and through the area of blockage. Try sitting in a warm bath, and with a wide-toothed comb gently massage the skin over the lump, to ease it out.

Inverted nipples

Some women have nipples that do not protrude, but this does not mean that you will be unable to breastfeed. Some inverted nipples are righted during pregnancy, when they become erect, but if yours don't, try not to worry. It is suggested that you begin wearing a small breast shield made of rubber, glass or plastic, inside your bra from the fifteenth week of pregnancy, as the suction will help to draw them out. If they remain inverted by the time you have had your baby, you will be able to breastfeed, but you may find it more difficult, and need more time to relax in preparation. Try to remove your clothing completely on your upper body,

Expressing milk

There are many reasons why you may wish to express milk, including engorgement or mastitis, or simply at times when your baby does not seem to need as much and you want to keep your supply up. It helps to have some expressed milk on hand, perhaps for your partner to offer the occasional feed, or in the event of an emergency, when you are unable to be with your baby.

It is possible to express milk by hand, and the best way to do it is to apply a warm compress – or even sit in the bath – and gently rub your breasts towards the nipple, catching the milk in a sterilized bottle. Many women find a pump easier to manage, and it will be much quicker and more efficient. To use a manual pump, fit the funnel of the pump over your areola in an airtight seal, and then use the lever to draw out the milk. If you have trouble 'letting down', it may help to have your baby nearby, or to think about him feeding. A battery-operated or electric pump will also be effective, and is not so hard on your hand muscles.

Store your milk in a sterilized bottle with a tight seal, and refrigerate it for up to 48 hours. You can keep it for up to six months in the freezer, and simply defrost in the refrigerator, and reheat in a pan of water. It is not recommended that you microwave breast milk, as it can alter the nutritional quality. Always wash your hands and sterilize all equipment before use.

One of the great advantages of breastfeeding is that it can be done anywhere, at any time. Many mothers find it easier to bring their baby into bed with them for night feeds – and you may even find that you can sleep a little while your baby feeds. Try to stay awake long enough to wind your baby, however, or she may suffer some discomfort. Don't worry about rolling over on your baby – even asleep, your mind is alert enough to know there is a baby in the bed.

and ensure that the entire areola is in your baby's mouth. If you have trouble, contact a breastfeeding counsellor (see page 133).

Mastitis

Mastitis is an inflammation or infection of the breast, and it is characterized by red patches, a temperature and flu-like symptoms. It can be caused by a blocked duct that is not cleared, or by an infection, which enters the breast tissue, perhaps from your baby's nose.

● If your mastitis is not caused by infection, try to encourage any lumps towards the nipple (see 'Blocked ducts', above), and express milk from the affected breast (even if it is painful). Always feed on the affected side first – it can actually be a huge relief to feel the milk flowing through the inflammation.

● Flatten a cabbage leaf with a rolling pin, and put the leaf in your bra. The enzymes will help soothe your breast and draw out any infection.

● If you do have an infection, antibiotics may be necessary.

Lack of milk

Many women are concerned about the amount of milk their baby is getting, and give up breastfeeding for just that reason. If your baby is growing normally, and has regular, wet nappies, you should have no cause for concern. If you wish to increase your milk supply, cut out any bottle feeds, and feed your baby on demand, which will ensure that you make enough for his needs. Offer both breasts at each feed, even if your baby doesn't seem hungry. Make sure you get plenty of rest, and a good nutritious diet, which will help to keep supplies even. There are some good natural remedies which may help, including:

● Lavender oil, in the bath or in a vaporizer, can encourage the let-down reflex. Better still, try massaging your baby with one drop in a little light carrier oil before a feed, to relax you both.

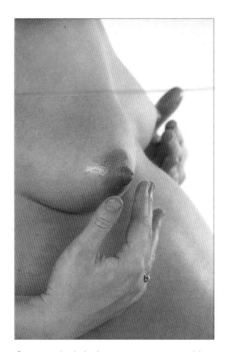

Sore, cracked nipples are a common problem associated with breastfeeding, particularly in first-time and fair-skinned mothers. Keep your breasts lubricated with a healing cream or oil, and leave them open to the air as often as possible.

● Caraway, aniseed, dill and fennel are all herbs which can be used to promote the flow of milk, and can be taken in the form of teas or infusions as required.

● The homeopathic remedy Agnus will help with milk production, and can be taken at 6x dilution, three or four times daily as required.

Sore, cracked nipples

There are many causes of nipple problems, including the action of the baby suckling on tender breasts, and dry or chapped nipples, which then crack and even bleed. The bleeding won't harm your baby, but it will certainly be painful, and may cause you to become frustrated with the whole process.

● The best advice is to take care of your breasts – use breastpads, and change them when they become damp.

● Rub a little olive oil or Vitamin E oil into each breast, and leave them open to the air to heal.

● Creams which contain calendula are safe for your baby to take orally, and some of them have ingredients which not only encourage healing but also act as a mild analgesic.

● Make sure your baby is latched on properly, otherwise pain and cracking can occur.

Bottle-feeding

Feeding your baby from a bottle is a viable alternative to breastfeeding, and it may be the right choice for you, particularly if the idea of breastfeeding does not appeal, or you have a busy lifestyle and will be unable to feed your baby on demand. Infant formulas available today are very nearly equivalent in nourishment to breastmilk, and you will be able to bond equally well with your baby, for it is the care that counts, not the breast or the bottle.

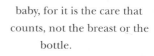

Milk formulas

Many formulas come as a dried powder in a tin, although some are available in a ready-to-drink form. Everything on the market should be safe, with balanced nutrients and added vitamins, although you may need to choose between brands according to your baby's age and special requirements. Most formulas are based on cow's milk, but there are soya-based formulas available for babies who have difficulty digesting cow's milk, or who have allergies or intolerance. You can also get a goat's milk preparation, although some babies do not like the pronounced taste. If you are unsure which to choose, ask for advice from your health visitor or midwife, who will be able to recommend something suitable.

Read the label on your baby formula to ensure that it is appropriate for your baby. If he seems sensitive to cow's milk, or you have a history of allergies in your family, you may want to try a Soya-based brand.

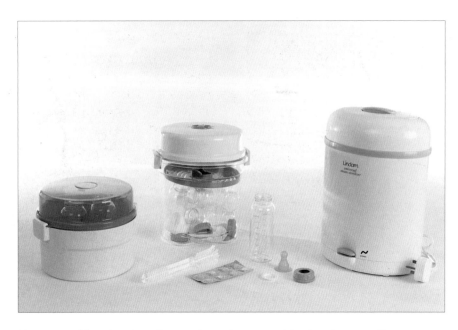

There are a wide variety of sterilizers on the market, and each has its advantages. The chemical 'soaks' may be the least time-effective, since you will have to rinse everything carefully before use, and change the water often. Remember that anything that comes in contact with your baby's mouth should be sterilized, from teething rings and soothers, through to feeding equipment.

than 24 hours; try to make up formula when you need it rather than making dozens of bottles in advance. Never reheat an existing bottle, even if he has had just a few sips.

There are many types of sterilizers available, including steam sterilizers, microwave sterilizers, dishwasher sterilizers and chemical sterilizers, all of which will do the job with varying amounts of effort from you. If you have a dishwasher, you can clean the equipment in it on the normal cycle, which will be hot enough to kill germs, but you should clean the teats separately, and it is recommended that you rub the insides with salt to loosen any milk residue. If you are washing by hand, you'll need a bottle brush, and plenty of hot, soapy water. Rinse both bottles and teats under hot running water, and store in a safe, dust-free place.

Preventing infection

● Perhaps the only major drawback to bottle-feeding is the increased risk of infection, so it is extremely important that you keep everything you use to feed your baby and prepare his formula scrupulously clean. Newborn babies are very vulnerable to infection, particularly of the gastro-intestinal tract, and you will need to sterilize anything that comes

into contact with his mouth, including bottles, teething rings and pacifiers (dummies), and all the equipment used to prepare his feed, such as knives, spoons and jugs, until he is at least four months old.

● Always use cooled, boiled water for making feeds.

● Never store formula milk for more

Preparing a feed

Always follow the manufacturer's instructions carefully, and never be tempted to add more formula, even if your baby is larger or seems to be hungrier than most.

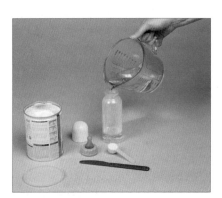

Measure out the warm, pre-boiled water in the sterilized bottle or jug. Don't use just boiled water, which can evaporate and change the balance of water and powder.

Using the scoop provided in the formula, measure out the quantities carefully, levelling off the scoop with the blade of a knife. Don't pack or heap the formula in the scoop.

Add the formula to the water, stirring with a sterilized spoon, or if you are making up the feed directly into the bottle, tighten the teat and cap and shake vigorously.

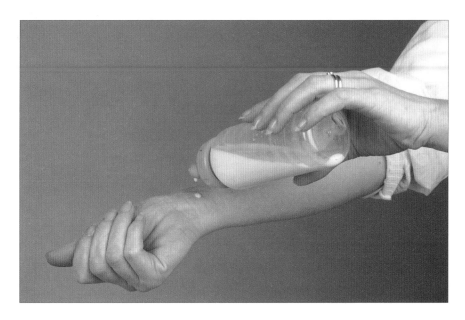

The quickest way to ensure that your baby's bottle is at the right temperature is to shake a few drops onto the inside of your wrist. The milk should be body temperature, and it will feel tepid on your skin. If you can feel any heat, the bottle is too hot. Remember that milk bottles can contain 'hot spots', and should be shaken carefully before testing the heat.

Burping your baby

It's a good idea to help your baby bring up any air she has swallowed during a feed, to prevent it from causing discomfort later. There are three easy ways to do this:

Hold your baby over your shoulder and gently tap or rub her back until she burps. Don't forget to place a muslin square or clean towel over your shoulder to catch any possetting (sick).

Bottle-feeding your baby

1 Heat the bottle of formula in warm water, and when it is the right temperature, test a few drops on your wrist. It should feel tepid.

2 When you feed your baby, hold her at an angle so that her head is slightly raised and she can swallow easily. Let her take as much of the teat as she wishes.

3 Find a quiet, comfortable place to feed her, make sure you have plenty of eye contact, and hold her securely. Let her feed for as long as she wants, and don't worry if she has not finished the entire bottle. She'll let you know when she is hungry again.

Always hold the bottle at an angle, so that the teat is full of milk and there is less likelihood of your baby swallowing air. If your baby seems to be choking, you may have to invest in teats with tinier holes, to ensure that the flow is slower.

You may need to insert a clean finger into the corner of her mouth to break the seal when she is finished feeding. Newborn babies have amazing powers of suction, and sometimes pull the teat from the bottle when you try to remove it from their mouths.

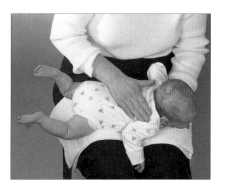

You can wind your baby by laying her across your lap, and gently rubbing her upper back until she releases air. If your baby is sleepy, or suffers from colic, she may respond well to this position.

Sit your baby upright on your lap, holding her chin in one hand. Lean her forward slightly, and gently rub or tap her back.

Changing nappies

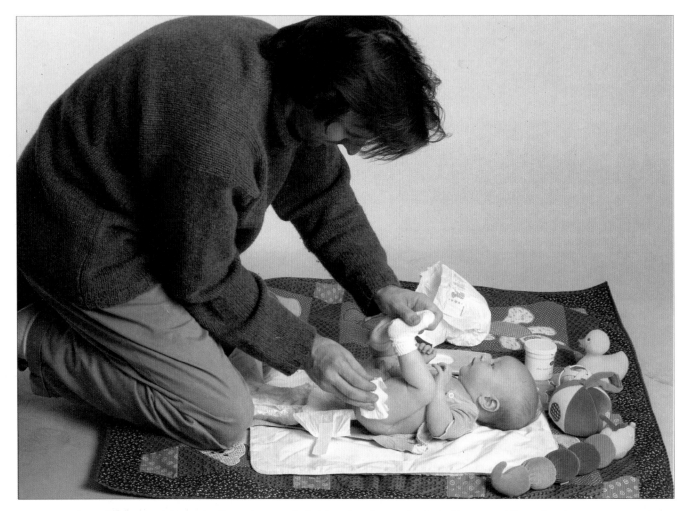

Whatever the type of nappy you choose, you will spend a great deal of time changing nappies in the first years of life, so it makes sense to organize a changing table, with all the necessary items to hand. Keep a supply of nappies, disposable baby wipes and creams in a bag that you can take with you whenever you go out.

Nappy changes present a good opportunity to talk to your baby, and to play a little while he kicks his legs without the constraints of a nappy. You will need to choose between disposable or cloth nappies, and always have a good supply to hand. In the first few days, you may find your baby gets through an endless supply of nappies – and clothing.

Cloth or disposable nappies?

Many people believe that the environmental advantages of using nappies made of cloth or terry towelling far outweigh the convenience of using disposables. A major problem with some disposable nappies (although this is changing) is that their plastic backing is

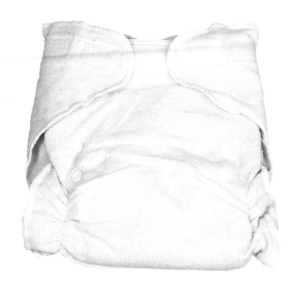

Disposable nappies are available in many sizes and qualities, and prices vary according to the various features. Look for nappies which are absorbent without being too bulky, and which have an adjustable waist for a better fit. Try not to buy too many 'newborn' size nappies, which will be outgrown quite quickly. On average, your baby will go through about eight nappies a day in the early days.

More and more parents are choosing washable cloth or terry nappies, and you can choose between shaped and rectangular, and self-fastening with Velcro or poppers, or nappy pins. You may need to purchase extra liners, and most nappies available require plastic pants of some description.

not biodegradable, which contributes to pollution. Furthermore, the average baby uses up five whole trees' worth of nappies by the time they are potty-trained. There is also a risk of infection (passed through the baby's faeces, and traces of the substances used to vaccinate), coming in contact with other members of the public, due to the disposal problem.

Interestingly, your baby is more likely to get a rash from disposable nappies, if he is frequently changed, than cloth, because of the chemicals and perfumes used to produce them.

Practically speaking, it is suggested that you consider using cloth nappies most of the time, and disposables only when they are necessary or helpful.

● There are now nappy services available that will take care of cleaning them, and deliver freshly laundered cloth nappies to your door. If you can afford it, this might be a good option.

● If you choose to use cloth nappies, you may wish to invest in fitted nappies, which are fastened with Velcro. These are much the same shape as disposable and are much easier to put on and take off.

● Cloth nappies will work out to be cheaper in the long run, especially if you have more than one child, and there is no problem with their disposal. Worn with waterproof pants, they are now pretty much leakproof.

● Cloth nappies do, however, require soaking, rinsing, and possibly washing and drying, and if your drying facilities are minimal, you may want to think carefully about the prospect of having drying nappies hung around the house.

If you do choose cloth, you'll need

● at least twenty-four nappies

● at least a dozen pins, unless you choose the self-fastening type

● at least eight pairs of waterproof pants

● nappy bins (one for soiled nappies, and one for those that are only wet)

● cleaning solution

● perhaps some disposable nappy liners, which make cleaning easier

Disposable nappies

Disposable nappies work out to be quite expensive, and create a great deal of rubbish, apart from the other environmentally unfriendly issues. However, they are quick and easy to put on and take off, and you won't be saddled with constant washing and drying. Try to choose disposables that are biodegradable, and which are not perfumed or bleached with chlorine, which will be easier on the environment and on your baby's bottom.

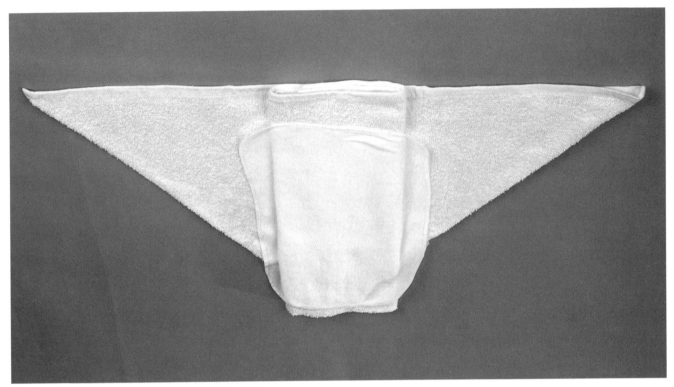

1 Lay a terry nappy flat on the changing table and fold it into a triangle by lifting the bottom right-hand corner to top left and then the bottom left to top right. Slide it underneath your baby.

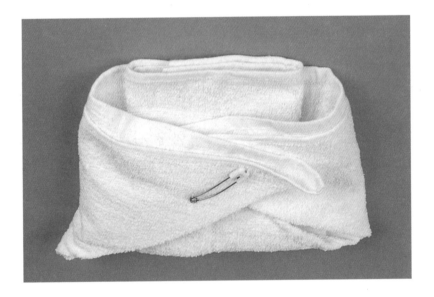

2 Pull the nappy up between your baby's legs and fold one side over the central panel and then the other, securing in the middle with a nappy pin.

Cloth nappies

Many cloth nappies are pre-folded and even have Velcro tabs much like the adhesive tabs of disposable nappies, so you will have no need for pins. If you are using an unfolded nappy, follow the instructions above to fold it into shape. If your baby is male, you will need to tuck down the penis, which has a tendency to shoot urine straight out the top of a nappy. In fact, all babies are prone to urinating just as you've cleaned them, applied cream and are about to secure a fresh nappy in place. There's nothing you can do except sigh and start all over again.

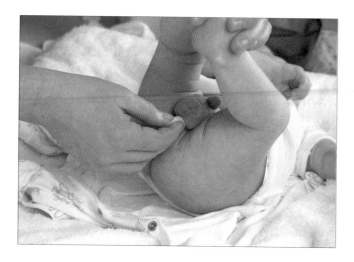

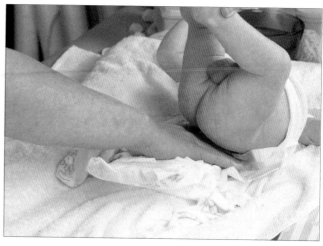

1 Always clean him carefully when removing a nappy, using dampened cotton balls, bottom wipes or a warm washcloth. Pay particular attention to skin folds and creases. Always dry him before you put the nappy back on.

2 Holding his ankles in one hand with your finger between his heels, lift him up so that you can clean the crease of the buttocks, and wipe from the front to the back. Do not use talcum powder.

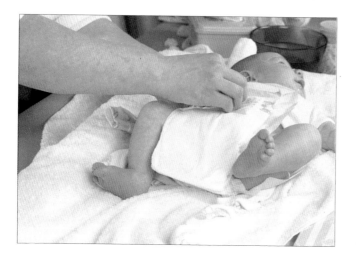

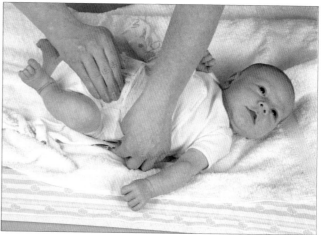

3 To put on a disposable nappy, open out the tabs and with his legs lifted as in step 2, gently slide the nappy underneath. Bring the front of the nappy up over between his legs, and smooth it across his tummy.

4 Stick down the tabs firmly, but gently, leaving space so that he can move a little in the nappy. Wipe your hands after using bottom cream, or the tabs won't stick.

Bathing your baby

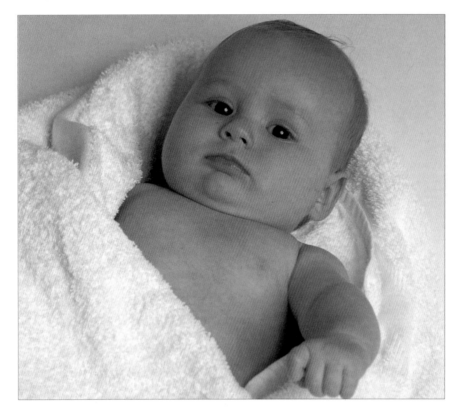

A newborn baby doesn't need to be bathed very often – and for most of the time, topping and tailing (see page 125) will be adequate. Don't feel that you have to invest in a baby bath: your baby can be bathed in any sink that is large enough to hold him, as long as the room is warm and draught-free.

Bathing your baby for the first time can be very disconcerting – a small, floppy body becomes an altogether different prospect when it is wet and slippery. Be assured that you are unlikely to drop your baby, or do her any damage, even if you do let her slip in the water. Make sure you choose a baby bath that is sturdy and stable. Your own bathtub or a sink will do just as well, but you might want to invest in a rubber mat to stop her from slipping. Take care only to use products that are specially created for babies – you can normally find a baby bath preparation that doubles as a shampoo, so there is no need to go in for a lot of expensive toiletries.

You'll need:

● a baby bath, or a rubber mat if you are using a sink or your own bath

● a washcloth

● a small sponge (the one you used when you were pregnant can be used again)

● baby bath preparation, preferably that doubles as a shampoo

● a soft towel

● cotton balls and cooled, previously boiled water

Bathtime should be fun, and if your baby is frightened, it may be helpful to take off her clothes and let her kick for a while on the bed, so that she becomes accustomed to being naked. She may not like the feeling of the water at first, so make sure you talk to her in a gentle voice, and keep your face close to hers so that she feels reassured. The most important thing to remember is that your baby must not get cold, so act quickly when you remove her from the bath, and give her a gentle but vigorous rub to keep the circulation going. Apply any creams or oils, and dress her as you would normally.

Once she is a month or so old, you can put her in a big bath; there she will have more room to kick and splash. Fill the bath only a couple of inches, so that when she lies flat the majority of her body is above the surface of the water. Always hold her with one arm and hand.

1 Fill the baby bath with warm water. Test it with your elbow, and if it feels warm, but not hot, it is the right temperature. Ideally, it should be about 98°F /37°C. Pour a few drops of baby bath in the water, and splash it until it foams. With cotton balls dipped in boiled water, wipe her eyes (one for each eye) from the inside corner to the outside corner, and wrap her in a clean, soft towel.

2 Hold your baby's head over the bath water, keeping her tightly wrapped in her towel, and with your arm supporting her along the length of her body. Splash or pour a little of the bathwater on her head, and shampoo her hair, talking to her all the time.

Washing your baby's hair

Some experts believe that a daily shampoo will help to prevent cradle cap, but it is not necessary to bath your baby every day to do so. You can now buy shampoo wipes, which are easy to use, and are less likely to drip anywhere near her eyes. Simply wrap your baby in a towel, and hold her over a sink filled with warm water (see above), or the baby bath. Moisten her hair with your sponge, and then shampoo. Rinse by squeezing a full sponge over her hair several times, and towel dry.

3 Unwrap the towel, and put your baby in the bath slowly, one wrist under her head and the other under the thigh that is closest to you.

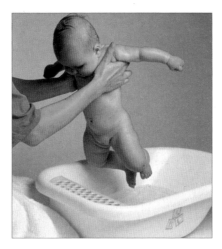

5 When you are finished lift your baby out carefully. Remember they will be slippery.

4 Keep supporting her head and neck on your forearm, with your hand holding her firmly around his far shoulder and upper arm. Move your other hand from under her bottom and gently splash the water, until she becomes accustomed to it. Take care to keep her supported, and partially upright, and gently clean her bottom and over and around her body with the washcloth.

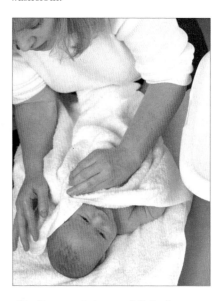

6 Dry your baby carefully before you dress her, paying special attention to the fingers, toes and skin folds around her bottom and neck.

7 Gently dress her in her usual clothes, talking to her in a gentle voice. She'll soon realize that bathtime is a comforting experience that she will enjoy.

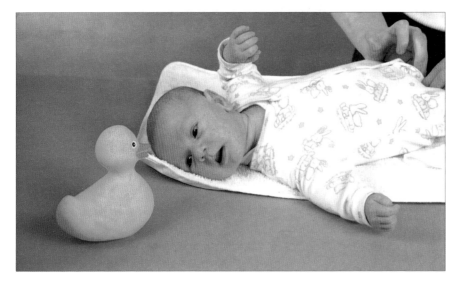

Holding and handling your baby

A newborn baby will need lots of attention and affection, and will feel most secure when he is being held close to you. Contrary to some schools of thought, it won't do you or your baby any good to let him cry when he wants to be held.

A happy baby is a secure and well-cared-for baby. If you leave him when he cries, it may teach him not to, but in the early days, crying is his only way of communicating with you, and if you ignore his needs, he will feel abandoned and uncertain, and he won't develop the trust in you that he needs to feel.

Your baby will feel instinctively nervous about being picked up, so try to do it gently and slowly at first, until he learns to feel safe. Arrange your hands and arms under and around him while he is still supported by his cot or cushions, and don't begin to lift him until he has felt the security your arms are providing. When you put him down, reverse the process, keeping your hands in place until he has time to feel the mattress and understand that he is safe. Picking up a baby can feel awkward at first, and it may take some practice before you do it naturally.

1 Put your hand under his neck, and your other hand under his bottom. Spread your fingers so that he is well supported.

2 Lean down so that your wrist and forearm follow his spine down to his waist, and slowly lift him. Your arms should support him in the same places that his cot or mattress did.

3 You are now in the right position to place him to your shoulder, and you will be able to hold him there with one hand if you tuck him along the length of your arm and into the curve your elbow.

Putting your baby down safely

Put your baby down using the entire length of your arm to support his spine, neck and head. When the mattress or mat is taking his weight, you can gently slide your hand from under his bottom, lifting his head slightly to release the hand still supporting his. Lower his head gently down.

Cradling your baby

Babies will be comfortable in many positions, and you can adjust his position from your shoulder (see above) to turn him so that he can see you, or the room around you. The cradling position, with your baby to your breast and his head in the crook of your elbow, is comforting for him because he will be able to hear your heartbeat, and he will feel safe with your arms wrapped round him.

Babies also enjoy facing outwards, so that they can see what is going on around them, and you can gently turn him, holding your hands between his legs and behind his back, until he is resting back against your chest. Hold him across his middle, so that his chin is supported on your lower arm, and use your other arm to support his bottom.

You may also like to hold his face down, with his chin and cheek resting on your forearm. This position is good if you want to stroke or rub his back, and it may help to soothe his if he is having difficulty settling.

There are a variety of car seats available, and most will double up as a baby chair, with a handle that makes transportation easy. This type of car seat is most appropriate for babies who waken easily – you'll be able to take him to and from the car with the least disturbance. When purchasing a car seat, look for models that conform with safety standards, and have straps that are easy to fasten. Many models have padding under the belt itself, to ensure that your baby is comfortable, and that a metal buckle won't burn him when the weather is very hot.

This cradling position makes your baby feel very secure. He is tightly supported in your arms and has the reassurance of being able to see your face.

Transporting your baby

● A baby sling is excellent for the early days, and it can be used both indoors and out. He will feel the warmth of your body, and be able to hear your heartbeat, and your hands will be free to get on with your daily tasks. Choose a sling with a padded headrest, and padding on the belt and shoulder straps. The belt should be wide enough to provide some support for your back, because even the tiniest babies become heavy after some time in a sling. Put on the sling while you are seated, holding him tightly against you, and slip the straps up over your shoulders. Lean forward slightly so that he falls back against the head rest, and you are ready to go!

● Car seats and prams are now designed for easy manoeuvring, and with a quick click of a safety belt, he will be in place. Choose a car seat that can be removed from the car, and which will also serve as a baby seat indoors. Even the most unsettled babies are comforted by the rhythm of a car, and desperate parents have been known to drive around the block in the middle of the night to settle a crying baby. If you can lift him into the house while he is still sleeping in his car seat, you may have a few moments' respite.

● Always strap your baby into his car seat, or his pram, no matter how small he seems, or how uncomfortable he may look slouched over in a little seat. If the belt seems to be uncomfortable, cushion him from the buckle with his blanket.

Your six week check

Both you and your baby will be given a post-natal check at about six weeks after the birth, although you may have seen your doctor or midwife several times before this.

You

You will be weighed, your blood pressure will be checked, and your breasts may be checked for lumps. You will have a pelvic examination to ensure that any stitching or tearing has healed well, that your cervix is closed, and that your uterus has contracted to its normal size in the abdomen. Your vagina will be checked to ensure that it has contracted and resumed much of its muscle tone. Haemorrhoids or varicose veins may also be examined, and treatment will be prescribed if necessary. If you are feeling particularly tired, or you suffered from

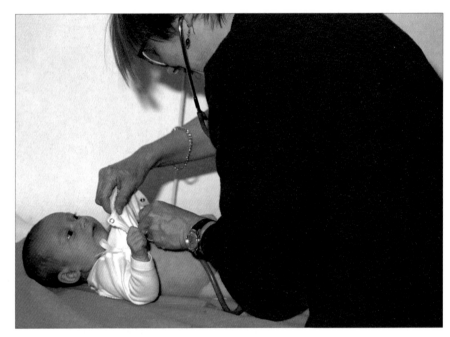

anaemia during pregnancy, your doctor may arrange for a blood sample to be taken to test your haemoglobin.

This check-up is a good opportunity to discuss things with your doctor – any concerns you may have about your own health, or that of your baby, and to talk through how you may be feeling emotionally. It is normal to experience some depression in the early days of motherhood, and your doctor will keep a close eye on you to ensure that it doesn't become anything more than that (see post-natal illness, below). You may also discuss the methods of contraception that you are or will be using, when you are ready to resume having sex.

Your baby

Your baby will also be examined around six weeks after the birth, and will usually have a separate appointment. Her eyes, muscles, ears, limbs and heart will be checked, and she will also be weighed and measured, to ensure that she is

developing well. Your doctor will check for hip displacement, and also measure the circumference of her head. Many doctors will provide you with a book to record your baby's weight, immunizations, health problems and size throughout infancy. If you don't receive one, you might like to keep your own record book, as it can be an invaluable reference in later days, and an important record of your baby's progress.

When you and your baby have received the all-clear, you will have passed an important milestone. After about six weeks of age, your baby will no longer be considered a newborn, but an infant, and her development will begin to increase dramatically.

Post-natal illness

Some mothers feel calm and happy from the moment their babies are born, but others (roughly 50 to 80 percent) experience some anxiety, fearfulness and mild depression that is known as the 'baby blues' around the third or fourth day. This normally disappears about a week after the birth.

Some women experience more severe postpartum or post-natal depression, which can range from mild feelings of depression to a state of limited functioning, which requires treatment with antidepressants. If the baby blues have not disappeared within two weeks, you should see your doctor because there is a possibility that it may become something more severe; about 10 percent of mothers develop post-natal depression in the first four to six weeks after their baby is born, but others may develop symptoms six months or more later. Symptoms can range from sleeping problems, obsessive worrying and anxiety, to feeling miserable, inadequate, and exhausted all the time. Post-natal depression is classified as an illness, and your doctor will be able to provide help, referring you to a counsellor or prescribing mild anti-depressants.

Post-natal depression is attributed to a variety of physical and emotional changes. The physical side includes alteration in hormone levels after giving birth, changes in your appearance after pregnancy, and weariness or exhaustion and fatigue from caring for a newborn.

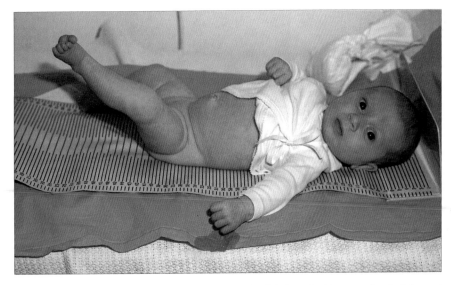

Your baby's growth can be a source of great concern, but it is important to remember that there are wide parameters for what is considered to be normal. You will likely be given a record book, in which you or your midwife will record your baby's height and weight on a regular basis.

Common emotional responses are feelings of anticlimax after the anticipation of the baby's arrival, fear of failure as a parent, loss of self-esteem as everything focuses on the baby, and marital stress. A good support system of family and friends can lessen the potential for post-natal depression.

What you can do
● If you have difficulty sleeping, talk to your doctor, or try some of the tips for sleeping in pregnancy (see page 86), which may help.

● You may need to talk to a professional about your feelings, and your doctor will be able to arrange this for you.

● Ensure that you eat good nutritious meals regularly, and drink lots of fluid. Exhaustion can cause paranoia and anxiety in even the healthiest women, and if you are eating well, you will have more energy and will be able to cope better. Avoid alcohol, which can exacerbate symptoms.

● There are some homeopathic remedies which can help with post-natal depression, and they can be taken two or three times daily, at 6c dilution. Try: Pulsatilla, for extreme weepiness; Natrum mur if you are feeling withdrawn, guilty and irritable; Sepia is an excellent post-natal remedy, and it will help if you feel uninterested in things, tired and irritable.

● Rescue Remedy, a blend of five flower essences, will help if you are feeling traumatized or shocked by motherhood, or by the birth. Gorse may be suggested for feelings of hopelessness; olive is for profound fatigue.

● Essential oil of clary sage is useful for a number of female complaints, and it will help to balance your hormones. Try putting a few drops in your bath water, or ask your husband to give you a comforting massage.

Your doctor will check for hip displacement by gently rotating your baby's hips. A male baby's genitals will be checked to ensure that the testicles have descended.

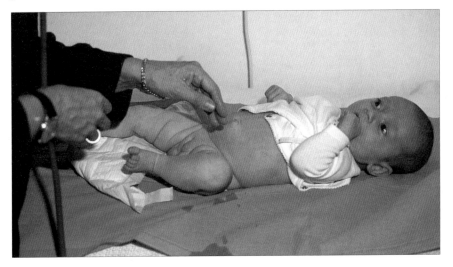

How much sleep does your baby need?

Most babies sleep about 16½ hours a day in the first few weeks, about nine of which will be at night, but no two babies are the same, and they will sleep exactly as much as they need to sleep – no more or no less. Yours may drift between sleep and wakefulness a great deal during the early days, and it may help if you encourage him to learn the difference between sleeping and being awake. If your baby is asleep, move him to his cot and wrap him tightly so that he feels secure. When he wakes, talk to him, and play with him, and encourage him to respond to you, and to his surroundings.

Many babies fall asleep when they are being wheeled around in pushchairs, finding the movements soporific.

Babies who learn early on to distinguish between being fully awake and fully asleep are those who usually sleep longer at night. You baby will waken at night for a reason – he may be hungry or uncomfortable, or he may have wind or perhaps colic (see page 153). Don't ignore his calls for attention at night; if

he learns that you are there, he will feel more secure, and will sleep better because of it. A baby who is left to cry in the early stages of life will feel anxious, which may disrupt sleep even further.

If your baby is restless and can't seem to settle down at night, you should be very cautious about assuming that he is

just a poor sleeper, or that he doesn't need as much sleep as other babies, as you will allow him to slip into bad sleep habits – your own expectations will have a strong influence on how your baby's sleep pattern develops from the day you bring him home from the hospital. Many babies sleep well from birth, and

A crying baby will respond to being held, and soothed by the sound of your voice. Never leave a new baby to cry – he'll feel insecure. He may 'learn' that crying does not bring a response from you, but he will feel miserable and very alone.

may even have to be woken for feeds. They will probably go on to sleep soundly throughout childhood. Other babies seem more susceptible to having their sleeping patterns disrupted, and illness, or any change in routine, can cause their sleep patterns to deteriorate.

Always put your baby to sleep on his back, which is now proven to be the safest position, and ensure that he is warm, but not hot.

It is important from the early days to set up a sleep routine – even from birth, your baby will benefit from a series of events that tell him that sleep comes next, and that it is a comforting and restful experience. Give him a warm bath or a gentle wash, maybe even a light massage to quiet and soothe him. Sing him a lullaby, or read him a nursery

rhyme in a quiet voice. Let him drift off to sleep while he is feeding, but continue talking to him as you lay him in his cot. Keep a soft, familiar toy or blanket close to his face or hands, so that he can feel it if he wakes. If he wakes at night, try to keep the lights low, and make it clear that it is sleeping time, not waking time. Talk quietly or not at all, and encourage him back to sleep with cuddles and soothing strokes. Keep night-time feeds and changes brief, and put him back in his bed when he has been burped. He'll soon get used to the routine, and realize that there is no point in waking for fun and games.

Coping with exhaustion

Lack of sleep or consistently broken sleep can cause even the most patient parents to become irritable and feel that they cannot cope. It is helpful to remember that most babies do settle down by the time they are three months old, although that may seem like a very long time away when you are in the middle of a period of severe sleep deprivation. There are some things you can do to help:

● You might consider having your baby in your bed with you. If you are breastfeeding, you will soon be able to feed him without really waking. Babies who sleep in their parents' bed often wake much less frequently than other babies as they get older, and it may help them to feel secure. Be warned, however, that it can be a hard habit to break.

● Go to sleep early, after your baby's early evening feed – if you wait for the last feed and he doesn't waken till later, you have wasted valuable time. You might even want to wake your baby deliberately before you the time you plan to go to sleep, and to feed him then, in the hopes that you get at least a few hours of unbroken rest at the front end of the night.

● Feed your baby as soon as he wakens, so that he doesn't fret and wake up completely. Although he may have cried himself back to sleep without a feed, he is now less likely to waken again from hunger.

● Find ways for your partner to help. Perhaps you could express some milk, if you are breastfeeding, and a middle-of-the-night feed could be undertaken by your partner. Have a bottle ready in the refrigerator for just that purpose. Try to take turns with the waking, so that at least one of you has had a good night's sleep under your belt the next day.

● Don't be tempted to get up and have a drink or something to eat after you have settled your baby. Get in the habit of going right back to bed, and perhaps practise a little visualization (see page 59) if you are finding it difficult to get back to sleep.

● If your baby is sleeping with you, it may help to move your baby's bed out of your bedroom – particularly if you are a light sleeper and are disturbed by snuffling and movements in the cot.

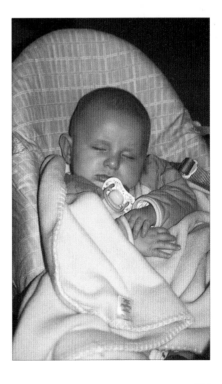

Common problems

Newborn babies are generally healthy during the first few weeks of life, particularly if they are breastfed and have the benefit of your immunities being passed on to them. There are, however, a number of common ailments that can occur in early infancy, most of which are not serious. If you are in any doubt about your baby's condition at any time, do not hesitate to contact your doctor (see page 236).

Cradle cap

Cradle cap appears on the scalp of babies as a thick, yellowish crust, sometimes in patches, and sometimes covering the entire surface of the scalp. It is caused by over-productive sebum glands, and most babies who suffer from cradle cap have slightly oily skin. It can last for up to three years in some children, but as the hair grows in it becomes less noticeable. Many babies outgrow the condition in the first few months of life.

What you can do
● Massage a few drops of lavender or lemon essential oil, mixed in a light carrier oil, into the scalp before bedtime. Rinse gently each morning.

● Olive oil can be massaged into the scalp each evening, and then gently shampooed away in the morning. Gently loosen flakes of skin with your fingers or a soft brush, but never use a sharp comb, which can cause bleeding and lead to infection.

● Cradle cap is not caused by inadequate hygiene and over-washing will make the condition much worse, although some experts recommend a daily shampoo.

Nappy rash

Nappy rash occurs around the genitals and anus, and may extend up the abdomen or down the legs in more severe cases. It results from contact with urine or faeces, which cause the skin to produce less protective oil and therefore provide a less effective barrier to further irritation. Friction may also exacerbate the condition.

What you can do
● Avoid using soap or other detergents on the nappy area. Rinse carefully with clean water at each nappy change. Frequent nappy changes are suggested, and using a disposable nappy liner may help to reduce irritation. Allow your baby to go for as long as possible with a bare bottom, to allow it to dry and heal.

Cradle cap is one of the most common ailments affecting new babies, and it can appear quite alarming, particularly when crusts of skin build up. Always be gentle when loosening the crusts, and use a healing oil to prevent infection and encourage the growth of healthy skin.

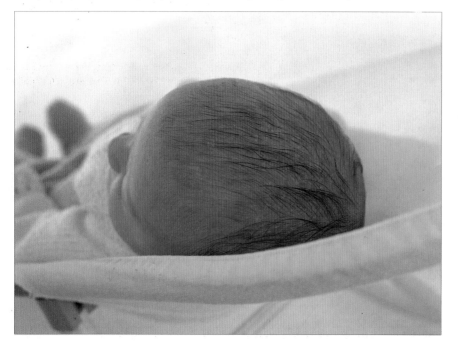

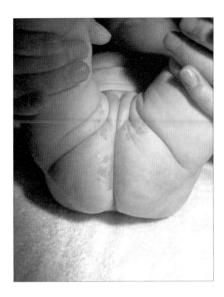

Most babies will suffer from nappy rash at some point, and unless it is causing her pain, or is linked to 'thrush', which is characterized by white patches, a soothing cream, plenty of to drink, and lots of time with the nappy off, will sort it out in a few days.

● Give your baby lots of soothing drinks, such as diluted chamomile tea, to reduce the acidity of the urine. There are many herbal formulas available for newborn babies, but be sure they do not contain any sugar.

● Rub a little calendula (marigold) ointment on to the cleaned nappy area to soothe and to reduce inflammation. If you use a chamomile or calendula cream on your breasts, they may be suitable for use on your baby's bottom as well.

● Rescue Remedy cream may be gently massaged into the affected area to reduce inflammation and ease any pain or itching. A few drops of Rescue Remedy on pulse points may calm a baby who is distressed.

● Egg white can be painted on the sore bottom and allowed to dry before putting on a nappy. This will encourage the skin to heal and prevent further irritation.

Caution: Nappy rash that does not heal within a week or so should be seen by a doctor.

Colic

Colic is a condition affecting almost a quarter of all infants – a large percentage of which are male – and frequently begins at about two or three weeks, often continuing until the baby is eight to twelve weeks old. It is characterized by inconsolable crying (usually at the same time each evening), wind, severe pain in the abdomen which causes the legs to be drawn up against the body, and bloating. The cause is unknown, but it may stem from contractions of the colon, an allergy to something in the formula (if bottle-fed) or the mother's diet (if breastfed), or simply excessive air which is gulped in through repeated bouts of crying.

What you can do

● A hot-water bottle, wrapped in a towel, can be applied to the abdomen.

Colic can be agonizing for both parent and baby – and it is important to keep your baby calm and relaxed before feeds, particularly around the time of day that she suffers from attacks. Try a gentle abdominal massage before your evening feed, if her colic is worse at that time, and during an attack, to soothe and relax.

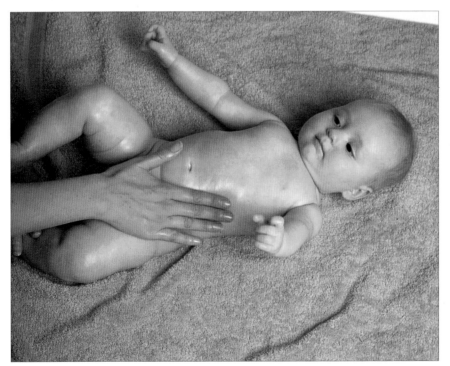

Diluted chamomile tea can make the urine less acidic, thus easing the pain of nappy rash.

Chamomilla 200c

Jaundice is quite common in new babies, and is usually mild, beginning a few days after birth. The skin takes on a yellow tinge, and in black babies, the yellow can be seen in the whites of the eyes. Jaundice occurs when your baby's liver is less efficient in disposing of red blood cells which were necessary while in the womb, causing pigment to remain in the blood, and to be deposited under the skin. Mild jaundice doesn't usually need treatment and will disappear within a week or so. More serious jaundice is treated by phototherapy, or 'light' therapy.

● Try a few drops of lavender or chamomile oil in a warm bath, just before evening feeds.

Caution: If colic is accompanied by vomiting or diarrhoea, see your doctor.

Sticky eye

Sticky eye is a mild infection of the eyes causing a yellowish discharge and crusting. It is most common in the first few months, and is most often caused by a blocked tear duct. At birth, the end of the duct closest to the nose is sometimes covered by a thin membrane, which will break open during the first few weeks, allowing tears to drain through to the corner of the eyes. Babies begin producing tears at around three weeks, but in some babies the membrane does not open fully, and the ducts may remain partially or entirely plugged. Accumulated tears may become infected and yellow. Sticky eye can also be caused by infection contracted during childbirth, or from contact with childbirth blood or amniotic fluid.

● Most babies respond to being rocked and gently massaged.

● Colic can be very distressing for parents, and this can often be passed on to the baby. Try to stay calm and enlist a little extra support from a friend or family member. If you are breastfeeding, give up dairy produce for a few days to see if this helps. Other foods which should be avoided are wine, very spicy foods, citrus foods, gassy foods (beans, onions, cabbage, etc.) and sugar.

● If you think your own distress or nervousness is causing your baby to become tense, drink a cup of passion flower or chamomile tea just before feeding.

● There are several useful homeopathic remedies for colic, including: Chamomilla, for babies who seem better when they are held; Pulsatilla for babies who are better in the fresh air, and when they are rocked; Cuprum met is used when the tummy rumbles, and the child curls his fingers and toes in discomfort. Most of these remedies will be available at your local healthfood

shop, and they can given safely to newborn babies as required, in 6c dilution.

● A gentle massage of the abdominal area with one or a blend of essential oils of chamomile, dill, lavender or rose, will help to ease symptoms and calm a distressed baby. If your baby is wakened by discomfort, place a hanky with a few drops of lavender oil by the bed.

When to call the doctor

Until they are able to talk to you, it is difficult to know when babies and young children are ill, and when they require medical help. Trust your instincts. If you feel that something is wrong, don't hesitate to contact your doctor at once. Important signals that all may not be well are:

● a high temperature that does not immediately respond to cooling (see opposite).

● unusually drowsy, listless, quiet or restless behaviour

● when your baby consistently refuses feeds, or does not demand one, for any length of time.

● when your baby cries much more than usual, sounding different to his usual requests for attention or feeding

● diarrhoea or vomiting

● convulsions of any description

● trouble breathing, or blueness around the mouth

● an unusual rash

There are a variety of herbal treatments that are gentle and safe enough for babies. When in doubt, consult a registered herbalist, and stick carefully to the recommended dosages. Most herbal remedies can be applied externally – for nappy rash or cradle cap, for example – and they will encourage your baby's natural healing mechanism, which makes them infinitely preferable to chemical treatments.

What you can do

- Clean your baby's eyes regularly with warm, sterile water, always using a separate cotton ball for each eye, and working from the inside corner out.

- There are two good homeopathic remedies which may help: Euphrasia can be given if the eyes are watering, but they become clogged with sticky mucus, or Allium cepa, if the eyes are burning, red and watery, but improve in warm air.

- If the yellow discharge persists, take your baby to a doctor.

Fever

There is advice on page 245 about what to do for a high temperature.

Babies' temperatures can fluctuate quite dramatically and it is important to monitor a fever, particularly in a young baby, because of the risk of febrile 'convulsions' (fits). Many mothers can tell when their baby's temperature is high simply by placing their lips to baby's forehead. If you are unsure, use one of the easy-to-manage thermometers on the market. This one records temperature by placing a strip on your baby's head, which 'lights up' the relevant details.

Essential oils should be used sparingly on new babies, and carefully diluted. An excellent way to experience the benefits of aromatherapy is to use a vaporiser in your baby's room – try lavender or roman chamomile to relax, or tea tree when he has a stuffy nose.

Developmental stages

From the very earliest days your baby will have a personality of her own, with clearly defined tastes, preferences and characteristics. As you get to know one another, you'll slip into a comfortable sort of companionship, and before you know it, life has become more predictable again, and you will be able to settle down to the uniquely satisfying but frustrating task of raising a child.

There will always be days when you feel anger and frustration, and even complete helplessness, but your baby will have become a known quantity and you will be able to anticipate her

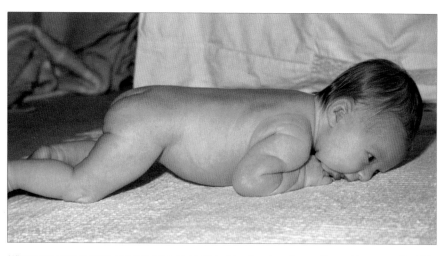

When your baby is born, she will have no control of her head, and you will need to ensure that it is supported at all times. This 'floppiness' can be alarming, particularly for first-time parents.

demands, and deal with her needs without having to pause to consider how. Most importantly, perhaps, you will begin to have confidence in yourself as a parent.

Your baby will grow and develop a great deal over the first six months, and her blossoming personality and increasing responsiveness to you and the

world around her will enchant even the most seasoned mother. When your baby first smiles at you, when she gurgles and waves her fists, and reaches out to stroke your breast or your cheek, a passionate tie is formed between you that will help to make the considerable work of new parenthood worthwhile.

After only a few weeks, your baby will be able to lift her head up for a few seconds, as her muscles strengthen and she becomes more co-ordinated.

By six weeks your baby will be able to raise her head and look around – and by three to four weeks, she will be able to push herself up on her arms and raise her chest from the ground.

The stages of development

There are a number of milestones in your baby's first six months, as she develops from a helpless, dependent and unpredictable creature into a sociable and responsive baby. Babies progress at different rates, and you have no reason

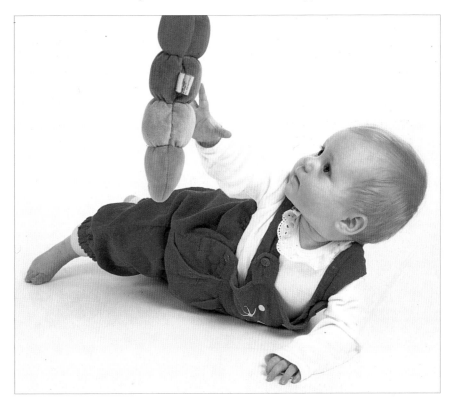

for concern if your baby is slower than most to achieve the recognizable stages of early life. Your baby is unique, and she will do things in her own time. All babies catch up in due course, and you may find that your early crawler doesn't walk for months after the neighbour's baby, who didn't crawl at all.

Growing stronger

Your newborn baby will not be strong enough to move around with any purpose until she is several months old. When she is born, her movements are spontaneous, taking the form of reflexes. As her muscles strengthen, she will gain control her limbs, and she will feel less floppy, and her movements will

Before long, your helpless baby will be able to reach out for a favourite toy, or anything that catches her eye, pushing herself up on her arms. Beware! A baby who can lift herself up and reach out will soon be able to roll, and your bed or the changing table may no longer be safe.

be more graceful. By three months, she will enjoy kicking her legs and reaching out for things with some purpose.

A newborn baby maintains the vestiges of the fetal position for the first few weeks, and she will lie curled up against you, with her legs and arms tucked under her body and her bottom slightly raised. As the weeks pass, her body will gradually flatten out, and she will learn to lift up her head for a few seconds, and then a little longer. You will need to support her head when you lift her in the first weeks, for her back and neck muscles will be too weak.

By six weeks, your baby will start to raise her head and look around, and by three to four months, she will be able to push herself up on her arms, and raise her chest from the ground.

As her neck and back muscles become stronger, she will also be able to hold her head still as she watches something that engages her – a mobile, her own hands, a colourful button, or your face, which she will be content to examine for long stretches of time. Encourage her interest in the world around her, and when she is ready – at about two months – place her in a specially designed baby chair or a bouncing cradle, so that she can investigate her surroundings more easily.

By about five months, your baby will be able to support herself on her arms, as she looks around, turning her head when she sees movement, or hears the sound of your voice. It won't be long before she is able to sit, well supported by cushions, for short periods of time. By six or seven months, her back will have straightened, and she will be able to draw her head back and up to look around him.

Your baby may be active from the beginning, and many begin to roll from their sides to their backs as early as nine or ten weeks – which can make nappy changing a completely new experience. By three months your baby will learn to roll from her back on to her side, and may even be able to turn herself right over on to his tummy. Try to encourage these first attempts to assert her independence, and take care not to make clothing or blankets too tight. The baby who loved to be swaddled and needed the constant comfort of your arms may now reject anything that hampers her determination to move.

Young babies will not require many toys – in the early months they will be fascinated by your face, your smile, your skin, and their own fingers and toes. Your baby will be most interested in 'visual' entertainment in the early days, and mobiles hung over cots or change tables can provide hours of entertainment. By four

Young babies will enjoy lying on their backs and taking in their surroundings, with a little freedom to kick their legs and assert their independence. Place toys close by, so that your baby can reach out for them. Avid kickers may prefer a baby gym, with hanging toys that respond to movement from their hands and feet.

baby will soon begin to put anything that she can grasp straight into her mouth, so toys may need to be sterilized as carefully as feeding equipment – or at

months, your baby will enjoy shaking a rattle, and batting at toys hung from the side of a cot, or a baby gym. Remember that your

least washed in hot, soapy water on a regular basis.

A bouncing seat is a great investment, and it can save your sanity when your arms are occupied elsewhere and your baby is not content to lie on her own on her back. Parents soon become adept at the art of rocking a chair with one foot while preparing food, taking a well-earned break, or even in the bath! Baby chairs are also useful for feeding and allow your baby to play with toys. If you have a baby who likes to have you in her vicinity at all times, a portable chair is a must! She can see you as you move around the room, and she will be able to follow your voice. Be careful never to place a bouncing seat on table tops or work surfaces in the kitchen. Your baby will love it when you get down on her level, and talk to her. Bounce her in her chair, sing to her, and encourage her to learn that you are there, and available for play and comfort, even when she is not in your arms.

Smiling

No parent can fail to be won over when their baby smiles for the first time, and even smiles that are associated with wind can be endearing. There is no set time for the first smile, except that most babies can smile by about four to six weeks. There are three distinct stages in 'smiling'. First there is the pre-smile or reflex smile, which can be observed as early as three days after birth, and continues on and off for the remainder of the first month. You may find that baby smiles 'instinctively' when you tickle her, or speak in a high voice. The second smile is an 'unselective' or 'general' smile which normally occurs around four weeks of age. Each smile lasts longer and is accompanied by some expression. In unselective smiling, the reaction smile has matured and developed, but your baby will not be able to understand why she is smiling, or be able to sort out the appropriate stimuli. It is not until four to six months that your baby smiles 'specifically', when smiles are fully formed and delivered with expression. It is difficult to discern between the last two smiles – unselective smiles will be aimed at any adult face or object. Specific smiles are those that occur when your baby smiles with recognition, and becomes 'selective' about who she will and will not smile at.

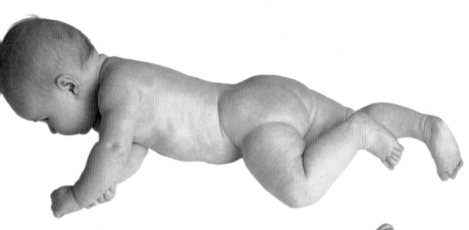

Some babies roll over for the first time by three months old – others do not do so until nine or ten months. When your baby can push herself up on her hands, and rock her body, the first roll is close at hand.

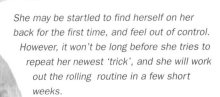

She may be startled to find herself on her back for the first time, and feel out of control. However, it won't be long before she tries to repeat her newest 'trick', and she will work out the rolling routine in a few short weeks.

Sitting up

From about three or four months, your baby will enjoy being pulled up by her arms into a sitting position, and carefully held so that she can look around. She will be able to hold her head upright, although she may need a great deal of support to prevent her from toppling straight over again. Those first glimpses of life beyond her cot and the mobile may inspire in her a greater determination to learn more about her surroundings, and you may find that she is happiest when she is sitting upright in a baby chair, on your lap, or propped up on some cushions, from where she can get a better view.

By five or six months, her ability to control her muscles and hold her head, neck and shoulders upright have improved enormously, and she will be able to sit with only a little support around her hips and the base of her spine. She will begin to reach out for things in this position, which will inevitably result in a spectacular topple, but she will be well on her way to sitting by herself. Propping her up helps to strengthen the muscles she will need to sit on her own, at around the six-month mark, and it encourages her to practise her balance.

Early crawling

Soon after your baby is able to push herself up on her arms, and push her bottom up into the air, she will begin to make the first concerted attempts to move. She learns to straighten her knees, and by four to five months she can do it in a series of motions that will propel her forward inch by inch. She will bounce against you or the floor as she learns that she can shift his body, even very slightly, by her movements. She will begin to lift her shoulders by pushing up with her hands, and she may begin to use her feet to push herself forward. Progress is often slow, but

From the earliest days, and in the safety of her chair, your baby will take interest in the world around her, and many babies are not happy unless they are in an upright position, with a bird's-eye view. When your baby is strong enough to support her head, and shows interest in sitting up – responding, perhaps when you pull her up by the hands – try propping her up with cushions around her for support (and safety). She will enjoy the freedom and independence that sitting on her own gives her. Gone are the straps of the car seat and the baby chair – she can now reach out and grasp anything that catches her fancy, and make the first steps towards moving, perhaps beginning with an inefficient bottom shuffle, or a 'topple-roll-sit-up-again' type manoeuvre. Don't be surprised if your baby finds the early days of sitting frustrated. Until she achieves reasonable co-ordination and balance, she will fall often.

beware of a baby who has learned to move her body forward (or backwards) in a rhythmical fashion – the edge of the bed or the top of the stairs may be closer than you think.

Your baby may not enjoy being placed on her tummy, and she may not make an effort to crawl until she is much older, but she will manoeuvre herself by rolling or stretching out in progressive movements until she is able to reach whatever she is after.

at you for seemingly endless periods of time, but when she begins to respond by smiling, and grimacing, and even mimicking the faces that you make, it is clear that everything she does is a learning exercise. By three months, she will move her head to look around her, and by the time she is about six months old, she will be able to move her eyes enough to follow movement around the room. She will be delighted with her fingers and hands, and as she learns to move them, she will start to reach out for toys and touch them. She

may hold a toy that is placed in her hands, and she may instinctively bring it to her mouth, before dropping it again. Some children can find these early learning experiences frustrating, and you may spend a lot of time picking up toys and placing them back in her hands again. By six months, however, she will be able to reach out and pick up toys herself, and even play with them a little. She will pass things from one hand to another, and look with considerable interest at toys held in both hands.

Reaching and holding

From the beginning, your baby will be able to focus on your face, if you hold her about 8 to 10 inches (20–25 cms) away, and she will be fascinated by faces, patterns, lights and colours. You may feel disconcerted by her ability to stare

Hand-eye co-ordination

For the first eight weeks, your baby can only see and focus on things that are quite close to her face, and you will be able to tell when something comes into her line of vision by her excited reaction, or when she stops stock still. She can follow a toy with her eyes for a limited range, and when it is reintroduced, she will act as though she has never seen it before. Help your baby by placing things within her visual range, and spend time with her, so that she can learn from watching your face.

● By two to three months your baby is quicker to focus, and she will follow a moving object with her eyes. She will reach up for things that interest her, and when they jingle or make a shaking sound, she will be amazed, and try it again. She will soon realize that her hands are capable of doing the most

Every baby learns to crawl in a different fashion – and some babies never crawl at all. Encourage her to move, by placing toys just out of her reach, or calling to her from a few feet away.

Your baby will soon learn to use her hands in order to draw things to her face for a closer look, and a good chew. It is important, therefore, that any toys conform to safety standards, and that there are not any loose pieces that may cause choking. If your baby is fond of furry toys, ensure that the fur is non-toxic, and washable!

wonderful things, and she will begin to swipe at toys or even your face. She won't be able to grasp hold of most things, although by four months she will be able to lift her hands towards an object and practise moving things together.

● By six months she will be able to focus on an object, and bring her hands straight up to grasp it. Try to provide her with lots of stimulating things to play with, for she will enjoy practising and experimenting with new and ever more interesting household items or toys.

Early toys

In the beginning you will be your baby's favourite toy, and she will need you to stimulate her with your hands, your voice and your face. Don't be embarrassed to exaggerate facial expressions, poke your tongue out at her, or play clapping games. Your baby will respond and will learn from your movements, and soon try to mimic them herself. Mobiles provide good stimulation from the beginning, and rattles, placed in her hand, will inspire periods of rapt attention. She will like the sound of the rattle, and will be stimulated by the rhythm.

Try to find toys that are colourful, and which make noise or move when she touches them. Hang things safely above her head to stimulate her, and to encourage her to reach out to touch them.

A baby gym or a row of beads or even shiny or soft balls dangling above her cot or chair will help to entertain her, and she will soon realize that by waving her arms, she can make something happen. Teething rings and safe, plastic toys without detachable pieces provide an excellent opportunity for oral experimentation, as she will put most things that you place in her hand

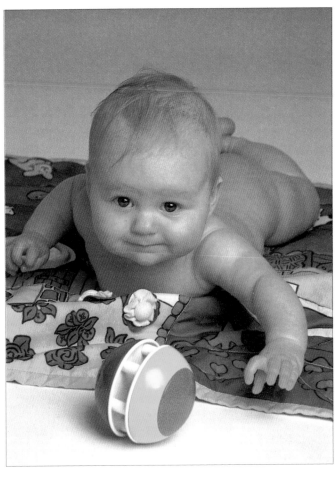

Your baby will soon fix on a toy, and as she becomes more mobile, show great determination in reaching it. Try to ensure that she has plenty of stimulating toys or household goods to play with, to encourage her to reach out, and to test her newly developed skills.

- Enjoys soft music and being rocked gently to a lullaby

- At about one month, she can recognize her mother's face, and usually her father's, too

Six to twelve weeks

- Can focus for longer on mobiles and cot toys at a greater distance

- Shows preference for bright colours by looking at them longer

- Is interested in faces, and pictures of faces

- Enjoys a wrist rattle, musical toys and squeaky toys (if they are not too loud)

Three to six months

- Can now grasp a toy placed in her hand, and will begin to reach for toys

- Favourite early toys are lightweight rattles and colourful teething rings

- Learns to use both hands to play with foam bricks, soft balls, grip-toys with internal squeaks or bells, pram beads; cuddles soft toys.

straight into her mouth. She will suck and chew toys, and she will like different textures and sensations.

You don't need to buy expensive toys. Everything is new to her, and a clean wooden spoon will be as fascinating as any plastic toy. Take care not to give her anything sharp, or that has long ribbons or strings. Avoid anything that is small enough to fit into her mouth, or heavy enough to hurt your baby if she inadvertently swings it round. Otherwise, anything goes – and you can have fun creating colourful mobiles from bits of aluminium foil, colourful balls and plastic bottles that she can beat at and explore with her hands and feet.

Toys and awareness

The first six weeks

- She will enjoy human faces and voices

- Focuses best on hand-held toys about 8 inches from her face

- Enjoys mobiles, wind chimes, cot toys, if they are clearly in her view

Everything that your baby comes into contact with is new and exciting for her, whether it is the bag of carrots from the grocery cart, or your old wooden spoon. Many parents improvise with pieces of aluminium foil tied on strings, to catch the light, or empty soap bottles filled with beads (the lid must be firmly closed), which will make a satisfying sound when shaken. Try to involve your baby in your activities, and look out for safe and interesting 'toys' for her to play with. Despite what manufacturers would have us believe, there are very few advantages to new 'shop bought' toys, as your baby will learn from the world around her and practise her skills with whatever is to hand. Expensive toys may be unnecessary, but toys are essential for your baby's development. She will learn through play, and anything you give her to encourage that learning will help her to develop.

Communicating with your baby

In the early days, your baby learns everything from you and your family. Babies do require stimulation, and they develop primarily through play, and through interaction with people. It may be difficult in the beginning to find time to sit down and play with your baby, but his needs are essential, and it is more important to him to have someone to keep him company, and to entertain him, than to have a sparkling clean kitchen, or a pile of well-ironed clothes. The days will fly by as your baby gets older, and you may regret not spending time with him when you had the chance. Always try to make time – play can be rewarding, as you see your baby develop.

Your baby will try to communicate with you from birth, by crying, and then by making different facial expressions. He will begin to listen to voices, and may turn his head from a feed to investigate. He will show pleasure or relax when he hears familiar songs or sounds. From about six weeks old, he will begin to gurgle and coo when you speak to him. Talk to him in an exaggerated voice, and leave silences for him to respond. He'll soon realize that he is part of the conversation, and add his own sounds to fill the silences. He will smile at you, and he will wave his arms and legs when he is excited and happy, and smiles soon turn to laughter.

Your baby will love the sound of his

own voice, and experiment with different sounds, which he will repeat over and over again. He will be able to anticipate feeds, bath-time and playtime with his parents, and he will wriggle with happiness when he knows something that he enjoys is just around the corner.

Talk to your baby whenever you can, even if you find it difficult at first. Set up situations that make it easier for you to chat with him. Try reading a story to him, and showing him colourful pictures. Take him for a walk, and point out all the new and different things he will never have seen before. If you are in the kitchen cooking, or busy with the housework, explain to him what you are doing, and try to involve him. Point out different things in his home, and play

with him when you are bathing him, or undressing him. You don't need to talk to him in baby talk, or make silly sounds, unless you want to. Your baby will just be happy to have your company, and will enjoy the rhythm and inflection of your voice, and he will soon respond in kind.

Early play

Play games with your baby that he likes – every baby has a different temperament, and some may like to be tickled, or even tossed gently in the air and caught. Others may like to hear music, or will respond to gentle chatter. Your baby's smiles and, by about five months, his ability to laugh out loud, will guide you in your choice of playtime activities. He will want to use his newly developed

senses – to taste things, stop and listen to sounds that interest him, watch movements and reactions, and smell the familiar and comforting scent of your body, a favourite blanket, or even an early food. He will love repetition – whether it is in the form of a rhyme recited over and over, or playing with the same group of toys. As he learns how things work, he will begin to try to do things for himself. He may try to imitate the cadence of your voice, or lift and shake a rattle, as he has seen you do. He will be endlessly delighted by one or two toys placed in front of him.

An interesting 'baby gym' can be the source of hours of entertainment for your baby. Choose one with a variety of shapes, sounds and textures, with hanging toys well within reach. Alternatively, you can make your own baby gym by stringing toys between two chairs at a height that he can both reach and kick at.

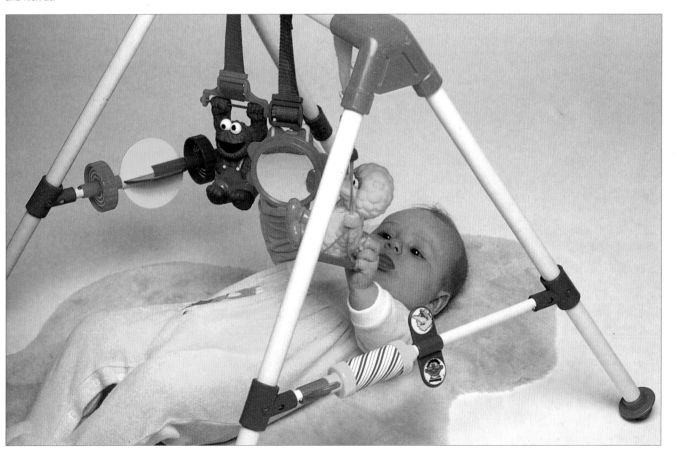

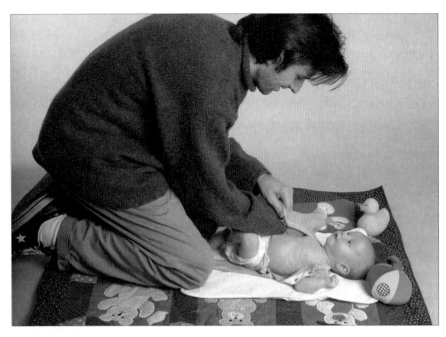

Nappy changing time is an ideal opportunity for a chat and a gentle play. If your baby associates changing with fun, he will be less likely to resist when he is older.

How you can help your child's development

Watching your child's development is fascinating. In what seems to be no time at all, your baby will have learned to sit, begun to crawl, stand, and then walk. As well as acquiring these 'motor skills', your baby will also be developing intellectually, socially and emotionally. He will begin to talk, play and interact with other people, and start to explore, understand and respond to the world around him. You have an important role to play by talking to him and reading with him, joining in his games, helping him to practise his new skills, praising and encouraging him, and eventually by answering his questions.

By monitoring your child's well-being and development, and detecting any abnormalities, you can ensure that he grows up as healthy as possible. You will be working in partnership with professionals such as health visitors and doctors, and there will be programmes set up to ensure that your baby has a series of health and developmental checks, up to the age of about five years old. The aim of these programmes is to detect any problems early, to prevent illness, and to promote good health and development.

In the first six months of life, your baby will probably have two checks – one around six to eight weeks, and another at about six months. In between checks you can visit your local baby clinic, or contact your doctor or health visitor if you have any concerns.

During routine checks, your doctor will measure your child's skills or developmental progress. Although all children develop at their own pace, the majority will have acquired basic skills by the time they reach a certain age. The following lists provide guidelines on the stages of development for most babies. These are only guidelines, however, and you should always talk to your doctor if you are worried. If necessary, an assessment can be done by a team of specialists at your local health centre, or hospital. (If your baby was premature, his development is assessed from his expected date of delivery rather than his actual birth date.)

By three to four months:

● grasps an object placed in his hand

● smiles spontaneously and begins to laugh

● makes cooing sounds and starts to babble

You will be the most fascinating person in the world to your baby, and she will love listening to your voice, and gazing at your face. Before long, she will begin to respond with her own 'chatter', and copy your facial expressions.

Your baby will watch your lips to see how you form certain sounds, so that she can imitate them.

- kicks vigorously without restricting clothes
- gets excited and waves his arms in the air
- holds up his head

Check with your doctor if he:

- does not smile
- does not startle when he hears loud sounds
- appears unresponsive
- has poor head control
- has a squint
- is stiff in his movements

By six months:

- grasps and holds objects in one hand
- transfers objects from hand to hand
- rolls over and back
- plays with his feet
- bears his weight when held in a standing position, and bounces

- drinks from a cup held to his lips, and can hold his own bottle
- finger feeds and begins to chew
- a cough, or a facial expression
- laughs, squeals in annoyance and uses double syllables, such as 'Mama', 'Dada' and 'ahgoo'
- turns to the sound of his mother's or father's voice
- watches adults move around a room
- sits when propped up
- starts to move on his tummy
- pushes up on his arms
- starts to be wary of strangers

Check with your doctor if he:

- appears unresponsive or uninterested
- has poor head control
- does not grasp or transfer objects
- does not turn to sounds
- has a squint

How development is helped by play

For your child, play is a serious learning process, which begins in the first weeks of life and continues throughout childhood. Through play your baby learns to use his five senses, at first by watching and listening, and then by touching, tasting, and smelling everything within reach. Play enables him to explore, discover, experiment and practise new skills, and once he has mastered them, go on to tackle greater challenges.

You are your baby's first teacher, and his very best toy. You and your baby will constantly learn from each other. Your baby will try to imitate your facial responses, and mouth movements when you talk or sing to him. You will respond when he touches you, or when he makes his first sounds, which will encourage him to do more to attract your attention. Your baby will be happy when you encourage and admire his achievements, and he will have a great need for praise and approval. Without even having to think about it, many parents will automatically provide the sort of stimulating environment that a baby needs for learning.

Teach your baby about different noises she can make using everyday household objects.

The importance of routine

Setting up your life in a series of ordered, sequential events may seem tedious and you may feel tied down by the monotonous regularity. However, babies thrive on routine, and you will find that your baby settles easier if he knows what to expect. As your baby slips into the routine that you have designed to suit both you and him, you'll know when to expect him to sleep or to want to feed, and you'll soon learn when you can snatch a few moments for yourself.

Long before they understand the words, babies will enjoy being read to and looking at the pictures in a story book.

Setting up routines doesn't mean that you have to be entirely inflexible or give up spontaneity. Good routines make it easy to comfort and settle your baby wherever you are, which can be a huge advantage, and provide you with freedom to go a little further afield. There is no point in trying to force a routine on a small baby, who will have his own agenda and timetable – unfortunately one that runs around the clock. You will need to set up a routine that fits into your baby's inborn schedule, and gently adapt it to suit your lifestyle.

The bedtime routine is one of the most important you can establish – even from the first days of motherhood. When your baby begins to recognize his own routine, he will relax and feel secure, and he will know what to expect. That means that you will be able to set the routine in motion wherever you are – in the spare bedroom of a friend's house for dinner, or perhaps on holiday.

Choose night-time rituals that you know your baby enjoys, or which comfort him. You may wish to begin after the evening feed or meal with a short playing session, winding down to some cuddling on the bed, or perhaps a

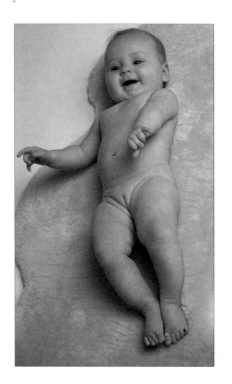

Babies love to roll around naked but watch out for accidents on your rug.

short massage session with some relaxing aromatherapy oils. A bath every day is not necessary, but many babies feel settled and calm after one. Take time to rub him dry and talk to him about what you are doing, and then settle down for a story together. Even a newborn baby will respond to colourful picture books, and the sound of your voice. You may wish to sing to your baby, or rock him for a while before you give him a final feed, or settle him down to sleep. Whatever you do, try to repeat the same order of events every night, and bedtime will soon be associated with pleasurable sensations, rather than the fear of being left alone.

Try to plan your day around a series of regular events. You may wish to dress him about the same time each day, and perhaps take him for a walk in the park, or to a friend's house in the mornings. If he is agreeable, you may begin to settle him down for naps around the same time each day. In the early days, most of your time will be spent feeding your baby, changing him, bathing him and getting him off to sleep, with very little time for yourself in between, but you will soon begin to discern a pattern in his activities, and that is the time to swoop down with a routine that both he and you can

As your baby grows older, she will probably not fall asleep immediately, and may need reassurance when you lay her down. Babies do need to learn to fall asleep on their own, and to associate bed with comfort and relaxation, so it is important not to get into the habit of waiting until she is asleep before putting her in her cot.

recognize and work with. Paradoxically, a routine will give you freedom, and will help your baby to be confident as he goes about his familiar activities. You will also find that even if you are feeding on demand your baby will slip into a rhythm of waiting to feed at particular times and you should encourage this regularity.

A healthy diet

Your baby's main food for the first year of her life will be milk – it is easily digested and provides all the nutrition that she needs. There comes a time, however, around the fourth to the sixth month (later in some children), when she will need a little more. Weaning your baby from the breast or bottle can be a time-consuming and long-term project, and it is best to start gradually by introducing new tastes one at a time.

Don't be surprised if your baby isn't interested, and rejects anything that doesn't come with a teat on the end of it. If that's the case, try a few new tastes, and if she still won't have it, give up and wait for a few weeks and then try again. Early foods merely supplement milk feeds, and there is no reason to worry if your baby has nothing but milk for the first six or seven months of life.

You may be impatient to begin solids for various reasons – perhaps because you are returning to work, and you think your baby will be able to go a little longer between milk feeds, or perhaps you wish to stop breastfeeding altogether. But try not to rush it – your baby will let you know when she is ready,

and if you force solid food on her any earlier, you can be setting up all sorts of problems that will be manifested in later months and years.

Your baby may be ready when she shows signs of being interested in food – perhaps she has begun reaching out for food on your plate when you are eating, or she seems determined to eat her toys. Some mothers decide that their baby needs 'more' when she continues to wake repeatedly at night, but beware! Many babies have wakeful periods at night during the first six months, and their waking may be unrelated to hunger. Their need to feed in the night – towards the end of the first six months – is more likely to stem from a need for comfort. You may end up starting her on solids earlier than you would like in the

hope that she will sleep better when, in fact, solids introduced too early can have quite the opposite effect.

Some babies will thrive on milk for the first twelve months, so don't panic if you have a slow beginner. If you wish to stop breastfeeding, you can switch to the bottle long before you need to give solid foods. Similarly, it is not advisable to give solid foods to a baby that is younger than three months. It is now believed that babies' digestive systems are not mature enough to cope with solids before this time, and they will be more prone to food allergies, rashes, diarrhoea and tummy ache if you do. Wait as long as you can, and the chances are that your baby will welcome those first tastes.

Changing from breast to bottle

If you have been breastfeeding and want to change over to bottle-feeding with formula for any reason, you should try to do it gradually. First of all, your baby may not take kindly to the idea of a rubber alternative to your breast, and she may not like the taste of formula. Secondly, and most importantly, you must give up gradually so that your milk supply diminishes slowly, in line with the reduced demand for it. When you are ready to change from the breast to the bottle, talk to your health visitor or

You may wish to invest in some specially designed baby feeding equipment. Choose cutlery with chunky, easy-to-manage hands, and a beaker that your baby can grasp with ease. A plastic bowl is a must, since your baby will soon find it an exciting game to pitch the bowl and its contents over the side of the high chair.

doctor before you begin, and she will be able to provide you with some expert advice, to make the transition easier. Some women find that a baby who will not take the bottle is more eager to try it if you wrap a scarf, or another article of your clothing, by her face, so that she can smell you, and will come to associate the bottle with a pleasurable and comforting way of feeding. Or you could try smoothing a little of your nipple cream on the end of the teat, which will provide a first familiar taste to get her to suck.

First foods

Your baby's first foods are intended to be tastes, rather than nutritional supplements, although it is important to choose foods that are nutritious, and which will not put any strain on her immature digestive system. In the

Remember when giving your baby either water or milk from a bottle, to hold it at an angle so that the teat is completely full, and they won't get wind.

When your baby has progressed from baby rice and puréed fruits, you may wish to try a good brand of baby muesli, with a variety of grains and fruits.

beginning you will need to purée everything, making it as sloppy as possible, as she will suck it rather than eat it, until she becomes accustomed to the different consistencies.

The best first foods

Puréed:

- apple, pear, peaches, apricots, bananas
- parsnips, swede, green beans, squash, sweet potato, cauliflower, carrots, spinach, potato (thinned with a little milk), peas, broccoli
- baby rice

From about four to five months, you can begin to introduce other cereals, such as wheat, oats and barley, to add some variety. Whichever solids you decide to offer, remember to introduce one new food at a time, for three to four days, to give your baby a chance to grow to like it, before offering another food. It may take some time for her to become accustomed to a new taste, and it will also give you an opportunity to pinpoint any adverse reactions to certain foods.

Only offer a small amount to begin with – about a teaspoonful at first, which you can increase a little more each day. When she is used to the first tastes, let her guide you as to how much she wants to eat – within reason: your baby may love the taste of pureed apricots or pears, and may be happy to eat them in unlimited quantities.

To begin with, offer her solid food once a day, and over the next few weeks this can be gradually increased to three or four times a day. The speed at which you can increase the frequency of her first solid foods will depend on her appetite, and how quickly she becomes accustomed to eating.

Choose a time that suits her. Although it is preferable for her to eat with the family, it is not essential, nor does she need three balanced main meals. Offer the first foods halfway through a feed, so that she is not starving enough to demand her favourite food (milk), but she still has appetite enough to want more. Let her finish her meal off with milk, if you like. You can also try the first tastes at the end of a feed, if she is not too full.

Prepare the dish in advance, and have it ready to give to your baby at the right moment. Baby foods should be gently heated to lukewarm (test a little on your

Make sure that your baby seat or high chair has a safety harness.

wrist, or your lip) to make them more palatable and appealing.

You will need:

● bibs

● plastic spoons or small weaning spoons, which are soft on your baby's mouth and gums, and which are the right size to fit into her mouth

● a small bowl or dish. If your baby is old enough to reach out for things, or swipe them off a surface, you are probably better off with plastic.

● a blender or liquidizer, if you are planning to prepare food yourself

Remember that until at least four months of age, your baby's feeding equipment must be sterilized, and that means everything that will come into contact with your baby's food or mouth when starting solids.

What to do

You may wish to feed your baby the first tastes while she is sitting on your lap, or in her favourite chair. It may be daunting for her to find herself in a new highchair, with a variety of new equipment and tastes being introduced

Mix puréed vegetables with some baby pasta for a nutritious supper.

at the same time. Leave a high chair until much later, unless she accustomed to sitting in one.

Scoop up a tiny bit of food purée and put the spoon just inside her mouth. She may reject it first of all, but you can rub a little on her lips, so that she will get used to the new taste and consistency. Don't be surprised if she

Try puréeing a blend of different vegetables and fruits when your baby has experienced her first tastes. Carrots and apple are a good combination, or try potatoes with a little parsnip or puréed courgette.

sucks the food off the spoon, and then spits it back out again. Babies probably take in only about a quarter of what you feed them over the first few weeks. Gently scrape what she has spat out back up her chin and into her mouth as you go.

These first tastes are not intended to be meals, merely an introduction to the idea of food, so don't panic if she gets very little. Let her enjoy the food, and make a mess if she wants to. She will need to learn that food, and mealtimes, are a pleasant experience, and if she feels forced to eat, or picks up tension from you, food will begin to have negative associations for her.

After a couple of weeks, if all goes well, you can try solid food twice a day, building up the quantities gradually, when she seems ready for them. You can also make the food slightly thicker as she becomes accustomed to it, and when she reaches the point where she takes enough at one meal, you can give up that milk feed altogether. When she has tasted her way through a variety of fresh fruits and vegetables, you can introduce some fish or lean meats such as chicken or turkey. These will need to be cooked and puréed before eating, and you will probably need to add a little milk or water to make them more palatable.

Drinks

Initially, your baby will be getting enough liquid from the milk she is drinking, but as she starts to eat increasing amounts of solid foods, she may become thirsty and require a little to drink. Some mothers offer the bottle alongside a meal, but it may be easier to buy a lidded plastic beaker specially designed for younger babies, which has a spout with small holes, and offer her small sips from that, so that she gets used to the idea of drinking from something other than a bottle. If she sucks too hard, and chokes or splutters, try offering her drinks on a spoon, and let her sip/suck them off in smaller quantities.

Let her have the beaker to hold, even if she is clumsy with it. Most babies won't be able to hold it properly, or bring it to their mouths until well after six months, but she should be given the opportunity to experiment with it until she learns what to do.

The best drink is water – and it should be boiled and cooled before serving. If you plan to use fruit juices, dilute them

until there is not much more than flavour.

Try not worry about the mess. New babies are notorious for splattering both themselves and the kitchen with even the tiniest quantities of food and drink, but that is all part of the learning experience, and she should feel comfortable to practise her new skills.

Preparing first foods

You may choose to use ready-prepared foods rather than make your own in the early days, particularly when she is taking very little. Try to make sure that you give your baby foods that do not contain salt, sugar or any additives, and if you can afford it, organic will be more

When your baby begins to teethe, you may wish to give her specially prepared, sugar-free teething biscuits or rusks. Other foods should be puréed to a fairly liquid consistency, as she will begin by sucking it off the spoon.

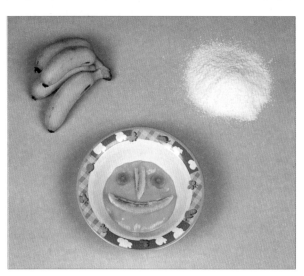

Baby rice is an ideal first food, and all your baby will need for the first few weeks of weaning. When she has adjusted to the idea that food can come from a spoon as easily as a teat, try introducing puréed fruits, one at a time, and allow her to experiment with different textures and flavours.

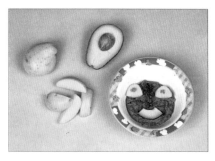

Choose a variety of fresh vegetables to purée, and introduce them one at a time to let her get used to the taste, and ensure that she doesn't have an allergic or other reaction to them. She may wish to hold a suitable 'finger food', such as firm avocado or gently toasted bread, while you feed her.

nutritious and less likely to contain pesticides and fertilizers.

You may wish to prepare your own food – using leftover carrots from your family meal, for example. Lightly cook foods like apples and vegetables before you puree them, and add a little cooled, boiled water if the consistency seems to be too thick. There are a number of liquidizers and blenders available for making small quantities, or for puréeing in the dish or the pan, and if you plan to make most of your baby's meals, it might be worth investing in one.

First finger foods

Your baby may like to hold some foods and try to eat them herself. In the early days she will probably do nothing more than gnaw on them, and make a mess. Don't ever give her anything that can break and cause her to choke. Ideal first finger foods are teething biscuits, rice crackers (without salt), rusks, or even a raw, peeled carrot, which she will not be able to chew. Finger foods are not intended to supply nutrition, they will simply get her used to putting food in her mouth, and encourage her to explore new tastes and textures.

Many foods are considered to be common 'allergens', which means that they are more likely to cause an allergic reaction, or sensitivity in your baby, particularly if they are introduced too early. Wait until your baby is around a year old before introducing citrus fruits, strawberries and cow's milk, and watch her carefully to ensure that she doesn't react in any way. Nuts, in the form of nut butters, are usually fine after about a year, if your child is not allergic, but whole nuts should not be given to pre-school children, because of the danger of choking.

Foods to avoid

● Egg white should be avoided until after six months old, because of the risk of allergy.

● Pork and lamb should wait until she is older, too, because they are too fatty for her to digest easily; oily fish will be too rich.

● Strawberries, blackcurrants and tomatoes should be avoided until after six months because they are common allergens, and they contain pips which may cause her to gag.

● Avoid food with any salt, which can put unnecessary strain on her kidneys.

● Spices can be very gradually introduced after about six or seven months.

● Sugary foods or drinks, which can encourage a sweet tooth, and promote tooth decay.

● Cow's milk, which should not be offered until after at least six months. Give breast milk or formula until this time. Cow's milk is a common allergen, and the later you leave it, the more likely she is to take it without problems.

● Fried foods are not good for her. Lightly steam foods when you cook them, and avoid using butter or oil.

● Wheat and other grains that contain gluten should be avoided for as long as possible if you have a history of food allergy.

● Nuts are also common allergens, and should not be introduced until your baby is much older.

Always hold your baby while she drinks from a bottle to minimize the risk of choking.

Common problems

Crying

Babies cry for different reasons, and although we are told that the average baby cries for about four hours a day, there are few that conform. If your baby cries inconsolably for hours, she may have colic (see page 153), or she may simply be hungry, uncomfortable, or she may require constant physical comfort. She may have nappy rash (see page 152), or she may have a problem with formula milk, or if you are breastfeeding her, with something that you have eaten.

Many babies cry because they are tired. Lack of sleep causes irritability just as it does in older children and adults, and makes it even more difficult to fall asleep. Babies are also very sensitive to their environment, and if you are feeling angry or tense for any reason, she may sense it and cry even harder. As your baby becomes more settled – usually around the six-week to three-month mark – her crying will change and you will be able to distinguish between the cries that indicate her different needs.

What you can do

● Many babies respond to being held and rocked, although you may find, frustratingly, that something that worked one day may not work the next. If your baby does require constant comfort, you may want to carry her next to your body in a sling, as you get on with things around the house.

Most babies will cry when they are hungry or uncomfortable, or just lonely. Never leave your baby to cry – check first to see if she is hungry, or if her nappy needs to be changed. It may just be that she wants the comfort of your arms, which will make her feel secure.

● Rhythmical sounds soothe many babies, and you can buy a recording of a mother's heartbeat as your baby would have heard it in the womb, which can be very effective. Low music may also help, and many babies will settle instantly at the sound of the vacuum cleaner – mothers have admitted to taping the sound of the cleaner, and replaying it to their baby when things get tough.

● If your baby is eased off to sleep by rocking, bring her pram or pushchair inside, and settle yourself in a position where you can comfortably rock the cradle with a free hand or foot.

● Many babies like to feel securely wrapped, and you can make her feel more comfortable by swaddling her – that is, wrapping her quite tightly in a blanket – before settling her down. Other babies may feel too constrained by blankets and covers, and want only a light blanket.

● Some need to suck to get to sleep, or to settle, which is why they feed almost constantly when they are upset. Sucking will not stop a hungry baby from crying, unless he gets milk from it, but it will certainly soothe a crying baby who is not hungry. Your baby might benefit from a soother (dummy), which can always be used as a last resort, or you can help her to find her thumb or fingers, which she might want to suck to quiet herself.

● Make sure she is not hungry – calm her down before a feed by giving her a light massage with a soothing oil, perhaps blended 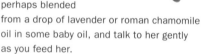 from a drop of lavender or roman chamomile oil in some baby oil, and talk to her gently as you feed her.

● If she is frightened of the bath, avoid giving her a whole-body bath, and concentrate on topping and tailing (see page 125), which will be adequate until she is old enough to cope better.

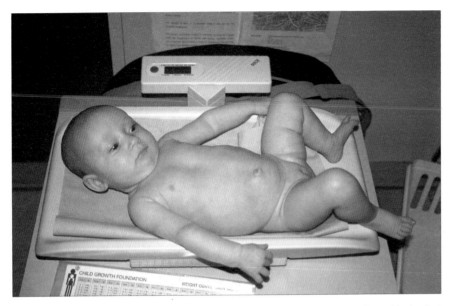

Your baby's weight is often used to assess whether or not she is growing normally, and in the first months of life, she will be weighed regularly to ensure that all is well. Babies all go through periods of slow weight gain, and some babies may appear to put on weight much more quickly than others. The average-sized baby will put on about an ounce (30g) per day until the age of about three months, and anything well above or under that figure may be noted by your doctor or health visitor.

● If you are tense, and find it difficult to cope with her crying, take a few drops of Rescue Remedy on your tongue, which normally provides nearly instant relief. Take time for yourself, perhaps giving her to your partner while you have a soothing bath with lavender oil, or drink a cup of chamomile tea. If you are feeling exhausted, see pages 148-9 for some tips.

● Flower essences are also gentle enough for babies, and if your baby is distressed and fearful, she may respond to mimulus, or try chicory if she needs constant attention and reassurance.

● You may find that if you set up a routine that makes her feel secure (page 168), she will calm down and feel more comfortable in the day.

● If crying begins after feeding, after switching from breastmilk to formula or a change in formula, talk to your health visitor or midwife. There may be problems with the formula she is taking.

Weight gain

Most parents keep a watchful eye on their baby's weight gain. In some baby clinics there is a positive rivalry between new mothers, while others may be worried that their babies are becoming too chubby. Try to remember that every baby is different, and if she is fed the correct diet, she will grow at the rate that is right for her. A baby who begins with a weight advantage – a higher birthweight – is likely to

remain heavier than babies with a lower birthweight, but each of these is likely to fall within the norm.

Your baby's weight will be checked regularly at a baby clinic, and recorded on a weight chart. In the early months, her weight gain is likely to be rapid, doubling between four and six months of age. It should ideally follow a steady curve as she grows bigger. If your baby's weight falls too far below her average, she may not be getting enough to eat, and you can address this by changing your method of feeding, or perhaps changing the formula if you are bottle-feeding.

Teething

Most babies get their first teeth between about four and six months of age, but there may be problems with teeth coming through until the age of two or three. The majority experience some discomfort, which can range from simply being clingy and fractious, to dribbling, loosened stools and problems sleeping. Many experts insist that there is no evidence to confirm that babies may become unwell with teething, but mothers have quite different experiences, and your happy baby may experience a variety of complaints.

What you can do
● Offer your baby a cool teething ring to gnaw on, and rub her gums with a clean finger. If she has trouble sleeping, rocking may help.

● The homeopathic remedy Chamomilla is standard for teething, and can be taken as required for up to six times a day to ease symptoms and relieve the distress.

● Rub a little Rescue Remedy directly into the gums, or apply to pulse points if your baby is crying inconsolably. A few drops at night will help her to sleep, as will a few drops of lavender on the bedclothes.

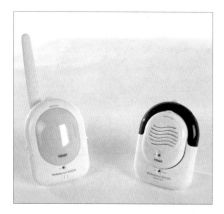

A baby monitor is a must if you have a big house, or if you are unable to hear your baby when you leave the room. You may find a baby monitor reassuring, particularly when your baby is very young.

● A little of the essential oils of chamomile and lavender can be added to the bathwater to calm a distressed baby.

Worrying about cot death

It is normal for parents to be concerned about the possibility of cot or crib death, and you may feel anxious about the safety of your baby when she is very small – particularly if you know someone to whom this tragedy has occurred. Cot death is the sudden death of an apparently healthy baby between two weeks and a year old, due to unknown causes. About 95 percent of all cases occur between two and four months of

age. The condition occurs more frequently in male babies; low-birthweight babies, particularly premature babies; babies born to mothers who used narcotics during pregnancy; babies of parents who smoke; and babies with recent respiratory infections.

What you can do

● European studies have shown that babies who sleep on their stomachs are more vulnerable to cot death, as are babies who sleep on soft bedding or in overheated rooms, and overbundled babies. Some studies suggest that babies who sleep with their parents are less at risk, possibly because parents are more alert to changes in their baby's breathing.

● Certainly the incidence rises when your baby is in contact with tobacco smoke, so make sure that no one smokes in her presence, or even in the same house, if you can help it.

● If you are concerned, keep a baby monitor in your baby's room while she is sleeping, or bring her cot into your room when she is small.

Household safety

As soon as your baby is old enough to reach out, or to roll, it is wise to take simple precautions to ensure her safety, including:

● keeping a first-aid kit on hand (see page 248)

Keep alcohol, matches, cigarettes, hot drinks and other hazardous substances well out of your baby's way.

● installing stair gates at the top and bottom of the stairs

● getting a fire guard if you have an open fire or gas fire

● putting plastic plugs in unused wall sockets, and turning plugs off

● never placing your baby's chair, basket or carry cot on a raised surface – only the floor will be completely safe

● keeping babies away from the cooking area, and ensuring all sharp or hot items

Fix stairgates to the top and bottom of stairs until your baby is confident enough to manage them without supervision.

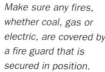

Make sure any fires, whether coal, gas or electric, are covered by a fire guard that is secured in position.

Cupboard locks are essential for any cupboard that contains items that are heavy, dangerous or inappropriate for children. You may wish to keep your stereo, books, or articles of value in a locked cupboard, until your baby is old enough to understand that your possessions are not toys.

are kept well out of reach and not left on the edge of a table.

● keeping flexes coiled up on the counter, or using a flex guard, so that she can't pull appliances down on herself

● fitting a refrigerator lock, and child-resistant catches on drawers

● placing a guard around the cooker, and keeping your pan handles turned away

● installing a thermometer in your baby's bedroom, and checking her frequently to ensure that she is not too hot or too cold, and that she is sleeping on her back

● using flame-resistant bedding and sleepwear

● positioning the cot away from the window, and always locking windows that are within a baby's reach.

● keeping your hot drinks, alcohol, cigarettes and matches and all other poisonous substances well out of the reach of little hands.

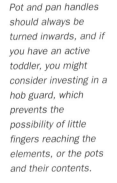

Pot and pan handles should always be turned inwards, and if you have an active toddler, you might consider investing in a hob guard, which prevents the possibility of little fingers reaching the elements, or the pots and their contents.

A toilet lock may seem unnecessary, but if your baby or toddler is particularly adventurous, he may be tempted to try to reach the water, or to empty the contents of the bathroom cupboard into the bowl.

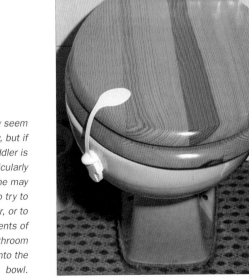

Immunization

Immunization involves giving a mild or inactivated form of an infectious disease to a healthy baby or child, so that she will fight it off and in this way build up an immunity against it. Your health visitor or doctor will explain to you that immunization is one of the most important ways that you can protect your child from some severe infections.

Why immunize?

Whooping cough, diphtheria, tetanus, polio, measles, mumps, rubella and Hib (Haemophilus influenza type b) are diseases which babies and children are liable to catch, and they can often be more serious than you may realize. Many of these illnesses have severe complications, and sometimes they can be fatal. Through widespread immunization, polio and whooping cough are now very rare in the West, but they could still recur. There are still epidemics of whooping cough and measles, and both these illnesses can lead to complications such as brain damage. Mumps is the most common cause of viral meningitis in the under-15s, and may even cause permanent deafness. Meningitis and other serious infections could follow Hib. Tetanus causes painful muscle spasms, and can be fatal. Rubella, if caught by a woman in the first four months of pregnancy, may lead to the baby being born with heart, sight, hearing defects and brain damage.

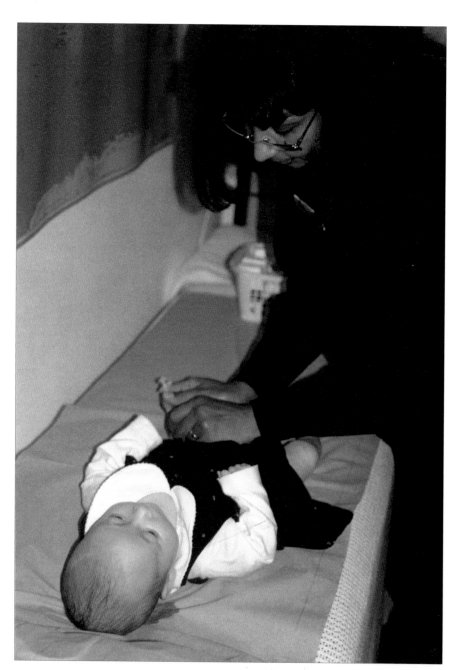

Most babies will receive their immunization shots in the muscle of the upper leg or buttock, although in some cases the arms are used. Don't be surprised to see an immediate 'local' reaction, including some redness, swelling and a hard bump. Many parents are distressed when their babies cry after the innoculation, but it is important to be calm and reassuring. The injections are not painful, and if you continue to smile and offer comfort, your baby will not become frightened.

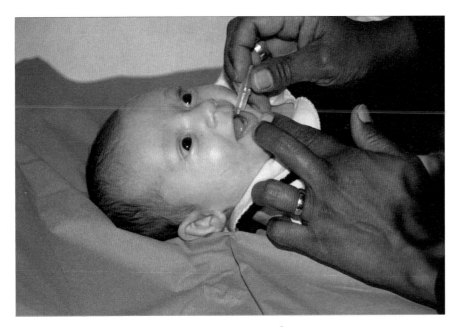

The polio vaccine is given orally, from a small phial, and most babies do not object to a little taste of something sweet! If you have not been vaccinated, your physician may recommend that you have some too!

Immunization has been the focus of intense debate over the last years. The conventional view is that mass immunization is necessary, both for the protection of the child and the community at large. Other schools of thought have argued that acquiring childhood illnesses is a natural part of childhood, that a healthy child will successfully fight off the disease, and through that develop a natural immunity. There are risks pertaining to vaccination, of varying severity. Doctors insist that the risks of vaccination are minimal compared with the risks of the disease in question, and that there are no real dangers involved for children who have no contra-indications to vaccinations (see box). There are a number of possible short-term side-effects, such as fever, local reactions to the injection and headaches, and some claim that there are more long-term effects, including allergies and chronic disease patterns which may manifest themselves later in life. There is also some evidence to suggest that the effect of vaccines is short-lived, and that some children go on to contract the disease later in life even after immunization.

Parents who instinctively balk at the idea of immunization may be put under considerable pressure from the medical profession to reconsider, and should bear in mind the threat to pregnant women, the elderly and adult males that exposure to some childhood illnesses pose, before finally coming to a decision.

Contra-indications to immunization

Some children should not be immunized, including those:

● with a history of convulsions;

● with a family history of epilepsy;

● with a weakened immune system (this can be due to current illness, convalescence, or chronic illness);

● who have already had the disease in question (medically confirmed);

● suffering from hyperactivity

● with an allergy to eggs; a special vaccine made without egg protein can be made

Caution: Side-effects of immunization should not last longer than a week or two, and a small reaction is usually interpreted as a sign that your child is fighting the infection and developing an immunity. When side-effects last longer or appear more serious than the general malaise, fever, bad temper and diarrhoea, see your doctor.

If you have concerns about immunization, talk to your doctor or health visitor, or perhaps a registered complementary health practitioner with experience in this field. You must make the decision to the best of your ability, based on the advice of a doctor you trust.

In many countries, immunization is required by law. In the UK, your young baby will be immunized as follows:

Hib

One injection	2, 3, 4 months

Diphtheria , Whooping cough, Tetanus

One injection known as DPT	2, 3, 4 months

Polio

By mouth	2, 3 4 months

There are many natural remedies that can help your baby to cope better with any side-effects of immunisation. A homeopath may recommend Arnica (at 6x) hourly for the first day, which prevents bruising, and Ledum, for puncture wounds. If your baby is more difficult to settle in the days immediately after the injection, try a daily massage with a few drops of Roman chamomile oil in a light carrier oil. This will help to soothe, and to relax your baby. Tea tree oil is a great immune stimulator, and you can add a drop to your baby's bathwater to encourage a good response.

Baby landmarks

By the second half of the first year, your baby will be taking an increasingly active part in life, and will have become an established member of your family. He will be aware of everything going on around him, and it won't be long before he is on the move, making sure he is not left out of anything. This is a fascinating period of physical development, and it may seem that no sooner have you helped him to sit on his own than he is off, following you when he can, and getting into virtually everything he can lay his hands on.

Every baby has their own method of movement, and an inefficient bottom shuffle or see-sawing crawl soon turns into the real thing, and he will become adept at outwitting you and escaping your clutches. Your previously safe home may now become a minefield of potential dangers, and if you haven't done so already, you will need to childproof it (see pages 178–9). The days of moving him with you as you go about the house are over – he will be off and crawling in the other direction without a moment's hesitation, and into trouble before you know it. He may laugh when you say 'no', and continue in his carefree way to explore his surroundings. You will need to be one step ahead at all times, and keep yourself sane by remembering that all babies do eventually learn what is acceptable and what is not. He will learn by feeling, tasting and smelling, as well as by looking and hearing, and everything he comes into contact with will end up in his mouth, so beware of leaving sharp or small objects where he can reach them.

Many parents find this period emotionally rewarding, as they are given the honour of being their baby's 'special people', and there is nothing more loyal than a baby of six to ten or eleven months. Your baby will want to be with you at all times, and, around nine months, may experience separation anxiety when you are out of sight (even for a few moments). His face will light up when he sees you, and he will gurgle with delight when you join in his games. He will smother you with affection, and make it very clear that he would rather spend his time with you than with any other person.

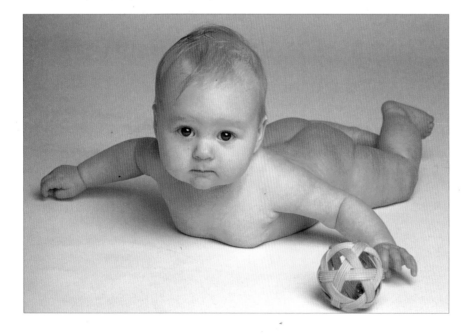

Your baby will love the occasional session 'au naturel', free of the confines of nappy and constricting clothes. Place a towel on the floor of a warm, draught-free room, and allow her to kick and roll as she pleases.

As well as being rewarding, this period can, however, be frustrating, as you may feel so tied to your baby. You may be daunted by the constant affection and attention given and required by your baby, and by the fact that he may cry or become unable to occupy himself if you are out of his sight. He will also become suspicious of strangers for the first time, and you may find him clingy and difficult when others are around.

Feeding will settle down, and you may wish to give up breastfeeding altogether during this period, or limit it to the evenings, or first thing in the morning. Your baby will be generally happier, and less likely to cry as your routines are established and he knows when to expect to play, to eat, to sleep, and to share your company. He will have learned to use his voice in other ways, by shouting at you, laughing, and chattering, and he will begin to really

She will quickly become more adept at crawling and some babies can move astonishingly fast.

play with you – mimicking your actions and facial expressions, and even your sounds.

Sleeping habits are usually established by your baby's first birthday, and you may be able to persuade him to take two regular naps during the day, and to sleep through the night without waking (see page 188), which will help to ease the exhaustion that may have you for plagued the first six months of his life.

Your baby will love experiencing the pleasures of the park, or indeed any trip outdoors. Remember that everything is new and exciting to her, and she will find the things that we take for granted – trees, cars, flowers, other children – endlessly fascinating. Talk to her as you take her out for walks, pointing out people at work, clouds, buses – anything that catches her interest. A daily trip out can be relaxing for both of you, and form a part of a good daily routine.

Eating and growing

By the age of six months, your baby will probably be beginning to want to assert his independence by feeding himself. His nutritional needs will be growing, and he will need less milk and more in the form of nourishing food. His weight gain slows down so that he will gain only two or three ounces (on average) per week, and his rate of growth will probably be less of a preoccupation.

Weaning your baby

You will probably want to begin weaning your baby when he drops the fourth milk feed of the day, and begins to settle down to a regular pattern of three meals per day. A gradual start to weaning is probably easier for you and for him, and you may want to begin by putting his lunchtime milk in a beaker that he can sip, or be helped to sip, himself. Breastfed babies can continue to take their milk from you, until they are ready to have all of it from a cup, although you may use bottles or beakers for juice or water, if you wish.

Weaning a bottle-fed baby

Babies are less likely to grow bored of bottles than they are of the breast, so you may have to make a concerted effort to wean him, particularly if he is becoming too attached. If your baby starts needing it more and more as a comfort object, he may begin to demand it in the middle of the night, or at odd times of the day – at which point, you may need to draw the line. Ease in the changes so that he does not suddenly lose an important source of comfort, and you can be hopeful that he will not notice when the bottle is gone completely. Introduce a cup by six months old, and abandon the lunchtime bottle completely in favour of solid foods. As soon as your baby is able to sleep through the night, try giving up the night-time bottle, too. Make sure that he doesn't use the bottle as a cup, and that you lie him down and feed him in your arms when you give him milk from the bottle. He'll soon get bored with the idea of lying still for long periods of time, and will probably begin to take less and less.

Solid foods

As you wean your baby, the foods he eats will become more than first tastes – they will form the backbone of his growth

Weaning a breastfed baby

Some babies decide for themselves when they want to stop breastfeeding, and you may find that your baby is too independent and interested in his surroundings to settle down sufficiently to feed, or suddenly rejects your breast. Other babies are happy to carry on breastfeeding until they are toddlers. Choose the time to wean that is best for both of you. It is important, however, to take things gradually. Avoid stopping suddenly, which can make your baby feel rejected, and which can cause you some discomfort, as your breasts continue to make milk. Try offering milk in a cup for one meal at a time, and gradually decrease breastfeeds between meals. As your baby requires less from you, your breasts will produce less milk, which means that even when he is hungry there will be less for him. He will soon realize that he is more satisfied by solid foods, and suckling will become a comfort rather than a need. The night-time feed is usually the last to go, and you can decide when it feels comfortable to give it up. Your baby may find it difficult to sleep without the comfort of the last feed, and you may enjoy sharing this time together, particularly if you have gone back to work and you are seeing less of him. Most babies will give up of their own accord by about twelve months, but do not force the issue, unless you are finding that it is a habit you really want to break.

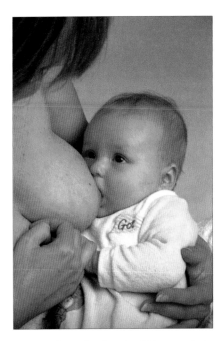

Giving up breastfeeding should be a gradual process.

and development, and you will have to plan his nutritional intake carefully to ensure that he gets enough of the necessary vitamins and minerals, as well as proteins, fats and carbohydrates. From about six months, your baby can probably drink cow's milk, but if you have allergies in your family, or he has proved to have trouble digesting it, stick to the formula you have been using throughout the first six months of his life, or try a soya-based milk. Your baby will need full-fat milk, as his need for energy will be great as he grows bigger.

A healthy diet

If you are busy, and have little time for food preparation, you may wish to use commercially prepared baby foods, which can be both convenient and easy to use. Try not to feed your baby on these products exclusively, as they usually work out to be more expensive, and they tend to be of similar consistency. Commercially prepared foods can also be bland, and you have no control over

the ingredients used to prepare them. Your baby needs variety, and good, wholesome food, with different tastes, textures and consistencies. If he has spent the second six months of his life eating from a jar, he is not going to adjust easily to family foods when the time comes. If you do decide to use ready-to-eat brands, avoid foods with preservatives, artificial colours, flavour and added sugar or salt. Don't feed straight from the jar, and store uneaten food for no more than 24 hours.

Your baby will need about 800 calories a day by now, some of which he will be getting from his milk. You can base the remainder of his caloric intake around a well-balanced diet.

Foods for six- to eight-month-olds

- Choose fresh foods that can be mashed or minced to the texture of cottage cheese.
- Add water or milk to thin if necessary.
- Peel fruits and vegetables carefully, removing any pips and strings.
- Trim fat off fish and meat.
- Try mincing foods such as chicken, fish, boiled egg, fruits or vegetables, and then add finger foods.
- Suitable finger foods for this age group include fruits, cubes of cheese, bread, bread sticks, rice crackers

(without salt) and unsweetened cereal.

Foods for eight- to nine-month-olds

- Your baby will be able to chew more, and you can now introduce food with a lumpier, or chunkier consistency.
- Try chopping food rather than mincing it, and offer small portions of your own food, if it does not contain too many seasonings.
- Good foods may include mashed beans, scrambled eggs, rice, baby-sized pasta, lean minced beef, shepherd's pie, soups, chopped fresh vegetables and fruits, and mashed potatoes and bread.
- Suitable finger foods may include carrots, celery, apple (grated or in pieces), avocado, peaches, apricots, oat biscuits made without sugar or salt, and breadsticks.

Foods for ten to twelve-month-olds

- As he nears his first birthday, your baby will be able to eat what the rest of the family is eating, but ensure that it is chopped into manageable, bite-sized pieces.
- You can now introduce tinned tuna, well-cooked pork, lamb with the fat cut off and drained, and some fruits such as oranges and raspberries, which were not appropriate in early babyhood.

Try to choose a good-quality brown bread for your baby, but try to stay away from wholegrains that are too dense, as his immature digestive system will not be able to manage it. White bread is all right for babies, but the nutritional content is low due to the refining process.

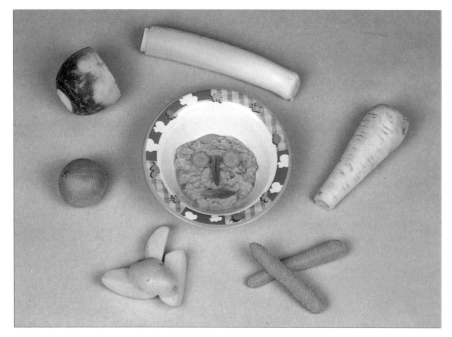

As your baby becomes accustomed to a variety of different foods, you will be able to purée, or mash whatever your family is having, blending vegetables with lean meats and even adding a fresh fruit pudding course!

● He will be able to pick up a broccoli 'tree' and try to eat it himself, or gnaw at a Brussels sprout.

● Try to include some foods that require feeding (which he will be learning to do himself) and others that he will be able to pick up and eat himself.

Helping your baby to feed himself

At some point between six and twelve months of age, your baby will want to start feeding himself, and he will attempt to explore and examine his food in much the same way as he does his toys. Help him by continuing to feed

Eggs and cheese are not normally recommended for the first months of weaning, as they are common allergens.

him yourself, but let him play with his food, and try not to think about the mess, which is a necessary part of his experimentation. He will want to see what happens when he squishes cereal through his fingers, or mixes his fruit into his cheese. Don't worry if he seems to eat odd combinations of foods, and it doesn't matter if he chooses his dessert before his main course.

Keep a warm washcloth available to wipe his face, but don't be over-fussy, or he will become frustrated. Show him how to handle his spoon, and let him use his hands. Be patient, and encourage him to think of mealtimes as a happy time. They are undoubtedly a learning experience, and as he grows his co-ordination will develop.

Hold his beaker for him, and encourage hom to take sips. Place it in his hands and show him how to bring it to his mouth. Don't be surprised if he is

Preparing your own baby foods

If you have a liquidizer, it will be easy to prepare small quantities of whatever you are eating for your baby to try. Preparing your baby's food allows you to decide on the nutritional balance of the meal, and to choose ingredients which are fresh and healthy.

● Food for your baby should be cooked without salt and with very little fat.

● Fresh vegetables are best steamed or lightly cooked.

● Don't pre-cut fruit and vegetables and leave them in water, or in air, for long periods of time, or their nutritional value will be compromised.

● Don't use stock cubes or yeast extracts, which are high in salt.

● Young babies will find too much fat indigestible, so choose lean cuts of meat.

● Remove the skin from chicken, and cut the fat off meat.

● Use butter and margarine sparingly.

● Purée baby food to a smooth consistency, adding a little milk or water if necessary.

● As he grows older, you will be able to chop rather than purée his foods, and he will learn to chew.

● Make large casseroles, or prepare large quantities of fruits and vegetables, and freeze them in small containers. Most foods will freeze well, and you will soon build up a variety of ready-prepared meals to have on hand for busy times.

● When reheating food, place it in a heat-resistant cup within a pan of gently boiling water. If you use a microwave, take care to stir it constantly, to avoid 'hot spots'.

● Try to include at each meal: some brown bread, cereal or potato (carbohydrates), a little fish, chicken, milk, beans or meat (protein) and some fresh fruits and vegetables (fibre and extra vitamins and minerals).

more interested in shaking its contents into his food, or spraying you and the walls with his enthusiastic waving.

Choose a stable highchair with a safety

Mashed potato is a filling, nutritious meal, and a great 'base' for other chopped or minced foods. Try a basic 'shepherd's pie', with puréed minced meat and carrots in the base, and a mashed potato topping.

- See that your child gets at least two good, nutritious hot meals each day.

- Like adults and older children, babies will need five servings of fresh fruits and vegetables each day. If vegetables or fruits are unpopular, try grating them and adding them to other dishes, or use a juicer to extract juices and add them to foods and drinks that your child will like. Fresh carrot juice is sweet and delicious, high in vitamins and other nutrients, and most children love the taste. Other vegetables, such as cucumbers and beets (after the age of six months), can be added to juices or drunk on their own.

- Don't eliminate fats from your baby's diet. Unlike adults, children do need fat. Try to stick to 'healthy' fats, such as olive oil, and use butter instead of margarines.

- Offer your child lots of fresh water to drink between meals, which can help the body to work more effectively. Avoid sweet drinks, and only offer fruit juices with food, to reduce the risk of damage to their teeth.

strap, and an easy-to-clean tray. Wooden chairs may be more aesthetically pleasing, but they can be difficult to keep clean. You may need to use an antibacterial cleanser on his highchair after feeds.

Is my baby getting enough?

When your baby begins to feed himself, you will have no guarantee of what he is actually eating, so you should continue to feed him with a spoon, and a bowl (out of his reach) while he experiments. As he becomes more reliable with a spoon, or even with his hands, you will be able to gauge his intake and offer spoon-fed foods only when necessary.

Practical advice

- If you have a fussy or faddy eater, be patient and consistent and try not to offer fast or convenience foods – which are high in artificial ingredients – as a substitute. Children who become accustomed to the enhanced flavours of commercially prepared foods will find it difficult to be satisfied with home

cooking. Look convenience foods that use only natural ingredients.

- Peel and cut grapes into manageable, bite-sized pieces, which will help to ensure that your baby does not choke.

Try to offer foods that your baby can pick up and eat himself. Many parents find it easier to feed a distracted baby when he has something to do on his own. You can slip him spoonfuls of his main meal while he experiments with different tastes and textures of fingerfoods.

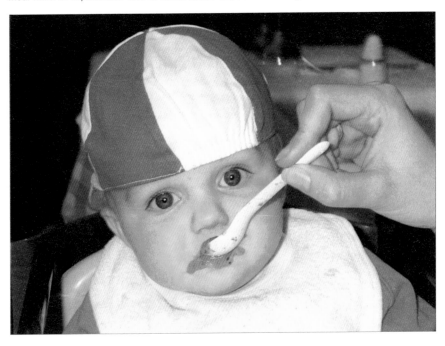

Sleeping

Many babies will have settled down to a good sleep routine by the time they approach their first birthday; however, as always, your baby will develop her own patterns, and you may find it difficult to convince her to adapt them to yours. She may also become difficult to settle at night, and seem to require rocking, comforting and extra feeds to get her to do so. She may be a wakeful baby, and decide early on that naps are not for her. She may also continue to wake in the night, and sometimes with increasing frequency. It is not uncommon for parents to decide at this point that sleep is an issue that they can't let slide; the time has come to establish a routine.

Sleep patterns are continually changing because any of the things that affect your baby during the daytime, such as teething, illness or seasonal changes, can also affect her sleep, as can dreaming. At between five and eight months, your baby will be more mobile, and she won't lie still when she is put down. Try to use a slow, calming routine to wind down, and allow her to move

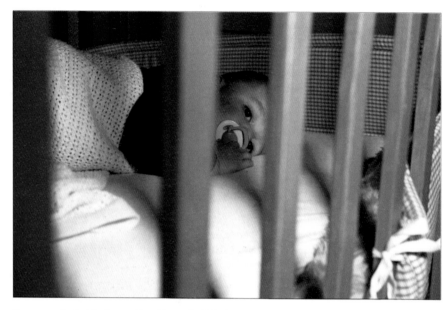

Some people find that a soother (dummy) will help to settle their baby at night.

around until she feels comfortable – but don't expect her to fall asleep immediately.

At around eight months, even good sleepers may begin to wake at night with the onset of separation anxiety (see opposite). When she wakes, make your response as matter-of-fact as possible. Try not to pick her up, just settle her down and talk quietly but firmly. If she senses that you mean business, she may not bother to try to play or chatter, or even insist on cuddles.

Try to find a balance between being supportive and firm, and control your anger or distress. If you communicate in a cheerful, but matter-of-fact manner, your baby will effectively 'borrow' your confidence until she develops her own. Reassure her that you are nearby, and call out to her, or even visit, if that helps. Tell her that you will be there when she wakes up.

Try to set up a bedtime routine that

you baby enjoys (see page 168). She will know what to expect, and will soon realize that the routine ends when she is tucked lovingly into bed. As she gets older, she will remember the nice parts of the routine, and will find the settling down to sleep a natural progression.

Allow your baby to become attached to a special object, such as a blanket, a soft toy or, if she needs it, a dummy.

Sleep needs

By six months old, your baby may sleep about four hours in the day, and ten at night. By nine months, she will need only two or three hours in the day, although her night-time sleep requirements are likely to remain the same. By the time she reaches her first birthday, she may need only a couple of hours of sleep in the day, but she may go for longer at night – up to twelve or even fourteen hours. These are average requirements, however, and individual babies' needs will vary.

Some babies suck their fingers or thumb for comfort when they feel insecure.

Attachment is a healthy way to deal with fears, and there are numerous studies that show that children who have comfort items feel less afraid or isolated when left on their own. If your baby doesn't have a special object, try to encourage her to choose one. Place a teddy in her cot, and bring it along with you on outings. Encourage her to hug it, and put it next to her at both stressful and happy times in the day.

If your baby is still waking in the night for a feed, continue to make it a 'non-event' by proceeding quietly, in the dark, with the minimum of fuss and conversation. Burp her and place her straight back in her cot. If she is waking for comfort rather than because of hunger, she will soon realize that the period at your breast, or on the bottle, is no longer as rewarding as it used to be, and night waking should tail off.

Early risers may be worse than night-time wakers if you are not a morning person, and it is difficult to be cheerful when the clock reads 5am, and you have had less than half a dozen hours of precious sleep. Try to encourage your baby to play in her bed. After she has gone to sleep, place a few favourite toys where she can reach them, towards the bottom of the cot, so that she can keep herself busy when she wakes. You could try putting her to bed slightly later, but unfortunately early risers often continue to wake at the same time, regardless of the amount of sleep they have had. It might be worth considering giving in to your baby's patterns while she is still young enough to require your care. Babies are usually cheerful and happy in the morning, and it can be a good opportunity to play together without interruption from other members of the household. Take turns getting up with your partner, so at least one of you gets some sleep.

Put toys in the cot to try and encourage early risers to let you have a little more sleep.

What is separation anxiety?

Separation anxiety occurs around eight or nine months of age, when previously happy babies experience insecurity, alarm and even panic when left alone, even for a few minutes. The degree to which your baby experiences this anxiety is dependent upon her stage of development. If your baby can crawl when these feelings first surface, she is likely to crawl after you and feel less uneasy. If she is still immobile, she may feel greater anxiety whenever you move from her view.

WHAT YOU CAN DO

● Always tell your baby that you are leaving the room, and wave good-bye. Never sneak away, or try to slip out when she is occupied with something else.

● When you return, greet her, and confirm that you are back. Your baby will soon realize that absences are preceded by information that you are leaving, and that you will always come back. If she feels that you are out to 'trick her', and that you can't be relied upon actually to be there when she thinks you are, her fears will increase.

Learning and playing

Your baby's body, and her character, will be developing and growing as the months pass. She will change a great deal physically – and make progress, as she learns to crawl, sit, move, stand and eventually walk. She will not hesitate to inform you of her likes and dislikes, and she will make her presence felt. She will recognize the people she knows well, and familiar places and routines, and respond when you call her name. Toys and games are now becoming increasingly important to her as she begins to experiment more and more.

Movement

Your baby's body has become stronger and more controlled, and she will learn to sit. As she becomes confident sitting on her own she will begin to reach out for toys, and then return to the sitting position. She may find herself on her tummy, or on her hands and knees, and move forward into a crawl. From there, it is only a short time until she will be ready to pull herself up to her feet.

Most babies begin to sit unsupported somewhere between five and eight months old, and you can help her to achieve this by propping her up, and

Be prepared for plenty of topples, scrapes and banged heads as your baby learns to control her body, and becomes ever bolder and more adventurous.

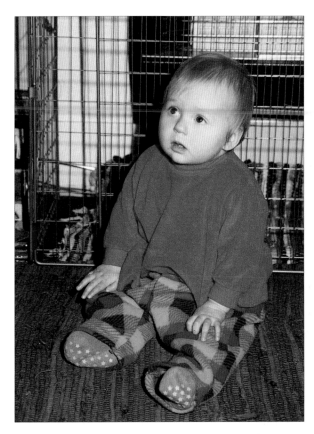

Many babies who found the first six months of life frustrating, relax and become happier when they are able to move about under their own steam.

helping her to learn to balance. As her muscles become stronger and more controlled, she will be able to reach forward, and then to the side – finally being able to run and stretch for things that are out of her reach.

Rolling will be the first real attempt your baby will make towards independent movement, which she will do from her side or tummy on to her back, and then a little later, from her back on to her side, and then her front. By the time she is about ten months old, she will be able to use a combination of movements to get around – perhaps shuffling on her bottom, pulling herself upright, or wriggling to get closer to things. She will roll, and then learn how to use her legs to propel herself along on her bottom. She may alternate between frustration and pleasure as she struggles without success to reach for something, or to edge towards something that has caught her eye and then manage to co-ordinate her movements to reach it.

First crawling may be backwards, as she pushes more efficiently with her arms and hands than with her feet and legs. As soon as she is able to move, however, she will learn to change direction and make her way with considerable speed towards what she wants.

As the months pass, she will be gaining control over all parts of her body. By about six months she will be able to lift her legs off the mattress when she is lying on her back, and catch them in her hand. She may engage in a little foot-sucking, and examine her feet with as much interest as she would any toy. She will kick excitedly when on her back, and when you hold her against you she will use the new power of her legs to jump and bounce. It won't be long before she pulls herself up on her feet, by grabbing hold of you or perhaps a piece of furniture. She will bounce excitedly when she is on her feet, and as her confidence grows, she will begin to take a few steps while still holding on.

Helping your baby to crawl

Your baby will decide when she is ready to crawl, and within a few short days she may go from confident sitting to a serviceable crawling position. You can encourage her crawling by:

● Holding out toys a short distance from her. Don't hold them too far away, or she will become frustrated and be tempted to give up. Encourage her, and as she comes closer, proffer them to her.

● Protect her knees by dressing her in trousers, or something soft. Make sure her clothing is loose enough for her to manoeuvre, but not so big that she gets tangled up.

● Keep anything sharp or dangerous out of her way – it will set her back if she associates movement with injury.

● Most importantly, never underestimate how quickly she will be able to travel, once she has got the knack.

● Don't leave her alone in a room or try to keep her strapped down when she is experimenting. If you have to leave the room, bring her along with you, or ensure that she is safe while still having room to move.

Your baby will learn to balance and become more confident as her muscles develop.

Make sure the objects your baby chooses to support her are sturdy and won't topple over.

or your clothing, or the nearest piece of furniture. Make sure that whatever she has access to will support her weight and not topple over. Don't put shoes on her when she is learning to stand – she will need to spread her toes to get her balance right, and she will need traction in order to pull herself up.

Hand control

When your baby first learns to pick up toys, she will be unco-ordinated, may hesitate and seem to lack confidence. Soon, however, she will learn to stretch out, reach and pick up whatever catches her eye, using her whole hand to cup the object she wants. She will pass toys from one hand to another, and to her mouth, and she may bang toys together. Gradually she will learn to pick up small things, with her thumb and her first finger. She'll learn to control her fingers separately, and will be able to poke and prod things, and then to point.

Her arms will also become more co-ordinated, and she will be able to lift things – such as blocks or stacking cups – and knock over towers or piles of toys. She can tug a pull-along toy towards her

Helping your baby to stand

Your baby will learn to stand by herself when she is able to pull herself up. Don't try to rush the event, because her muscles may not have developed or strengthened to the point where it is actually possible. You can help her by placing her in a safe area where she has something to grasp onto, in order to pull herself up. She may begin by pulling herself up on the bars of her cot

Everything she finds on the floor will end up in your baby's mouth.

Baby milestones, six to twelve months

● 6 months: transfers an object from hand to hand

● 6 to 8 months: sits unsupported

● 9 months: explores surroundings

● 9 months: probes with forefinger

● 10 to 12 months: uses two words appropriately

● 12 months: develops pincer grasp. Lets go of an object.

● 12 months: imitates actions. Responds to own name.

● 12 to 18 months: walks

by its string, clap her hands and wave good-bye.

Toys to help her learn

As she learns to move and to become more independent, toys are less important than the space to manoeuvre and explore. She will need plenty of floor area in a childproofed room (see pages 178-9), with sturdy furniture to draw herself up on.

When she can crawl, she will enjoy things that move, such as a ball, or a toy with wheels, crawling after them, and learning to push them along. She will enjoy using her new skill of picking things up and setting them down, and will soon co-ordinate her muscles enough to throw things.

She will like toys that have a definite purpose – a car that moves when pushed, a soft toy that squeaks when pressed, or a whole baby gym with different sounds and sensations that she can explore and establish the meaning of cause and effect. She will learn that she is capable of making things happen by performing certain actions, and it will empower her and make her feel secure. Good toys for this age group include cubes with bells in them, musical instruments such as tambourines,

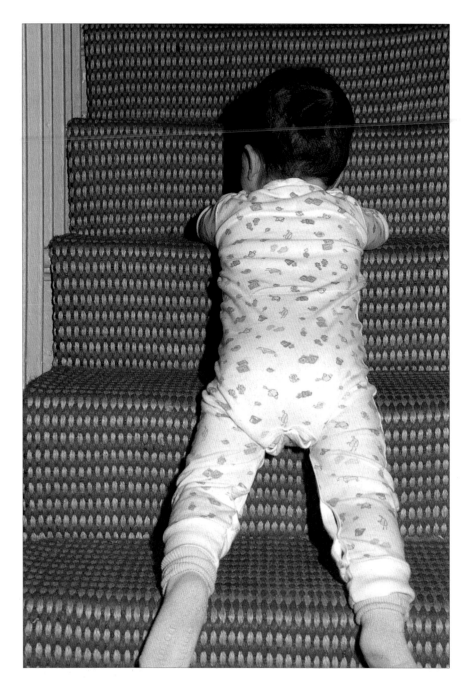

As soon as he can crawl, your baby will be unstoppable. Make sure that you have stairgates in place to prevent accidents, and teach him to crawl upstairs, and slide down again on his bottom or tummy.

drums, and bells, pop-up toys that respond when she pushes a button or a lever, durable books, blocks, balls and toy farm animals.

She will need physical play. Games such as 'This little piggy' or 'Round and round the garden' will help her to learn about her whole body, and how it feels when it is touched – and how it feels to touch you, and other things in the world around her. Roll a ball to her, and teach her how to roll it back, or try to catch it

Toys that fit one inside the other will both challenge and amuse your baby, and it won't be long before he has figured out that small fits inside large, and so on. Loading and unloading is a favourite baby occupation, and you can improvise with the contents of your larder and a big plastic box with equal success.

Solving problems successfully is a major achievement and you should offer lavish praise. React with excitement to his triumphs and he will try to emulate them next time.

she can see herself. She won't recognize the baby in the mirror, but she will respond to it, and will get hours of pleasure smiling at herself, and reaching out to touch the 'other' baby.

She will love to wrap and unwrap parcels, and you can involve her with

when she throws it. She will watch carefully and eventually copy you, so try to incorporate many different activities into your playtime session. Continue to sing to your baby, and talk to her as often as you can. She will respond to your voice, and may even try to sing back.

When she is pulling herself up and beginning to walk, a toddle truck should be popular, or an animal on wheels or soft toy to push in a buggy, which will encourage her to gain stability and confidence.

When she begins to crawl, she will need toys that are big enough to catch her eye across a room. She may love 'wrestling' with a big stuffed toy, and it will help her to practise lifting and rolling.

Set up a mirror in a safe place so that

As soon as your baby is confident on his feet, you may wish to invest in a 'push' toy, such as this one, with a tray to load and unload, and a good sturdy base.

Younger babies like games such as peek-boo or clapping and will remain amused for long periods as you repeat the same actions. In fact, you will almost certainly get bored long before they do.

supermarket, and being shown how to drop them into the trolley. While you work in the garden, give her some clean, empty flowerpots to play with, and she will be happy for hours.

Try to find some good, colourful and sturdy books that your baby will be able to handle herself. She will enjoy reading with you when you have time, and will likely enjoy 'pretending' to read on her own. Try to choose books with pictures of familiar objects, which your baby will

be able to recognize and identify with.

Another source of entertainment is a mirror. It will be many months before your baby recognizes herself as the baby in the reflection, but she will be endlessly amused by the 'other baby', and will reach out to touch her, and experiment with different facial expressions. Make sure you choose a mirror that is firmly fixed to a wall, or a specially designed child's mirror, with plastic rather than a glass surface.

your own activities – perhaps opening the mail with you, or playing with tins from the cupboard while you unpack your groceries. Your larder will be an endless source of amusement, and she may enjoy loading potatoes and carrots into a pan, and then taking them out again.

Help her to feel part of any activity – whether it is grocery shopping, gardening or doing the laundry. She will enjoy splashing her hands in a bowl of warm water, with a few floating toys, and will love holding things in the

A trip to the grocery store can be exciting, or torture, depending on your baby's temperament. Try to include her in your visit – asking her to hold things, or place them in the cart, and explaining what you are buying and what you might make with it later.

Listening and talking

Playing with your children is a good opportunity to help them develop their conversational skills in a relaxed atmosphere.

Your growing baby will have plenty to say to you, and she will be anxious to know that you are listening, and will even begin to wait for your response before she continues.

Her voice should become yet another tool for experimentation, and she will be able to make a wider range of sounds, which she will enjoy practising. She will soon learn to differentiate between your voice tones, sensing when you are cross or pleased with her. She can laugh and may giggle uncontrollably when you tickle her, or play peek-a-boo.

By seven months your baby will be alert to speech, and will look for you when you call her, and try to establish the source of a sound – such as music from the radio, or someone talking in another room. Her words will expand from one-syllable sounds to two-syllable 'words', by repeating the sounds.

From nine months, her two syllable words will have expanded into single, unique words, such as 'ibi', 'ahgoo' and 'imi', and she will begin the next stage of verbal development – babbling. When

Reading a story to your baby while he looks at the pictures is a good way to help him understand the meaning of words.

she babbles she may make long strings of noises that echo the cadence of your own speech. She may begin to use her first words in a long stream of babbling sounds, and she will understand basic words that you use – including the all-important 'no'.

By ten or eleven months, your baby will probably have spoken her first real words, although they may have been well hidden in a stream of babble. She will soon understand that every object has a sound attached to it, and that by using

Try to make books and reading an important part of your baby's regular routine. A night-time story can be comforting and relaxing, and you will inspire in your baby an interest in books and reading. On his own, he will enjoy looking at familiar pictures, and even tasting the pages!

that sound, she can get what she wants. She may begin by using words that seem completely unrelated to the name of the object, but she will adapt her speech as she grows older, and will imitate what you say, rather than developing her own sound for what she sees.

● Let her hear talking as much as possible – read to her, play story or rhyme tapes, talk to her constantly, and sing whenever you can. Explain what you are doing as you go about changing her, doing housework, shopping for groceries, picking or smelling flowers – it will give her the opportunity to grasp the meaning of the words she hears. When she responds, listen carefully, and respond back, and she will soon learn that chatter and talk is sociable, and elicits a response.

● Talk about things that interest your baby, and show her pictures of babies doing the things that she does. Point to objects and say their names. Point to her and call her by her name. Point to yourself and say 'mummy'. Repeat words several times in the same sentence, for

The word 'no'

● Don't overuse 'no', but gently correct her with positive speech instead. When you do use the word, say it gently and firmly, so that she understands you are not happy.

● Try not to begin phrases with 'don't', such as 'don't touch that radiator, it's hot'. She will understand you more readily if you say 'it's hot! don't touch!'

instance: 'Look, here is your ball. You hold the ball. Can you throw the ball?' She'll soon understand that the object is called a ball, and will try to use the word herself.

● Try to keep eye contact with your baby when you are speaking to her, so that she will understand you are addressing her, and she will respond in kind.

● Show encouragement when she finds words for things – even if they are wrong. Use her word and then the correct word, but don't ever make her feel as though she has not communicated.

Everyday care

As you begin to establish routines, bathing and caring for your baby will begin to become much easier in these later months, and you will treat him with increasing confidence, and probably enjoy the rituals of everyday life.

Nappy changing

Your baby's bowel movements and bladder control will have improved, so that the number of nappy changes required decreases dramatically. As he begins to eat solid foods, his bowel movements will be more solid, and usually a little less frequent, although they will begin to smell, and you will not have to check to see if a nappy change is required.

Your baby will probably not waken at night with a wet nappy unless he is very uncomfortable, and you can help to prevent night-time discomfort by ensuring that he wears a specially absorbent night-time nappy, if you are using disposables, or two layers, or perhaps an absorbent pad, if you are using cloth.

His nappies won't be as obviously wet during the day, so you may need to remind yourself to change them, to avoid nappy rash and discomfort. Try to set up a routine during which you change nappies mid-morning, after lunch, late afternoon, and just before bed, adjusting this time-table to your baby's bowel movements and altering it according to the number of drinks he has had!

Make bathtime fun by offering your baby a selection of toys and waterproof books to experiment with and enjoy. Even when your baby is old enough to sit, he should not be left on his own in the bath, and you should continue to use a slip-proof mat, to prevent accidents.

Bathing your baby

Your baby will soon be able to graduate to the big bathtub, and he will probably love the freedom he will experience with the extra space. Bathtime should be fun – try to include singing games, and don't hesitate to play with him. He may enjoy being splashed a little. Always talk to him, and if he is nervous, maintain eye contact.

1 Run a little water in the bath, pouring cold water in first, and then adding hot until it is warm.

2 Make sure the room is warm, and never leave your baby in the bath alone, even for a second, or let go of him completely.

3 Wash his face, eyes and ears on a changing mat first, and then gently lower him into the bath. Keep his head and shoulders supported, and the ears above the waterline.

4 Always support him with one arm, using the other to lather soap, or to rub his body with the washcloth.

5 Splash him to rinse off the soap, taking care not to get it into his eyes.

6 Lift him out by placing your hands under his armpits, and hold him carefully.

7 Dry your baby gently on a clean, dry towel, taking care to remove moisture from the skin folds.

When your baby becomes mobile, it is a good idea to cover both taps with washcloths or towels, to prevent him from burning or injuring himself.

Washing your baby's hair

The majority of babies are not pleased to have their hair washed, and indeed, many do not have enough hair to warrant it. If you have a bald baby, or one with only a little hair, a wipe with the washcloth will probably be sufficient. When your baby's hair does grow, however, you will need to keep it clean.

● Avoid wetting his face by scooping water over his head as he lies in the bath.

Older babies may wander off to explore the soapdish while you're trying to wash their hair. Make sure you have a slip-proof mat on the bottom.

● Always use a gentle shampoo, specially formulated for babies.

● Use a sponge or a washcloth to wring water out over his head to rinse, keeping him lying flat, well supported by your hand.

● As your baby gets older, you may be able to use the shower attachment on your tap, but remember to check the temperature of the water first.

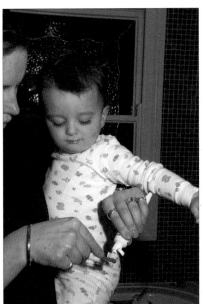

Brush your baby's teeth as soon as they appear, using a pea-sized drop of child's toothpaste on a soft toothbrush or flannel.

● You may want to brush your baby's hair after washing, but towel it rather than blow it dry, which will be frightening, and may burn his tender skin.

Tooth care

You will need to begin caring for your baby's teeth as soon as they appear – initially by rubbing them with a soft cloth and then, when there are more

Clip or cut your baby's toenails and fingernails regularly, using specially designed children's clippers, or a pair of blunt-edged nail scissors. If your baby objects to the procedure, you might consider doing it while he is feeding, or asleep.

than three or four, with a soft toothbrush. You may wish to brush your teeth at the same time – handing him his own toothbrush to play and practise with after you have given his teeth a good rub. Don't worry if he swallows the toothpaste – rinsing is not necessary!

● Using a pea-sized drop of fluoride toothpaste specially prepared for young babies and children, rub his teeth and gums gently.

Trimming your baby's nails

Your baby's nails will gradually harden as he gets older, but you may be able to continue to bite them off if you are daunted by the prospect of using nail scissors or clippers. If you do use slippers or scissors, hold one finger at a time, and cut the nail, following the shape of the fingertip. Don't cut the nails straight across, which can encourage hangnails. If your baby hates having his fingernails cut, try doing it while he is asleep at your breast, or on your lap, when he will hardly notice. When cutting toenails, cut them straight across, rather than curving, which can cause ingrown toenails.

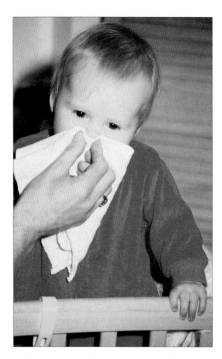

Always use a cloth handkerchief to wipe your baby's nose, rather than a tissue. Parts of tissue could break off and be inhaled, causing her to choke.

Baby massage

Babies and children usually enjoy being massaged, but they will often only keep still for a short time. You don't need to learn any special strokes to massage your baby – just explore her body with gentle rhythmic or stroking movements, and she'll soon let you know what feels good. Massaging your baby is an excellent way of settling her, and of establishing a close physical relationship. She will feel loved and cared-for, and you may find that you bond more easily and more deeply if you spend a little time massaging her on a regular basis. Touch is very therapeutic, and you will both benefit from close, loving contact.

Babies love physical contact, and it can be enormously rewarding to take the time to play with her as you are dressing her, changing her nappy, or preparing her for bed. Baby massage is also an ideal way to soothe and relax her, and to enhance the bonding process.

If your baby is small enough, you can sit on the floor and massage her on your lap. Otherwise spread a towel on the floor or on any safe, raised surface.

Basic baby massage

Front of the body

● Starting with your baby on her back, gently stroke her face, starting in the middle of the forehead and working out to the temples.

● Stroke across the cheeks from nose to the ears and then from the cheeks down to the chin.

● Gently stroke across the eyebrows, and back around under the eye.

● Make gentle circles around the temples

● Stroke up the front of the body and out along the arms.

● Make clockwise circles around the navel using both hands.

● Do gentle 'wringing' strokes across the abdomen and up the body.

● Lift arms one at a time and stroke the length of the arm from the shoulder to the hand.

● Use one hand to squeeze the arm, starting from the shoulder and moving down the arm.

● Massage the hand and squeeze and rotate each of the fingers in turn.

● Repeat for the other arm.

● Gently wring or squeeze up the leg.

● Stroke down the leg using a light feathering stroke.

Back of the body

● Turn your baby onto her front and gently stroke her back.

● Stroke up and over the back and along the arms.

● Gently knead shoulders.

● Make a gentle wringing stroke up over the body.

● While your baby is still quite young, massage her bottom using gentle kneading or pinching strokes.

● Smooth down the spine using alternating hands, starting at the base of the neck and working down to the base of the spine.

● Use gliding strokes down the legs.

● Bend the knee up and work on the foot.

● Work around the anklebone with fingertips.

● Sandwich the foot between the heels of your hand and massage, moving both hands in a circular motion.

● Squeeze the heel with one hand and massage up the sole of the foot using your thumbs.

● Massage each toe, gently squeezing, rotating and pulling each in turn.

● Sandwich the foot between your hands and hold firmly for a few seconds.

● Stroke from one foot up the leg, across the sacrum (base of the spine) and back down the other leg.

● Use light strokes down the body, starting from the top of the head right down to the feet.

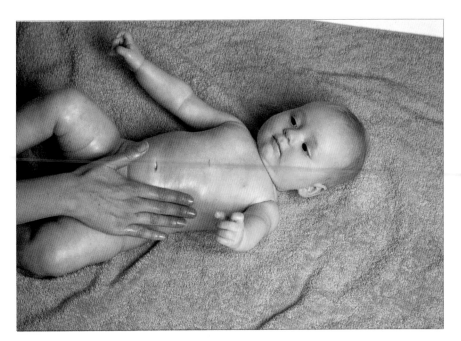

Use a gentle oil when you massage your baby, perhaps adding a drop or two of a good aromatherapy oil, such as lavender or Roman chamomile. Warm the oil gently before you begin, and use long, gentle strokes, across the abdomen, and down the limbs. If your baby has difficult settling to sleep, a pre-bed massage can help to make her sleepy and content.

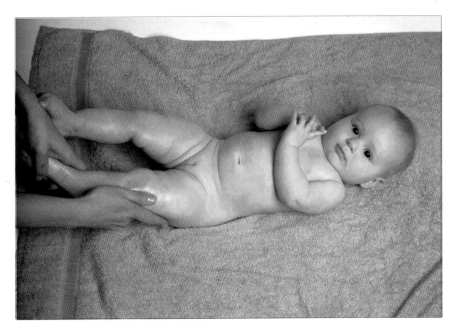

Massage up the leg with a gentle squeezing stroke, and then stroke down the leg lightly. Talk quietly to your baby as you massage her, and adjust your movements according to her response.

Teething

The first teeth may have already poked through the gums by the time your baby is six months old, and 'teething' will continue until she has twenty teeth – ten on the top and ten on the bottom. The first teeth are normally the bottom centre teeth, although this can vary from baby to baby. The two front teeth are often the next to show, joined by the neighbours on either side.

Brush your baby's first teeth carefully each night, and let her have a toothbrush of her own to chew on, and 'practise'.

When your baby is teething, offer her a variety of sterilized, non-toxic toys to chew on, which will help to ease the discomfort. Some teething rings can be chilled in the refrigerator, which helps to soothe sore gums.

Some babies get their first teeth as early as 4 months, and it can be difficult to recognize the signs, especially if it is your first baby. If your baby is drooling more, and seems desperate to chomp on anything that goes into her mouth, or seems fractious although she is not ill, chances are the first teeth will appear shortly. Some babies sail through teething without a murmur, and others experience great discomfort.

Your baby's milk teeth (his first set of teeth) are almost entirely formed in the gums before birth. Early teething can interfere with breastfeeding, and you may be treated to a powerful bite, followed by a look of delight when your baby realizes that clamping his jaws down on your breast has caused a violent reaction. Babies do usually become a little disturbed when teeth start to erupt (see page 177), and they will like to bite on something hard, such as a teething ring. Rubbing the gums also provides relief.

Don't worry if your baby does not produce teeth until a little later – some babies are still giving gummy, toothless smiles until the end of their first year.

Despite what parents of early teethers may have you think, teething in the first six months of life does not indicate advanced development or super intelligence.

You should rub your baby's first teeth with a soft toothbrush, or a clean cloth and take care not to offer sweet drinks between meals.

6–8 months
lower front teeth

7–9 months
upper front teeth

9–13 months
incisors

12–15 months
back molars

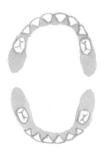
16–18 months
canines

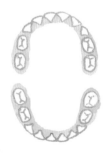
20–30 months
remaining molars

203

Safety points

Don't leave your child unattended in public places.

Make sure the high chair has a harness to hold her in place.

Use plastic covers on plug points.

SAFETY POINTS CHECKLIST

Once your baby is mobile, watch out for the following:

- Remember that anything she can lift will go straight into her mouth so become extra vigilant about small objects dropped on the carpet. ☐

- Keep everything poisonous and breakable in inaccessible places. ☐

- Make sure that furniture is solid and won't topple over. ☐

- Place hot drinks, cups and plates well out of reach. ☐

- Fit stair gates, fire guards, cupboard locks and power point covers. ☐

- Always use the harnesses and straps in car seats, bouncy chairs and high chairs. ☐

- Never leave your baby alone with a dog, cat or other animal. ☐

- Don't leave them alone in public places, even for a moment, and at home, they should only be left in their cot or a play pen. ☐

- Fit flex guards to be doubly sure they can't pull that boiling kettle onto their heads. ☐

- Make sure your cooker is toddler-proof. ☐

- Keep doors and windows securely closed unless you are there to watch. Remember that toddlers can move very swiftly. ☐

- In the garden, watch your toddler at all times and protect her from pools, fish ponds and even puddles. ☐

- Lock the garden shed and garage, both of which can contain dangerous substances and tools. ☐

- Buy good-quality toys and check the age recommendations on the packaging. Some fabrics are unsuitable for babies, as are toys with small parts that could be swallowed. ☐

Learn basic first aid techniques (see page 248) and keep a first aid kit to hand. There are further safety suggestions on page 251.

Tests and immunization

During the second half of the first year, your baby can be weighed and measured on a monthly basis (or more often if you like) at your baby clinic, and you will need to bring him along for his immunizations (see page 180). In the eighth or ninth month, you can expect to have the first major developmental check.

The eight- or nine-month check is normally carried out by a health visitor. She will be looking to see how alert your baby is, and will ask about patterns of eating, sleeping and behaviour as well as about any illnesses your baby may have had. By eight months, most babies can sit unaided, push themselves up on their forearms when lying on their tummies, and reach out to grab an object, such as a brick placed in front of them. She will test his hearing by making a series of sounds behind him, and seeing if he turns his head in response. If your baby fails to respond to the noises, it is probably not because his hearing is in any way impaired, but because he is tired, distracted by something else, not interested, not familiar with the test sounds, or has wax blocking his ears. The test will be repeated a few weeks later, and if he fails to respond again, he will be referred to a specialist.

By nine months, your baby:

- Crawls or attempts to crawl
- Sits alone on the floor for 10 to 15 minutes
- Says 'Mama' and 'Dada' with meaning
- Understands 'no'
- Claps hands, plays pat-a-cake and peek-a-boo
- Looks for fallen toys
- Pulls up to standing position in the cot or in front of a chair
- Shouts to attract attention

Check with your doctor if he:

- Is too quiet, or does not make any sounds
- Does not appear to hear
- Is unable to sit without support
- Does not move around on the floor
- Is unable to crawl or bottom shuffle
- Cannot point to small objects, such as raisins, or pick these up with finger and thumb

Immunization

Your baby may be offered his MMR around his first birthday – the Measles, Mumps, Rubella vaccine, which is given in one injection. A few children experience side-effects, or 'reactions' to the vaccine but you can help to prevent a negative reaction by giving him a dose of the homeopathic remedy Ledum, at 6c dilution, every three or four hours for the first day.

Family relationships

The year after your baby's first birthday marks the transition from babyhood to toddlerhood, and by this time, life will have settled down into a recognizable routine that helps both you and your baby to feel more confident about your relationship. This period bridges the gap between infancy and childhood, and your baby will be learning a great deal – particularly about being his own separate person – and is able to do more things for himself.

These rapid changes will be both encouraging – as your baby becomes inquisitive and energetic, trying out new things and constantly testing himself, fired by an inspiring zest for life – and frustrating, as you will lock horns for the first time. His developing personality will be interspersed with periods of rest, or regression back to babyish ways, and he will need the comfort of familiar routines, games and cuddles, as he learns more, and struggles to meet the demands of the world around him.

Until now, your baby has been totally dependent upon you for his every need. You have been his favourite person, and may have felt both flattered and enslaved by his focus and dependence on you. By the time his first birthday

As your baby becomes a toddler, you may begin thinking about having another baby. A second or subsequent pregnancy can be exhausting with a toddler in the house, and you will have to take great care in introducing the new member of your family to existing children – particularly if one has been 'ruling the roost' until the new baby arrived.

comes around, however, this situation is slowly changing. Your baby will now have a firm grip on life, the result of your

constant care during the first year, and he will be consumed with the task of growing up. By now well established as

Young babies may notice each other but they rarely pay much attention, preferring to watch and respond to any adults present.

part of the family, he will widen his horizons to encompass other family members apart from his mother and father. This period is unique in that he will develop physically at a tremendous rate – learning to crawl, if he hasn't already done so, walk, and then run. He will delight in activity and be into everything with enthusiasm and unending curiosity. His determination to learn everything he can about his environment and the world around him means that he will be capable of disappearing without a moment's notice, or creating chaos in a room in just a few minutes. This focus and drive may fill you with pride and amusement one minute – and exasperation the next.

The difficulties of this period are compounded by your baby's single-minded resolve to do exactly as he pleases – but he will require the comfort of the knowledge that you are there when he needs you, and you will certainly hear about it when you are not. He will shun your attempts to help him, because he will be confident that he is capable of doing everything for himself – from changing his own nappies to feeding himself, from carrying the groceries, to building his own block towers. He won't understand danger, and you will need to intervene constantly to ensure his safety, and to pick up the pieces when he dissolves into tears of frustration.

Help siblings to play with each other and treat them equally at all times to avoid one feeling less cared for than the other.

Teach older children how to hold a new baby safely.

Toddlers can't control their emotions, or understand the concept of 'later'. They think in terms of the here-and-now, and he will battle determinedly for what they want, even in the face of your obvious displeasure. Most toddlers are not deliberately naughty – they genuinely forget what they have been told, or attribute little significance to it. Your toddler will not yet be able to discern between what is acceptable and what is considered naughty, and if the inspiration strikes him, he will do exactly as he pleases. His overwhelming curiosity may drive you to distraction. Some people call this period the 'Terrible Twos', and for many babies, with good reason.

But your toddler will be enormously rewarding, and will make you helpless with laughter. You will share his pride in new achievements – from learning to walk, to feeding himself, from possibly making his first steps towards potty training, to speaking his first clear words and even sentences with purpose. Try to take pleasure in his boundless enthusiasm and delight, and show your approval whenever you can. He will move forward with great confidence into childhood.

Your baby's increasing mastery of his body, his capacity to explore his environment, and his ability to use words enables him to take a more active and assertive role in the family dynamic. He will be making relationships with other members of the family, and with friends, and the type of relationships he makes are deeply rooted in, and influenced by, the early relationship with his mother, father or primary carer.

Whichever parent is the primary carer, your baby may have mixed feelings towards the other. A toddler is more able to consider the idea that you are a couple, and he may find this a threat or feel jealous. Obviously a stable and friendly relationship between you and your partner will make your baby feel secure and reassured, but on a day-to-day basis, he will want to be included

Introducing your baby to a range of new experiences can make her more confident.

Encourage your older child to help look after the new baby, making him feel involved.

will delight in playing with and encouraging younger family members, and conspiring with them against Mummy and Daddy.

Children who are closer in age may feel threatened by their siblings' growing achievements, and perhaps jealous when they perceive that the division of attention is not always even.

You will have to be fair and consistent with your attention and your discipline, for according to the number of children you have, you may have several sets of eyes watching you suspiciously.

You may consider having another baby as your toddler reaches his second year, and a new arrival will undoubtedly cause some disruption in your toddler's life, but what he will notice and mind most is that your attention will be focused elsewhere. If you are lucky, your children will grow up to love each other and be good friends, but you cannot insist that they do so, and too much intervention in their relationship will not do it any good. Try to maintain an equilibrium, and encourage respect and toleration, but let them get on with things. As they grow up, continue to make time for each child to be on his own with you, and encourage them to have time away with friends.

As your toddler requires your attention less exclusively, and he begins to eat and feed on his own, he will probably develop a special relationship with his father, or another family member, and you will want to encourage independent activities away from the home – perhaps trips to the local swimming pool, the library, or shopping with another member of the family – which will help him to feel special and secure. If you have not already done so, you may now consider going back to work, and your childcare arrangements will extend his social network even further.

in this love affair that seems to be going on without him. He is desperate to be seen as an individual part of the family, but if he can't be included in every discussion or show of affection, he will want to keep you separate. He may suddenly be reluctant to go to bed in the evenings, or he may turn up in yours in the middle of the night. He may position himself firmly in the middle of your embrace, and chatter incessantly or even shout and cry when he feels excluded from conversation. Your

toddler's preference for one parent can be so obvious at times that it becomes difficult for their partner to cope with the rejection.

Until the coming of a new baby, first-born children know the joy of a special relationship without the pain of sharing affection. A younger member of the family learns from the outset that he has to compete for your attention, but will benefit from the general chaos of family life, with its existing networks and relationships, and many older children

Eating and growing

For much of the first year of his life, your baby's activities and your relationship with him will have inevitably been based around his need for food and for comfort. To some extent this will carry on into toddlerhood, although his routine and the kind of food he will be eating will have changed. As he becomes completely weaned, you will no longer have the same control over how much he eats, and many mothers become anxious when toddlers refuse to eat, or eat so little that it seems impossible that they will ever grow.

The average one-year-old will be having three meals a day, a mixture of solid food and milk, and perhaps a bottle or breastfeed at night or early in the morning. But children vary enormously in the amount they eat, from day to day, and from month to month. Minor illness, teething and even periods of intensive growth can throw your toddler off for days at a time, and a change in routine can have the same effect. Some children will refuse to eat outside the home, and others will be encouraged by company to eat more than they would ever do with their mother hovering over them.

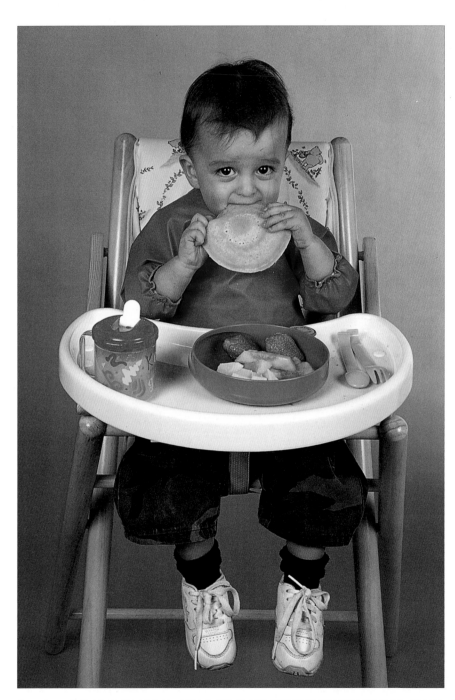

It can be a challenge to feed a fussy eater, but try to stay calm and never force the issue. Choose foods that appeal to him, and which have as much nutritional value as you can manage. Pancakes are much more appealing than scrambled eggs, and contain plenty of nutrients. Top them with pure, organic maple syrup or a little honey, if he needs encouragement.

It is not unusual at this stage for your toddler to have intense likes and dislikes, and he may insist upon a particular food almost exclusively, and then reject it and go on to something else. Try to respect your baby's choices and preferences, and simply offer other foods in an appetizing way, until his passions shift.

Mealtime battles

One of the most frustrating problems that characterizes this age group is the sudden refusal of food. In your role as provider, you may feel rejected by this refusal, and you may feel helpless, angry and concerned about what he is – or is not – eating. You may find that you become locked in a battle of wills, and mealtimes become a battleground, as you cajole, tempt and maybe even try to force your toddler to eat. Food is the ultimate weapon between parent and child, and the best advice is to relax and avoid making a fuss. Very few babies starve themselves, and although you may not be happy with his choice of food, if it isn't an issue, he will soon be curious to try what you are eating – or be tempted to sample something that has been attractively prepared.

What to do

● If your child is a difficult eater, make sure that he is not ill. Chronic earaches, colds and other ill health can put him off his food.

● If your toddler is in good health, and not losing weight, try not to worry.

● Your baby may be drinking too much milk – cut his milk intake by half, if he is still drinking several bottles a day, and he should become hungrier, with a renewed interest in other foods.

● If your toddler seems only to graze, and never eat a single major meal, don't panic. As long as he is offered only nutritious foods for snacks and mealtimes, he'll be fine – at least something is going in.

● If your baby will only eat one variety of meat or vegetables, concentrate on the fact that he is at least getting something nutritious, even if it isn't a very varied or balanced diet. Try to find vegetables that he will like, and grate them into sauces and stews, or in little piles for him to treat as finger food.

● Keep calm and avoid forcing the issue. If your toddler senses that he has lost his best weapon, he may dispense with it. If you become anxious, and he gets a constant reaction, or requires spoon-feeding when he is perfectly capable of feeding himself, he will have won. He has your attention and concern, which is usually what he is after.

● Invite your baby to share family meals. Eating together is important both for social reasons and to let him see that people eat a variety of foods and seem to enjoy it. If mealtimes are fun and cheerfully presented, your baby will want to join in – after all, a toddler hates to miss any of the action.

● Don't offer him a different meal. If he learns that what is on his plate is all he will get, he is less likely to demand substitutes, and if he is hungry, he will eat.

A healthy diet

There are three main groups of foods: those that should be encouraged, those that are allowed, and those that should be avoided wherever possible. The main rules of healthy eating remain the same for both baby and child, which means, in practice:

● plenty of cereals, bread, vegetables and fruit
● moderate amounts of lean meat, fish, milk, cheese, yoghurt
● small amounts of raisins, fried foods, sweet drinks, butter, margarine, cakes, sweets, honey and sugar.
● After about five years of age, your baby will switch from full- to low-fat milk and dairy produce, but until that time,

Fish and chicken may have been unappetising in a puréed form, but as your toddler gets older, he will be able to manage chunks, and feed himself. Try to feed him what the rest of the family is eating, and he will be intrigued enough to taste it, and flattered to be included.

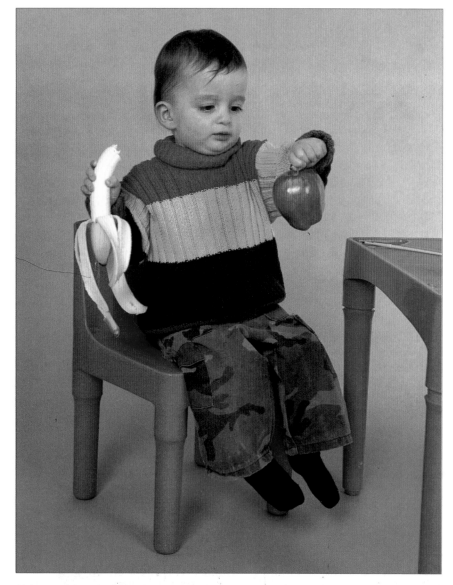

Make snacktime special by serving your toddler at his own table. Snacks are often necessary to get a toddler through the long periods between meals, and they should be chosen with the same care that you give his main meals.

Presenting your baby's food

Your baby will be able to manage foods with a greater variety of textures and flavours, and if he is a good eater you will have nothing to worry about. He will probably be able to eat most things you do, and will enjoy being part of family mealtimes. If, however, you have a fussy or faddy eater on your hands, there are a number of things you can do to make meals more appealing:

● Make faces with your food – or cut things like bread, cheese, apples, carrots and meat with cookie cutters so they appear as stars, animals, or other shapes

● Thread grapes, melon, orange segments, cheese and cubes of meat on a blunt-ended stick (this will require supervision when eating) and encourage him to make his own.

● Ask him to help you with meals – babies who have pulled the ends off tomatoes, or have helped you wash the salad, are more likely to want to eat it too.

● Make fish fingers or fishcakes into cars, with cherry tomato wheels, strips of green pepper and other vegetables or bits of cheese.

● If your baby is passionate about chips (a common problem when there are older children about) and finger foods, cut his food into strips and present it in appealing piles that he can manage himself. Try cutting parsnips, sweet potatoes, carrots and potatoes in chip form, and roast them in the oven with a little olive oil.

● If your baby won't eat eggs or milk, try making pancakes, which simply contain those ingredients in another form. Don't be hung up on making him eat things that don't appeal – try different methods of cooking, or combine foods in sauces or casseroles.

he will need the energy it provides, so don't be tempted to cut down on his fat intake.
● reducing salt intake
● cutting down on highly sweet and refined foods.

Try to work your diet around these foods with as much variety as possible, bearing in mind that the occasional treat will not harm your baby.

Foods to focus on:

● yoghurt (low-sugar, organic, if you can get it)

● rice

● potatoes

● pasta

● fruits and vegetables – fresh or frozen, and lightly cooked

● liver

Sometimes it's best to give in to a fussy toddler and serve his favourite foods, so long as they have some nutritional balance. When he is a little older, he can help you to make his meals and he will then be more likely to eat the finished result.

Foods that can be allowed:

- baked beans
- rusks
- tinned fruits and vegetables (without sugar and salt)
- lean minced beef or lamb
- cereals such as rice krispies, corn flakes or puffed rice
- white bread
- lentils
- lean meat
- fresh fish
- chicken
- brown bread (wholemeal may not be digested properly by your baby yet)
- cereals such as oatmeal or porridge
- cheese
- dried fruit
- eggs
- fruit juice
- fish fingers and other prepared fish products
- ham
- butter
- fruit yoghurts or fromage frais
- plain biscuits and cakes

- nut butters (but not if your baby has shown an sensitivity to foods, or there is someone with a nut allergy in your family)
- low-fat sausages
- honey

Foods to avoid or serve only occasionally:

- deep-fried foods
- fatty meats, such as salami or processed meats
- jam
- jelly
- ketchup
- salt
- sugar
- sweet or salty biscuits and cakes
- sweetened breakfast cereals
- fruit squash and fizzy drinks
- tinned fruits in syrup
- refined or processed foods
- crisps and pastry

Offer your toddler a drinking cup to encourage independence and skill. Don't be surprised to have most of its contents sprayed around the room.

Sleeping

In the year following his first birthday, your baby's sleep will normally establish a pattern, although you may have a struggle with certain parts of the routine – such as settling him down at night, or urging him to sleep through. You can expect your baby to sleep somewhere in the vicinity of eleven to thirteen hours a night, and perhaps sleeping slightly less, between one to two hours, in the daytime. His increased mobility will mean that he is more physically exhausted, which may improve both the quality and the duration of his sleep.

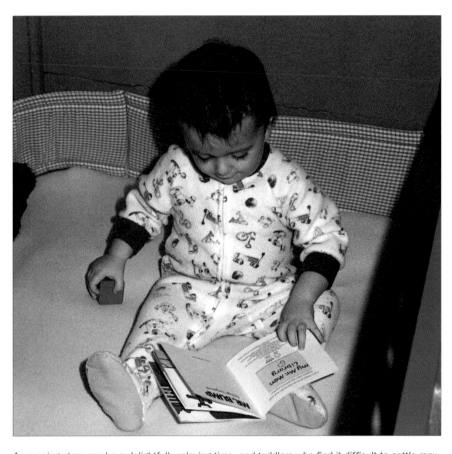

An evening story can be a delightfully relaxing time, and toddlers who find it difficult to settle may enjoy 'reading' on their own after sharing a story with you, or listening to a story tape.

Establishing regular daytime naps

● If you baby tends to have a sleep in the morning, after breakfast, don't let him sleep for too long. Tempting though it is to let him stay asleep, it will make him too lively for a nap later in the day. So gently wake him and play with him, or take him out for a short walk.

● Try to put him down at roughly the same time each day, so that his body will become accustomed to it, and experiment to see how much sleep he needs. If he has a good afternoon nap, but won't settle in the evenings, you may

need to cut the length of time he is sleeping in the afternoon, and perhaps move it closer to midday.

● Use a variation of your night-time routine to get him to sleep – a short story, a song, and maybe a gentle massage and a drink of milk will settle him, and he may feel sleepy and content when you lay him in his cot.

Sleeping through the night

There is no reason why a healthy baby shouldn't sleep through the night by the time he is a year old – some manage it at

only a month or so. If you have a sleep rebel on your hands you will need to get a routine established now more than ever (see page 168), and arrange some sort of regular sequence of events now that your baby can understand and remember more. If he continues to wake at night, here's what you can do:

● Check him regularly to make sure he is warm enough, and that there isn't a light shining nearby (a streetlight is a common culprit) which may wake him up.

● Relax him before bedtime with a drop of lavender or roman chamomile oil in his bathwater, or use a drop or two of oil in a light massage (see pages 200–201).

● If your baby is afraid of the dark, invest in a dimmer switch or a nightlight, or leave the door open so that light from the hall can shine in.

● If he finds a wet nappy uncomfortable at night, use a more absorbent nappy (or two cloth ones).

● If you take your baby a drink make it a small one, and gradually water it down until eventually it will only be water. If you are still breastfeeding, make the feed as short as possible, and stop as soon as you see him start to fall asleep.

● If you normally sing a lullaby, just sing a short refrain, and then stop.

● Don't take your baby out of his bedroom.

● If you normally lie down with him, sit instead.

● Stop taking him to your bed, and if he climbs in, gently and firmly return him to his bed.

● When your baby is about eighteen months old you can begin some sort of explanation for your new regime, and explain how mummy and daddy need to sleep at night so that they won't be cross and tired the next day, and encourage him to conspire with you. It may work!

● Provided you are consistent about keeping night-time contact to an absolute minimum, this process is likely to be successful after a few nights for some children, and for others after a few weeks.

Chamomile and lavender oil in the bathwater may help your child to calm down at bedtime.

Problems settling

If your evenings seem to be a series of trips to and from your baby's bedroom, you may need to take a firm hand at bedtime. Use a consistent approach, and think about modifying any habits you have inadvertently set up, such as rocking him until he is completely asleep before moving him to his cot.

● Teach your baby to fall asleep by himself, by putting him down in his cot while he is still awake. Use your normal bedtime routine, and speak softly and firmly to him, making it clear that you are saying goodnight.

● Establish and stick to your bedtime rituals, and refuse to do any more. Say 'no' to your child and mean it.

● Make it clear that your baby is expected to stay in bed for the night. Say goodnight, and leave the room.

● If he cries, leave him for a couple of minutes and then return. Repeat the kind and firm goodnight, but do no more than soothe him with a back rub or a quick cuddle and a few words of

A nightlight can calm babies who are afraid of the dark.

reassurance. Then leave the room again.

● Repeat the process for as long as it takes for your baby to realize that he has nothing to gain from crying. Remain firm, and try not to show any irritation or frustration. Don't weaken and allow your baby to get out of bed.

● You may find his cries distressing after many months of tending to his every whimper, but by this age he will need to learn that bedtime is for sleeping, and that you are not available to spend 24 hours a day with him.

Your toddler's first bed

Many parents choose to leave their babies in a cot until they are more reliable sleepers, or can be trusted to stay in bed when they are put there. You may need the cot for another baby, and choose this time to move him into his own bed. If your baby felt confined by his cot, moving him may help with sleep problems. But like any change, it can lead to an unsettled period. If your baby is inclined to play at bedtime, he may launch a series of missions to find you. With time and patience, he will learn that it is unacceptable to leave his bed in the evening, and that there are no rewards when he appears.

Developmental stages to watch for

Once your baby has learned to pull herself up on the furniture, she will be confident enough to let go first with one hand, and then both. Walking a few steps between chairs will soon follow, and she will soon 'forget' to hold on at all.

Your baby will begin to exercise his body and mind over the second year of life, and you will notice profound developments in the way he thinks, and is able to manoeuvre. Learning to walk is an incredible achievement, and one that should be encouraged but never forced.

There is a wide variation in the time at which different children learn to walk, and he may skip whole stages of preparation, and seem to go straight from an awkward crawl to walking with a staggering gait. Many babies learn to walk in stages:

1 Your baby will have learned to pull himself up to standing position, and he will move along the furniture or the cot by sliding his hands to one side, and then moving his feet afterwards. He will take care to hold on, and will not trust himself to let go.

2 He will stand back a little from his support, and carry his weight on his legs and feet, using his hands only for balance. He may use only one hand when he moves alone, or use the hand-over-hand technique.

3 He will learn to cross small areas between his support systems. Try to arrange your furniture so that he can move easily between pieces. He will always hold on to something, and won't let go until he has firmly grasped another means of support in the other hand.

4 He will begin to take his first unsupported steps, attempting to cross gaps that are ever larger. He may hold on, and then quickly step forward.

Even a confident walker may find it difficult to get to his feet without some support. Be prepared for many frustrating attempts and topples. It may help to ensure that he has sturdy supports in the early days, so that he can stand up with the minimum of fuss.

When he can walk around the furniture with some confidence, he will reach down to get toys, and move to things that interest him. Make sure he has bare feet in the early days of walking – shoes will inhibit his movement and make it more difficult for him to balance.

6 He will walk independently, although he may not be able to go very far before he needs to rest, or to get some support.

Many children experience a setback after walking a little for some time. They may have hurt themselves while toppling over and be anxious about trying again, or they may become a little nervous when they realize what they are actually doing, and the independence it brings. He may also move on to another developmental 'stage', and be much more interested in sedentary activities than in walking. Setbacks are normal, and you should not force your baby to practise his new skill if he doesn't want to.

By the time he is about eighteen months old, he will be moving about quite freely, carrying a doll or pushing a toy as he walks. He may be able to run a little, and every part of his body will be focused on the effort involved. He will soon be able to squat down, and to climb up on the furniture, and to try to make his ride-on toys move as well.

His movements will become more controlled, and he will enjoy showing you his new tricks. Continue to show enthusiasm, and praise him for his considerable achievements – even if they do create a mess, or interfere with the activities of the household.

Play and how it can help your baby's development

Children will learn about their world through play, and they will use whatever is made available to them. Don't worry about buying the best or most expensive toys – a few simple toys will give hours of pleasure, and your baby will learn most from the things you have already in your household. Most of his play will probably be home-based, although as soon as he is steady on his feet, and has overcome his fear of strangers, you may wish to take him to a mother-and-baby group,

He will soon begin to stand alone, although he will be easily unbalanced and frequently plop down on his bottom. He may begin to stand unwittingly – perhaps loosening the grip of his hands to reach out for something, or turn to look around, and 'forget' that he needs to hold on.

5 When he is confident to take a single step, he will begin to walk with less and less support. He may walk two or three steps to get where he is going, but he will probably sit down if he gets frustrated. He may love holding your hands and 'walking'.

217

where he will meet other children and learn social skills. The toys and games you choose at home will enhance his development in a variety of ways, so it is helpful to keep a supply of different toys and activities on hand.

● Reading to your child will encourage his use of words, and his understanding of them. He will also learn to pick out objects and give them a name.

● Water play – in a bucket with warm, soapy water, or even in the bath – will teach your child how things move in water, how they sink, or bob up and float.

● Playdough, clay or other modelling materials. As soon as your baby is reliable enough not to put everything

Outdoor play can provide hours of enjoyment. As soon as your toddler can be relied upon not to eat everything he picks up, a sandbox is an ideal place to play.

directly into his mouth, you can begin to give him toys that will encourage him to use his hands to make shapes, or even just to feel the sensation of squeezing and pounding.

● Toys on a string are fun for your child because he will be able to control them, and bring them along with him as he moves. He will learn how to make things move by his own volition, and may try to make other things move after him as well.

● Bricks are excellent first toys, and he will do everything from chewing them to building ever-larger towers. He will have to learn how to make them work herself, which will build his confidence and teach him the basic skills of engineering.

● Threading toys encourage his hand-

He will learn from the texture and properties of sand, even if early sand-castles don't work out.

Encourage your baby to build towers of bricks, which encourages hand-eye co-ordination, and teaches him to learn how 'small' and 'large' work.

Shape sorters encourage your toddler to understand the basic shapes, and how things of the same size go together. Fitting small shapes into larger ones will also improve her hand-eye co-ordination.

eye co-ordination and will also help him to group things and create sets.

● Shape sorters help him to recognize shapes, and to learn that things of the same size go together (fit into the sorter). One of your child's most important tasks

is to notice similarities and differences between things and learn to group them together. He will also practise his hand-eye co-ordination as he learns to fit small shapes into larger ones.

● He will enjoy emptying and filling

things – which teach him about quantities, weights and measuring. He will put bricks in a bucket, pour water in and out of cups, and fill containers with sand.

● Give him miniature farmyards, or

Every child becomes frustrated at some point, as the skills he is learning never seem to keep apace with his active mind. Gently encourage your child if he is finding something difficult, and when the going gets tough, change activities.

Creative expression is enormously important for your toddler, and he will love using his imagination, and a variety of different media, to create masterpieces. Show him how to use a brush, or try finger-painting, which is often easier to manage.

shopping. He will learn by copying you, and he will feel pleased to be able to do 'grown-up' things with you.

● He will love to do active things, such as climbing, sliding, balancing, swinging and running, and if your house or garden do not allow this, make time to take him to your local park where he can experiment with his body and practise his growing skills.

● Toys that he can push, pull or ride on will please him as he will enjoy taking things along on his travels, as long as they are easy to control.

● Throw a ball to him and encourage him to throw it back. His hand-eye co-ordination will improve, and he will enjoy playing games with someone he loves.

● Let him listen to music, and play with drums, tambourines, keyboards and instruments that he can blow. He will enjoy the sounds they make and develop his sense of rhythm. Music can be used

Toddlers can be a great help with household tasks.

train stations, which he can move around with his hands. He will begin to use his imagination, and make them do the things he wants them to do. It will also help his confidence, as he will feel in control of things that are smaller than him.

● Let him help you with the washing up, sorting the laundry (toddlers are very good are loading washing machines), basic dusting and grocery

Everyday kitchen objects can provide as much entertainment as the most expensive toys.

Your toddler will take great pride in his achievements, and you should offer plenty of positive encouragement when he is successful.

At one year

● walks around the furniture competently

● may walk around the floor on arms and feet

● many can now walk alone (between nine and eighteen months)

● drops from a walk to sit with a poorly controlled bump

● picks up small items with a good pincer grip

● gives and takes objects from you

● puts small blocks into a container

● throws toys to gain attention

● has a tuneful babble

● usually says two meaningful words

● turns when his name is called

to soothe, or to encourage a sense of fun, and if he has lots of music in his young life, he will learn to appreciate it.

● By drawing and colouring simple shapes, he will control and exercise his imagination.

● Most importantly, leave plenty of time for one-to-one talking and cuddling. Your toddler is growing up but he will

need your comfort and the knowledge that you are still there for him. It will give him the courage and the security to try new things if he knows he has your constant back-up, and can revert to baby comforts when he wants to.

Basic developmental milestones

Your baby may begin to achieve his first milestones around the ages listed below. Every baby is different, however, and unless his skills are developing a number of months behind those of his peers, you have no need to worry.

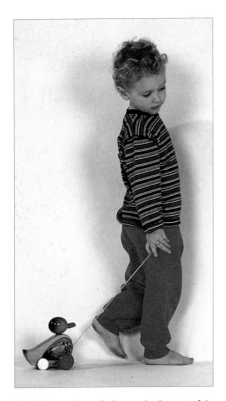

Toys that can be pulled or pushed are useful when your toddler is learning to walk. He will enjoy anything that 'follows' him, and doesn't require carrying, when arms are still required for balance.

- starts to show an interest in things he wants
- starts to show an interest in pictures
- looks for a toy hidden under a cup, and knows where to find it
- holds out arms to help with dressing

At fifteen months

- usually walks alone with broad, high steps
- can crawl upstairs
- plays with wooden blocks, and will post them into an open container
- enjoys throwing toys
- uses two to six words with meaning
- babbles away to himself and to others
- makes an attempt to feed himself

- starts to climb
- explores his environment with no sense of danger
- is often frightened by loud noises
- may be clingy and likes to be close to his immediate family
- will eat a cut-up version of the family dinner
- starts to show a dislike for wet or dirty nappies

At eighteen months

- walks well, with feet close together, and some flow of movement in his arms
- runs
- throws a ball without falling over
- holds a crayon or a pencil and can scribble with it
- uses between six and twenty words with meaning
- understands more words than he can use
- points to several parts of his body when asked
- points to items in a book
- starts to enjoy nursery rhymes
- demands what he wants by pointing
- is impatient and eager to do things for himself
- likes putting things in and taking them out of containers
- pushes wheeled toys around
- explores, climbs and gets into everything

- likes to be close to his family, and may be deeply suspicious of strangers
- begins to imitate you – pretending to write, to wash the floor, to read, or to tell you off!

Most toddlers will enjoy toys that can be pushed or ridden – particularly those that are miniature versions of things he has seen his parents use!

Cars, trucks and other vehicles will excite your toddler's imagination, and encourage him to create his own games, based on what he knows and has learned.

At two years

- holds on and can walk upstairs
- comes down again on his bottom or his tummy
- kicks a ball without falling over
- turns the pages of a book
- can do a simple puzzle
- can build a tower of six or seven blocks
- can copy a vertical line
- talks incessantly
- asks questions
- calls himself by his name, and gradually begins to use the words 'I' and 'me'
- can put two or more words together in a basic sentence or command
- plays beside but not with other children
- starts to pretend and to use his imagination
- may begin potty training

Learning language

You will have been communicating with your baby from the earliest days after the birth, and your baby will have become accustomed to 'talking' and listening to you as part of your daily life together. Towards the end of the first year, as your baby is becoming more independent, more complex sounds emerge, which spring from his desire to make contact, and from her experience of hearing you talk. Your baby will love it if you repeat words and sounds back to him. The first sounds are usually 'Mama' or 'Dada', and later the word 'no' will make itself a firm fixture in his limited vocabulary.

The words your baby learns next are likely to be those that reflect his experience, and the interests of your family. The time of a baby's first word, and the rate at which he continues to learn to talk, vary tremendously. Some children develop a huge vocabulary early, while others prefer to watch and consider what is going around them.

After his first birthday, he will begin to learn to ask for things, and to use words rather than signals and gestures, although for the first little while he may do both together. You will want to

You are your baby's first teacher, and you will be amazed at how quickly he picks up sounds and learns to speak, if you take the time to talk to him, and allow him time to respond. Share books with him, pointing out familiar words. Encourage him to repeat words and sounds, and praise his attempts at responding, even if they are wrong.

Stories are an excellent way to expand your child's vocabulary.

involve him in your activities so that he becomes accustomed to new words and experiences, and learns the context in which they should be used

read to him, and show him pictures in books – the more contact he has with words and their associated meanings, the more easily he will use them

Children in large families may be slow to speak, despite the amount of talking going on, because there may be no one person taking the time to listen to what a child of this age is trying to say. Sitting down quietly to look at a picture book with your baby, perhaps at bedtime, is one of the best ways of helping him understanding of words, while enriching the experience. He will enjoy hearing his mother or father talk about the pictures and will be encouraged in

this way to begin to say the words himself. To be able to look at a picture, to imagine it, to think about it, and then to find a word for it, is a major intellectual achievement for a baby. If he associates learning with comfort and fun, he will be much more likely to try for himself.

continue to encourage him to use new words and always acknowledge his attempts to communicate, even if he is using the wrong word.

Continue to:

sing to him and talk to him constantly

encourage him to listen and to respond when you talk

listen to what he says and respond to him

use single words with meaning, and repeat them often

ignore mistakes or the 'wrong' word, repeat the correct word but make it clear that you have understood what he meant

encourage him to repeat sounds and words and praise him when he does

It is important that children learn to communicate effectively before mixing with their peers at playgroups.

Potty training

There is no ideal time to start potty training, and there is no method that is guaranteed to work. Many mothers begin the process somewhere around the second birthday, but you may have more success if you wait until he is closer to his third birthday. Eighteen months is generally considered to be too early, and the average toddler will not be trained at night until he is about 33 months old (for many it will be much later). As your child approaches eighteen months, he will begin to have some control. By age of two, he will have some warning, and he may understand that you want him to control the urge until you have a potty beneath him.

There is a great variation between children, and much of it is connected with family history; parents with late bladder training, particularly at night, find their children have the same characteristics. Girls tend to become trained earlier than boys.

You will know when your child is ready by watching his responses and reactions:

The first week of potty training is, in most cases, a complete nightmare. Just when you are about to give up and buy the next size nappy – lo and behold, you have success! Try to make light of accidents, and offer encouragement and distractions when your toddler is seated on the potty. After a few successful 'seatings', he will begin to understand what it is you want him to do, and take great pleasure in pleasing you, and being independent.

226

● Is his nappy occasionally dry (does he have some bladder control)?

● If he is left without his nappy, and he urinates, does he understand what is happening, and understand the link between his body and the growing puddle?

● Can he understand and carry out simple requests?

● Has he expressed interest in sitting on a potty lavatory?

If he seems to be more or less ready to get on with training, you may want to begin by introducing a potty. If he doesn't seem ready for it after a few attempts, don't hesitate to abandon the whole operation until he is feeling more confident.

Bladder training

At some point, babies start to realize that they are wet, and many do not like the feeling. They may actually train themselves – after seeing mummy or daddy doing it every day, they will copy and know what to do when they are on the potty. Other babies do not mind being wet, and it might be a good idea to begin using training pants, or nappies that are slightly less absorbent, so that he will feel some discomfort and want to do something about it.

Some children are keen to try potty training, and if you reward them for their efforts, they will be pleased, and want to do it again. If your toddler decides to use potty training as another form of power over you, ignore it, and

It usually takes much longer to tackle bowel movements, and you should be prepared to spend some time with your toddler on the pot, in the event that one might be imminent. Keep an eye out for the signs that he might need the pot – a grimace and a grunt are usually a good warning!

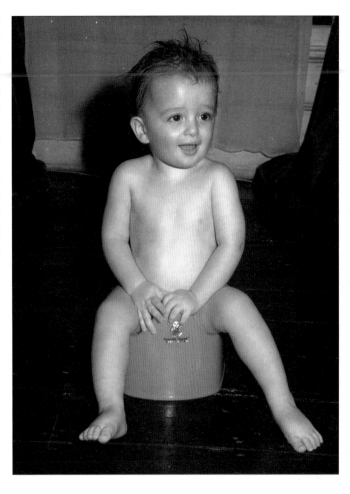

try later. If nothing happens, don't comment. Brightly say that you will try again later. Take care not to get angry with your child – encourage and reward when something does happen. If there are constant accidents, mop them up and lead him gently to his potty to explain what is expected. If he gets a reaction from you – even a negative one – he will repeat his actions. If he gets no response except when he is successful on the potty, that will be the action that is reinforced.

● Begin by leaving your child's nappy off in the house, but ask him regularly and without any pressure, if he wants to use the potty. Leave it in an accessible place, so that you can grab it quickly, and encourage him to use it if he seems to need to.

● Take the potty with you when you go out, and try not to revert to nappies, which will be confusing when he is learning to control his bladder. It's better to risk the odd accident. Increase the frequency of sessions on the potty, as long as your child is happy to do so.

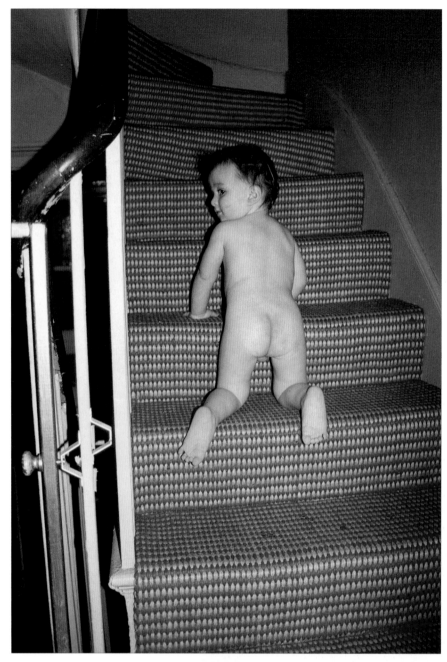

It is a good idea to keep nappies and pants off for the first days of potty training, since your toddler will not have mastered the art of holding on while you unfasten clothing. He will also be able to witness his own body's functions when accidents do occur, and make the connection between the potty and the interesting things he is now able to do, more quickly.

Bowel training

Your child may be dry long before he is able to control his bowel movements. Try to get him to sit regularly on the pot – perhaps after meals, or while you read him a story. If he has a bowel movement, praise him and make a fuss. If he sits regularly, and is relaxed and encouraged, he will eventually produce something. If he has an accident, don't chastise him, but lead him to the potty and seat him there. If you keep an eye on him (crucial while potty training) you will probably notice when he is about to begin a bowel movement. He may begin to screw up his face in concentration, or even grunt. Get him on the potty as quickly as you can without upsetting him, and gently encourage. Always wipe his bottom for him – he can't be expected to do this efficiently himself for another year or two.

Staying dry at night

Few babies can manage to stay dry at night, and you may want to keep on the night-time nappy for some while after he has been potty-trained. Try to encourage him to use the potty before bedtime, and if you want to, lift him in the night. This is unlikely to teach him to waken and go when he is soundly sleeping, but it may save you having to change bedding and pyjamas. As he becomes accustomed to holding his bladder during the day, it will sink in at a

If he resists, try again later, and slow down the pace.

● Make sure he is wearing clothes that can be easily removed.

● Keep a change of pants and trousers at hand for emergencies.

● Seat boys on the potty rather than teaching them to stand – it is easier to control the flow, and they will feel more comfortable sitting while they wait for something to happen.

Potty dependence

Use a variety of potties – perhaps at other people's houses – as well as the lavatory, with a seat fitted in the centre so that he doesn't fall in, to avoid him becoming dependent upon his own potty. Let him see that all lavatories serve the same purpose, and show him that he can achieve the same good results in other places that he does at home.

subconscious level, and he will automatically do so at night. Night wetting is not considered to be a matter that warrants concern until your child is five years old, after which you may need help. There are many four- and five-year-olds who are still wetting the bed at night, and it is something that the majority of babies and children grow out of in time.

The worst thing you can do is chastise children and tell them they are naughty for wetting the bed, as this will make them more anxious and more likely to have accidents.

If all your efforts fail ...

Wait. There is a certain amount of convenience involved in using nappies – you won't be summoned dozens of times each day to wipe bottoms and settle your baby on the potty, and you won't find that every important telephone conversation you make is punctuated by a singsong 'I've finished my poo...'. Choose a period when your child is being co-operative, and don't apply any pressure. Take heart from the fact that all babies are trained eventually, and it doesn't matter if yours is the last!

If your baby manages to wake in the night and warn you of an impending bladder or bowel movement reward him with warm praise. Night-time accidents should be dealt with swiftly and without fuss. Make sure you always have clean pyjamas and bedclothes standing by.

Everyday care

Let your child have time to play in the bath but don't leave him unaccompanied in case of accidents.

Your one-year-old will be keen to begin doing things for himself, and you will want to encourage him to put on his own boots, or to brush his own hair. He will be able to use a washcloth – probably inefficiently – and he may begin the early stages of potty training, which will be a huge source of pride for him. He is bound to become dirtier, and messier, as he is out and about, and both eating by himself and bathtime will become more than a routine!

Changing nappies

Until your baby is potty-trained, you will have to continue to change nappies as frequently as required. Most toddlers hate having their nappy changed, as it interrupts whatever activity they are engaged in, and they may squirm, twist, cry or even refuse point blank to open their legs. Try to find ways of distracting him – with toys, talk, tickling and games – while you change him, and do it as quickly and efficiently as you can. You may want to involve him by asking him to hold and hand you the baby wipes, or to smooth down the tab of a disposable nappy. If he finds nappy-changing fun, he will be less likely to resist.

Try not to get angry if he resists – use every distraction technique you can think of – and rest assured that this stage will pass. Your rebellious 15-month old, may, at 18 months, come and tell you when he has a wet or dirty nappy.

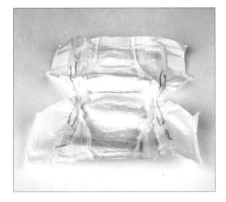

Some independent babies will attempt to take off their own nappies – whether they are wet or not.

Hair washing

Unless your child's hair is particularly dirty, there is no need to wash it any more than once or twice a week. If he hates having him hair washed, involve him in the activity. Ask him to hand you the shampoo, and maybe pour a little into your hand (be prepared for messes!). Explain what you are doing when you lather, and take extra care not to get water in his eyes. Allow him to pour water over his own head – some babies find this fun! Invest in a

Give your toddler his own toothbrush, and let him practise while you brush your own teeth.

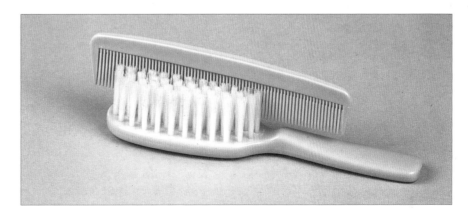

A soft brush and comb can help keep hair tidy and tangle-free, and your toddler will enjoy brushing your hair and his own.

protective ring that sits along the hairline, and keeps water from his face. Ask him to help you wash your own hair over the sink or the bathtub, so that he sees it is a normal activity and one which can be pleasurable.

As his hair grows longer, it may be difficult to comb. Use a wide-toothed comb and a good leave-in conditioner, to help ease out tangles without hurting him.

Bathing and washing

You will inevitably face battles when you need to wash your baby's face and hands, and you can begin teaching him how to do it for himself even from eighteen months (although he will not be reliable for many months to come). Do it quickly and maybe play a game with the washcloth, which will make him laugh. Use soft cloths that don't scratch his face, and gentle soap that won't irritate his eyes if it should get in them.

Bathtime will now be fun, and your baby will be able to sit largely unsupported in the tub. Give him his own sponge or washcloth, and encourage him to use it. He will be able to hold his own toothbrush, and he can have a turn at 'brushing', after you have cleaned his teeth. If he hates having his teeth brushed, do it in the bathtub as part of your cleaning routine, and let him help.

Give him plenty of bath toys that will inspire him – buckets, floating balls and ducks, boats and sponges will all have different uses, and bathtime can be as much of a learning experience as any other daily activity. Show him how to pour water from one bucket to another, and how a duck bobs back up to the surface when you push it under. Bubbles are fun, and if your baby does not have sensitive skin, they can be an excellent way of cleaning him while he plays. Water is enormously therapeutic, and even the most fractious baby will relax in the bath. If you need to calm him down, add a few drops of a relaxing aromatherapy oil, such as roman chamomile or lavender, but give him the opportunity to play, as it will help him to unwind.

Mealtimes are a time of confrontation for most parents. Refusing food is one of the few ways in which toddlers can express their independence. Let him have the freedom to feed himself with reason.

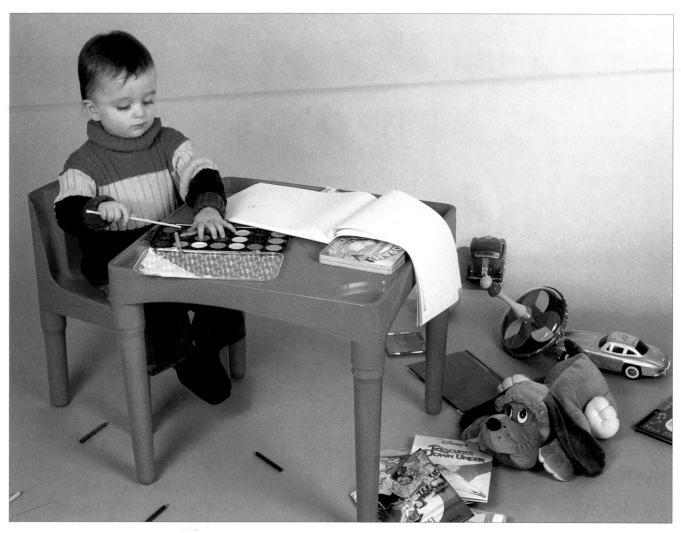

There is no point in worrying about the mess your toddler makes while he is playing, whether of his clothes or your room. Learn to be laid back about it and clear up at the end of the day.

Clothing

Choose clothing that is machine-washable and allows as much freedom of movement as possible. As you near the days of potty training, you may want to avoid things like dungarees or tights, which may take some time to manoeuvre down and off. Don't dress your child in clothes that you mind getting dirty, or which are fussy and difficult to clean. Clothing is designed to keep him warm and to protect him, and he is bound to get things grubby in his ever-greater exploration of the world both inside and outside your home.

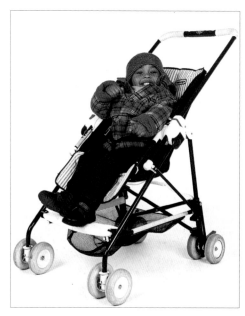

Independence only goes so far and little legs will get tired on long walks to the shops, so make sure the pushchair is still at hand. You don't want to have to carry them far at this age!

Discipline

As your baby strikes out on his own, and enjoys his independence, one of his first words is likely to be 'no' – and you may find that you are in for a series of constant battles. It is essential for a baby to progress and to learn to do things for himself, and he will naturally resist your wishes to do things for him.

Let your baby say 'no', and listen to him. If his natural inclination to say 'no' is not respected, he will become either over-obedient, desperately needing your approval, or he will become obstinate and difficult to manage. In the end, you will want to encourage your child to have a mind of his own, and to stand up for himself, and therefore you must respect his attempts to stand his ground. He must be able to feel that he can express his feelings without being punished, or made to feel that he is being naughty. If you give him some freedom to explore things, he is more likely to submit to rules when it is important. Save your own use of the word 'no' for emergency situations, and gently distract or explain rather than slamming down rules and regulations that will, in the end, not matter. Think about the things that are most important to you – safety, for example – and avoid making unimportant events into issues. You may be house proud, but it is not the end of the world if your child gets a muddy hand-print on the wall. You will not want him to be

Discipline can be difficult for parents of young children, particularly when you have more than one, both of whom need time and considerable attention. Try to remember that your toddler will learn by example, and if you are polite, calm and co-operative and, above all, respectful, he will be much more likely to respond in kind. Try to be positive and clear, and take the time to explain why he must do something, so that he will be able to apply his 'knowledge' in the future.

destructive, and you will need to guide his behaviour gently, but once gain, it isn't an intentional act of vandalism if he rips up the letter you were writing, or tips the contents of the wastepaper basket all over the floor. Show him positive things he can do, and try not to over-react to the normal messes and high spirits of toddlerhood.

Discipline does not mean punishment, but it does mean being firm, deciding when to set limits and when you have to say 'no'. You will have to occasionally, but if you are respectful of his own use of the word, he will be much more likely to understand that he must respect your wishes too.

● Try to decide in advance on how you wish to raise your child – there is nothing more confusing for a child than

parents who are battling with each other!

● It is healthy to allow your child to get away with things occasionally, and let him think he can trick you, but it is equally important to be clear when it is a game and when it is serious.

● Your child will recognize by your face and your voice when you are displeased, and in most cases, he will want to do something to make you happy again. If you always encourage productive and non-destructive behaviour, and ignore the bad, or simply greet it with a frown, he will realize that he must behave in a certain way to get the response and attention he loves.

● Try to avoid hitting or slapping your child, which will insult him, and

Some toddlers sail through the 'terrible twos' without a tantrum in sight. Others find life more difficult, and react to any discipline with full-scale drama. Try not to respond with anger – and encourage him to reason and discuss things rather than throw a tantrum. While it is not a good idea to completely ignore a distressed child, make it clear that this type of behaviour will not win him attention. Reward him when he behaves well and he will soon get the message.

encourage his own violent response to situations that make him unhappy or angry. However, a slap on the wrist in very exceptional circumstances – when he has, for example, repeatedly done something that endangers either himself or someone else – and the shock of being hit by the person he loves most will probably stop him dead in his tracks, and make him think the next

time he considers the same activity again.

● Never save punishment or discipline for later. Young children have short memories and they may be bewildered if you seem to be angry with them for a whole day – the 'naughty' event having long since passed. Deal with him firmly when he needs to be disciplined, immediately after he does something

that you consider naughty or dangerous.

● Don't hold grudges. Your carefree baby will not understand why you are angry after the event, and he may begin to associate his now positive behaviour with you being angry.

Coping with temper tantrums

There will be times when your baby responds to being thwarted with a tantrum, or a fit of temper. Toddlers do not know how to 'wait' for things, and to him you are saying 'no', even if you do mean to give in at some stage. Don't become angry when he flies into a rage – he will be frightened by his own lack of control, and will probably be afraid that he will lose your affection. Let him cry, and get out his frustration while you talk quietly and gently. Hold him when he calms down a little, and he will feel more secure and in control. If he throws a temper tantrum while you are out of the house, scoop him up and change locations. Don't worry about what other people think. Whenever possible, ignore tantrums and he'll eventually learn that they get him nowhere, and that your response was not the one he had hoped for. Above all, don't give in. If you give in once, you give him the message that tantrums are an appropriate way to get what he wants.

Crying babies are trying to communicate a need – hunger, fear, loneliness or a dirty nappy.

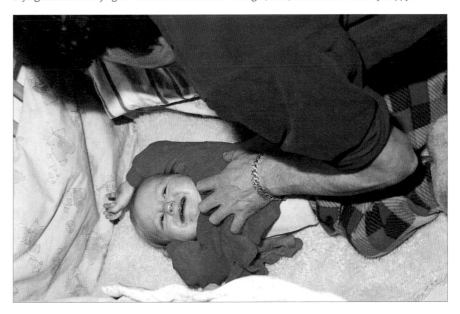

You and your doctor

The doctor with whom you were registered before you became pregnant may not be the right one for you once you have had a baby, and in some countries you will need to choose a specialist paediatrician. The relationship you have with your doctor is an important one, and you will need to feel that you can call upon him or her when you are anxious without feeling embarrassed or over-anxious. Select a doctor of a particular sex, if you prefer – it is perfectly within your rights so to do.

While your children are small, you need to be able to trust your doctor, and to know whether it is possible to have home visits in an emergency, or night calls. You will want to feel that your doctor has time for you, and doesn't

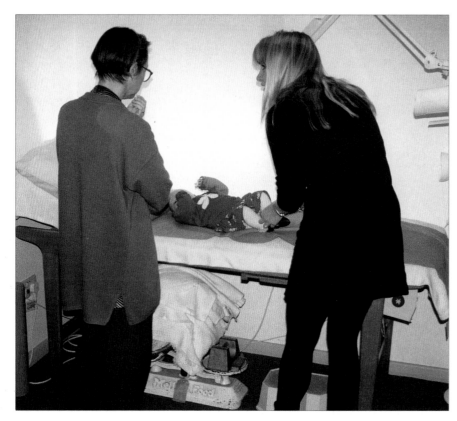

Your doctor is an important ally when you have young children, and you must never be concerned about being a too-frequent visitor, or asking too many questions. A good doctor recognizes that parents will be concerned about what may be minor health or behaviour problems, and will take the time to help you through difficult periods.

Contacting your doctor

You are responsible for your baby's health and well-being, and you have the right and duty to see your doctor if you need medical advice. Don't worry about wasting your doctor's time, and ensure that you understand his advice or explanations, so that you can learn from the experience, in the event that it may recur some time in the future. Checking babies and children to ensure that all is well is not a waste of your doctor's time, but a part of his or her job.

usher you out of his office before you are satisfied, or fully understand a diagnosis or proposed method of treatment.

Babies and young children can become ill quickly, and if you are concerned about anything at all, you should contact your doctor – do not be put off by fears that you may be an over-frequent visitor. You know your child better than anyone else, and you are, therefore, the best judge when things are not right. Instinct plays a large part in diagnosis and every good doctor will respect your intuition.

New babies in particular cause a huge

degree of anxiety in their parents, and it will obviously take you some time before you come to recognize abnormal behaviour and perturbing symptoms. You must feel comfortable asking for help whenever you are anxious, and let your doctor advise you accordingly. If you need more support during the first few weeks of your baby's life, your doctor can normally arrange for someone – a nurse, a health visitor or a midwife – to visit you regularly. You could also join a post-natal group, where you will be able to share your concerns.

An older baby should be taken to the doctor if he seems unwell, or if there is any radical change in his behaviour. In many cases, changes in patterns of behaviour are the main indicators of illness setting in, and you are in the best position to notice these and get the appropriate treatment before full-scale symptoms set in.

As your child gets older, you will probably be calmer about his health, and about his ability to throw off illnesses, and you may find that you have learned a great deal about child health yourself, and may feel confident in making basic diagnoses and dealing with common ailments at home on your own.

If you do plan to go 'alternative', talk to your doctor and explain your reasons for doing so. Make sure he or she is aware of any complementary treatments you are using, and ensure that you choose a practitioner who is both registered and approved by a major governing body. Never discontinue medication without the approval of your doctor.

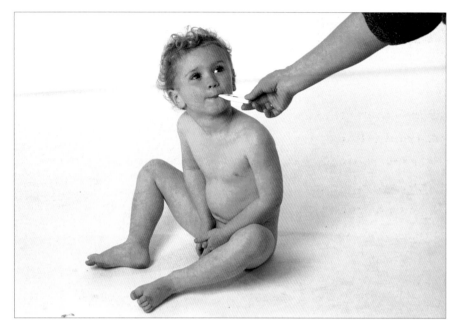

Your child's temperature will rise as a natural response to fighting infection. In many cases, it is a good sign, for it means that his immune system is working. Small rises in temperature (to about 37.4°C/99.4°F) are not usually caused by illness, and can normally be ignored. Anything above this should be monitored, and you should take steps to keep him cool. Take his temperature every hour or so, using a fever-tester, or a mercury or digital thermometer, used under the arm. As soon as your child is old enough to be trusted not to bite the thermometer, you can take his temperature in his mouth, using a non-glass, non-mercury thermometer.

Home visits and night calls

Most parents will find themselves in the position of requiring urgent medical care at some point, and anxieties can be more acute in the early hours of the morning. If you are genuinely worried,

and feel that your child either needs hospitalization, or a prescription immediately, don't hesitate to call your doctor. Many doctors will be able to provide advice over the telephone, and will visit if they feel it is necessary.

Try not to bother your doctor if it can wait until a visit can be arranged for the following day. Ask your doctor to come to your home only if you cannot move your child, or transport him safely. Above all, use your intuition — if you are

seriously alarmed, chances are you have a reason to be, and no doctor will mind following up on your concerns.

Complementary treatment

Some health conditions can be safely addressed by complementary medical practitioners, and the alternatives to conventional drugs can be appealing for a variety of reasons. Many doctors now endorse the use of complementary medicine, which is often successfully combined with conventional treatment. You may wish to see a homeopath, for example, if your child has a chronic condition such as asthma or eczema, which is controlled rather than cured by conventional medicine, or a nutritional specialist or a herbalist may also be successful in treating a condition that has not responded to the remedies offered by your doctor. Babies who have had traumatic births may benefit from cranial osteopathy, and aromatherapy is excellent for minor complaints.

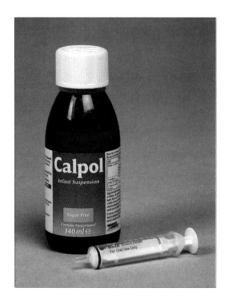

The best way to administer liquid medicine is a plastic 'syringe', which allows you either to 'shoot' the contents into your baby's mouth, or to allow him to suck it out. Syringes are useful for all children, particularly babies who are too young to suck from a spoon, or older children who are too active to sit still long enough for medicine to be administered, or who are resistant to the idea of taking medicine from a spoon.

Common ailments

Asthma

Asthma is a very common respiratory disease affecting about one in ten children, and it appears to be on the increase. In conventional terms, the disease is not curable but is treatable and tends to get less severe as children enter their late teens or early twenties.

Symptoms

● Recurrent cough
● Wheeze
● Chest tightness
● Shortness of breath

Not all the symptoms are present in each child, and often a child's only symptom is a recurrent cough which does not respond to courses of antibiotics.

Asthma is usually worse in the night, and night-waking with chest symptoms is a good indicator of under-treatment.

Asthma is often triggered by:

● Exercise
● Change in air temperature
● Fumes, including perfume
● Animals
● House dust

Asthma, eczema and hay fever often run in families. The incidence of asthma is rising but the reasons for this are unclear; the likely causes include increased environmental pollution, and food allergies and intolerances.

Treatment is with two types of drug: relieving drugs and preventing drugs.

● The relieving drugs such as salbutamol (Ventolin) and terbutaline (Bricanyl) act within minutes to open the airways and bring relief from symptoms, but wear off within a few hours and fail to deal with the underlying inflammation of the airways.

● Preventing drugs such as beclomethasone (Becotide), budesonide (Pulmicort), or sodium chromoglycate (Intal) tackle the root of the problem – the inflammation in the airways. They act slowly over several hours and their full effect may not be apparent for several days. These drugs should be used regularly, whether the child is well or ill, in order to keep the inflammation at bay and prevent long-term or permanent damage to the airways.

NATURAL TREATMENTS

● A homeopath will be able to prescribe constitutional treatment – in other words, treatment that is designed to suit your child's individual constitution. All remedies are compatible with orthodox treatment, and the success rate for cures is very promising. If your child has a sudden asthma attack, especially after shock or exposure to cold, try Aconite 30c, which can ease the symptoms.

● A nutritional therapist will decide if the underlying cause is linked to nutritional deficiencies, or allergies or intolerance to foods or other substances. Treatment would be once again aimed at your child's specific needs.

● Roman chamomile essential oil can be diluted in a little grapeseed or even olive oil and rubbed into the chest to ease spasms and help to relax your child.

Balanitis

Balanitis is inflammation and soreness of the foreskin of the penis. It is common in boys with a very tight-fitting foreskin, making it difficult for the urine to flow out easily. The foreskin often balloons when the child passes urine.

Symptoms

● Pain when urinating
● Inflammation, redness around the end of the penis
● General discomfort

Treatment

● Your doctor will probably first try a local antibiotic or anti-inflammatory cream – eye ointment is commonly used for children. If this does not work, a course of antibiotics may be necessary.

● Circumcision may be required for recurrent balanitis.

NATURAL TREATMENTS

● Add salt water to your child's bath, and gently bathe the area to encourage healing. If there is obvious infection, one or two drops of tea tree oil can be added to the bathwater to help fight it off.

● Make sure your child has a good diet, rich in foods containing Vitamin C, such as citrus fruit, broccoli and leafy green vegetables, which will help him to throw off the infection more quickly.

● The homeopathic remedy Mercurius can be taken up to five times daily, for several days, at 6c dilution.

Chickenpox

Chickenpox is a contagious, common viral infection characterized by fluid-filled blisters which appear first on the trunk and then spread to the rest of the body. There is headache, fever and fatigue, and as they progress, the spots become very itchy, and then dry up and form a scab. The incubation period is ten to fourteen days, and sufferers are contagious from just before the spots appear.

Treatment

Your doctor may suggest calamine lotion to ease the itching, and paracetamol to relieve the temperature. In most cases, children will recover within about ten days.

NATURAL TREATMENTS

● There are some good homeopathic remedies, which work well for children, including: Variolinum, which can be taken once in cases where there is an epidemic of chickenpox, before your child acquires the illness, and symptoms should be less severe. Rhus tox can be taken for a few days after contact with an infected child, and then again as soon as the first spots appear. Aconite is useful in the early stages of the illness, as is Belladonna, for the fever.

● The flower essences chicory, hornbeam and cherry plum are usually suggested to help relieve some of the discomfort. Impatience can ease irritability.

● Essential oil of lavender can be dabbed directly on spots to ease the itching and encourage healing. Lavender also has an antibacterial action, which will help prevent a secondary infection.

● Eat plenty of fruit and vegetables, and drink raw vegetable juices in order to help cleanse the body, which will reduce the severity of the condition.

● Cool the itchy spots with cold compresses, and make your child comfortable.

● Try to discourage your child from scratching the spots. Scratching can lead to bacterial infection and scarring.

Caution: When fever lasts for more than a couple of days, or there is an obvious chest infection accompanying the rash, see your doctor. Very rarely, chickenpox pneumonia can occur as a secondary infection.

Colds and flu

Small children are more susceptible than adults to the viruses causing colds and flu because their immune systems are immature, and antibodies have not yet been developed against them. At school age, children often develop a new crop of illnesses as they come into contact with viruses carried by other children. Symptoms of a cold include a running nose, headache and sometimes a cough. There may be a mild fever and a feeling of general malaise.

Treatment

Your doctor may suggest you take steps to lower your child's temperature (see page 245) and advocate paracetamol. Antibiotics will only be prescribed for a secondary infection.

NATURAL TREATMENTS

● Chamomile will soothe an irritable child and help her to sleep. Chamomile also has antiseptic action, which will help to rid the body of infection, and works also to reduce fever and feverish symptoms. Make an infusion using a herbal teabag, and allow it to cool. Sweeten with a little honey, which also helps to relieve the symptoms of a cold.

● The homeopathic remedy Pulsatilla is useful if your child is clingy and irritable, and when there is thick yellow discharge. Administer every four hours, at 6c dilution. Bryonia helps an irritable child who is thirsty and wants to be left alone. Mercurius is for a child with an earache, and swollen lymph nodes in the neck.

● Try a few drops of lavender or tea tree oil in a warm bath to encourage healing and help to open up the airways.

● Position your child's head over a steaming bowl of water with a few drops of essential oil of cinnamon. Place a towel over her head to make a tent, and let her sit there for 4 or 5 minutes to ease congestion.

● Encourage your child to drink plenty of water, fresh fruit and vegetable juices, particularly those rich in Vitamin C. She should get lots of rest to help her shift the infection. Avoid dairy produce and foods that are difficult to digest, until the illness has cleared.

Cough

Cough is the most common symptom presented to doctors. It may be due to a respiratory infection, usually viral, to asthma or to a post-nasal drip. If the child has not lost his appetite and has no difficulty breathing through his mouth, then the cough will usually settle within a week or two without any treatment. Recurrent or prolonged cough may be due to asthma.

A cough associated with a runny nose is often worse at night because the mucus runs backwards when the child is lying down and trickles down the throat. This triggers a reflex cough which protects the lungs by throwing the mucus forward to be swallowed. In babies the mucus may be so indigestible that they vomit to get rid of it from the stomach. In this case the child may vomit only once in 24 to 48 hours, the mucus is clearly visible in the vomit and the baby is otherwise well and happy with a good appetite and no temperature.

Treatment

If the condition is caused by a virus, there is little that can be done, other than to keep your child warm and dry, and set up with plenty of fluids, until he throws off the illness. If there is reason to suggest a bacterial infection, antibiotics may be prescribed. Some doctors may advocate a cough suppressant, but this is not advised unless the cough is non-productive and exhausting. Paracetamol may bring down any fever, and reduce the discomfort.

NATURAL TREATMENTS

Recurrent coughs may respond to constitutional homeopathic treatment (see above), and a number of remedies can be useful for acute conditions, including:

● Belladonna, when the cough is accompanied by a fever, and the child has bright red cheeks and neck.

● Ant tart is useful for a cough that causes the chest to rattle and makes breathing painful.

● Bryonia is for a painful, dry cough, which is made worse with movement.

● Spongia is excellent for croup (see below), and for a loud, crowing cough.

● Drosera for a tickling cough which is worse for lying down.

● Try Aconite if the symptoms come on suddenly.

● Chamomilla will soothe a child who is inconsolable, but better for being held.

● Dr Bach's Rescue Remedy, which is a blend of five different flower essences, is useful when your child experiences distress, or panics because breathing is difficult. Rescue Remedy will also help your child to sleep. A few drops can be taken internally, or applied to pulse points, and Rescue Remedy cream can be rubbed into the chest.

● Use lavender, myrrh, eucalyptus or thyme essential oils in a vaporizer in your child's bedroom, or add a few drops of eucalyptus and sandalwood to a carrier oil, or some petroleum jelly, and rub into the chest and upper back.

● Give your child lots of pasteurized honey, which has antibacterial action and will also soothe a sore throat.

● Plenty of fluids and bedrest will make it easier for your child to shift a cough. Offer only fluids for the first couple of days, and then just light meals, avoiding dairy produce altogether until the catarrh has shifted. Children (not babies) should be encouraged to sleep on their side rather than on their back.

Croup

Croup occurs when the larynx (voice box) becomes inflamed and swollen. It can be the result of a bacterial or viral infection, or even simply a cold. Because the larynx swells and blocks the passage of air, breathing can be very difficult, which can panic a child (and her parents). The cough is a loud bark or whistle, caused by inflammation of the vocal cords.

Treatment

● Your doctor will recommend steam inhalations (filling the bathroom with steam is useful), and if the cause is bacterial, a course of antibiotics.

Paracetamol, which has anti-inflammatory action, may also be recommended.

NATURAL TREATMENTS

● Spongia is the traditional homeopathic treatment for croup, and can be taken every 20 minutes during an attack. Aconite can be taken alongside.

● Rescue Remedy will help to calm the child, which will make breathing easier. Parents may also benefit from a few drops! Alternatively, rub a little Rescue Remedy cream into your child's chest and upper back.

● Rub a drop of lavender oil mixed with petroleum jelly into your child's chest and upper back.

● Offer a warm honey and lemon drink to ease the symptoms. Honey has strong antibacterial properties and will be useful if the cause of the croup is bacterial infection.

● Steam will help to open the airways and reduce spasm of the larynx. Put your child in a bathroom with the door shut and the hot taps running, or fill a bowl with boiling water and gently position your child's head over it, covered by a towel. Raise the upper end of the cot or bed so that breathing is easier. Provide lots of reassurance and comfort and try not to panic. Serve only light meals for the first few days after an attack, until your child is entirely clear of symptoms.

Caution: If your child turns blue, call a doctor immediately.

Diarrhoea

Diarrhoea is common, especially in warm weather. It may be accompanied by vomiting and abdominal pain

and is usually due to an infection or toxin in the bowel, when it is known as gastro-enteritis. Avoiding solid foods and taking plenty of fluids for 24 to 48 hours will usually settle it, but close attention should be paid to hand-washing, food hygiene and refrigeration, so the problem does not spread to other members of the household.

Toddler diarrhoea is a profuse diarrhoea in an otherwise well toddler who continues to have a good appetite and gain weight. It often contains undressed food particles. No treatment is needed if it lasts less than 48 hours, and the problem shouldn't recur once the child is potty-trained.

Treatment

● In prolonged diarrhoea or diarrhoea following foreign travel, medical advice should be sought so that a sample can be sent for analysis. Very occasionally the analysis will indicate that an antibiotic is needed.

● If your child is becoming dehydrated because of the diarrhoea, you may be advised to give him an electrolyte mixture to replace body salts and water being lost.

NATURAL TREATMENTS

● It is a good idea to avoid milk initially, and if you are bottle-feeding it may be recommended

Caution: Call your doctor urgently if your baby or child shows symptoms of dehydration, including a sunken fontanelle, unresponsiveness, drowsiness, prolonged crying, glazed eyes or a very dry mouth.

that you use a formula that is low in lactose.

● Children (not babies) may take a little herbal tea, such as peppermint or blackberry, which act as astringents to the gut and may help to ease the condition.

● Offer your child plenty of fresh, bottled water to drink, which will help to cleanse the system, and avoid fruit juices if possible.

● If the diarrhoea is linked to gastro-enteritis, the homeopathic remedy Arsenicum may be useful. Or you might try Colocynth, for diarrhoea accompanied by gripping spasmodic pains, with copious, thin, yellowish stools.

Ear infections

Infections of the ear are common in children during the first four years of life, and there is frequently ear inflammation with colds and sometimes with teething.

Symptoms

Your child will appear:

● unwell
● feverish
● off his food
● tearful
● in pain
● tired

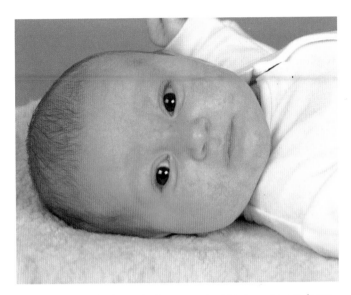

Eczema is becoming increasingly common in children, and tends to run in families. It usually begins with a bright red, scaly and itching patches on the cheeks, and there may be an itchy rash or scurf on the scalp itself.

Older children can say clearly that the pain is in the ear, but younger children may not give a clear indication of what is wrong.

The child pulling the ear is a good clue. Infections of the outer ear extend right down the hole to the eardrum, and commonly present a milder illness with a discharge from the ear. Beyond the eardrum, where even the doctor cannot see with his auroscope, is the middle ear. It is here that most ear infections occur – and the eardrum will become bright red.

Treatment

Treatment with antibiotics and paracetamol is usually effective, but some deafness may persist for a week or two until all the pus has drained away via a narrow tube to the throat.

NATURAL TREATMENTS

● There are a number of homeopathic remedies which can help, including Hepar sulph, if the pain is throbbing and your child seems to be soothed by warmth, and Chamomilla if your child is distressed and requires constant comforting. Aconite will help if the condition comes on very suddenly.

● Crush up some fresh garlic and soak it in some olive oil; strain and gently heat the oil to body temperature. Soak a cotton ball in the oil, and insert into the outer part of your child's ear. This acts as a natural antibiotic, and helps to draw out infection. The heat will also soothe the pain of the earache.

● A few drops of neat lavender oil can be placed in the ear on a cotton ball, or gently eased in with a cotton bud to act as a local anaesthetic, and to help fight infection. Lavender oil will also help to calm your child and help her to relax.

● Tea tree or lavender oil can be used in a vaporizer for their antiseptic properties.

● Make sure your child's diet is rich in foods containing Vitamin C and zinc, which boost the immune system and help to treat infection.

Eczema

Atopic eczema is a skin condition which often occurs when there is a history of asthma and hay fever in the family. This form is treatable but not curable conventionally, and frequently goes through good and bad spells. Other forms of eczema are due to sensitivity to certain chemicals in contact with the skin (contact dermatitis) or to certain foodstuffs.

● Contact dermatitis is present on or near the skin exposed to the allergen; for example, nickel dermatitis is found where cheap jewellery is in contact with the skin under necklaces, bracelets or earrings. Biological soap powders produce dermatitis under clothes, sparing the hands and face.

● Eczema, often severe and widespread, can be due to a protein in cow's milk. The common infant formula milks are based on cow's milk so it is worth trying a soya-based or goat's milk infant formula to see if the eczema settles.

● In atopic eczema, and in other eczemas where the cause cannot be eliminated, treatment needs to be continuous.

Treatment

Your doctor will probably prescribe antihistamines, which help with the itchiness or scratching, or antibiotics, if the skin becomes infected. As a rule, steroid ointments are only prescribed when the itching is so severe that it prevents the child from sleeping, or if the skin is severely infected.

NATURAL TREATMENTS

● Expert homeopathic advice, prescribed constitutionally, has a good chance of entirely curing the condition, but it will be necessary to see a therapist to ensure that the treatment is appropriate for your child. Some short-term remedies that can help in flare-ups include: Psorinum, when the eczema is worse on the legs and the skin looks dirty; Sulphur, when the skin is dry, itching and red, specially in bed or after bathing, and your child has a tendency to morning diarrhoea; Petroleum when the skin is bubbling, with yellow crusts, and worse at night; Rhus tox when the skin is blistered, particularly on the wrists, and worse in damp conditions.

● Oatmeal baths may be helpful, to ease itching and help to encourage healing.

● A nutritional therapist will be able to pinpoint any nutritional deficiencies or food allergies that may be causing or exacerbating the problem, and may prescribe a diet to encourage the action of the liver.

● Rescue Remedy cream, which is a blend of flower essences, can be rubbed into the affected area to soothe and encourage healing.

German measles (rubella)

Rubella is a viral infection characterized by symptoms which mimic a cold, and go on to include loss of appetite, sore throat, mild fever and swelling of the lymph nodes in the neck. There is an accompanying rash, made up of pale pink dots which usually cause only mild discomfort. The incubation period is fourteen to twenty-one days. The condition itself only lasts three to five days.

Treatment

Your doctor will suggest paracetamol to bring down any fever and reduce discomfort. Creams and ointments can be prescribed if the rash is very itchy; these include calamine and mild steroid preparations.

NATURAL TREATMENTS

● Some of the best homeopathic remedies include: Pulsatilla, when there is thick yellow discharge and hot, red eyes; Belladonna, for fever, a bright red rash and hot face; Phytolacca for painful ears and swollen glands, better on taking cool drinks; and Aconite if there is a high fever and not too much mucus.

● Merc sol where there is yellow discharge and a fever.

● Rescue Remedy may ease any distress.

● A few drops of lavender oil on the bedclothes, or on a hanky near the bed, will help ease symptoms and calm the child.

● If there is a build-up of phlegm, use a few drops of tea tree or eucalyptus oil in a vaporizer to encourage easier breathing.

● Frequent, cool baths will relieve any itchiness and bring down a fever.

Glue ear

Glue ear is a chronic condition affecting a large number of children. It is characterized by a thick, often bad-smelling mucus which builds up in the middle ear, impairing hearing, and causing the eardrum to perforate to allow the mucus to be discharged. The

condition arises mainly because the middle ear is unable to drain its secretions into the nose by way of the Eustachian tube. Unlike the other common forms of earache, glue ear is not primarily caused by infection.

The condition is usually symptomless, the only effect being deafness, and this, too, may be unsuspected as the affected child is often unaware that anything is wrong and may not complain. Such children are often accused of inattentiveness.

Treatment

Glue ear can fairly easily be treated by a simple operation in which a tiny cut is made in the eardrum and a small plastic drainage tube – a grommet – is inserted. This allows immediate equalization of pressure on the two sides of the drum and free drainage of middle-ear secretions.

NATURAL TREATMENTS

● Chamomile and echinacea herbs are antiseptic, and can be taken internally, or added to a foot or hand bath, to reduce subsequent infection and to relieve symptoms.

● There are number of useful homeopathic remedies, although it might be a good idea to see a homeopath for constitutional treatment, particularly if the condition is long-standing. You could try: Kali bicrom, if there is mucus in the throat and pain in the sinuses; Graphites, if there is a yellow discharge from the ear; Sulphur, if there is a thick, yellow, smelly discharge from the ear; or Calcarea, if there is discharge accompanied by swollen glands and night sweats.

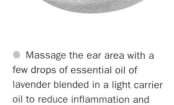

● Massage the ear area with a few drops of essential oil of lavender blended in a light carrier oil to reduce inflammation and encourage healing.

● A steam inhalation of eucalyptus, chamomile or lavender can help. Avoid foods which cause the mucus to be produced – dairy produce, refined sugars and wheat are the main culprits. Offer foods rich in Vitamin C and zinc. Ensure that your child is not in contact with cigarette smoke or other pollutions. Make sure his room is clear of dust.

Caution: Glue ear should be treated to avoid later hearing problems caused by scarring on the eardrum.

Headache

Headache in children is a common symptom with most feverish illnesses. Most are due to infections such as a cold, ear infection, gastro-enteritis or tonsillitis. However, headache and fever are also the signs and symptoms of the much rarer meningitis which can cause brain damage, fits, or even death, if untreated.

In meningitis typically there is headache, fever, vomiting, neck stiffness and photophobia (dislike of bright light). In the dangerous form, meningococcal meningitis, there may also be a faint rash but this is an unreliable sign. Not all the signs and symptoms are present in every case. If meningitis is suspected then medical help must be sought at once because a child with meningitis can get worse rapidly.

Headache without fever may be due to:

● Stress (tension headache) caused by problems at home or at nursery school

● Food allergies or intolerance

Treatment

Analgesics may be suggested for chronic headaches, but your doctor will investigate to uncover the cause before prescribing anything. If your child is troubled and is getting tension headaches as a result, some family counselling may help. Meningitis should be treated as a case of extreme medical emergency, and will be addressed in hospital.

NATURAL TREATMENTS

● If your child is feeling stressed by anything, try to spend time with her talking things through. She may just need a listening ear rather than advice; never undermine her confidence by saying that she is only being silly – treat all of her concerns with respect and acknowledge them, and gently reassure her.

● A few drops of lavender oil in the bath will calm her, and you can blend a drop or two in a little apricot kernel oil and gently massage her temples, and the back of her neck, to provide relief and encourage relaxation.

● Flower essences are extremely useful if there is an emotional cause to the headaches, and there are dozens to choose from. A good blend is Jan de Vries' Child Essence.

● If the headache comes on suddenly, try Aconite, at 6c strength. If headaches are chronic, or are manifested as abdominal pain, see a homeopath for constitutional treatment.

Impetigo

Impetigo is an infection of the skin which causes weeping and scabbing sores to develop and spread rapidly to adjacent areas of skin. It is highly contagious and the child should not mix with other children until the lesions are dry. It commonly starts on the face, the sores growing and spreading over a few days. The child remains otherwise well and happy with a good appetite.

Treatment

Treatment is usually very effective and involves antibiotics, either by mouth or in an ointment. Some doctors also prescribe a type of liquid soap to sterilize the rest of the skin and scalp, too, where the bacteria may be lurking with no outward sign.

NATURAL TREATMENTS

● Ensure your child has a diet rich in Vitamin C, which will encourage her immune system to fight off the infection.

● Add a few drops of echinacea to her juice three times a day. Echinacea is a herb that acts as a natural antibiotic while stimulating immune activity.

● Blend a little tea tree oil in some Vitamin E oil, and apply to the sores, using a fresh cotton ball or Q-tip for each application.

Kidney disease

Urine infections, common in adult females (cystitis), need investigating carefully in children. Passing urine frequently, burning or stinging when passing urine, blood in the urine, abdominal pain, wetting the pants and bedwetting are the signs and symptoms of a urine infection, although they may not all be present. In some children the only signs are loss of appetite or being 'off colour'.

Left untreated, the infection may rise further to the kidneys, causing abdominal pain and often fever and malaise. Kidney damage may ensue and, if recurrent or untreated may eventually lead to kidney failure, dialysis or kidney transplant.

Treatment

● Investigations are aimed at seeking a cause for the infection, because in some children a congenital abnormality makes them prone to urine infections. Surgical correction can prevent recurrent infection and thus prevent lifelong kidney problems.

● Nephrotic syndrome is an uncommon disease of the kidneys in which the child looks very puffy, particularly in the face. An abnormality develops which causes the kidneys to leak protein into the urine. The mainstays of treatment are a high protein diet and steroids, which usually lead to a cure.

NATURAL TREATMENTS

● Make sure your child drinks plenty of fresh, bottled water, which will help to flush the system.

● Cranberry juice helps to ease the symptoms of urinary infections by dealing with the bacteria.

● Give your child plenty of fresh, live yoghurt (not suitable for babies), which will help to build up her body's healthy bacteria, and will prevent future attacks.

● Mild chamomile tea, slightly cooled and mixed with a little honey, will help to ease symptoms.

Measles

Measles is a viral illness which can be very serious, particularly in children with reduced immune activity. It is characterized by white spots on the lining of the cheeks, and a very high fever as the rash comes out. The rash itself is brownish red, and the spots may join together. There may be diarrhoea, vomiting, pain in the neck (around the lymph nodes) and cold symptoms, including a cough and occasionally conjunctivitis. The incubation period is between eight and fourteen days, and the illness itself can last up to two or three weeks. Thankfully the spots are not itchy.

Treatment

Fever is generally controlled with paracetamol, and plenty of liquids should be taken. Antibiotics are not prescribed for the measles itself, but may be necessary if any additional complications develop. In the unlikely event of encephalitis, a brain infection which may occur secondarily, strong antiviral drugs may be used in the hospital. In Britain, children are routinely offered the combined MMR (Measles, Mumps, Rubella) vaccine between the ages of twelve and twenty-four months.

NATURAL TREATMENTS

● A compress of ginger (either a tincture, which your can buy in a bottle, or a ginger tea) may encourage the toxins to be released from the body.

● Some of the best homeopathic remedies include: Morbillinum, which can be taken for three days if your child has been in contact with a sufferer and will help to reduce the severity of the symptoms; Aconite and Belladonna for high fever; Pulsatilla is suggested when there is diarrhoea, yellow discharge and a cough; Stramonium is recommended when there is a high fever, a red face and convulsions.

● A few drops of roman chamomile in the bath will ease symptoms and help encourage sleep.

● Lavender oil can be dropped on the bedclothes or on a hanky by the bed as a calmative. It can also be applied neat to spots, to encourage healing.

● When there is a build-up of phlegm, and other symptoms of a cold, a gentle chest massage with a drop of tea tree oil in a light carrier oil base will help.

● Avoid all solid foods until the fever has gone. Offer plenty of fresh, cool water – fever can lead to dehydration. Bedrest is recommended until symptoms are completely clear.

Mumps

Mumps is a viral infection of the salivary glands which run from the ear down to the angle of the jaw and then wrap around the angle of the jaw on each side (the parotid glands). These glands become swollen and tender making the child look like a

Caution: Watch your child carefully as he recovers from measles. There is a risk of complications, including pneumonia, ear infection and bronchitis, and very rarely, encephalitis. If fever recurs several days after the spots have begun to heal, see your doctor.

hamster. Usually the child also feels unwell, runs a fever and loses his or her appetite.

Treatment

Treatment is with fluids, paracetamol for the pain and fever, and rest. Complete resolution is usual in a week or two. All children in Britain are now offered a vaccine to protect against Measles, Mumps and Rubella (MMR vaccine) between the ages of twelve and twenty-four months.

NATURAL TREATMENTS

● A number of homeopathic remedies will help to treat mumps, including Belladonna, for high fever accompanied by a red face, Aconite, at the onset of the condition, and Phytolacca if the neck glands feel hard and your child's ears are painful.

● Cold compresses may help to reduce swelling in the neck. Add a little lavender oil to the water before applying the compress, which will act as a local analgesic.

Nits or lice

This is an infestation of tiny insects which bite the skin to feed from the blood. These parasites lay their eggs, which are visible as tiny grey dots, on the hair shafts. Head and body lice are itchy and are highly contagious. They are a common problem among schoolchildren and seem especially to like clean hair.

Treatment

A shampoo, purchased from your pharmacist, will deal with the problem, but

wash all towels, clothing and bedding in boiling hot water, and disinfect combs and hair brushes after treatment. There is some evidence that treatment available from the pharmacist may cause some neurological damage in a small percentage of children, so it is worth consulting your doctor before purchasing anything.

NATURAL TREATMENTS

● Blend some lavender, tea tree and eucalyptus oils in some warmed olive oil, and apply to your child's head. Leave overnight, and rinse off in the morning. Apply every 48 hours as required. This works as a strong insecticide, and also helps to prevent infestation.

● Children who are prone to nits may benefit from a single dose of the homeopathic remedy Psorinum, at 30c dilution.

Rashes

In a small baby, a rash on the body is often heat rash, as babies have ill-formed sweat glands. The rash disappears on cooling down. Rashes in children are very common, most of them being caused by acute viral illnesses. Most of the viral rashes are

accompanied by a fever, loss of appetite and malaise, although some (such as rubella) are not.

Many of the rashes have a typical appearance, such as sparse itchy blisters in a spot of red skin (chickenpox). Others produce a generalized non-specific rash, frequently mimicking rubella (German measles), to which it may be impossible to attach an accurate label without unnecessary blood tests.

Treatment

Calamine lotion may soothe itchy rashes, paracetamol is useful if they come with a fever. Your doctor may prescribe antibiotics if there is a risk of infection from scratching, or if there is a bacterial cause.

NATURAL TREATMENTS

● Apply calendula cream to the affected area, to encourage healing and soothe inflamed or itchy skin.

● Rescue Remedy cream soothes sore and itchy skin, and encourages the healing process.

● Add a handful of chamomile flower, or a drop or two or roman chamomile oil, to your child's bath, to ease the symptoms.

Stomach ache

There are many causes of stomach ache in small children and babies. In infants, colic can be a problem (see page 153), or simply wind. In older children, a bowel movement may relieve any abdominal pain or discomfort. Over-eating, tension, gastro-enteritis and abdominal migraine are other causes. If vomiting or diarrhoea is present, contact your doctor.

Treatment

A warm drink, a hot water bottle on the tummy and avoiding solid food should ease the pain. If stomach ache is recurrent and eased by a bowel movement, constipation may be the problem. In those circumstances, increase your child's intake of fluids and fibre-rich foods, and cut down on refined and processed foods.

NATURAL TREATMENTS

● Ensure that your child gets plenty of fresh, bottled or previously boiled water, to flush the system of anything that may be causing the condition.

● Add a drop of chamomile oil to a little apricot kernel oil, and massage into the abdominal area to ease the symptoms.

● The homeopathic remedy Bryonia is useful if your child is very irritable, and screams at the slightest movement, and Chamomilla is good if your child seems better for comforting, but otherwise almost impossible to please.

Temperature

The child with a raised temperature will feel hot or cold, may perspire or shiver, will feel hot to touch and usually look flushed. He will lack energy, wanting to flop around or sleep rather than run everywhere as usual, be miserable and off his food. Babies may cry despite being cuddled, and be difficult to settle. If untreated, a high temperature will commonly cause a child to vomit, and rarely the child may have a fit (febrile convulsion).

The fever can be confirmed by measuring the temperature with a thermometer. A mercury thermometer should first be shaken down so that all the mercury is below the beginning of the scale.

● With a baby or young child, the bulb should be put in the armpit and the arm held to the child's side to keep it in place for at least a minute, preferably two, before it is read.

● With an older child, the bulb should be placed under the tongue with instructions to close the mouth without biting it. After removing it, rotate the thermometer between your fingers until the mercury can be seen clearly against the scale.

● The temperature is raised if it is greater than 98.4°F/37°C.

Treatment

● The child should be cooled down by removing clothes and excess blankets, and if necessary sponging with tepid (not cold) water, which is then allowed to evaporate.

● Paracetamol should be given regularly, four times a day.

● Cool drinks should be offered frequently.

In most childhood illnesses the temperature will subside in about 24 hours (a disturbed night!). If it persists any longer, medical help should be sought.

NATURAL TREATMENTS

● There are a number of homeopathic remedies which will be useful, according to the symptoms. The best one is

usually Belladonna, for fever, a bright red rash and hot face; Phytolacca helps when there are painful ears and swollen glands, better on taking cool drinks; Aconite should be tried if there is a high fever and not too much mucus; Merc sol is suggested where there is yellow discharge with a fever.

● Rescue Remedy can be taken to ease any distress and calm the child. Chicory, hornbeam and cherry plum are useful for all childhood illnesses that may cause fever.

Urticaria

Urticaria is an itchy blotchy rash commonly called hives. It is a harmless form of allergic reaction which will not make you feel unwell, but which can be very irritating. The causes of urticaria are many and vary from person to person. In some a particular food or drink may provoke it, in others simply getting hot or too cold may bring it on. In these cases the rash recurs whenever the stimulus recurs, but sometimes the rash is manifested only once.

Treatment

Your doctor may prescribe antihistamines to ease the itching, or a topical cream.

NATURAL TREATMENTS

● The best homeopathic remedies to try are Apis, for burning or swelling,

particularly of the lips and eyelids; Urtica, for a rash that feels like a nettle sting, worse for touching or scratching, and Rhus tox, for burning, itching and blisters. These remedies should be taken every 3 hours.

● The Bach Flower Remedy Impatiens is very useful for itching. Take internally or mix into a neutral cream and apply to the affected area.

● Urtica urens cream, which is available from healthfood shops and some good pharmacists, will soothe and promote healing.

● Aloe vera can be used topically to soothe the rash.

● A warm bath with essential oil of chamomile or melissa will soothe the skin and help to prevent stress-related attacks.

● Add a few tablespoons of baking soda to the bath to relieve itching.

Vomiting

Children vomit for many reasons, including a raised temperature or food poisoning. Whatever the cause, the treatment is initially the same – starvation and fluid replacement.

● Starvation should be for 24 hours at first, with no solid food at all.

● The best fluid replacement is a mixture of clean water (one pint), sugar (one tablespoonful) and salt (one or two pinches). Flavouring such as squash may be added if the child refuses to drink without it. When the first pint has been drunk, another should be prepared. If this gets vomited, sips should be offered rather than a cupful. In this way the stomach can usually be persuaded to keep some down.

● Babies may be offered full-strength or half-strength milk.

For babies that are vomiting, dilute their usual formula milk to half strength.

If the vomiting has not stopped after 24 hours, then the starvation needs to be continued for a further 24 hours. When feeding is restarted, it is wise to begin with a quarter of a slice of dry toast (no butter), then to wait for an hour. If it stays down, more can be offered. Then a small quantity of another food can be tried, followed by a further hour's wait. If a food causes vomiting, then revert to the foods which were safe. If they cause vomiting as well, return to starvation and fluids.

NATURAL TREATMENTS

● The essential oils of peppermint or lavender can be used in a vaporizer and inhaled to alleviate nausea and vomiting. Check with an aromatherapist about what will be suitable for a very young child.

● Make a cup of very weak blackcurrant or chamomile tea and offer to your child in small sips after it has cooled. This will help to soothe the digestive tract, and boost the immune system.

● Chewing a little fresh ginger, or drinking ginger ale, will help to settle the stomach, and is particularly useful for travel sickness.

Caution: If you are concerned about your child's vomiting, or it has no recognizable cause (an accompanying fever or excess mucus, for example), contact your doctor immediately.

Whooping cough

Whooping cough (pertussis) causes bouts of coughing and frequently vomiting, especially in younger children. It gets its name from the characteristic whoop when the child draws in his breath for the next bout of coughing, but the whoop may be absent in older children.

It starts with a runny or snuffly nose for about a week, together with the cough, which is always worse at night. There may be as many as fifty paroxysms of coughing which can be so severe that the face goes red or blue and the eyes bulge. The cough improves slowly over many weeks, often taking months to settle completely.

Whooping cough is highly infectious. Children should not attend nursery school or playgroup for twenty-one days from the onset of the cough.

There is no treatment to shorten the illness, only time will cure it. However a very effective vaccine is available and offered to all babies.

NATURAL TREATMENTS

● A few drops of tincture of the herb thyme, available in a healthfood shop, can be taken to loosen and expel the mucus. Thyme also works as an antiseptic.

● Elecampane is commonly used for children's coughs, and can be purchased in easy-to-use syrup form.

● After the bath, massage a little comfrey ointment into the chest and back to relax and expand the lungs.

● The homeopathic remedy Aconite can be taken during an attack, or at the beginning of the illness; Ant. tart is particularly good when there is a rattling cough with gasping; try Sanguinaria, for a harsh, dry cough; Drosera is useful when the cough is made worse by lying down, and there are pains below the ribs; Bryonia is suggested when there is a dry, painful cough and vomiting.

● Dr Bach's Rescue Remedy is excellent for calming a child who has difficulty drawing breath, and who is frightened by the condition. A few drops on pulse points, or sipped in a glass of cool water, will help.

● Mix a few drops of lavender and chamomile oils in a light carrier oil and massage into the chest and back area to calm your child, and to relax tensed muscles.

● Tea tree, lavender, chamomile and eucalyptus can be used in a vaporizer to help open up the lungs and reduce spasm.

● Increase the intake of foods containing Vitamin C and zinc, to aid the action of the immune system.

Caution: There is a risk of secondary infection, in particular pneumonia and bronchitis. All cases of whooping cough should be seen by a doctor. If the cough is accompanied by vomiting, make sure there is adequate intake of fluid to prevent dehydration. Call your doctor immediately if your child becomes blue around the lips.

Sleep disorders

All babies and children need different amounts of sleep, and most of them experience some difficulty sleeping at some point. Common causes of sleeping problems in babies are nappy rash, teething, colic, illness, being too hot or cold, or simply being wakeful. Older children may be worried about something at school, or a stressful event in the family home. Illness usually disrupts sleep patterns in some way. Some children experience night terrors, which may cause them to waken suddenly, screaming.

Children who will not sleep can pose tremendous problems for the parents. It often starts after an episode of illness in which the parents have to attend the child through the night for very good reasons. When the illness is over the normal sleeping pattern does not resume and the parents continue to stay with their child at night.

Disturbed sleep is regarded by many experts as a behaviour disorder. If a child does something good, he is praised by his parents and given 'rewards', such as extra attention and cuddles, which the child responds to by doing the same thing again. Unfortunately these are exactly the same rewards

parents tend to give to a child who wakes. The child is likely to wake again for more, and so a sleep disorder is founded.

Treatment

If your child is not ill, the cure is to withdraw the rewards.

● If the child might need lifting, it should be done without cuddling.

● If the child craves a drink, water only should be offered. If possible, leave it on the bedside table and do not administer it.

● Requests for anything else should be firmly but pleasantly refused with an explanation that it is time for sleep.

● If the child cries the moment the parent leaves the room, then the parent should stay, all night if need be, but refuse to give into any other demands. Alternatively, controlled crying (waiting for 5 minutes and then re-entering the room, then 10 or 15 minutes, with each subsequent cry) is also a successful technique, and teaches the child that it's not

acceptable to waken his parents, but leaves him secure in the knowledge that they are still there.

● Getting into bed with a child is also a reward (cuddling). Save the rewards, which may be fulsome, for the morning after a full night's sleep.

● Only a few nights of this firmness will usually cure the problem. But weaken and all the child has learned is to cry and make a fuss for longer!

NATURAL TREATMENTS

● The herb limeflower is useful for children who are nervous and sensitive, and it can be prepared in much the same way as a herbal tea. Take care to give your child only the recommended dosage.

● A crying baby may be soothed with an infusion of chamomile, offered an hour or so before bedtime, or when he wakens.

● A strong infusion of chamomile, lavender or limeflower can be added to a warm bath to soothe and calm a baby or child.

Caution: If you are concerned about the cause of your child's sleep problems, see your doctor.

● Some of the best homeopathic remedies for sleep problems include: Pulsatilla, for a weepy, clingy child; Chamomilla, if sleep is being disturbed by teething; Nux vomica, for irritability, and after a busy day; Bryonia or Colocynth for constant crying; and Calcarea or Ant tart if there are night terrors.

● A distressed child or baby can be given Rescue Remedy, which will calm him. Offer rock rose, another flower essence, for night terrors, or aspen if your child is afraid of the dark.

● Lavender oil, on a hanky tied near the cot or bed, will help your baby or child to sleep.

● A gentle massage before bedtime, with a little lavender or chamomile blended with a light carrier oil, may ease any tension or distress.

Your baby should enjoy the comfort of his bed, and should never be 'sent to bed' as a punishment, which sets up negative associations. If your bedtime routine is comforting and pleasurable, the final step – bed – will not seem a daunting or unhappy prospect. Babies under the age of one should never be left to cry for any length of time.

Basic first aid

By their nature, children are prone to accidents and mishaps. The likelihood of an emergency situation arising is greater than for any other age group and above all it is important for parents and carers to be prepared to deal with these emergencies.

Many emergency situations are handled differently for children, and you should, therefore, never assume that your child should be treated as an adult. Children are not always able to describe their symptoms and it is all the more important to be familiar with the features of a condition or situation so that you can act swiftly.

What to do in an emergency

There are certain steps to remember in any emergency. Above all, stay calm.

1 Assess the situation. Do so quickly. Think of:
● The nature of the accident and how it happened.

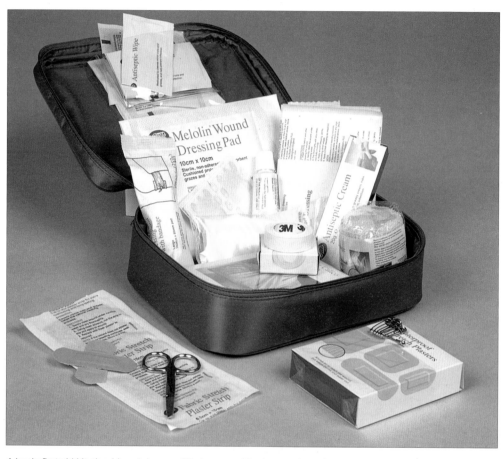

A basic first-aid kit should contain everything you need to dress cuts and grazes.

● Who is injured and how badly.

● Is there any existing or continuing danger or is the child causing danger to anyone else?

● Should the doctor or emergency services be called?

● Do I need help?

2 Assess the safety aspect. Do so quickly. Think of:
● Will you or anyone else be injured by treating the child?

● Can you remove the source of danger from the child easily and safely?

● Should you move the child – bearing in mind that you should not move a casualty unless absolutely necessary.

3 Ring for help. Call the emergency services, or call for a doctor.

4 Stay with the child and provide constant reassurance. If she is seriously injured, check her pulse and breathing constantly.

An emergency situation

1 Check the airway.

Tilt the head back and lift the chin.
Check that the airway is clear.
If it is blocked, try to swipe your fingers into the throat to clear any obstruction.

Caution: Remember not to panic. Children are sensitive and they will respond to anxiety.

2 Check breathing.

Is the child obviously breathing? For example:
● Is the chest rising and falling?

● Place your hand across the mouth and nose – can you feel any air movement? Can you hear any sounds of breathing?

● Place your head against the casualty's chest – can you hear any breathing?

If the child is not breathing, begin artificial respiration.

3 Check circulation.

To check for a pulse in a baby:
● Place two fingers in the inner arm, halfway between the shoulder and the elbow.

● Press into the bone.

● If you do not feel a pulse in 5 seconds, begin external cardiac compression and artificial respiration.

To check for a pulse in a child:
● Tilt back the head and find the carotid artery in the neck which runs up either side of the Adam's apple. You'll find the pulse in the hollow between the Adam's apple and the neck muscle.

● Press lightly into the hollow.

● If you do not feel a pulse in 5 seconds, begin external cardiac compression and artificial respiration.

Artificial respiration
Babies

When a baby is unconscious and not breathing, but has a good pulse, resuscitation should be done through the nose and mouth. This is called mouth-to-mouth and nose ventilation.

1 Tilt the baby's head back and ensure the airway is clear.

2 Seal your lips around the baby's mouth and nose and breathe into them until the chest rises.

3 Remove your mouth and allow the baby to exhale as the chest falls.

4 Continue for one minute, breathing in once every 3 seconds.

5 Check the pulse every ten breaths.

Children

Children should be ventilated through the mouth, unless there is a mouth injury. Breathe in every 3 seconds (about twenty per minute) and a little less if the child is older.

CPR (Cardio-Pulmonary Resuscitation)
Babies

1 f there is no pulse in the baby, put her on a firm surface and place two fingers a centimetre or so below the point on the chest between her nipples.

2 Press at a rate of about a hundred compressions per minute – nearly two per second – about 2cm into the chest.

3 Artificial respiration must be combined with this action in order for oxygen to reach the brain and other parts of the body.

4 Compress five times for every breath of air.

Children under five

1 If there is no pulse in the child, lay him on a flat surface and place the centre of the hand two finger breadths above the angle of the ribs.

2 Using the heel of one hand only, press into the lower part of the breastbone at a rate of a hundred compressions per minute – almost two per second – about 2.5 to 4cm into the chest.

3 Artificial respiration must be combined with this action in order for oxygen to reach the brain and other parts of the body.

4 Compress five times for every breath of air.

Some common emergency situations:
Bites and stings

Bites and stings should always be treated immediately. Stings from a bee, wasp or hornet are not usually dangerous unless your child suffers from an allergy. Bites may be more serious, partly because germs from the animal's mouth can be injected deep into the flesh, causing infection, and partly because a bite may break bones and damage tissue.

What to do

● Always remove a sting before beginning treatment. Animal bites should be carefully washed with soap and warm water.

● Prevent insect bites by diluting essential oils of eucalyptus or citronella in half a mug of water, and then gently applying to exposed areas, avoiding the eyes and mouth. Use cider vinegar in the same way.

● Witch hazel is useful on mosquito bites.

● Apply a paste of bicarbonate of soda and water to a bee sting to relieve pain.

● Apply garlic and onion to ant bites, and cucumber juice to ease the discomfort.

● Make a compress from a pad of cotton wadding soaked in lemon juice and apply to a wasp sting.

Minor burns

Minor burns are those that do not cover more than 9 per cent of the casualty's body, and which are superficial.

What to do

1 Cool the affected area with cold running water for at least 10 minutes.

2 Remove all constrictive clothing.

3 Dress the burn with a sterile burn sheet, or any sterile (or very clean) fabric which is not fluffy.

4 If you are concerned about the extent or severity of the burn, call your doctor immediately.

First aid kit

Your basic first aid kit – which can be purchased complete – should contain:

● Plasters
● Sterile dressings
● Sterile eye pads
● Triangular bandages
● Roller bandages
● Safety pins
● Moist cleansing wipes, preferably antibacterial
● Antiseptic lotion
● Cotton wool

Choking

Choking occurs when a foreign body, such as a piece of food, becomes lodged in the airways, preventing air from reaching the lungs. Without an air supply, the body becomes starved of oxygen. A blocked airway is a serious medical emergency, and should be treated immediately.

Signs of choking include:

● Clutching at the throat

● Turning blue or very pale.

● Breathing with difficulty or sometimes not at all.

● Becoming unconscious within a few minutes.

What to do

BABIES

A baby who is choking may turn blue and breathe noisily or not at all. Call for help immediately.

1 Lay the baby face down along your lower arm with her head supported in your hand.

2 With the heel of your other hand, slap her back sharply, four or five times, just between the shoulder blades.

3 With your fingers, try to clear her airways.

4 If she is still choking, turn her on her back along your other arm and support her head with your hand.

5 With two fingers placed at the line where the ribs meet, just below the

Caution: Multiple stings, or stings to the eyes, ears or mouth should be treated in hospital. Animal bites that cause bleeding should be seen by a doctor – particularly if there is any possibility of contracting rabies.

breastbone, thrust upwards four or five times. Make sure her head is below the level of her lungs, but do not hang her upside down.

6 Continue this process: slap four or five times; clear the airways with your fingers; thrust four or five times, until the obstruction is cleared or help arrives.

Children

A child who is choking will probably be able to cough to eject the obstruction. If this does not work, follow these steps.

1 Lay a small child across your lap face down and slap her sharply, four or five times, between the shoulder blades, or until the obstruction clears.

2 With the heel of your hand placed below the ribs, between the chest and abdomen, thrust four or five times upwards, until the obstruction is cleared.

3 If the obstruction does not move, try clearing the airways with your fingers, and then begin to slap her back again.

Work as quickly as you can; if you cannot clear the obstruction, you should ring for an ambulance immediately and continue to try to clear it.

Cuts and bruises

Children are the recipients of a huge variety of bruises and cuts, and if they are not serious, you can easily treat them at home. If there is extensive bleeding, or any other unusual symptoms, such as dizziness, difficulty breathing, or head injury, take

your child to the hospital for emergency treatment.

What to do

1 For minor cuts, carefully clean the wound with soap and water, and cover with a sterilized piece of gauze or a bandage. Apply gentle pressure to stop bleeding.

2 For bruises, soak a clean cloth in witch hazel, and apply to the affected area. A cold compress will also help. Give your child an arnica tablet, to help disperse the bleeding and encourage healing.

Febrile convulsions

Febrile convulsions are the result of a high fever, which interferes with the activity of the brain. All cases of high fever and convulsions in small children should be taken to hospital; treated immediately, they should not cause any damage.

The priorities are:

● Protect the baby or child from anything which may cause injury; for instance, place him on the centre of the bed and watch him carefully.

● Take steps to cool him in order to reduce the fever.

● Call for emergency help.

What to do

1 Remove any constrictive clothing and place the baby somewhere safe.

2 Sponge him with lukewarm water. Take care not to overcool.

3 Place him on his side, if possible, and call for help.

4 If he becomes unconscious, prepare to resuscitate (see page 249).

Nosebleeds

The lining of the nose is very thin, and even heavy blowing or a minor jolt can rupture a capillary and cause bleeding. Unless there is an accompanying blow to the head, or intense pain, nosebleeds are not usually serious.

What to do

● During a nosebleed, gently pinch together the nostrils, and lean forward. Hold for several minutes, until the bleeding stops. Avoid blowing the nose for several hours after a nosebleed.

● A cold compress of witch hazel can be applied to the nose (externally).

● The homeopathic remedy arnica should be taken, particularly if there has been a blow to the nose.

● Apply lemon juice to a cotton wool swab to dab inside the nose and staunch the bleeding.

Poisoning

Each year hundreds of children attend emergency departments having swallowed a drug or chemical which may cause poisoning. Most of these poisonings are preventable.

● All medicines should be kept out of reach of children, preferably in a locked cupboard.

● Ask your pharmacist to dispense medicines in containers with childproof lids.

● Household detergents and bleach should also be stored out of reach and not in the cupboard under the sink. Many of these now also come in childproof containers. When you have a choice, choose one that does.

● The garage or shed provides endless fun as a place to explore or build a den, so the same precautions should apply here, too, with creosote, white spirit, petrol, weedkillers and similar noxious substances.

What to do

● If you suspect that your child has swallowed something, ring the hospital or your local poison control centre immediately for instructions on what to do, and if necessary, get him to hospital as soon as possible.

Sunburn

Sunburn is the result of overexposure to the ultraviolet rays of the sun, or a sun lamp. Sunburn is normally superficial, characterized by redness, some swelling and pain. More severe cases will blister and may be accompanied by heat-stroke. Children are much more sensitive to the sun than adults, and you should take every precaution to keep them covered up, applying a good sunscreen with a high sun protection factor, and ensuring that they do not go out into the sun during the middle hours of the day.

What to do

1 Cool the skin by pouring cold water over the affected areas, or by very gently sponging the skin. A cool bath might be helpful, but avoid a sudden very cold bath for fear of hypothermia.

2 Offer sips of cold water and dress the skin with a soothing lotion like aloe or calamine.

3 Watch for signs of blistering, which should be brought to the attention of a doctor.

Travel sickness

Although the exact cause is not known, it is believed that travel sickness occurs because of a disturbance of the balancing mechanisms of the inner ear. Common symptoms are nausea, dizziness, tiredness, pale and clammy skin, and vomiting. Travel sickness is very common in children, which can make car journeys very difficult.

What to do

● It may be helpful to offer small sips of ginger ale, or offer some candied ginger root, to ease the nausea.

● Ensure that your child has lots of fresh air while travelling. Make sure they eat a light meal before you travel, and take care to avoid sugary, greasy foods.

● There are acupressure points on the wrist which are said to prevent the symptoms of travel sickness when stimulated. You can now purchase slim wrist bands to do this.

Safety points

● Watch out for strange or over-zealous dogs both at home and out of doors.

● Don't leave a dog or a cat and a child alone together.

● Keep knives, scissors, screwdrivers and all sharp tools out of reach.

● Keep sewing materials out of reach.

● Keep electrically powered appliances out of reach.

● Never leave a baby or toddler alone in a room unless they are in a cot or in playpen.

● Furniture which is not solid or steady should be replaced or put to ne side until the child is older.

● Beware of swing doors and those with automatic closures.

● All fires need guards.

● Avoid araffin heaters if you can.

● Watch the hob – make sure all handles are turned inwards. Even the outside of an oven can be very hot and cause serious burns.

● Check the hot water temperature. If it runs too high, radiators and taps can lead to serious burns.

● Avoid using hot-water bottles for small children. Use only hand-hot water for older children.

● Never leave a child or baby alone with food or a bottle.

● Don't let a baby or child play with anything small enough to be swallowed.

● Don't give nuts to pre-school children.

● Don't give grapes or cherries to children unless they are cut up.

● Never leave a child alone in the bath.

● Help your child learn basic swimming skills and help her to feel confident in water but to be aware of the risks.

● Cover garden pools or water butts.

● Empty paddling pools at the end of every session.

● Teach your child to avoid power sockets and light switches. Invest in plastic covers for power sockets.

● Don't give a child an electric blanket.

● Make sure all of your appliances are earthed.

● Avoid trailing flexes.

● Never leave a child in a room with an iron.

● Take care around balconies.

● Beware of rugs on polished floors.

● Use safety gates on the stairs at the top and the bottom.

● Watch steps in the garden. Consider a safety fence.

● Buy a medicine cabinet with a safety lock. Do not keep medicines anywhere but here.

● Don't allow your child to play with empty medicine containers.

● Be vigilant in other people's homes.

● Keep all cleaning substances in a locked or high cupboard.

● Lock garden sheds and garages.

● Teach your child how to cross the road safely, but do not allow him to do so on his own until the age of eight.

● Safety-check all bicycles.

● Use an approved car seat for babies and children until the age of seven.

● Keep children away from plastic bags and empty trunks or boxes.

● Do not give a baby a pillow when he is sleeping.

● Use a high SPF (15 –25) sunscreen if your child is in the sun. Babies should not be exposed to sun at all.

● Put a wide-brimmed sunhat on children and avoid midday sun.

● Sterilize all your baby's feeding equipment.

● Always use a safety harness in a high chair and pushchair.

● Never leave your front door open.

● Buy toys that have an approved safety mark.

● Buy only non-toxic paints and writing materials.

● Make sure your baby's cot is deep enough to prevent him from attempting to climb out.

● Always put your baby to sleep on her back or side, which is believed to reduce the risk of cot death.

● When your child begins to climb out of her cot, move her to a bed.

● Make sure your child cannot climb out of any windows in the house. Fit safety catches.

Acknowledgements

Our grateful thanks to the following for their generous assistance with the photography:

The models:

- Brad, Sylvia and Charlie
- Charlie
- Charlotte
- Christina and Ruby
- Emily and Alfie
- Francesca
- Gaynor, Max and Joe
- Joy and Henry
- Lee
- Lisa Carr
- Lisa Chapple
- Norma, Nadine and Sophia
- Racheal and Joshua
- Sandy, Tone, Billy and Maya
- Sasha, Nick and Lola
- Serge
- Tara and Lucas
- Tess and Cinnamon
- Vesna and Alexander

The practioners:

- Michelle Denny (midwife & acupuncturist)
- Dr F.A. Loughridge
- Dawn Thein (massage)
- Yvonne Moore (Yoga teacher)
- Jutta Russell (make-up)

Grateful thanks to the following for their help:

- St John and Elizabeth Hospital, St John's Wood, London
- The Studio/Perfumery, Primrose Hill, London
- Living Well Health Club, London
- U.C.L.H. Hospital, Huntley Street, London
- Yvonne Moore Yoga Class, London
- Beehive Photographic Centre, Camden, London
- St Mary's Hospital, Paddington, London

Photographic assistants:

- Serge Boon
- Peggy Cole
- Lawrence, Malcolm, Ken, Mark and Roger (Beehive)
- Lee Ryda
- Duncan Sanderson

All photos by Christina Jansen except for medical scans and pages 187, 197, 208 and 220, which are by Duncan Sanderson, and 107 and 108, which are by James.

• •

Useful Addresses

Alcohol Concern
Waterbridge House
32–36 Loman Street
London SE1 0EE
Tel: 0171 928 7377

AIMS (Association for Improvements in Maternity Services)
40 Kingswood Avenue
London NW6 6LS
Tel: 01812 960 5585

APEC (Action on Pre-Eclapsia)
61 Greenways
Abbots Langley
Herts WD5 0EU
Tel: 01923 266778

The Association for Post-Natal Illness
25 Jerdan Place
Fulham
London SW6 1BE
Tel: 0171 386 0868

The Active Birth Centre
55 Dartmouth Park Road
London NW5 1SL
Tel: 0171 267 3006

Centre for Pregnancy Nutrition
University of Sheffield
Dept of Obstetrics and Gynaecology
Clinical Sciences Centre
Northern General Hospital
Herries Road
Sheffield S5 7A
Enquiries: 0114 243 4343
Helpline: 0114 242 4084

Foresight
The Old Vicarage
Church Lane
Withey, Goldalming
Surrey GU8 5PM

La Leche League of Great Britain
BM 3424
London WC1N 3XX
0171 242 1278

Maternity Alliance
15 Britannia Street
London WC1X 9JP
Tel: 0171 837 1265

The Miscarriage Association
c/o Clayton Hospital
Northgate, Wakefield
West Yorkshire WF1 3JS
Helpline: 01924 200799

The National Childbirth Trust
Alexandra House
Oldham Terrace
London W3 6NH
Tel: 0181 992 8637

SATFA (Support after Termination for Abnormality)
78 Charlotte Street
London W1P ILB
(0171) 631 0285

Stillbirth and Neonatal Death Society
28 Portland Place
London W1N 4DE
Helpline: 0171 436 5881

Twins and Multiple Births Association
PO Box 30
Little Sutton – South Wirral L66 1TH
Tel: 0151 348 0020

The Register of Chinese Herbal Medicine (RCHM)
PO Box 400
Wembley
Middlesex HA9 9NZ

British Acupuncture Council (BAC)
Park House
206–208 Latimer Road
London W10 6RE

Health Education Authority
Hamilton House
Mabledon Place
London WC1H 9TX

Society for the Promotion of Nutritional Therapy
PO Box 47
Heathfield
East Sussex TN21 8ZX
Helpline: 01435 867007
(Send an SAE plus £1 for a copy of the register)

Dietary Therapy Society
33 Priory Gardens
London N6 5QU
0181 341 7260

Institute of Optimum Nutrition
5 Jerdan Place
Fulham
London SW6 1BE

Women's Nutritional Advisory Service
PO Box 268
Lewes – East Sussex BN7 2QN

Yoga Therapy Centre
Royal London Homeopathic Hospital
Great Ormond Street
London WC1N 3HR

The Yoga for Health Foundation
Ickwell Bury
Biggleswade
Bedfordshire SG18 9EF

British Wheel of Yoga
1 Hamilton Place
Boston Road, Sleaford
Lincolnshire NG34 7ES

Health Education Authority
Hamilton House
Mabledon Place
London WC1H 9TX

Society for the Promotion of Nutritional Therapy
PO Box 47
Heathfield
East Sussex TN21 8ZX
Helpline: 01435 867007
(Send an SAE plus £1 for a copy of the register)

Dietary Therapy Society
33 Priory Gardens
London N6 5QU
0181 341 7260

Institute of Optimum Nutrition
5 Jerdan Place
Fulham
London SW6 1BE

Women's Nutritional Advisory Service
PO Box 268
Lewes
East Sussex BN7 2QN

Aromatherapy Organisations Council
3 Latymer Close
Braybrooke, Market Harborough
Leicester LE16 8LN

International Federation of Aromatherapists
Stamford House
2–4 Chiswick High Road
London W4 1TH

The Bach Centre
Mount Vernon
Sotwell, Wallingford
Oxfordshire OX10 9PZ

Homeopathic Development Foundation
19A Cavendish Square
London W1M 9AD

National Association for Parents of Sleepless Children
PO Box 38
Prestwood, Great Missenden
Buckinghamshire HP1 0SZ

The Faculty of Homeopathy
The Royal London Homoeopathic Hospital
Great Ormond Street
London WC1N 3HR

The British Homeopathic Association
27A Devonshire Street
London WC1N 1RJ

Index

Figures in italics refer to illustrations.